UNIX®
System V Bible

UNIX®
System V Bible

Commands and Utilities

Stephen Prata
Donald Martin
The Waite Group

SAMS
PUBLISHING

A Division of Prentice Hall Computer Publishing
201 West 103rd Street, Indianapolis, Indiana 46290

© **1987 by the Waite Group, Inc.**
A Division of Macmillan, Inc.

International Standard Book Number: 0-672-22562-X
Library of Congress Catalog Card Number: 87-60535

95   94   93   11   10

Interpretation fo the printing code: the rightmost double-digit number is the year of the book's printing; the rightmost single-digit number, the number of the book's printing. For example, a printing code of 92-8 shows that the eighth printing of the book occurred in 1992.

The following people contributed to the publication of this book:

From the Waite Group, Inc.
Development Editor: Mitchell Waite
Editorial Director: James Stockford
Series Editor: Harry Henderson

From SAMS
Acquisitions Editor: James S. Hill
Cover Artist: Kevin Caddell
Project Coordinator: Kathy Ewing

From Info Express Inc.
Editor: Joyce Cox
Proofreader: Dale Callison
Designer: Ken Sanchez
Artist: Nick Gregoric

Composition: The Type Gallery, Inc.

Printed in the United States of America

UNIX® is a registered trademark of AT&T.

Contents

Acknowledgments

From the authors:

First, we would like to thank Mitchell Waite for his continuing interest and input into this project. We would like to thank Ashley Crooker at AT&T for her help in providing us with access to an AT&T computer system running under System V. Thanks also to Santa Cruz Operations for providing us with a copy of XENIX System V. Also, we thank Jeff Bowles of AT&T for his useful review of *UNIX System V Bible* and his valuable suggestions. And, finally, we wish to thank Harry Henderson for his helpful, thoughtful editing.

Stephen Prata
Don Martin

From Mitch Waite:

I would like to thank Don Martin for being the best physics teacher I have ever had, and for helping me during a hard time. And I would like to thank Stephen Prata for meeting our insane schedules and for continuing to create such great work. I also extend my sincere appreciation to Harry Henderson, editor of the Waite/SAMS UNIX series, for his meticulous editing and for his detailed and encouraging letters to the authors.

I would also like to thank THE WELL computer conferencing system in Sausalito, California, for providing the platform that the authors and editors used for communications while working on this book.

I would like to extend my appreciation to the people at Info Express: to Joyce Cox for her diligent editing and patience with the manuscript; to Salley Oberlin for her help in managing the project; and to Ken Sanchez, the designer of the book, who turned my crude idea for a friendly design into something usable in the real world.

I give my sincere thanks to the people behind the scenes at SAMS, who took our manuscript and turned it into a smooth, marketable product we are all proud of: to Jim Hill for seeing the vision of a user-friendly reference book in the crowded UNIX market, and taking the risk of acquiring the book in the first place; to Wendy Ford and Kathy Stewart Ewing for managing the book's production; to Kevin Caddell for his wonderful cover painting, which perfectly captures the expression of the two authors as they held the UNIX documentation ("This is documentation?"); to Glenn Santner for turning my ideas into something Kevin could understand; and to all the other people at Sams who, in one way or another, were involved with making *UNIX System V Bible* a success.

A nine-track tape containing "help" files based upon the contents of this book is available directly from the authors. The files are arranged so the UNIX commands and utilities covered in *UNIX System V Bible* can be read on-screen and easily accessed. For more information, write to Don Martin, College of Marin, Kentfield, CA 94904.

Mitchell Waite
The Waite Group

Preface

Why did we write *The UNIX System V Bible*? Because we wish we'd had a book like this when we first began learning UNIX® several years ago. Most introductory books on UNIX do a good job of outlining its philosophy and of guiding you through the basic commands. But UNIX has so many commands that an introductory guide can't possibly cover them all. And the more advanced texts have other priorities, such as discussing shell programming and explaining the UNIX file system. So if you want to find out how a particular command works, you often have to go to one of the UNIX manuals. The manuals, in order to cover all the material, present information in a concise, sometimes hard-to-read fashion, and they are notably poor in examples. What we would have liked, and what we have tried to provide here, is a manual that explains the commands more fully and offers more examples.

The penalty for more explanation and examples is that more text is needed per command. To keep this book manageable in size, we have restricted ourselves in two ways. First, we cover Bell Lab's UNIX System V Release 2 and include some additions and changes implemented in Release 3. This means we ignore many commands found in Berkeley's BSD UNIX. However, some of the more popular Berkeley commands, such as the **vi** editor, have found a place in System V and, therefore, are covered here.

The second restriction is that we do not cover all System V commands. Our selection of commands is based on the command classification scheme outlined in *The UNIX System User's Manual*, prepared by AT&T and published by Prentice-Hall (1986). That manual, in turn, is based on a document called the *System V Interface Definition*, which describes a standard computing environment to be shared by all System V implementations of UNIX.

The UNIX System User's Manual divides UNIX commands into four groups: basic utilities, advanced utilities, administered system utilities, and software development utilities. We cover the two groups of most general interest: the basic utilities and the advanced utilities. As a result, we have enough space to describe each command fully and to provide examples.

But simply expanding the command descriptions isn't quite enough. Understanding the use of many commands requires understanding such UNIX features as standard I/O, I/O redirection, pipes, the file and directory system, permissions, and so on. Because you will have to continually deal with these concepts when working with UNIX, we decided to include a

"UNIX Features" section to provide the background needed to understand, utilize, and coordinate the UNIX commands.

The topics in the "UNIX Features" section are arranged alphabetically and are cross-referenced to each other and to relevant commands. We assume, however, that you already have some familiarity with UNIX, so we don't offer basic tutorials on such things as how to log in, create a password, and so on. (If you have not yet been introduced to UNIX, we suggest you read a good introductory book, such as *UNIX System V Primer (Revised Edition)*, by Mitchell Waite, Don Martin, and Stephen Prata, published by Howard W. Sams & Company, 1987.)

So, if you want to know which commands do what, read the "UNIX Commands" section. If you want to know more about how UNIX works, refer to the "UNIX Features" section.

Other UNIX Versions

What about using this book with other versions of UNIX? The most important difference between System V UNIX and Berkeley's BSD UNIX is that System V's default shell is **sh** (the Bourne shell), while BSD UNIX uses the **csh** shell. Aside from that, some commands available in one version are not available in the other, and some commands common to both versions work differently. But most commands described in this book will work much the same on BSD UNIX as on System V.

With XENIX, the correspondence is closer—XENIX System V is particularly close to the AT&T standard. Indeed, we tried most of the examples in this book on a Zenith 200 running under SCO XENIX System V, Release 2.1.3, and noted only these major differences: the XENIX **mail** command corresponds to neither the UNIX System V **mail** nor **mailx** command, although it is closer to the latter; and XENIX lacks the **shl** (shell layer) command and the **tabs** command. Also, XENIX has many additional commands that are not part of the UNIX System V definition, including some BSD UNIX commands and some commands for dealing with MS-DOS floppy disks. These commands are not covered here.

Additional Reading

If you wish to read more about UNIX, here is a list representative of the different levels of reading material available.

☐ Waite, Mitchell, Donald Martin, and Stephen Prata, *UNIX System V Primer (Revised Edition)*. SAMS, 1987.
     A friendly introduction to UNIX System V.

☐ Prata, Stephen, The Waite Group, *Advanced UNIX—A Programmer's Guide*. SAMS, 1985.

A deeper look into the workings of UNIX , exploring shell programming and C programming on a UNIX system. Also describes **grep**, **egrep**, **fgrep**, **sed**, and **awk**.

☐ Sage, Russell G., The Waite Group, *Tricks of the UNIX Masters*. SAMS, 1986.

Real-life applications for UNIX commands and shell scripts.

Conventions

Throughout this book, we use a few organizational and typographical conventions to make it easier for you to spot what you are looking for. Although both the "UNIX Commands" and "UNIX Features" sections are organized alphabetically, we also have included a table of contents at the beginning of each section to help you quickly locate the information you need. In both "UNIX Commands" and "UNIX Features," we start each command or topic on a new page, and we repeat the command names and topic titles, dictionary-style, at the top of subsequent pages (an arrow head (▶) indicates when a command or topic continues from page to page).

To distinguish our program examples from the surrounding text, we have put them in a monospace font. Within the program examples, we use blanks not only when UNIX requires them, but also for readability (you should check specific command entries to find out whether or not the blanks are actually needed). In addition, we have followed the convention of beginning directory names with a capital letter. This causes them to be listed before lowercase filenames, since uppercase precedes lowercase in the machine collating sequence. Of course, we can use this convention only for user-created directories, since the names of system directories are fixed.

When we discuss our examples, or when we refer to command names, options, filenames, and directory names in the text, we put them in boldface type to make them stand out, and we put the names of keys between the < and > signs for the same reason; for example, we use <enter> to represent the key labeled "enter" or "return" on your terminal.

Other conventions are specific to their individual sections and will be discussed as they come up, so we won't duplicate those explanations here. UNIX is a powerful, versatile, and broad system, and we hope this book makes it easier for you to learn UNIX and to use it effectively.

Overview

UNIX, in a narrow sense, is a computer operating system. In a wider sense, it encompasses a broad set of commands, or "utilities," that are provided along with the operating system. Most of this book explains and discusses these commands. However, it will be helpful if we all start out with a common idea of what the operating system does. And, while we are discussing such conceptual matters, let's also look at the UNIX file system and its "shell," and talk a bit about UNIX philosophy.

The UNIX Operating System

A computer has many resources to manage—not a simple matter. It typically has several input/output devices with which it must interact. For example, when you type something at a terminal keyboard, the computer must receive and interpret your keystrokes. Or when a computer sends something to be printed, it has to communicate correctly with the printer. In addition, a computer typically maintains an internal clock and keeps track of the date and time. It has to run disk drives and store files, keeping track of where they are, how big they are, who owns them, when they were last used, and so on. At the same time, because UNIX is a multi-user, multi-tasking system (meaning that it can handle more than one user or one task concurrently), it has scheduling problems to handle: which user and which task should be attended to next. And the computer must keep track of who is allowed to use the system, what their passwords are, how much time a particular user spends on the system, and other forms of accounting.

This is a representative, although not complete, list of some of the computer's chores. They involve a lot of the grungy, detailed work that people find tedious but at which computers excel. The sensible way of getting these chores done is to write a program that tells the computer how to perform the work; that program is an operating system.

The UNIX operating system, then, is a computer program that operates a computer. When a computer that runs under UNIX is started up, or "booted," the UNIX operating program is loaded into the computer's memory and then run. This program then attends to all the chores we mentioned, including the running of other programs. The operating system

1

program contains many subroutines, each concerned with some particular task; this is where the "system" in "operating system" comes from.

Now that we have an idea of the range of jobs the operating system undertakes, let's take a closer look at some particular features.

TIME-SHARING We've said that UNIX is a multi-user, multi-tasking operating system. However, at present most standard UNIX systems run on computers that can do only one thing at a time. The way UNIX gets around this limitation is to use "time-sharing." This means that UNIX maintains a list, or "queue," of tasks waiting to be done. It then shares the available time among these tasks. Typically, it works on one task for a little bit, then puts it aside and works on another task, and so on. Eventually, it comes back to the first task and works on it some more. After enough of these cycles, it finishes that task and takes it out of the queue. Because computers are rather fast, you often have the impression that the computer has your undivided attention when, in fact, it is sequentially attending to the tasks given to it by several users.

Even if you happen to be the only user, time-sharing still goes on. First, the operating system has some programs, such as system-wide accounting programs, that it automatically runs from time to time. Second, UNIX allows you to run a program "in the background." This means that UNIX places the program in the queue of programs to be run, but instead of forcing you to wait for it to finish before prompting you for a new command, it *immediately* prompts you for the next command. Thus UNIX time-shares between your immediate command and the one you ran in the background. The Processes entry in the "UNIX Features" section and the **sh** entry in the "UNIX Commands" section describe how to run programs in the background. (Incidentally, in this book we use "running a program" to mean both running a standard UNIX command like **cat** or the **vi** editor, or running other programs that you have written or acquired.)

SYSTEM ADMINISTRATION AND THE /etc/passwd FILE One aspect of system administration is that the operating system should keep track of authorized users and their passwords. To do this, the operating system (with the help of the system administrator) maintains a file named /etc/passwd. (This name is an example of a "pathname," in which the filename is preceded by a directory list enclosed in slashes, indicating where the file is.) Each time a user is added to the system, an additional line is added to this file. Such an entry might be

```
joy:xxZYz1.9zw0a1:25:2:JOY USER:/usr/joy:
```

The first field (**joy** here) is the user's "login name," the next field is an encrypted password, the third field is the user identification number (**25** here), and so on. The encrypted password may initially be chosen by the system administrator or left blank, but **joy** can choose or modify her password by using the **passwd** command described in the "UNIX Commands" section of this book.

The **/etc/passwd** file contains other information about each user, but your login name and password are the most critical, because when you "log in" on the computer, the operating system asks you for them. If you don't enter them correctly, you won't get on the computer.

The Kernel, the Shell, and the UNIX Commands

UNIX, in the wide sense, is an operating system plus a host of supporting programs. The essence of the operating system is called the "kernel," and the "shell" is one of the most important of the supporting programs.

THE KERNEL The kernel is the set of programs that carry on the resource management we discussed earlier. When the computer is started up, the kernel is booted, or initiated, and it takes charge. You interact with the kernel through the shell program.

THE SHELL Once you log in, the operating system places you in your home directory (we'll discuss directories in the next section) and starts up a shell program for you. As we've said, a shell is a program that acts as an interface between you and the kernel. Several shells have been developed for UNIX, but the standard one used with System V is the Bourne shell, named after its creator, Stephen Bourne. Each person who logs in has a shell program, called **sh**, started up for him or her, so usually the time-sharing system handles several shells concurrently. *Your* shell program interprets *your* commands, *Minnie's* shell interprets *her* commands, and so on. It is the shell program, for example, that is responsible for sending you your screen prompt (usually a $ or %) to let you know that UNIX is ready for your next command. It also is responsible for fetching your next command and interpreting what it means. For instance, if you type **date**, the shell searches through the system files for the file that contains the **date** program. When it finds it, it runs that program.

The role of the shell, then, is to facilitate your interactions with the computer. You don't have to know where the **date**, **vi**, or **cat** command is stored, nor do you have to know the internal identification numbers used by the kernel for those files; the shell takes care of these details for you.

The shell, in fact, has many capabilities. These are outlined in the entry for **sh** in the "UNIX Commands" section, and much of the "UNIX Features" section is devoted to presenting shell concepts and facilities.

THE COMMANDS The power of UNIX is augmented by the great number of programs that come with the operating system but are not part of it. These programs are the UNIX commands: **cat**, **sort**, **lp**, **vi**, **ls**, **mail**, **awk**, and the like. Each is a separate program (or set of programs) kept in the /**bin** or the /**usr**/**bin** directory.

For the most part, the UNIX commands are designed to work with each other and with the kernel. One of these programs is the **sh** program. As we have seen, it communicates with the kernel and facilitates the use of the other programs.

Files and Directories

As you work with UNIX, you most likely will begin to accumulate files of your own. The UNIX operating system manages the computer's resources, but it is up to you to manage *your* resources. Fortunately, UNIX provides the framework and support to help you manage the files that you create and use in the course of your work.

The framework UNIX supplies is its file system. Conceptually, the multitudes of files on the UNIX system are organized into separate directories that are themselves organized into a tree-like structure. There is one master directory, called the "root directory." Various subdirectories branch off this root, and sub-subdirectories can branch off them (see Figure 1).

As we've mentioned, each user is assigned a "home directory." When you log in, your home directory becomes your "current working directory." This means that files you create are stored in this directory and that commands you give are assumed to apply to files in this directory. (You can

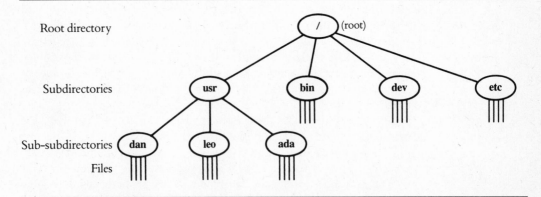

FIGURE 1. *A directory tree*

use the **cd** command to change your current working directory, and you can use pathnames, as discussed in the "UNIX Features" section, to access files in other directories.)

UNIX offers several tools to manage your files:

TOOL	PURPOSE
ls	Lets you display a list of your files.
ed, ex, vi	Let you create new files and modify existing ones.
rm	Lets you delete ("remove") old files.
cp, cpio	Let you make copies of files.
mv	Lets you rename (move) files.

To help you organize your files, UNIX lets you create your own system of subdirectories (with **mkdir**) and copy or move files easily from one directory to another (with **cp** and **mv**).

For more details on files and directories and on the workings of the shell, scan the list of entries in the "UNIX Features" section that follows the command discussions and read the ones that interest you. These entries also will direct you to related commands.

UNIX Commands

Introduction

This section discusses those commands classified as basic utilities and advanced utilities by the *System V Interface Definition*. In this introduction, we will go over the format used to present these commands. Perhaps the best way to do this is to look at the headings found in a representative entry and at what is discussed under them. Here's how each command is presented:

HEADING	DESCRIPTION
Purpose	Contains a short summary, usually one sentence, of what the command is for.
Format	Gives the format, or syntax, for using the command. In it, items in **boldface** are to be typed literally. Items in *italics* represent generic names or values for which you substitute actual names or values. And items in [square brackets], whether boldface or italic, are optional (you don't type the square brackets when you use the command). For example, the **cat** command uses this format:

    cat [**-s**] [*file(s)*]

To use the command, you type **cat** literally. You may use the **-s** option, and you may list the names of one or more files.
    If options are shown together, as in

    [**-ls**]

they can be invoked either in that form or separately, as in

    -l -s

Options shown separately in the format, as in

    [**-f**] [**-d**]

are incompatible; only one or the other (or neither) can be used.
    When there are a lot of options or when they are complex, we often use the form

    [*option(s)*]

rather than showing the actual options in the format. Consult the Options section to find out what the options are and how to use them.

Description	Describes the command, what it does, and how you use it.
Common Uses	Outlines a few representative circumstances in which you might use the command.

(continued)

9

HEADING	DESCRIPTION	_(continued)_
Other Headings	Not all UNIX command discussions can be conveniently squeezed under these headings, so some commands have additional ones. With the more involved commands, we use the Description section to provide an overview, then develop the discussion of the command usage in one or more additional sections.	
Options	Describes the options available with this particular command. Look here for detailed information about the options given in the Format section.	
Comments	In this section, we comment on any idiosyncracies of the command and on related commands.	
See Also	Lists related commands and relevant entries in the "UNIX Features" section.	
Examples	At the end of each command entry, we give examples that use the command (we've put them in a box so you can locate them easily). Typically, we show a basic usage, then illustrate an option or two; often, we also include a pipe or script that uses the command.	

As we've said, some commands do not have all these headings, and some have additional ones that are specific to that command.

Organizing the command discussions into this format should enable you to quickly find the information you need about each command. You can check the Purpose section for a quick overview of what a particular command does, glance at the Format section when you've simply forgotten the exact form of the command, turn to the Examples if you're unsure of how to use it, or consult the other sections when you need more detailed information.

The typographical conventions used in this section of the book are the same as those described in the Preface, so we won't explain them again here. Without more ado, here are the commands.

PURPOSE Use **ar** to build and maintain archive libraries. An archive library combines several files into one file and allows files to be added and removed. Typically, **ar** is used to manage program libraries.

FORMAT **ar** *key* [*posname*] *afile* [*file(s)*]

Here *key* specifies the action **ar** is to take (see the Main Key Characters section below). The *posname* argument is the name of a file in the archive; it is used to specify a position within the archive. Next, *afile* is the name of the archive file, and finally *file(s)* represents the names of the files to be processed.

DESCRIPTION The **ar** command combines several files into one archive file (called *afile*, short for "archive file," in the format above). The resulting file contains a header and tables detailing the archive contents. Once an archive file is created, you can use **ar** to modify its contents. Archive files typically hold object files (files of machine-language code) used by the link editor (**ld**), but they can be used to hold text files, too. A *key*, consisting of a main character and, perhaps, of one or more option characters, specifies the action to be taken; for instance, adding a new file or deleting an old one from the archive.

COMMON USES You can use **ar** to create an archive file of compiled C functions for use with the **ld** (link) command. You also can archive a group of related text files, such as correspondence relating to a particular project. You can add, remove, and update files in the archive. You can display the table of contents of an archive, as well as display the contents of specified files in the archive. In addition to allowing easy access to individual files, an archive lets you treat a collection of related files as a unit. This is especially useful for copying.

MAIN KEY CHARACTERS The *key* argument consists of one of the characters **d**, **r**, **q**, **t**, **p**, **m**, or **x**, along with, perhaps, one or more of the optional key modifiers listed below. The *key* can include a hyphen prefix. Here are the functions of the main characters:

CHARACTER	ACTION
d	Deletes the named files from *afile*.
r	Adds or replaces the named files in *afile*. New files are placed at the end of *afile* unless the **a** , **i** , or **b** key modifier is used.
q	Quickly appends the named files to the end of *afile*. **ar** does not check first to see if the file is already archived.
t	Displays a table of contents of *afile*. If a list of filenames is given, only names from the list are sought.
p	Displays the named files.

(continued)

CHARACTER	ACTION	*(continued)*
m	Moves the named files to the end of the archive.	
x	Extracts the named files; extracts all files if no names are given. The indicated files are copied into the current directory. The archive file is not altered.	

KEY MODIFIERS Here are the functions of the optional key modifiers, along with the main key characters they can be used to modify:

MODIFIER	ACTION
v	(Stands for "verbose.") Gives a file-by-file description of the making of a new archive file. When used with **t**, it gives a long listing of file information. When used with **x**, it displays the name of each file it extracts.
u	When used with **r**, replaces only those files that have been modi- fied since they were last archived.
a	When used with **r** or **m**, places the named files after the file named by the *posname* argument.
i, b	When used with **r** or **m**, places the named files before the file named by the *posname* argument.
c	Suppresses the normal message given by **ar** when *afile* is created (as opposed to modified).
l	Uses the current directory instead of /**tmp** for temporary files.
s	Forces regeneration of the archive symbol table. This is useful when an archive file has been modified by some other com- mand, such as the **strip** software-development command, which removes symbolic information from a file.

COMMENTS The **ar** command does not compress text, so there is no saving of disk space. However, by combining several files into one, you do save on file accounting; only one i-node is needed instead of several.

UNIX versions prior to Release 2 do not accept an initial hyphen in the *key* argument.

The **ar** command uses a file format that allows the UNIX link editor (**ld**) to search an archive file for given files. XENIX and some UNIX versions require that an archive library be processed by the **ranlib** command before it can be used with **ld**. Your system may require that you get administrative approval to make a new archive usable by **ld**.

The **ld** command is classified as a software-development tool, and thus is not covered in this book.

The **tar** command provides tape-oriented archive facilities, and **cpio** provides archive services oriented toward the directory system and inter-system copying. The **ar**, **tar**, and **cpio** commands each use a different archive format.

SEE ALSO   UNIX Commands: **cpio**; **tar**

EXAMPLES

---

1. Create an archive file of compiled C functions.

```
$ ar -qv libgrph.a circle.o line.o arc.o rect.o
ar: creating libgrph.a
q - circle.o
q - line.o
q - arc.o
q - rect.o
$
```

This creates the **libgrph.a** archive file containing four object code files. The .a extension is used because the **ld** command expects archived libraries to have the form **lib*.a**, where * represents up to seven characters. The **q** key character tells **ar** to append the named file to the archive file, and the **v** (verbose) modifier generates the list of files being processed.

2. Add files to an archive file.

```
ar -q libgrph.a tri.o
```

This adds the **tri.o** file to the end of the archive, even if a file by that name already is present.

3. Delete files from an archive file.

```
ar -d libgrph.a tri.o
```

This removes the **tri.o** file from **libgrph.a**.

4. Update an archive file.

```
ar -r libgrph.a line.o
```

This replaces the **line.o** file currently in **libgrph.a** with another version.

(continued)

---

5. Display the contents of an archive file.

```
$ ar -t libgrph.a
circle.o
line.o
arc.o
rect.o
$
```

This displays a list of the files contained in the **libgrph.a** archive.

6. Extract a file.

```
ar -x libgrph.a arc.o
```

This places a copy of the **arc.o** file in the current directory; the name of the copy is **arc.o**. The archive file itself is not changed.

PURPOSE Use the at command to run a list of commands at a later time. There may be restrictions as to who can use this command (see the Access to at section below).

FORMAT at *time* [*date*] [**+** *increment*]
command(s)
[**<control-d>**]
at -l [*job(s)*]
at -r *job(s)*

DESCRIPTION The at command takes a list of commands typed at the keyboard and runs them at a time specified in the command. You need not be logged in when the command is scheduled to run. Type the commands on the line following the at command, and terminate them by typing a <control-d> on the line following the commands. By using input redirection, you can use a previously created file of commands instead of typing them in. The output of commands run using at is mailed to you unless you redirect it to a file.

The at command preserves environmental variables, **mask** and **ulimit** values, and the current directory setting for the tasks it runs. This ensures that the delayed commands run in the same manner that they would if run immediately.

COMMON USES You can use at to schedule a lengthy job to run at a time when the computer is less busy. It's also useful for such things as sending reminders via mail at later dates and running database queries late at night.

OPTIONS The at command has two options that allow you to view and manipulate the jobs scheduled for future execution.

OPTION	ACTION
-l	Lists the "job numbers" (identification numbers created by at) for tasks scheduled by at.
-r	Removes the indicated job numbers from the queue of jobs scheduled by at.

SPECIFYING THE TIME AND DATE The *time* part of the at format is the time, in hours and minutes, when the command is to be run. If *time* is one or two digits, it is interpreted to be the time in hours. If it is four digits, the first two are hours and the second two are

15

minutes. Thus **9** is 9 o'clock, while **0911** is 9:11. UNIX assumes a 24-hour clock, unless you optionally use an **am** or **pm** suffix. Thus **0911pm** is 9:11 pm, as is **2111**, the 24-hour equivalent. Also optionally, you can use a colon; instead of **0911**, you can use **9:11**. If the time is before the current time and if no optional *date* is provided, the time is assumed to be the next day.

Other special terms recognized in the *time* specification are these:

TERM	MEANING
zulu	A suffix denoting Greenwich Mean Time.
noon	Noon (of course).
midnight	Midnight.
now	Right now (used with *increment*).
next	Used after *time* and before *date*.

The optional *date* can consist of the following:

TERM	EXAMPLE
Month and day	**Aug 22**
Month, day, and year	**Jan 3, 1988**
Day of week	**Wednesday**
"Special" day	**today** or **tomorrow**

Three-letter day abbreviations, such as **Tue** and **Thu**, are recognized, too. If the given month precedes the current month in the calendar, it is assumed that it refers to next year.

The *increment* is a number followed by one of the following: **minutes, hours, days, weeks, months,** or **years.** (The singular form can be used, too.) For instance, to run a task two hours from now, specify **now + 2 hours** as the time.

ACCESS TO at The system administrator may choose to make the **at** command available to everyone, to only some users, or to no users. Two files control who can use **at**. If the file **/usr/lib/cron/at.allow** exists, then only users listed in that file can use **at**. Otherwise, the system checks the **/usr/lib/cron/at.deny** file to see who cannot use **at**. If that file exists but is empty, everyone can use **at**. If neither file exists, ordinary users are denied use of **at**; only the system administrator and other superusers can use it.

COMMENTS The **batch** command is similar to **at**, except that it runs tasks when the system finds time for them, rather than at particular times.

The **cron** command allows for commands to be run periodically.

SEE ALSO UNIX Commands: **batch**; **cron**

UNIX Features: Standard I/O, Redirection, and Pipes; Processes

EXAMPLES

1. Run a job at 2 am the next day.

```
$ at 02 tomorrow
spell enormous
<control-d>
537271200.a
$
```

This will run the **spell** program on the **enormous** file at 2 am tomorrow. The **at** command causes the job number (**537271200.a**) to be displayed. The output (the misspelled words found by **spell**) will be sent to you via **mail**. To collect the misspelled words in a file instead, use redirection, as in the next example.

2. Run a job using output redirection.

```
$ at now + 2 hours
spell enormous > badwords
<control-d>
```

Two hours from now, the **spell** command will be run and the output will be collected in the **badwords** file.

3. Run a job using input redirection.

```
$ at 6:00 next week < commandlist
```

The list of commands in **commandlist** will be run at 6 am, one week from now.

4. Run a job at noon on Thursday.

```
$ at noon Thu
mail dinky < surprise
<control-d>
```

This will mail the **surprise** file to **dinky** at Thursday noon. Note that the **surprise** file must exist at noon on Thursday. (In general, none of the input to **at** is interpreted until **at** is executed—in this case, at noon on Thursday.)

awk

PURPOSE The **awk** command scans files for patterns or relationships and processes matching lines. It can therefore be used for many simple data management tasks.

FORMAT awk [-Fc] *program* [*param(s)*] [*file(s)*]

awk [-Fc] -f *programfile* [*param(s)*] [*file(s)*]

Here *program* is a sequence of one or more **awk** commands (see Description below); *programfile* is a file containing **awk** commands; and *param(s)* represents program variables you are providing to the program. A *param* has the form **x = 22**; this creates a variable **x** and initializes it to **22**. The *file(s)* argument represents the names of the files to be processed. If this argument is omitted, **awk** processes the standard input.

DESCRIPTION The **awk** command scans files line by line looking for particular patterns or relationships. It can act upon matching lines in a variety of ways. It also can match and act upon individual fields within a line, and it is capable of numeric as well as text operations. **awk** also provides decision-making and looping control statements similar to those of traditional programming languages.

To understand how to use **awk**, you need to know how it looks at input, how it selects lines, and what it can do with them once they're selected. We'll examine those topics in a moment.

COMMON USES You can use **awk** for tasks involving individual fields and numbers. For instance, **awk** can find the sum of a row of numbers, of a column of numbers, or of both. It also can reorder fields in a file and translate a data file from one form to another.

OPTIONS The **awk** command has only two options:

OPTION	ACTION
-F*c*	Makes the character *c* the field separator (see Records and Fields below).
-f *programfile*	Uses the *programfile* file instead of a sequence of command-line instructions (*program*) to provide the **awk** commands.

RECORDS AND FIELDS The **awk** command divides its input into records and fields. Records are identified by the record separator, which is, by default, the newline character. Thus the default record is one line of input. Fields are identified by the field separator, which is, by default, a space or a tab. Thus the default field is one word or any other string of characters containing no blanks.

The default field separator can be overridden by using the **-F** option. Follow the **-F** with the chosen separator. For example, **-F:** makes the colon the field separator. The built-in **awk** variable **FS**, discussed later, also can be used to change the separator.

Within an **awk** program, the notation $0 is used to represent the entire record, $1 the first field, and so on. For example, suppose the following is a line of input:

```
My kingdom for a horse!
```

Here $0 is the whole sentence, $1 is **My**, and $5 is **horse!** (note that because there is no space between the **e** and the **!**, the exclamation point is part of the fifth field).

awk PROGRAMS AND PROGRAM FILES An **awk** program can be specified either in a separate file or directly as a command line (or lines). In the second case, the program is enclosed in single quotes to prevent the shell from interpreting special **awk** characters as shell metacharacters and to cause the shell to treat the program as a single argument.

A program consists of one or more program statements, with the general form of a program statement being this:

pattern {action}

Each line of input is compared to the *pattern*, and if there is a match, the indicated *action* is performed. If you don't specify a *pattern*, the action is performed on every line. If you don't specify an *action*, all matching lines are displayed on the screen. Learning to use **awk** primarily consists of learning the possible forms of patterns and the possible actions.

PATTERNS The **awk** command recognizes three forms of patterns: special patterns, regular expressions, and relational expressions. Expressions of the last two types can be combined into Boolean combinations.

Special Patterns
There are two special patterns: **BEGIN** and **END**. **BEGIN** is used to label actions that are to be performed before any lines are read, and **END** is used to label actions that are to be performed after the last line has been processed.

Regular Expressions
Regular expressions are those recognized by **egrep**, and they are enclosed between slashes. For instance, the expression **/fudge/** matches any lines

that contain the string **fudge**. In general, a regular expression consists of a string of one or more characters, as interpreted in the following list:

EXPRESSION	PATTERN MATCHED
c	Matches the character c, if c is not a special character.
\\c	Matches the character c, even if it is a special character.
^	Matches the beginning of the compared string.
$	Matches the end of the compared string.
.	Matches any character other than the newline.
[*list*]	Matches any character in *list*, which represents a sequence of characters, as in [aeo], or a range, as in [a-m], or a combination, as in [a-mqz].
[^*list*]	Matches any character not in *list*.
(*r*)	Matches the regular expression *r*. Parentheses group several characters together for use with the *, +, ?, and ¦ special characters.
*r**	Matches zero or more successive occurrences of the regular expression *r*.
r+	Matches one or more successive occurrences of the regular expression *r*.
r?	Matches zero or one successive occurrences of the regular expression *r*.
r1 ¦ *r2*	Matches either the regular expression *r1* or *r2*.

For example, the expression

```
/^[Hh]i ¦ ^Hello/
```

matches **Hi** or **hi** or **Hello** at the beginning of a line.

The two comparison operators ~ and !~ can be used to compare a regular expression with a particular field instead of with the whole line, as in

```
$2 ~ /slime/
```

This matches lines in which the second field contains the string **slime**, whereas

```
$3 !~ /slug$/
```

matches lines in which the third field does not end with the string **slug**.

Relational Patterns

Relational patterns compare numbers or strings by using relational operators. There are eight relational operators. Two of them are the comparison operators mentioned above (~ and !~); the other six compare values:

OPERATOR	MEANING
<	Less than
<=	Less than or equal to
>	Greater than
>=	Greater than or equal to
==	Equal to
!=	Not equal to

When strings are compared, the comparison is lexicographic, and is based on the machine code for representing characters. Thus **C** is greater than **A** but less than **a**. If the first characters of the strings being compared match, the comparison moves on to the next character, and so on.

Here are some examples:

```
$4 > 100
```

This matches lines for which the fourth field is greater than the number **100**.

```
$5 < Smith
```

This matches lines for which the fifth field precedes **Smith** alphabetically.

Boolean Operators

The three Boolean operators !, &&, and ¦¦ can be used to construct Boolean combinations of regular expressions and relational expressions:

OPERATOR	MEANING
!	Negation
&&	And
¦¦	Or

These are listed in order of decreasing precedence. Parentheses can be used to indicate groupings. Boolean expressions are evaluated from left to right, and evaluation stops as soon as the truth or the falsehood of the expression is determined.

Here are some examples:

```
$4 > 100 && $5 > 300
```

This matches lines for which the fourth field is greater than 100 and the fifth field is greater than 300.

```
!($4 > 100 && $5 > 300)
```

This matches lines that do not simultaneously have the fourth field greater than 100 and the fifth field greater than 300.

```
$4 <= 100 || $5 <= 300
```

This matches lines for which the fourth field is less than or equal to 100 or for which the fifth field is less than or equal to 300. Logically, it is equivalent to the preceding example.

You can indicate a pattern range by providing two patterns separated by commas. Then the action is performed on all lines between the occurrence of the first pattern and the subsequent occurrence of the second pattern. For instance, the pattern

```
/pancake/,/waffle/
```

designates lines between (and including) the first line containing **pancake** and the first subsequent line containing **waffle**.

ACTIONS The **awk** command has a large repertoire of actions, including printing, performing arithmetic calculations, creating variables and arrays, using built-in functions, using control statements for making loops and decisions, and using redirection.

Printing

The basic print command, **print**, prints out its argument list (the list of items following it). Items in the list can be fields (such as $2), numeric values (such as 212), strings (such as "Hi ya'll"), **awk** variables, and combinations of some of these items (such as $2 + 3 * $1). Strings, in this context, should be enclosed in double quotes.

Items separated by commas in the list are separated by spaces when printed, and items not separated by commas in the list are run together when printed. Suppose, for example, that the first field is **22** and the second field is **37**. Then

```
{ print $1, $2 }
```

produces

```
22 37
```

and

```
{ print $1 $2 }
```

produces

```
2237
```

More generally, **print** commands can be used with line-matching patterns. For example,

```
$1 ~ /r/ { print $0 }
```

prints all lines that have an **r** in the first field, and

```
$2 == 4 { print $1, $2 }
```

finds all lines with a **4** as the second field and prints the first two fields of those lines.

By default, **print** uses the space as a field separator and terminates its output with a newline. These defaults can be altered by resetting the **OFS** and **ORS** special variables, which are described later.

You can control printed output more precisely by using **printf**, the formatted print statement. Its form is

printf *"format"*, *arg1, arg2, …*

The *"format"* argument is a string in which "format specifiers" specify how the other arguments are to be printed. Other characters in the format are printed literally, while the format specifiers are replaced by the corresponding arguments. For example,

```
printf "Field One is %d\n", $1
```

prints as

```
Field One is 22
```

The **%d** specifier indicates an integer is to be printed at that location. The argument is **$1**, so its value of **22** is printed after **is**. Similarly,

```
printf "%d plus %d is %d\n", $1, $2, $1 + $2
```

produces this output:

```
22 plus 37 is 59
```

In general, specifiers are identified by an initial percent sign. The following are the most common ones:

SPECIFIER	MEANING
%d	Prints as a decimal integer.
%f	Prints as a floating-point decimal.
%e	Prints in exponential form.
%g	Uses %e or %f, whichever is shorter.
%c	Prints as a character.
%s	Prints as a string.

A newline is printed only if explicitly included in the format string in the form **\n**.

The basic format specifiers can be further modified to indicate field widths, justification, and decimal places. To indicate field width, insert a digit between the percent sign and letter. Thus **%5d** means "print a decimal integer in a field five characters wide." Field widths automatically are expanded if numbers exceed their specified widths; strings, however, are truncated to fit.

By default, numbers are right justified; that is, the last digit is printed at the far right of the field. Use a minus sign for left justification: **%-5d**.

To indicate the number of digits to the right of the decimal point for the **%f** format, follow the field width with a decimal point and the desired number of digits. For example, **%20.3f** prints a number in a field that is 20 characters wide and uses 3 digits to the right of the decimal. (The default value is 6.)

Here's another example:

```
print "Pi is %8.2f\n", 3.14159
```

prints as

```
Pi is     3.14
```

The **printf** command is borrowed from the C programming language. See a C language reference manual or, if available, the on-line description of the C **printf()** function for more details on formatting.

Print Redirection

Both **print** and **printf** can be used with redirection. Thus the instruction

```
$3 > 1000 { print $0 > biggies }
```

causes lines in which the third field is greater than **1000** to be copied to a file called **biggies**, and the command

```
{ print $0 > $1 }
```

causes each line to be placed in a file that has the same name as the first field in the line. For example, if the input

```
oranges 200
apples 240
```

is used with the above **awk** program, **awk** creates two files (**apples** and **oranges**) with one line in each. If the input were

```
red 12 13
orange 14 15
yellow 16 17
green 18 19
blue 20 21
indigo 22 23
violet 24 25
```

seven files would be created.

Note that with some releases of System V, only 20 files can be created at a time using this mechanism.

Arithmetic

The **awk** command features several operators. First, it has the same arithmetic operators as those used in the C language:

OPERATOR	MEANING
+	Addition
-	Subtraction
*	Multiplication
/	Division
%	Modulus

In each case, the operation is performed using the two values (operands) flanking the operator; that is, the form 2 + 2 evaluates to 4. For division, if both operands are integers, then integer division is performed. This means the result is the largest integer in the answer and the remainder from the division is discarded; thus 7 / 4 is 1. If either or both operands are floating point, the result is floating point; thus 7.0 / 4.0 is 1.75 and 7 / (4 + 0.0) is also 1.75. The modulus operator requires that both operands be integers. It provides the remainder when the first operand is divided by the second; thus 7 % 4 is 3.

These arithmetic operators can be used with numeric fields:

```
{ print ($2 - $1) / ($2 + $1) }
```

This command prints the number that results when the difference between the second and first fields is divided by their sum. Note that parentheses are used for grouping operations; here they cause the addition and subtraction to be performed before the division.

Other operators work with variables, so let's look at them next.

Variables and Arrays

The UNIX field notation ($1, and so on) represents "field variables." Their values can be changed. For example, the action

```
{$1 = 1.05 * $1; print $1}
```

prints a value that is 5 percent greater than the original. (The original file is unaffected; it is the output that is altered.)

A variable can be created simply by assigning a value to it. For example, the action

```
{x = $1 + $3; print x, $1 / x, $3 / x}
```

creates a variable called **x**, assigns it the sum of the two field variables, and uses the value in the print statement.

In general, the value of a variable is assumed to be a string unless it is recognizably numeric. A string can be written using double quotes; if the string contains spaces, double quotes must be used, as in

```
mesg = "There ought to be a law"
```

This creates a variable called **mesg** and assigns it the indicated string.

Arrays also can be created simply by assigning them values:

```
{val[1] = $1; val[2] = $2}
```

creates two array elements and assigns them values. The array *index* is the value between the brackets. Here indexes of **1** and **2** are used, but an index need not be a number. Consider this assignment:

```
{thing[$1] = $2}
```

Suppose input consists of these two lines:

```
apples 200
oranges 240
```

Then the array element **thing["apples"]** is assigned the value 200, and the element **thing["oranges"]** is assigned 240.

Arrays typically are used with the looping structures we'll discuss later.

In addition to field variables, an **awk** program can use several other built-in variables. Here is a list of them:

VARIABLE	MEANING
FS	The input field separator (by default, a space).
FILENAME	The name of the current input file.
NF	The number of fields in the current record.
NR	The current number of records.
OFMT	The printing format used by **print** for numbers (by default, %.6g).
OFS	The output field separator used by **print** (by default, one space).
ORS	The output record separator used by **print** (by default, a newline).

For example, the following action prints each line with its line number:

```
{print NR, $0}
```

Remember, when you don't specify a pattern, all lines are matched.

You also can provide variables in the command line. For example, the command line

```
awk -f dok q = 10 file
```

initializes the variable **q** to **10**; presumably the program stored in the **dok** file will use **q**.

Other Operators

The C language assignment operators also are available: **=**, **+=**, **-+**, ***=**, **/=**, and **%=**. The **+=** operator adds the variable on its right to the variable on its left; that is, an action like

```
{sum += $1}
```

adds $1 to the current value of **sum**; it is equivalent to the following:

```
{sum = sum + $1}
```

A variable is initialized to the null string, which is interpreted as 0 for numeric operations. Thus the previous action computes a running total for all the first fields in the file. The next action prints the total:

```
END {print sum}
```

The other assignment operators behave similarly; that is, ***=** multiplies the variable on its left by the one on its right.

The C increment operator (**++**) and decrement operator (**--**) are available, too. The expression **s++** adds 1 to **s**, and **s--** decrements **s** by 1. If the operator is used in suffix form, as above, the current value of the variable is used before it is incremented; that is, in an expression like

```
y = s++
```

y is assigned the current value of **s**, then **s** is incremented. When used in prefix form, these operators cause incrementing or decrementing to occur first. Thus the expression

```
y = ++s
```

causes **s** to be incremented, and then the new value of **s** is assigned to **y**.

Multiple Statements

A statement is terminated by a semicolon, a newline, or a right brace. You use the first two when more than one statement is needed. For example, the following two actions are equivalent:

```
{ s = $1 + $2; print $1 / s, $2 / s }
{ s = $1 + $2
  print $1 / s, $2 / s }
```

In each case, the second statement is terminated by the closing brace.

Also, a long statement can be spread over several lines by terminating intermediate lines with a backslash:

```
{ print "The readjusted data have this form", \
  $1, $3, $6, $2 }
```

Additional brace pairs can be used to create compound statements; see the next section for examples.

Control Statements

The **awk** command's patterns imply an **if** statement: if the pattern is matched, perform the action. To extend the flexibility and power of **awk**, several control statements have been borrowed from C.

The **if** statement looks like this:

if (*expression*) *statement*

If the *expression* is "true," the *statement* is executed. As in C, any non-zero value is considered "true." Typically, *expression* involves using the relational operators and perhaps the logical, or Boolean, operators discussed earlier under Patterns. Here is a sample action:

```
{if ($1 > 500) print $0}
```

As in C, you can use the keyword **else** to designate an action to be taken if the test fails:

```
{if ($1 > $2 ) print $1 $2
  else           print $2 $1}
```

The entire **if else** structure comprises a single action, so just one set of braces is used.

The **while** statement creates a loop that executes a statement until the control expression becomes false. Its form is this:

while (*expression*) *statement*

For example, the following loop prints out the fields in reverse order:

```
{ i = NF
  while ( i > 0 )
     {
     printf "%s", $i
     i--
     }
  printf "\n"
}
```

Note that braces are used to create a "compound" statement for the loop; without them, only the first statement would be included in the loop.

The **for** control statement offers a second form of loop. It has this general form:

for (*exprs1*; *exprs2*; *exprs3*) *statement*

Here *exprs1* is evaluated once, before the looping is started. Then *exprs2* provides a test condition that is checked before each loop cycle. If it is "false" (numerically 0), the loop terminates. If it is "true," the loop continues, *statement* is executed, and *exprs3* is evaluated before the next loop cycle starts. The previous **while** example can be rewritten this way with a **for** loop:

```
{ for ( i = NF; i > 0 ; i--)
       printf "%s", $i
  printf "\n"
}
```

To handle arrays with non-numeric indexes, **awk** offers a special form of **for** loop. Its general form is

for (*i* **in** *arr*) *statement*

Here *arr* is the name of an array and *i* takes on all the subscript values. For example, earlier we gave this example:

```
{thing[$1] = $2}
```

When the input consists of these two lines,

```
apples 200
oranges 240
```

the **thing["apples"]** array element is assigned the value 200, and the **thing["oranges"]** element is assigned 240. This form of array also can be processed in this fashion:

```
END { for (fruit in thing)
       print fruit, "count:", thing[fruit] }
```

Then the variable **fruit** is set, in turn, to the strings **"apples"** and **"oranges"**, producing this output:

```
apples count: 200
oranges count: 240
```

The **continue** and **break** statements are used to modify the control flow in a loop. A **break** statement causes the program to break out of a loop, and the **control** statement causes the program to skip over the remaining part of the loop and to start the next cycle. Typically they are used in conjunction with an **if** statement, as in this example:

```
{ for ( i = 1; i <= NF; i++ )
    {
    printf "%s", $i
    if ($i > 1000)
        break;
    }
  printf "\n"
}
```

This prints fields, quitting after the first field greater than **1000** is printed.

An **exit** statement causes program execution to quit. The general form is

exit (*expression*)

The value of *expression* should be an integer; it becomes the exit status of the program.

The **next** statement causes the program to skip scanning the current input line and to start scanning the next input line.

Built-In Functions
There are seven built-in functions:

FUNCTION	PURPOSE
length(*s*)	Returns the length of the string *s*. If no argument is given, $0 is assumed.
exp(*x*)	The exponential function. Returns e to the *x*th power.
log(*x*)	Returns the natural logarithm (base e) of *x*.
int(*x*)	Returns *x* truncated to an integer.
substr(*s, p, n*)	Here *s* is a string, and *p* and *n* are integers. Returns a substring of at most *n* characters, beginning at position *p*. For example, `ns = substr("retraining", 3, 5)` assigns "**train**" to **ns**.
sprintf(*fmt, expr1, …*)	Formats values into a string. Here *fmt* is a format string as used by **printf**, and the following expressions are the values to be used. The return value is the resulting string. For example, suppose $1 has the value "donut". Then the statement `str = sprintf("%s is the next item", $1)` assigns the string "**donut is the next item**" to **str**.

COMMENTS The **awk** command is useful when individual fields of a file need to be used and when numeric calculations are required. Typically, it is much slower than an equivalent program in C, but is easier to create and requires much less storage.

SEE ALSO UNIX Commands: **egrep**
UNIX Features: Standard I/O, Redirection, and Pipes; Regular Expressions; Filters; Extending Commands over More than One Line

EXAMPLES

1. Print a file, adding a blank line between lines.

```
{ print; print "" }
```

Since no matching pattern is given, all lines are matched. Then **print** with no arguments prints the whole line, and **print** " " prints a blank line.

The program can be run two ways. First, the instructions can be given in the command line:

```
awk '{print; print ""}' samplefile
```

The quotes ensure that the instructions are passed from the shell to **awk** without confusing the shell. Second, if the instructions are in a file called **twospace**, the program can be run this way:

```
awk -f twospace samplefile
```

2. Find the sum of the first five fields and calculate the average per record.

```
{ sum += $1 + $2 + $3 + $4 + $5}
END { print "total =", sum, " average =", sum / NR}
```

Here **sum** maintains a running total of the sum of the first two fields. The program assumes the number of lines is the number of records; that is, the file is a pure data file. Suppose the instructions are in the **sums** file and that we have a **numbers** data file with these contents:

```
12 23 34 56 78
98 76 54 34 21
10 29 38 47 56
```

Then we get this result when using the program:

```
awk -f sums numbers
total = 666  average = 222
```

3. Find the sum and average of all the numbers in a file.

```
{ for ( i = 1; i <= NF; i++)
        {
        total += $i
        items++
        }
}
END { print "total =", total, " average =", total / items }
```

This time, we use a **for** loop to sum all the fields on a line and to keep a running total of the number of items summed. We use **NF**, the number of fields per record, to tell the loop how many fields to sum. Thus the program is not committed to a particular number of fields or even to having the same number of fields in each line. Here **total** and **item** are, by default, initialized to 0, and so represent cumulative running totals. Assuming these instructions are in an **ave** file and use **numbers** from the previous example, we get this output:

```
awk -f ave numbers
total = 666  average = 44.4
```

4. Use arrays to sum the numbers in each of a fixed number of columns in a file.

```
{ for ( i = 1; i <= 4; i++)
    col[i] += $i }
END { for ( i = 1; i <= 4; i++ )
        printf "%d ", col[i]
    print "" }
```

Here **col[1]** collects the running total for the first field, and so on. The **for** loop provides a convenient way to handle arrays. We use the **printf** statement so that the total appears on the same line; using **print** instead would print one column total per line.

5. Sum a variable number of columns in a file.

```
{ for ( i = 1; i <= NF; i++)
        col[i] += $i
  if ( NF > max) max = NF
}
END { for ( i = 1; i <= max; i++ )
        printf "%d ", col[i]
    print "" }
```

Here the program uses the built-in variable **NF** to keep track of the number of columns in a line. Because some lines could have more fields than others, the program uses **max** to keep track of the largest number of fields to date; that value, then, is used in the **END** statement.

(continued)

6. Read a file containing names in **first last** order and print them in **last, first** format.

```
{ print $2 ",", $1 }
```

The omission of a comma between **$2** and "**,**" is deliberate; it causes the name and the comma to be concatenated instead of being separated by a space. For example, suppose this program is kept in the **revnam** file and is applied to the **names** file, which looks like this:

```
Daniel Boone
Mia Farrow
Joe Louis
```

Then we get this output:

```
Boone, Daniel
Farrow, Mia
Louis, Joe
```

Note that each last name is followed immediately by a comma.

7. Print information found in particular lines.

```
$1 ~ /hardware/ { num += $3; cost += $4}
END { print "items =", num, "  cost =", cost}
```

This keeps a running tab on the number of items and the cumulative cost of items for which the first field of a line matches **hardware**. Suppose we apply the program to this sample file:

```
hardware   monitor     1    300
software   smallword  2    200
software   harpoon     1    100
supplies   paper       1     20
hardware   mouse       1    120
supplies   ribbons     5     30
```

Then we get this output:

```
awk -f inawk inv
items = 2    cost = 420
```

8. Use string–indexed arrays to collect information.

```
{ num[$1] += $3; cost[$1] += $4 }
END {   for (class in num)
        print class ":", "items =", num[class],\
                        "cost =", cost[class] }
```

The various values of **$1** for the different lines become the subscripts of the **num** and the **cost** arrays. The **END** statement causes **class** to assume each of these values in turn. Here is a sample output, using the same input file as in the previous example:

```
awk -f invawk inv
software: items = 3 cost = 300
supplies: items = 6 cost = 50
hardware: items = 2 cost = 420
```

Note, however, that you have no control over what order is used for the subscripts.

9. Redefine a field and search the **/etc/passwd** file.

```
BEGIN {FS =":"}
$4 == 60 {print $1, " : ", $5; ct++}
END {print "number of group members =", ct}
```

The **/etc/passwd** file uses a colon as its field separator, so this program resets **FS** to a colon. (You could, instead, use the **-F** option in the command line.) The program scans the file for lines that have the fourth field (the group number) equal to **60**. It prints out the first and fifth fields (the login name and comment field) for such lines and, finally, it prints the total number of entries for that group.

banner

PURPOSE Use **banner** to display or print banners.

FORMAT **banner** *string(s)*

DESCRIPTION The **banner** command displays its arguments in large letters across the page on the standard output. One argument is displayed per line. The maximum length that can be displayed depends on the equipment; it is 10 characters for an 80-column display. You can use quotes to make two or more words a single argument, so that they appear on the same line of the banner.

COMMON USES You can use **banner** to produce eye-catching titles for reports, to separate files from one another when printing a batch of files, to make signs for your office door, and so on.

SEE ALSO UNIX Features: Standard I/O, Redirection, and Pipes

EXAMPLES

---

1. Produce a motto.

```
banner HOME SWEET HOME ¦ lp
```

This causes the printer to print a banner bearing the words **HOME SWEET HOME,** thereby saving some embroidery. Each word is printed on a separate line. The pipe (¦) causes the output to be routed to the printer instead of to the screen.

---

2. Produce a warning.

```
banner "NO SMOKING" "" "NO JOKING" ¦ lp
```

This causes **NO SMOKING** to be printed on one line, followed by a blank line, followed by **NO JOKING** (see Figure 2).

FIGURE 2. *The output of a banner command*

3. Communicate with others.

```
banner "SEE ME" "AT ONCE!" -MUFFY > /devd/tty05
```

This sends a message to terminal **tty05**, providing it is open to receive messages. (It also interrupts and distracts the person at **tty05**, and if used too often, might be detrimental to **MUFFY**'s relationships with others.)

basename

PURPOSE Use **basename** to extract the basic filename from a pathname.

FORMAT **basename** *string* [*suffix*]

Here *suffix* is any string of characters you wish to be deleted from the end of the basename.

DESCRIPTION Each file has a "basename" and a "pathname." The basename is the name you use for a file when it is in your current working directory; for example, **razz** might be a basename. The pathname prefaces the basename with the sequence of directories leading from the root directory to the file; for example, **/usr/biggsie/umps/razz** is a pathname. The **basename** command deletes the directory portion of a pathname, deletes a pathname suffix (if given), and displays the result.

COMMON USES You can use **basename** to recover the basename from a pathname. You then can use the basename to construct a new filename. Most commonly, **basename** is used in shell scripts and with command substitution (`` ` ` ``), which allows the basename to be used rather than just be displayed.

COMMENTS If you would like to extract the pathname rather than the basename, use the **dirname** command.

SEE ALSO UNIX Commands: **dirname**
UNIX Features: Command Substitution; Pathnames and the Directory Tree; Shell Variables

EXAMPLES

1. Display the basename of a file.

```
$ basename /usr/hamlet/2bornot2.b
2bornot2.b
```

As instructed, this command removes the directory names and displays the **2bornot2.b** basename.

2. Obtain a basename and remove a suffix.

```
$ basename /usr/hamlet/2bornot2.b .b
2bornot2
```

If we had used **b** instead of **.b**, then **2bornot2.** would have resulted.

3. Assign the basename to a shell variable.

```
$ FILENAME=`basename /usr/hamlet/petard`
$ echo $FILENAME
petard
```

The command substitution backquotes (``` `` ```) cause the **basename** expression to be replaced by its value (**petard**), which then is assigned to the shell variable (**FILENAME**).

4. Assign the basename of a command-line argument to a variable.

```
FILENAME=`basename $1`
```

You might use this line in a shell script, using **$1** to represent the first command-line argument for the script.

batch

PURPOSE Use the **batch** command to run jobs as the system work load permits, even after you log out.

FORMAT batch
command(s)
<control-d>

DESCRIPTION The **batch** command takes a list of commands typed at the keyboard and runs them when the system has time, usually quite soon. You need not be logged in when the *commands* list runs. The commands are typed beginning on the line following the command, and are terminated by typing a <control-d>, also at the beginning of a line. By using input redirection, you can use a file of commands instead. The output of the commands run using **batch** is mailed to you unless you use output redirection to collect it in a file.

The **batch** command preserves environmental variables, **umask** and **ulimit** values, and the directory setting that was current when the command was given. This means the **batch** tasks will run as if you had run them directly.

COMMON USES You can use **batch** to arrange for a list of commands to be run and then turn your attention to another project or log out. Typically, you would use **batch** for long tasks that don't need your immediate attention.

COMMENTS The **batch** command is similar to **at**, except that you don't specify the time at which the commands will be run. It also is similar to running a job in the background, except that you can log out and still have the job processed. It is different from the **cron** command, however, which runs jobs from time to time rather than just once.

SEE ALSO UNIX Commands: **at; cron; sh**
UNIX Features: Standard I/O, Redirection, and Pipes; Processes

EXAMPLES

1. Run a command when the system finds time.

```
batch
spell warandpieces > sp.errors
<control-d>
```

This places the spelling job in the system's job queue. Spelling errors will be placed in the **sp.errors** file in what was the current working directory when you typed the **batch** command.

2. Run a command from a file.

```
batch < workfile
```

This places whatever commands are found in the **workfile** file in the job queue.

PURPOSE Use the **cal** command to display a calendar for a month or a year.

FORMAT cal [[*month*] *year*]

DESCRIPTION The **cal** command displays the calendar for the indicated year. If a month number also is given, just that month is displayed. If no month or year is provided, the current month is presented.

COMMON USES You can use **cal** to summon up a current calendar or to check the calendar for some other time period.

COMMENTS The **cal** command accepts years in the range 1 through 9999; it knows about calendar changes in the past.

EXAMPLES

---

1. Display the calendar for the year 1910.

   ```
   cal 1910
   ```

   Note that the full year value is typed; **cal 10** would display the calendar for the year 10 AD, not for 1910 AD.

   The calendar contains more lines than most screens hold (see Figure 3), so you may wish to pipe the results through **pg** and view the calendar one screen at a time:

   ```
   cal 1910 | pg
   ```

   ```
                                       1910

                 Jan                   Feb                   Mar
         S  M Tu  W Th  F  S    S  M Tu  W Th  F  S    S  M Tu  W Th  F  S
                           1           1  2  3  4  5           1  2  3  4  5
         2  3  4  5  6  7  8    6  7  8  9 10 11 12    6  7  8  9 10 11 12
         9 10 11 12 13 14 15   13 14 15 16 17 18 19   13 14 15 16 17 18 19
        16 17 18 19 20 21 22   20 21 22 23 24 25 26   20 21 22 23 24 25 26
        23 24 25 26 27 28 29   27 28                  27 28 29 30 31
        30 31
                 Apr                   May                   Jun
         S  M Tu  W Th  F  S    S  M Tu  W Th  F  S    S  M Tu  W Th  F  S
                        1  2    1  2  3  4  5  6  7              1  2  3  4
         3  4  5  6  7  8  9    8  9 10 11 12 13 14    5  6  7  8  9 10 11
        10 11 12 13 14 15 16   15 16 17 18 19 20 21   12 13 14 15 16 17 18
        17 18 19 20 21 22 23   22 23 24 25 26 27 28   19 20 21 22 23 24 25
        24 25 26 27 28 29 30   29 30 31               26 27 28 29 30

                 Jul                   Aug                   Sept
   ```

   FIGURE 3. *The screen output of a cal command*

2. Display the calendar for May, 1957.

   ```
   cal 5 1957
   ```

   Note that the month number, not the month name, is used.

---

calendar

PURPOSE Use the **calendar** command to provide a reminder service.

FORMAT calendar

DESCRIPTION The **calendar** command looks for a file called **calendar** in the current directory. It displays those lines that contain today's or tomorrow's date anywhere in the line. For weekends, "tomorrow" extends through Monday. **calendar** recognizes month-day formats such as *December 25, dec. 25,* and *12/25;* the European day-month order is not recognized.

COMMON USES You can include the **calendar** command in your **.profile** file so that you are reminded automatically when you log in of the things you need to do that day. This makes more sense than trying to remember to type the command every day.

SEE ALSO UNIX Features: The **.profile** File

EXAMPLES

First, use an editor to create a **calendar** file. Here is a possibility:

```
Christmas comes on December 25 this year.
3/13 Meet with Dr. Strangelove 1:30 pm
3/14 Meet with Mrs. Strangelove 8 pm
Apr 15: Are your tax returns done?
```

1. Assuming it is March 13, use the **calendar** command to remind yourself of things you need to do.

```
$ calendar
3/13 Meet with Dr. Strangelove 1:30 pm
3/14 Meet with Mrs. Strangelove 8 pm
```

Note that only appointments for 3/13 and 3/14 are shown.

cancel

PURPOSE Use the **cancel** command to cancel a printing request made with the **lp** (line printer) command.

FORMAT cancel [*id(s)*] [*printer(s)*]

Here *id(s)* represents the job identification number(s) that are created by the **lp** command (and are obtainable with the **lpstat** command).

DESCRIPTION The **cancel** command cancels printing requests made through the **lp** command. You need to specify either the request ID provided by **lp** or the printer name. Giving the ID halts the job whether it is already printing or waiting to print, while giving the printer name just halts a request that is in the act of being printed. When a currently printing job is terminated, the printer is freed to print the next request.

COMMON USES You can use **cancel** to halt a printing request made in error.

COMMENTS Use **lpstat -v** to obtain a list of all the printer names.

SEE ALSO UNIX Commands: **lp**; **lpstat**

EXAMPLES

1. Halt a printing job by using its ID.

```
$ lp surfsup
request id is printer1-343 (1 file)
$ cancel printer1-343
```

Note that the ID provided by **lp** specifies the printer.

2. Halt a job currently on the printer.

```
cancel printer1
```

For this to work, the job currently on the printer must be one of yours.

PURPOSE   Use the **cat** command to display files and to join files together.

FORMAT   **cat** [*option(s)*] [*file(s)*]

DESCRIPTION   The **cat** command reads input from a list of files and/or from the standard input, and copies all input, in order, to the standard output, which is, by default, the screen. The command's name is short for "catenate," or for "concatenate," which both mean "to form into a chain"; **cat** concatenates a series of files into one stream of output. Typing **cat** *filename* displays the contents of *filename* on the standard output.

COMMON USES   You can use **cat** to display a file on the screen, to combine two files into one, to append a file to the end of another, and to send a series of files to be printed.

OPTIONS   Before Release 3, the **cat** command had only one option (**-s**); Release 3 added four more:

OPTION	ACTION
-s	Suppresses the usual system complaints about nonexistent files.
-u	Output is unbuffered (by default, output is buffered). New with Release 3.
-v	Displays most nonprinting characters. Control characters are displayed using an initial caret; for example, **^H** represents a <control-h>. The DEL character (ASCII 127) is represented as **^?**. Tabs, newlines, and form feeds are not shown. Non-ASCII characters (those having the high-order bit set; that is, those with a code value in the range 128 through 255) are represented in the form **M-***c*, where *c* is the character specified by the lower seven bits. New with Release 3.
-t	(Works only with **-v**.) Displays a tab as **^I**. New with Release 3.
-e	(Works only with **-v**.) Displays a $ at the end of the line, just before the newline. New with Release 3.

INPUT SELECTION   If **cat** is given a list of files as arguments, it displays the contents of those files in the order listed; otherwise, it uses the standard input. By default, the standard input is the keyboard. **cat** ordinarily uses the end-of-file (EOF) signal to tell when input is complete. To simulate this signal from the keyboard, type **EOF** (by default, <control-d>) at the beginning of a line.

You can use redirection to make the standard input a file:

```
cat < bonkers
```

but it is simpler to provide the filename as an argument.

A pipe can be used to make the standard output of another command into the standard input for **cat**:

```
sort pickle | cat
```

This example makes little sense, since **cat** just passes on the input from **sort** as output. However, you can combine standard input with a list of filenames by using - as one of the filenames. When **cat** gets to the - "file," it uses the standard input. This allows you to, say, combine the output of a command with the contents of other files (see Example 4).

OUTPUT SELECTION The **cat** command sends its output to the standard output, which is, by default, the screen. By using redirection, you can send the output to a file instead (see Example 2). By using a pipe, you can send the output to another command (see Example 3).

COMMENTS Avoid commands like the following:

```
cat tuna chicken > tuna
```

Here the redirection (**> tuna**) begins by wiping out the original **tuna** file, before the **cat** command has a chance to read it.

The **cat** command often is used for viewing files, but it doesn't work well with fast terminals and long files, because the contents scroll too fast. Use **pg** for long files.

SEE ALSO UNIX Commands: **pg**
UNIX Features: Standard I/O, Redirection, and Pipes; Filters

EXAMPLES

1. Look at a file.

   ```
   cat ploys
   ```

   This displays the **ploys** file on the screen. Note that the file will scroll through to its end, so this use of **cat** is best confined to short files.

2. Combine two files into one.

   ```
   cat part1 part2 > report
   ```

   This example uses redirection to collect the output of **cat** in the **report** file. You can also use append redirection (**>>**) to append files to the end of a file, as in

   ```
   cat part3 part4 >> report
   ```

   If you were to use **>** instead of **>>** in this example, the new material *would replace* the contents of **reports** instead of being appended to the end of it.

3. Send a list of files to the printer.

   ```
   cat sample? ! lp
   ```

   This concatenates all the files in the current directory that match the **sample?** pattern and sends them to the printer. This command is different from **lp sample?** in that the latter prints each file separately, while the former runs the files together.

4. Blend file input with a pipe.

   ```
   sort data ! cat start - end > paper
   ```

   The first part of this command sorts the contents of the **data** file. The pipe (!) makes the output of **sort** become the standard input of **cat**. Next, **cat** concatenates the contents of **start**, the standard input (which is the sorted contents of **data**, as represented by the hyphen), and the contents of **end**. Finally, **cat** sends the result to the standard output, which is, by redirection, **paper**.

cd

PURPOSE Use the **cd** command to change your current working directory.

FORMAT cd [*directory*]

DESCRIPTION The **cd** command makes the directory given as the *directory* argument your current working directory. If no *directory* argument is given, you are switched to your home directory. **cd** uses the value of the **HOME** environmental variable to determine the name of your home directory. If you don't specify the directory path explicitly by providing a pathname, **cd** searches for a subdirectory of your current working directory, unless the **CDPATH** environmental variable is defined. **CDPATH**, if defined, is set to a list of directories that **cd** will search for the requested subdirectory.

You cannot change to a directory unless you have execute permission for that directory.

COMMON USES You can use **cd** to change to another directory in order to work on files kept there. This saves you from having to type pathnames for those files.

COMMENTS The **CDPATH** environmental variable typically is defined in the **.profile** file. It provides a list of directories that are searched in turn for the specified subdirectory until the directory is found, or until the list is exhausted. Directory names are separated by colons. For example, to set up a search list that looks first in the current directory, then in the parent directory, then in your home directory, you can do this:

```
CDPATH=.:..:$HOME
```

SEE ALSO UNIX Commands: **sh**
UNIX Features: Directory Abbreviations; Pathnames and the Directory Tree; Shell Variables; Permissions; The **.profile** File

EXAMPLES

1. Change to the **/usr/include** directory.

   ```
   cd /usr/include
   ```

2. Change back to your home directory.

   ```
   cd
   ```

3. Change to a subdirectory of your current directory.

   ```
   cd pliny
   ```

   No pathname is given, so the current directory is searched for a subdirectory of this name. If the **CDPATH** variable lists further directories, they are searched in order until **pliny** is found or until the list is exhausted.

4. Change to a second directory branching off the parent directory of your current directory.

   ```
   cd ../plautus
   ```

   Here .. indicates the parent directory. Since a pathname is given, **CDPATH** is not used.

chgrp

PURPOSE Use the **chgrp** command to change the group that has group access to your files.

FORMAT **chgrp** *group file(s)*

DESCRIPTION Users are divided administratively into groups, and the **/etc/passwd** file tells which group each user belongs to. Each group has an identifying group number and a group name, and the **/etc/group** file lists the group number and group members for each group name. Each file is identified by a group name as belonging to a specific group. Members of that group have access as specified by the group permissions. The **chgrp** command changes the group ID of the indicated files to that of the specified group. The group can be identified by the decimal group ID or by the group name.

    If the set-user-ID bit or the set-group-ID bit of the file mode is set, this command clears it, unless the user is the superuser.

    You must own a file in order to change its group ID.

COMMON USES You can use **chgrp** to grant a different group access to a file.

COMMENTS When you create a file, it is assigned your current group ID number. When you log in, your group ID is set to the value listed for you in the **/etc/passwd** file. If you are listed in several groups in **/etc/group**, you can use the **newgrp** command to switch your current group ID to one of these other IDs.

    The **chmod** entry discusses group permissions, as well as the set-user-ID and the set-group-ID bits.

SEE ALSO UNIX Commands: **chmod; chown; ls; newgrp**
UNIX Features: Permissions; Groups; The Superuser

1. Grant group number 210 group permissions for one of your files.

```
chgrp 210 chictalk
```

This gives members of group **210** group permissions for the **chictalk** file. The **ls -l** command shows what the group permissions are, and the **chmod** command lets you set those permissions.

2. Use a group name to change the group ID.

```
$ chmod o-r fueltable
$ ls -l fueltable
-rw-r----  1    jones    budget    12356  May 21   15:32:11  fueltable
$ cat /etc/group
...
rocket::55:braun,ley,olds,pocket
...
$ chgrp rocket fueltable
$ ls -l fueltable
-rw-r----  1    jones    rocket    12356  May 21   15:32:11  fueltable
```

First, the **chmod** command is used to deny read permission to the "other" class of users. The long listing then shows that the **fueltable** file has read and write permission for the owner, read permission for the group, and no access for others. It also shows that the owner is **jones** and that the group is **budget**. Next, displaying **/etc/group** (abbreviated here) reveals that **braun, ley, olds,** and **pocket** belong to the **rocket** group. Hence they do not have access to the **fueltable** file. Next, the **chgrp** command, given by **jones,** changes the group to **rocket,** as revealed by the next listing. (The group ID of **55** could have been used instead of **rocket.**) Now members of that group can read the file and members of the **budget** group are cut off from the file. However, **jones** can still read and write to the file, since that ID still is the owner of record.

chmod

PURPOSE   Use the **chmod** command to set the "file mode" (read, write, and execute permissions, and so on) for a file or directory.

FORMAT   **chmod** *absolute-mode file(s)*
chmod *symbolic-mode file(s)*

DESCRIPTION   The **chmod** command alters the file modes of the indicated files and directories. A file mode specifies who has read, write, and execute permissions for a file. The **chmod** command can use an "absolute" form, which indicates the exact settings for all permissions, or it can use a "symbolic" form, which indicates particular permissions to be set. **chmod** divides users into three classes: the "user" (the owner of the file), the "group" (people belonging to the group associated with the file), and "others" (everyone else). Permissions are set separately for each class.

Only the superuser and the owner of a file can change its permissions. The set-group-ID bit discussed below can be set only if the user's current group ID is the same as the file's group.

COMMON USES   You can use **chmod** to remove write permission from a file to protect it from accidental erasure. You can remove read permission for "other" users so that a file is private to you and to group members. Or you can remove group permission so that only you can read the file. You also can make a shell script executable so that typing the filename causes the script to run. And, with Release 3, you can cause a file to be "locked" when it is accessed, so that only one user or program can use the file at a time.

ABSOLUTE MODE   The absolute mode that describes the file permissions is a four-digit octal number, such as 0644. It is constructed from the following basic modes by adding the desired values:

MODE	MEANING
4000	Set user ID on execution.
2000	(Before Release 3.) Set group ID on execution.
20#0	(Release 3.) If **#** is 7, 5, 3, or 1, set group ID on execution. If it is 6, 4, 2, or 0, enable mandatory file locking.
1000	Reserved.
0400	The owner has read permission.
0200	The owner has write permission.
0100	The owner has execute (search) permission.

MODE	MEANING
0040	The group has read permission.
0020	The group has write permission.
0010	The group has execute (search) permission.
0004	Others have read permission.
0002	Others have write permission.
0001	Others have execute (search) permission.

For example, **0644** is **0400** (owner-read) plus **0200** (owner-write) plus **0040** (group-read) plus **0004** (other-read). (Technically, the combined mode is formed by logically ORing the basic modes.)

The set-user-ID bit is used with executable files. It means that whoever uses the program temporarily has the same permissions as the program's owner. For example, suppose **vote** is a program owned by **hal**. It uses a data file called **tally**, which only **hal** can open. Ordinarily, if **dick** tries to use the **vote** program, **vote** aborts when it tries to open the **tally** file, since **dick** does not have permission to use that file. But if **vote**'s set-user-ID bit is set, then **dick** has **hal**'s permissions while **vote** runs, so **vote** can open **tally** and complete its work.

The set-group-ID bit has a similar role. It grants the user of a program the same permissions as members of the program file's group. Mandatory file locking causes a file to have its read or write permission locked while a program is accessing the file. This prevents a file from being accessed simultaneously by two programs.

Read permission lets you read a file. "Reading" includes actions such as copying a file. For a directory, read permission allows you to list the directory contents.

Write permission lets you alter a file, including editing it and appending to it. For directories, write permission permits you to add or delete files in that directory.

Execute permission for a file means that you can run the file as a program by typing its name. An executable file should contain machine code, such as the code produced by a compiler, or a list of UNIX commands, as in a shell script. Execute permission for a directory gives search permission; that is, the power to make that directory your current working directory.

SYMBOLIC MODES A symbolic **chmod** mode basically consists of three parts; for instance, **o-r**. The first part is a "who string" indicating who is affected; the second is an operator indicating the action taken; and the third is a "permission string" indicating the affected permissions. In the **o-r** example, **o** indicates the "others" class, **-** indicates removal of a permission, and **r** indicates read permission. Let's take a more detailed look.

The who string can be a combination of the following letters:

LETTER	MEANING
u	The user.
g	The group.
o	Others.

In addition, the letter **a** (all) stands for **ugo**, as does omitting the who string entirely.

The three possible operators are these:

OPERATOR	MEANING
+	Adds the indicated permissions.
-	Removes the indicated permissions.
=	Assigns absolutely the indicated permissions.

With **+** and **-**, only the indicated permissions are affected. With **=**, all permissions are affected; those not mentioned are turned off.

The permission string is formed from the following letters:

LETTER	MEANING
r	Read permission.
w	Write permission.
x	Execute permission.
s	Set user ID (with o) or set group ID (with g).
l	Mandatory file locking during access. New with Release 3.

The permission string can be omitted if the = operator is used, in which case all permissions are removed.

The permission symbols are the same as those used by the **ls -l** (long listing) command.

As an example of a symbolic mode, **go+w** means "grant write permission to group members and to others."

More than one operator-permission sequence can be used with a given who string. For instance, **g+r-w** grants read permission and removes write permission for group members. Also, more than one symbolic mode can be used by separating modes with a comma. Thus the sequence **u+w,go-r** adds user write permission and removes group and others read permissions.

COMMENTS The symbolic mode is most useful when you wish to alter specific modes, while the absolute mode is better suited for setting all modes at once. Note that mandatory file locking is new with Release 3.

Groups and the association of a file with a group are discussed under the **chgrp** entry.

SEE ALSO UNIX Commands: **chgrp**; **chown**; **ls**
UNIX Features: Permissions; Groups; The Superuser

EXAMPLES

1. Make a file read-only.

   ```
   chmod 0444 gooddata
   ```

   This absolute-mode command gives everyone read-only access to the **gooddata** file. We can get the same result with this symbolic command:

   ```
   chmod u-w gooddata
   ```

   This removes the user's write permission, leaving all other permissions unchanged. (This assumes the default setting, in which no one else has write permission anyway.) Another approach is

   ```
   chmod ugo=r gooddata
   ```

   This gives everyone read permission and no other permission. It is equivalent to the **0444** version used earlier in this example.

2. Remove read permissions for others.

   ```
   chmod 0600 finestuff
   ```

   The user still has read and write permissions. All other permissions are turned off. Here is the symbolic approach:

   ```
   chmod go-r finestuff
   ```

   This leaves other permissions unchanged; that is, if **finestuff** were a shell script for which group members had execute permission, that permission would not be changed.

3. Make a shell script executable.

   ```
   chmod u+x prtfile
   ```

   This makes the **prtfile** executable; typing its name causes it to be executed.

4. Conceal a directory.

   ```
   chmod go-rx Rumors
   ```

   Removing read permission prevents the group and others from listing the directory contents, and removing execute permission prevents them from **cd**'ing to the directory.

5. Set the set–user–ID permission.

```
$ ls -l vote tally
-rwxr-xr-x  1  hal   polit    24245 Oct 23 12:43:31   vote
-rw-------  1  hal   polit    12096 Oct 28 15:12:36   tally
$ chmod u+s vote
$ ls -l vote tally
-rwsr-xr-x  1  hal   polit    24245 Oct 23 12:43:31   vote
-rw-------  1  hal   polit    12096 Oct 28 15:12:36   tally
```

Initially, all users can run **vote**. However, **vote** uses the file **tally**, which no one but the owner (**hal**) can use. Hence **vote** aborts when it tries to open **tally** for a non-owner. Setting the set–user–ID bit gives all users of the **vote** file **hal**'s permissions, so the program can proceed with its work.

6. Cause a file to be locked during access.

```
chmod a+l salesdata
```

Now only one program can update the **salesdata** file at a time.

chown

PURPOSE Use the **chown** command to change the ownership of files.

FORMAT **chown** *owner file(s)*

DESCRIPTION When you create a file, UNIX assigns you ownership of the file. The **chown** command changes the ownership of the indicated files to the specified owner. The new owner can be identified by name or by using the decimal owner ID, as given in the **/etc/passwd** file. You must own a file in order to use **chown** with it, unless you are the superuser.

If the set-user-ID or set-group-ID bit of the file mode is set, this command clears it, unless the user is the superuser.

COMMON USES You can use **chown** to let someone else own a file of yours and hence have owner permissions (but then you no longer have them). More typically, **chown** is used by the system administrator.

COMMENTS The **chmod** entry discusses owner permissions, as well as the set-user-ID and the set-group-ID bits.

SEE ALSO UNIX Commands: **chmod**; **chgrp**
UNIX Features: Permissions; The Superuser

EXAMPLES

1. Grant another user ownership of a file.

   ```
   chown delita furs
   ```

   This makes **delita** the official owner of the **furs** file.

PURPOSE Use the **cmp** command to see if two files have the same contents.

FORMAT cmp [-l] [-s] *file1 file2*

DESCRIPTION The **cmp** command compares two files. By default, it reports the location of the first difference, if any, and is silent if the files are identical. Options let you list all differences or suppress all output. The latter is handy for scripts that use the exit value of **cmp** rather than its output. (An exit value is a status report that a command provides to a shell. Many shell programming features use exit values.) The exit value is 0 if the files are identical, 1 if they differ, and 2 if a file is missing or not accessible.

COMMON USES You can use **cmp** to identify multiple copies of files so that you can remove duplicates.

OPTIONS The **cmp** command has two options:

OPTION	ACTION
-l	Prints the byte number (in decimal form) and the values of the differing bytes (in octal) for each difference.
-s	Prints nothing for differing files (typically used in shell scripts that look at the command's exit value).

COMMENTS The **comm**, **diff**, and **cmp** commands all compare files. However, **comm** is limited to sorted text files, and **diff** is limited to text files. The **cmp** command can be used both with text and with non-text files, including files of object code, such a those produced by a compiler.

SEE ALSO UNIX Commands: **diff**; **comm**
UNIX Features: Exit Values; Shell Scripts

EXAMPLES

1. Check whether two files differ.

```
$ cmp susy suzy
susy suzy differ: char 10, line 1
```

The output reveals that the first difference between the two files occurs at the tenth byte, or character, which happens to be in the first line.

2. Find all differences between two files.

```
$ cmp -l susy suzy
  10 163 172
  25  56  77
```

Here we find that the files differ in the tenth and twenty-fifth bytes. The **163** is the byte value (in octal) for the tenth byte in the **susy** file, while the **172** is the byte value of the tenth byte in the **suzy** file. (These turn out to be the ASCII codes for **s** and **z** respectively.) Similarly, the second line of output lists the values for the twenty-fifth byte of each file.

3. Use the **cmp** command as part of a shell script.

```
if cmp -s $1 $2
then
    rm $2
fi
```

Here $1 and $2 represent two arguments (presumably filenames) to the shell script. If the exit value of the **cmp** instruction is 0, the two files are identical, and the second file is removed. (The Bourne shell **if** statement treats a zero exit value as "true.") The **–s** option suppresses any printing of differences, since this script is concerned only with whether or not the files are the same, and not with what any differences might be.

PURPOSE   Use the **col** command to make text containing reverse line feeds and forward and reverse half-line feeds intelligible on displays and printers incapable of such motions.

FORMAT   col [-bfpx]

DESCRIPTION   Text formatted for printing may contain embedded codes to produce effects such as superscripts, subscripts, and reverse line feeds. These codes garble the text if it is viewed on a terminal. The **col** command deals with this problem by removing the special codes and modifying the text before displaying it. For example, if the input text contains a reverse line feed followed by a word, the reverse line feed is dropped and the word is inserted in the preceding line of the output text. The **col** command handles eleven control codes and ignores other nonprinting characters. Options control how certain characters are processed.

COMMON USES   You can use **col** to look at material containing nonprinting printer-control characters that are otherwise incompatible with terminal viewing.

DEFAULT BEHAVIOR   If no options are in effect, **col** causes any text following a reverse line feed to be placed in the preceding line. For instance, consider text like this, in which <esc-7> represents a reverse line feed:

```
See
Spot <esc-7>run
```

It is converted to text like this:

```
See   run
Spot
```

The control character has been removed, and the text has been changed.

Text that would be printed between lines is moved down to the next full line when viewed on the terminal. Instructions to back up to before the first line of a document are ignored.

OPTIONS This default behavior can be changed by using one or more of the following options:

OPTION	ACTION
-b	Assumes the output device is not capable of backspacing. In this case, if backspacing would place two or more characters at the same location, the last character placed there is displayed. For example, the sequence **x[backspace]_** would be displayed as _.
-f	Causes **col** to pass forward half-line feeds to the output unchanged. (By default, they are converted to forward full-line feeds.)
-p	Causes **col** to pass on control sequences even if it doesn't recognize them.
-x	Doesn't replace space characters with tabs. (By default, tabs are used when possible to replace lengthy sequences of spaces.)

CONTROL CHARACTERS Control characters are special characters used, for example, to control a printer. The **col** command recognizes the control characters listed below (notations like SP and VT are standard ASCII notations for the indicated characters).

CHARACTER	ASCII CODE (OCTAL)
Space (SP)	040
Backspace (BS, or ^H)	010
Tab (HT, or ^I)	011
Newline (LF, or ^J)	012
Vertical tab (VT, or ^K)	013
Return (CR, or ^M)	015
Start-text (SO, or ^N)	016
End-text (SI, or ^O)	017

Some control characters actually are "escape" sequences of more than one ASCII character. The **col** command recognizes the escape sequences listed below. Here <esc> represents the ASCII "escape" character (octal code 033), and ^H represents <control-h>.

COMMAND	ESCAPE SEQUENCE
Reverse line feed	<esc-7>
Reverse half-line feed	<esc>-8
Forward half-line feed	<esc>-9

The **col** command assumes that SO (start-text) marks the beginning of use of an alternate character set and that SI (end-text) marks the end.

COMMENTS Most typically, this command is used with the output of a formatting program, such as **nroff**.

SEE ALSO UNIX Features: Standard I/O, Redirection, and Pipes; Filters

EXAMPLES

---

1. Look at a file containing reverse line feeds.

   ```
   col < doc1
   ```

   Note that **col** reads the standard input, which means that redirection should be used to examine a file.

2. Print a file on a printer that does not allow reverse line feeds.

   ```
   col < doc1 ¦ lp
   ```

   Since **col** sends its output to the standard output, a pipe can be used to reroute the output to the **lp** (line print) command.

3. Route **nroff** output to a printer with limited capabilities.

   ```
   nroff doc.nr ¦ col ¦ lp
   ```

   Here pipes handle both **col**'s input and output.

---

comm

PURPOSE Use the **comm** command to examine two sorted text files for common lines.

FORMAT comm [-123] *file1 file2*

DESCRIPTION The **comm** command looks at two files, which should be sorted according to the ASCII collating sequence (the **sort** command can do the sorting). Then **comm** displays three columns, the first column containing lines found only in the first file, the second containing lines found only in the second file, and the third containing lines found in both files. Options let you suppress the printing of certain columns. You can use – as a filename to indicate the standard input.

COMMON USES You can use **comm** to compare two lists (contained in separate files) for common items or to find what one list contains that the other doesn't.

OPTIONS The following options are available with **comm**.

OPTION	ACTION
-1	Omits column 1.
-2	Omits column 2.
-3	Omits column 3.

Combinations like **-12** omit more than one column (in this case, columns 1 and 2).

COMMENTS The **comm**, **diff**, and **cmp** commands all compare files. However, **comm** is limited to sorted text files, and **diff** is limited to text files. The **cmp** command can be used both with text and with non-text files, including programs.

SEE ALSO UNIX Commands: **cmp**; **diff**; **sort**
UNIX Features: Standard I/O, Redirection, and Pipes

EXAMPLES

1. Find common and unique lines in two sorted files.

```
$ comm bugs1 bugs2
            ants
            bees
beetles
      dragonflies
      earwigs
            grasshoppers
            roaches
```

Here we find that the line **beetles** is found only in **bugs1**. The lines **dragonflies** and **earwigs** are only in **bugs2**, and the remaining lines are in both files.

2. Collect lines common to two files in a third file.

```
comm -12 bugs1 bugs2 > bugscom
```

Here the first two columns are suppressed, and the common lines are redirected to the **bugscom** file.

3. Find lines contained in an unsorted file but not in a sorted file.

```
sort newbugs ¦ comm -13 bugs1 -
```

The **comm** command can only compare sorted files, so first we must sort **newbugs** with the **sort** command. We could redirect the output of **sort** to a new file, and then compare the new file with **bugs1**. Instead, we use **comm**'s ability to read the standard input. The -, recall, stands for the standard input, and the pipe (¦) makes **sort**'s output **comm**'s standard input. Thus, the generic *file1* becomes **bugs1**, and the generic *file2* (the sorted output of **sort newbugs**) becomes -. The **-13** option means "print just the items unique to *file2*"; that is, unique to the sorted **newbugs** file.

cp

PURPOSE Use the **cp** command to copy files.

FORMAT **cp** *file newfile*

cp *file(s) directory*

DESCRIPTION The **cp** command can copy a single file to a new file, or it can copy one or more files to a given directory. The file permissions are copied, too.

COMMON USES You can use **cp** to create a backup file or to create a copy that you can then modify. You can copy a block of files to a given directory.

WHICH FORM TO USE The form

cp *file newfile*

creates a copy of *file* and gives it the name *newfile*. The form

cp *file(s) directory*

copies the indicated *file(s)* into *directory*, keeping the same basenames for the files (see Example 2).

To find out which form to use, **cp** looks at the final argument, or "target name," in the command line. If this argument is identifiable as the name of an existing directory, **cp** assumes you want to use the second form. If the target name is unfamiliar or it is the name of an existing file, **cp** assumes you want to use the first form.

If the target name is that of a file, the file is overwritten with the copied material. UNIX System V does not ask you if you are sure that you wish to overwrite; it just does it. So be cautious.

The **cp** command does not allow you to copy a file onto itself.

COMMENTS Although the **cp** command copies file permissions, the copy may not be accessible to the same people as the original. For example, suppose **ginger** copies **fred's steps** file and that **fred** has read and write permissions for the original file, while everyone else has only read permission. Then **ginger's** copy has the same permissions: read and write for the owner, and read for everyone else. But **ginger** is the owner of the copy, so owner write permission for the copy means **ginger** can write in it but **fred** can't, while owner write permission for the original means **fred** can write in it but **ginger** can't.

The **cp** command creates a new file that is a copy of the original. The **mv** command, on the other hand, changes the name of an existing file, while the **ln** command creates an additional name for an existing file.

By using redirection, you also can use the **cat** command to copy files, as in the following command:

```
cat original > notoriginal
```

This is particularly useful if you want to combine several files into one:

```
cat m1 m2 m3 m4 > mall
```

Note that **cp** preserves permissions, but **cat** doesn't.

SEE ALSO UNIX Commands: **ln; mv; rm; cat**
UNIX Features: Files and Directories; Pathnames and the Directory Tree; Filename Generation (wildcard characters)

EXAMPLES

1. Create a copy of a file.

```
cp resume resume.copy
```

This creates a new file called **resume.copy**, which is a copy of the original **resume** file.

2. Copy a group of files to a directory.

```
cp sterns broadmore clients
```

This copies the **sterns** and **broadmore** files to the **clients** directory. The copies have the same names as the originals; that is, the relative pathnames of the new files are **clients/sterns** and **clients/broadmore**.

3. Copy a related group of files to a directory.

```
cp *.c /usr/fimbol/cprogs
```

This uses the * wildcard character to copy a flock of C programs (indicated by .c extensions) to a directory.

PURPOSE Use the **cpio** command to copy files and directories into and out of archive files and to copy a directory tree (a directory and its subdirectories).

FORMAT cpio –o[acBv]   *Copy-out mode*

cpio –i[BcdmrtuvfSsb6] [*pattern(s)*]   *Copy-in mode*

cpio –p[adlmuv] *directory*   *Pass mode*

DESCRIPTION The **cpio** command has three basic modes. The **–o**, or "copy-out," mode copies a given list of files from a directory into an archive file. An archive file is used to store several files along with information about the stored files. The **–i**, or "copy-in," mode extracts requested files from such an archive file and places copies in the current working directory. Archives created by **cpio** are portable between different System V implementations.

The **–p**, or "pass," mode copies files from one directory tree to another; there is no archive file.

The three modes are discussed in more detail below.

COMMON USES You can use **cpio** to copy the contents of a directory or a directory tree into an archive file, from which you can later reconstruct the original files and directories. You also can copy a directory tree to another location. The **cpio** command can be used in shell scripts that create automatic backups.

COPY-OUT MODE The **cpio –o** mode reads the standard input to get the list of files to archive, and it sends the archived results to the standard output. Thus, by default, the input comes from the keyboard and the output goes to the screen. Neither of these defaults is particularly desirable, so normally redirection and pipes are used. For example, the following command copies the contents of the current working directory into an archive file:

```
ls | cpio -o > /usr/friples/save/old1
```

Here **ls** generates the list of files that **cpio** archives.

The output from **cpio** is padded to a multiple of 512 bytes.

When copying a directory tree (files, subdirectories, and so on), first use the **find** command to generate a complete list of filenames (see Example 5).

By default, using **cpio** to copy a file counts as accessing the file, and the access time for the original file, as shown by **ls –lu**, is updated.

COPY-IN MODE The **cpio –i** form extracts files from the standard input. In practice, this means redirection is usually used to obtain input from an archive file previously created by **cpio –o**. For instance,

```
cpio -i < /usr/friples/save/old1
```

places copies of the stored files in the current directory tree.

The actual directories used depends on how the files were stored. In our example, the stored files had pathnames relative to the directory that was current when they were stored, since they were generated by a simple **ls** command. If, for instance, the original directory contained a **smoof** file, then the **cpio –i** command above would copy a **smoof** file into the current directory. Suppose, though, the original archiving command were this:

```
ls .. | cpio -o > /usr/friples/save/old1
```

Then, if the parent directory contained a file called **fooms**, the filename would be stored as **../fooms**. As a result, the **cpio –i** command would attempt to place a **fooms** file in the parent directory of the current working directory.

By default, all files are extracted by **cpio**, but the optional *pattern(s)* argument causes only files whose names match the pattern to be extracted. For example,

```
cpio -i < /usr/friples/save/old1 *.f
```

extracts only those files whose names have a .f suffix. Multiple patterns can be provided.

The extracted copies have the same permission settings as the archived files. The owner and group identifications for the files are those of the user, unless the user is the superuser. In that case, the owner and group identifications of the archived file are used.

PASS MODE The **cpio –p** mode, like the copy-out mode, obtains the list of files to be copied from the standard input. But instead of combining the files into an archive file, it copies the listed files into a target *directory*. For example,

```
ls | cpio -p /usr/popo/junk
```

copies the files of the current directory (since that is what **ls** lists) into the **junk** directory. In this case, the result is the same as that produced by this command:

```
cp * /usr/popo/junk
```

However, the examples below show how **cpio** can be used to copy an entire directory tree, something **cp** does not do.

OPTIONS The Format section shows which options are allowed with each mode.

OPTION	ACTION
a	Resets the access times of input files to the values held before **cpio** was used (by default, they are updated). Files that are linked (see l) instead of copied are not affected.
B	Uses 5120-byte blocks for I/O. This is only meaningful when used with files representing character devices such as raw tape drives.
d	Creates directories as needed. This is useful when copying a directory tree.
c	Writes file information in text form for portability between systems.
r	Interactively renames files; a file is skipped if the user types <enter> at the beginning of a line.
t	Displays a table of contents of the archive file represented by the input; no files are copied.
u	Copies unconditionally. (By default, an existing file in a directory is not replaced by an *older* archive file of the same name.)
v	Prints the names of the files being processed; with **t**, provides a more detailed listing. This is useful for maintaining a log of **cpio** operations.
l	When possible, links files rather than copying them. This saves space, but a linked file is not a true backup, since it just provides a different pathname for the same file.
m	Retains the previous file modification time. This applies to regular files but not to directories being copied.
f	Copies all files except those in *pattern(s)*.
S	Swaps halfwords within each word (this option assumes four bytes per word). New with Release 3.
s	Swaps bytes within each halfword (again, this option assumes four bytes per word). New with Release 3.
b	Reverses the order of bytes within a word (this option assumes four bytes per word). New with Release 3.
6	Processes a file in the old UNIX Sixth Edition format. New with Release 3.

COMMENTS

The **cpio** archive format is not compatible with the **ar** or **tar** archive format. The **ar** command primarily is intended for object code files to be used with the **ld** (linker) command. **cpio** is oriented more toward archiving directories or directory trees and transferring files between systems. For saving archives on tape or other removable media, **tar** is more suitable. The **tar** command is block oriented; each new file is placed on a 1K boundary of the tape or disk; thus two 20-byte files would need 2K of storage. The **cpio** command saves material sequentially (a "streaming" backup), so less space is needed.

SEE ALSO   UNIX Commands: **ar; tar; ls; find**
UNIX Features: Standard I/O, Redirection, and Pipes; Groups; The Superuser

EXAMPLES

1. Copy all C programs (.c suffix) in a directory to an archive file.

   ```
   ls Cstuff/*.c ¦ cpio -o > Old/oldc
   ```

   The **ls** command generates the proper list of filenames, and redirection places the archived output in the **oldc** file.

2. Check the contents of an archive file.

   ```
   cpio -it < Old/oldc
   ```

   If the **t** is omitted, copies of the archived files are placed in the current directory.

3. Restore a set of files, renaming and deleting interactively.

   ```
   cpio -ir < Old/oldc
   ```

   As each filename is given, the user renames it. Typing <enter> at the beginning of the line deletes the file.

4. Archive material onto removable media.

   ```
   ls ¦ cpio -o > /dev/fd
   ```

   Since UNIX treats devices as files, the archive file can be a device. Here **/dev/fd** refers to a floppy disk drive.

   (continued)

5. Copy a directory tree into an archive file.

```
find . -print ! cpio -o > /usr/daffy/dstuff
```

The **-print** option causes the **find** command to print the names of all files in the current directory and all subdirectories. The files and archive information, including directory information, are placed in the **dstuff** file.

6. Recover a directory tree.

```
cpio -id < /usr/daffy/dstuff
```

The **d** option has **cpio** create directories and subdirectories as needed to reproduce the stored directory tree.

7. Copy a directory tree from one location to another.

```
$ cd /usr/sal
$ find . -depth -print ! cpio -pd /usr/pal
```

The contents of the **/usr/sal** directory, including subdirectories, are copied to **/usr/pal**. The **-depth** option causes subdirectories to be listed first so that the original directory is the last acted upon. This is useful when the person doing the copying lacks write permission for the source directory.

Why do we change to the **/usr/sal** directory instead of using **find /usr/sal**? Using **find .** causes **find** to generate filenames like **foo** and **Flo/fop**. But using **find /usr/sal** produces names like **/usr/sal/foo** and **/usr/sal/Flo/fop**. Thus **find /usr/sal** produces **/usr** and **/usr/Flo** subdirectories; that is, the **foo** copy is **/usr/pal/usr/sal/foo** instead of **/usr/pal/foo**.

cron

PURPOSE The system uses the **cron** command to execute commands at specified times.

FORMAT /etc/cron

DESCRIPTION The **cron** command normally is activated by the system administrator when the system is started up. It runs commands as scheduled in "crontab" files. Users may be allowed to create their own crontab files using the **crontab** command.

All actions taken by **cron** are recorded in a system log file.

COMMON USES You can use **cron**, via the **crontab** command, to run specified commands on a regular basis, such as once an hour or once a week.

COMMENTS The system administrator starts up the **cron** program. Other users access **cron** by using **crontab** to create files that **cron** will read. Use **cron** and **crontab** for commands that are to be run regularly, and use **at** for commands to be run just once.

SEE ALSO UNIX Commands: **at**; **crontab**

crontab

PURPOSE Use the **crontab** command to create files of commands to be run by the **cron** program.

FORMAT crontab [*file*]
crontab -r
crontab -l

DESCRIPTION The **crontab** command places a given "crontab" file in a directory read by cron. If no filename is given, the standard input is used. Each line in a crontab file contains a time pattern and a command. The **cron** program runs the command as indicated by the time pattern. Each user can have only one crontab file, and each call to **crontab** overwrites your previous crontab file. Options let you list and remove crontab files. Unless redirection is used, the output of commands run by **crontab** is mailed to you. Access to the **crontab** command may be restricted.

COMMON USES You can use **crontab** to create commands that are run once a month, every Sunday, every hour, and so on.

OPTIONS There are two mutually exclusive options for the **crontab** command:

OPTION	ACTION
-r	Removes your current crontab file.
-l	Lists your current crontab file.

ACCESS If there is a file called **/usr/lib/cron/cron.allow**, all users whose names appear in that file can use **crontab**. If that file does not exist, then UNIX checks the **/usr/lib/cron/cron.deny** file to see who cannot use **crontab**. If neither file exists, only **root** can use **crontab**. If only **cron.deny** exists but it is empty, everyone can use **crontab**.

CRONTAB FILE FORMAT Each line in a crontab file must consist of six fields separated by spaces or tabs. The first five fields specify the time, and the sixth field is a string representing the command to be run.

The time fields are integers in the following order and with the following ranges:

FIELD	RANGE
Minute	0–59
Hour	0–23 (midnight is 0)
Day of month	1–31
Month of year	1–12
Day of week	0–6 (Sunday is 0)

Each field can be a single integer; an asterisk (*) to indicate all legal values; a range, such as **1-5**; or a comma-separated list of integers and ranges, such as **4,6** or **4-10,12-15,18**. Here are some sample time patterns and their meanings:

PATTERN	MEANING
0 0 * * *	Every day at 0:00.
0 1 * * 1	Every Monday at 1:00 am.
0 1 1 * *	The first of every month at 1:00 am.
0 0,20,40 6-18 * * *	Every 20 minutes from 6:00 am to 6:40 pm every day.
0 1 2 * 2	The second day of each month and each Tuesday at 1:00 am.

Note that when both the day of the month and the day of the week are given, they are interpreted separately. For instance, in the last example above, the command is run as described and not only on those days that are simultaneously a Tuesday and the second day of a month.

In the sixth field, or command string, the end of the command string is marked by the newline character (produced by hitting <enter>) or by the % sign, whichever comes first. Text following the % is taken as standard input for the command.

COMMENTS This command most often is used by the system administrator to run system programs on a regular basis. These programs might, for example, perform accounting and housekeeping chores. Individual users may use it to run individually developed file-maintenance programs on a regular basis.

SEE ALSO UNIX Commands: **at; cron**
UNIX Features: Processes

1. Set up a crontab file.

   ```
   crontab do_file
   ```

   This copies the contents of **do_file** into your personal crontab file. Note that you can have at most one crontab file.

2. Show the contents of your crontab file.

   ```
   $ crontab -l
   30 2 1 * * echo PAY YOUR RENT
   0 1 24 12 * echo Christmas is tomorrow
   0 1 * * 1  /usr/franny/bin/listold
   ```

   The first line mails the message **PAY YOUR RENT** to the user on the first of each month. The second mails another message once a year. The third runs the **listold** command every Monday at 1:00 am. The **listold** command could be, for example, a shell script using the **find** command to generate a list of old files that are candidates for removal. Note that the full pathname is used for the **listold** command; **cron** is not run from the user's current working directory, so pathnames relative to that directory won't work.

3. Get rid of a crontab file.

   ```
   crontab -r
   ```

   That's all it takes to remove your crontab file.

PURPOSE   Use the **csplit** command to split a file into smaller files.

FORMAT   **csplit** [**-sk**] [**-f***prefix*] *file split-point(s)*

Here *prefix* is a name to be used with the new files, *file* is the name of the file to be split, and *split-point(s)* are arguments describing where to split the file.

DESCRIPTION   The **csplit** command splits a specified file into smaller files. The splitting can be done on the basis of line numbers or by context; that is, the file will be split at specified words or patterns. By default, the new files are named **xx00**, **xx01**, and so on. The original file is left unaltered. Portions of the original file can be skipped instead of copied, if desired. Up to 100 new files can be created. You can use **-** as a filename to make **csplit** read the standard input.

COMMON USES   You can use **csplit** to split a large file into more manageable sections, and you can use it to recover files that **cat** has joined.

OPTIONS   The **csplit** command has the following three options:

OPTION	ACTION
-s	Suppresses the character counts. By default, **csplit** prints the size, in characters, of each file produced.
-k	Doesn't remove previously created files when an error occurs. By default, if there is an error, such as when you specify a split point that doesn't exist, all the new files are removed.
-f*prefix*	Uses *prefix* instead of **xx** for the portion of the filenames that precedes 00, 01, and so on.

SPECIFYING SPLIT POINTS   There are several ways to specify at which points a file is to be split. In each case, the first file created will contain everything up to, but not including, the first split point. The first split point then becomes the new current line. The second file created will start at the current line and will contain everything up to, but not including, the next split point, and so on.

Here are the various forms for the split-point arguments:

FORM	ACTION
/exp/	Creates a file from the current line up to, but not including, the first line containing the regular expression *exp*. The **csplit** command recognizes the same regular expressions that **ed** does. This form of split-point argument can be followed by an optional *-n* or **+***n* offset, where *n* indicates the number of lines before or after the expression the split point should be put. For instance, /**Part 2**/**-3** indicates three lines before the next line containing **Part 2**. Note that no spaces are allowed before the offset.
%exp%	Works like /exp/, except the section of the original file from the current line up to, but not including, the first line containing the regular expression *exp* is skipped instead of being copied to a separate file. In other words, the current line is moved without a segment being copied.
lnumber	Creates a file from the current line number up to, but not including, *lnumber*, which is an integer representing a line number.
{num}	Repeats the preceding pattern *num* times. Thus /**Month**/ {10} means "use the first 10 lines containing **Month** as split points." When preceded by a line number, the split points are the first *num* multiples of that amount. For instance, 100 {5} means "use lines 100, 200, 300, 400, and 500 as split points". This construction is useful for files that organize data in a systematic fashion.

COMMENTS   The simpler **split** command can be used to split a file into equal-sized chunks.

SEE ALSO   UNIX Commands: **cat; split**
UNIX Features: Standard I/O, Redirection, and Pipes; Regular Expressions; Filters

EXAMPLES

1. Divide a file into three parts by context.

   ```
   csplit report /Part 2/ /Part 3/
   ```

   This splits the **report** file into three parts. Everything up to, but not including, the first line containing **Part 2** is copied into a file called **xx00**. Then the **xx01** file receives text starting with the line containing **Part 2** and continuing up to the line containing **Part 3**. Finally, the **xx02** file gets the text from **Part 3** to the end.

2. Split a document into four parts by line number.

   ```
   csplit -facc account 100 222 455
   ```

   Lines 1 through 99 of the **account** file are placed in the **acc00** file, lines 100 through 221 go into **acc01**, lines 222 through 454 into **acc02**, and lines 455 through to the end go into **acc03**.

3. Split a document using offsets from a pattern.

   ```
   csplit -k dearsam /Page/+4 {20}
   ```

   This splits the **dearsam** file four lines after the first 20 occurrences of the word **Page**. The **-k** option means that the output is retained even if the **dearsam** file contains **Page** less than 20 times.

4. Use **csplit** with the standard input.

   ```
   sort +2nr applicants | csplit -fgroup - 11 51 101
   ```

   This sorts the **applicants** file in reverse numeric order, starting with the third field. The top 10 sorted lines go into **group00**, the next 40 into **group01**, and so on. The **-** argument represents the standard input of **csplit** which, because of the pipe, is the output of the **sort** command.

PURPOSE Use the **cu** command to call up other systems.

FORMAT cu [*option(s)*] *telno*

cu [*option(s)*] -l *line*

cu [*option(s)*] *systemname*

The first form identifies the system by a telephone number, and the second identifies it by a connect line. The third form identifies the called system by its **uucp** system name.

The telephone number (*telno*) argument can include an **=** sign to indicate that a dial tone should be awaited; that is, if you have to dial 9 to get an outside line, use **9=5551212** to dial 555-1212 on an outside line.

DESCRIPTION The **cu** command is used to call other systems. The linkage may be by direct line or by modem. Typically, the called system is a computer system running UNIX, but it could be a computer running another operating system or a terminal. Once connected to another system, you follow normal procedures for logging in on that system, and your current terminal then becomes a remote terminal for the called system. In addition, the **cu** command allows you to transfer files between your system and the called system. To perform this and some other actions, **cu** recognizes special escape sequences, which are described later.

COMMON USES You can use **cu** to log in on another system on which you have an account. Then you can transfer files from one system to the other.

OPTIONS Note that not all options can be used with all **cu** format forms; restrictions are noted in the following option descriptions.

OPTION	ACTION
-s *speed*	Specifies the transmission speed in baud. By default, the speed is "Any," meaning that the system will use the speed of the next available communication device, as given in the device file. If you specify a speed with -s (and fail to use -l), **cu** uses the first available device having that speed. This option is not used in the *systemname* mode.

OPTION	ACTION
-l *line*	Specifies a device to be used as a communication line. If the line has a name of the form **/dev/ttyXX**, it is sufficient to type **ttyXX**. If the device is an autodialer, a phone number also must be supplied. If you use **-s**, **cu** obtains the speed of the line from a device file. If you use both **-s** and **-l**, **cu** checks the devices file to see if the combination is possible. If it isn't, the call is canceled and an error message is displayed. This option is not used in the *systemname* mode.
-h	Emulates local echo; this supports calls to non-echoing computer systems.
-t	Used to dial an ASCII terminal set to auto answer. The carriage return is mapped to carriage-return/line-feed pairs. Used only with the *telno* mode.
-d	Prints diagnostic traces.
-o	Generates odd parity for data sent to the remote system.
-e	Generates even parity for data sent to the remote system.
-n	Prompts the user to provide the telephone number interactively. Not used with the *line* or *systemname* mode.

OVERVIEW   The **cu** command runs two separate processes. A *transmit* process reads lines from the standard input (by default, the keyboard) and transmits them to the called system. However, lines beginning with a tilde (~) are processed as instructions rather than transmitted (see below). A *receive* process takes lines from the remote system and passes them to the standard output (by default, your terminal). Again, lines beginning with a tilde are exceptions, as described in the next section.

   Normally, **cu** uses a DC3/DC1 protocol to control input from the remote system and so protect the buffer from being overrun. (This protocol has the sender await a ready signal from the receiver. In ASCII code, DC1 is 17 and DC3 is 19.)

ESCAPE SEQUENCES A tilde (~) typed at the beginning of a line indicates that the line is to be interpreted as an instruction rather than as a line to be transmitted to the other system. Here is a list of commands available in the transmit process:

ESCAPE SEQUENCE	EFFECT
~.	Terminates the connection.
~!	Escapes to the local interactive command interpreter (normally, the **sh** shell).
~!*cmd*	Runs the *cmd* command on the local system.
~$*cmd*	Runs the *cmd* command on the local system and sends its output to the remote system as a command to be run there.
~%cd	Changes the directory on the local system. New with Release 2.
~%take *original* [*copy*]	Copies the *original* file from the remote system to the *copy* file on the local system. If *copy* is omitted, uses the original name for the copy, too.
~%put *original* [*copy*]	Copies the *original* file from the local system to the *copy* file on the remote system. If *copy* is omitted, uses the original name for the copy, too.
~~*line*	Transmits ~*line* to the remote system. This is used to call system B from system A, then call system C from system B. Then you use ~ to execute commands on system A, and ~~ to execute commands on system B.
~%break	Transmits a BREAK to the remote system; can be abbreviated to ~%b. (A regular BREAK would be interpreted by the local system.)
~%nostop	Toggles between the default DC3/DC1 input control protocol and no input control. This is used when the remote system does not respond properly to these characters.
~%debug	Toggles the –d debugging option on and off. This command can be abbreviated to ~%d. New with Release 3.
~t	Prints values describing the user's terminal. These values are useful for debugging. New with Release 3.
~l	Prints values describing the remote communication line (useful for debugging). New with Release 3.

CAUTIONS The ~%put command uses **stty** and **cat** on the remote system. It also requires that both systems use the same current erase characters and the same current kill characters.

The ~%take command uses **echo** and **cat** on the remote system. If tabs are to be copied on the remote system without being expanded to spaces, the **stty** command should be used to set **tabs** mode there.

COMMENTS The **cu** command can connect you to another UNIX system, but you still need to log in to that system; thus normally you would use **cu** to call only those systems with which you have an account. The **uucp** command, on the other hand, may allow you to transfer files to or from a UNIX system with which you do not have an account. And the **uux** command may allow you to execute commands on a system with which you do not have an account. However, system restrictions may heavily restrict the scope of these last two commands.

SEE ALSO UNIX Commands: **uucp**; **uux**

EXAMPLES

1. Call a computer that has the phone number 555-1000.

   ```
   cu 5551000
   ```

   The computer uses the first available device and baud rate.

2. Call a computer known to have a 1200-baud modem.

   ```
   cu -s 1200 5551000
   ```

   The local computer uses the first available device supporting that speed.

   (continued)

3. Call a system connected by a direct line identified as **/dev/tty88**.

```
cu -l tty88
```

4. Call a system using an autodialer identified as **/dev/mod02**.

```
cu -l mod02 5551000
```

5. Once connected, copy files and quit.

```
$ ~%take costs.86
$ ~%put parts parts.86
$ <control-d>
NO CARRIER
> ~.
$
```

The **take** command copies the **costs.86** file from the remote system to the local one; the copy also is named **costs.86**. The **put** command copies the local **parts** file to the remote system and names the copy **parts.86**. The **<control-d>** logs you out of the remote system, and the **>** is a modem prompt. The **~.** command quits **cu**. If you omit logging out, terminating the connection with **~.** generates a hangup signal at the remote UNIX system; normally, that signal will log you out (see the **stty** command).

PURPOSE Use the **cut** command to select columns or fields from each line of a file.

FORMAT cut –c*list* [*file(s)*]

cut –f*list* [–d*char*] [–s] [*file(s)*]

Here *list* identifies the columns or fields to be passed to the output, and *char* is the character to be used as the field delimiter.

DESCRIPTION The –c option of the **cut** command passes indicated columns from a list of files and displays the results. The –f option passes indicated fields. A column is a particular character position in a line, while a field is a group of characters whose extent is marked by a "field delimiter." The tab character is the default field delimiter, but the –d option allows you to select another character as the delimiter. Either the –c or the –f option must be used. Standard input is used if the list of files is omitted.

COMMON USES You can use **cut** to select just certain columns from a table or to print just certain fields in a data file. You also can use it to select certain values from a line for use in a shell script.

OPTIONS The **cut** command has four options:

OPTION	ACTION
–c*list*	Passes the columns indicated by *list*. For example, –c10–15 means "pass columns 10 through 15" (see the Lists section below for more details). Note that no spaces are allowed in typing the option.
–f*list*	Passes the fields indicated by *list*. For instance, –f1,3 means "pass fields 1 and 3" (see the Lists section for more details). Note that no spaces are allowed in typing the option.
–d*char*	Makes the character following –d the field delimiter. To use a space or other character with a special meaning to the shell, quote the character. Thus use –d ' ' to make the space character the field delimiter.
–s	Suppresses lines containing no field delimiter. By default, such lines are passed unchanged.

LISTS Lists used should contain no spaces. Use a hyphen to indicate a range: 5–25 indicates the range 5 through 25. Individual values and ranges can be listed by separating them with commas: 5,7,9 and 5,7–10,12–18 are examples. The combination –5 is the same as 1–5, and the combination 4– is the same as 4–end.

COMMENTS The **cut** command makes vertical cuts in a file. The **join** command can be used to glue together files vertically.

SEE ALSO UNIX Commands: **join**
UNIX Features: Standard I/O, Redirection, and Pipes; Filters; Shell Scripts

EXAMPLES

---

1. Display columns 10 through 25 of a table.

   ```
   cut -c10-25 table1
   ```

   If the table includes a heading, characters 10 through 25 of the heading are passed, too.

2. Display fields 3 and 5 of a table in which the fields are separated by tabs.

   ```
   cut -f3,5 table2
   ```

   If tabs have been used to separate field headings as well as the actual values, just the corresponding field headings are passed. If, however, the table has a tab-free heading, the whole heading is printed. (Using the **-s** option instead of the **-f** option would suppress the printing of lines without tabs.)

3. Look at the first and fifth fields of the **/etc/passwd** file.

   ```
   cut -f1,5 -d: /etc/passwd
   ```

   The **/etc/passwd** file uses the colon to separate fields, so the **-d** option is used to make the colon the field delimiter. (The fields contain information such as login names, encoded passwords, user ID, group ID, and comments.)

4. Use **cut** in a pipe.

   ```
   who ! cut -d" " -f1
   ```

   This takes the output of the **who** command and prints the first field, which is the user's login name. The **who** command uses spaces as separators, so the **-d** option is used to specify that a space is the field delimiter.

---

5. Get options from the command line of a shell script.

```
for ARG in $@
do
      if [ " `echo $ARG | cut -c1 `" = "-" ]
      then case $ARG in
            -a) do_option_a; shift;;
            -b) do_option_b; shift;;
            *)  do_error;;
            esac
      fi
done
```

This code would be placed at the beginning of a shell script that needs to process options, which are identified by a hyphen prefix. The notation $@ represents all the arguments in the command line. The **for** loop causes the shell variable **$ARG** to be set to each argument in turn and then be processed. The **echo $ARG** command outputs the argument, and the pipe makes the argument the input to **cut**, so each argument in turn becomes input to **cut**. The **–c1** option passes just the first character, and the backquote mechanism (command substitution) replaces the whole pipe with its output. This means that

```
`echo $ARG | cut -c1`
```

is replaced by the first character of **$ARG**. The **if** statement tests to see if this first character is a hyphen. If it is, then the **case** statement is executed to process the option. The **shift** statements discard the argument after it has been processed, so after the **for** loop completes, **$@** is the original argument list minus the options, assuming the options are the first arguments.

The most important thing about this example is that it illustrates that **cut** can be used to edit commands.

date

PURPOSE Use the **date** command to obtain the current date and time.

FORMAT **date** [**+***format*]

date *mmddhhmm*[*yy*]   *Superuser only.*

Here *format* specifies how the date is to be displayed, and *mmddhhmm*[*yy*] indicates the date to be set.

DESCRIPTION When used with no arguments, the **date** command displays the current date and time. The superuser can supply a date/time argument (*mmddhhmm*[*yy*]) to reset the system clock, and other users can supply a *format* argument to specify the form in which the time is displayed.

COMMON USES You can use **date** to check the time and to provide date information for log files.

DATE FORMAT If no *format* is specified, the date is expressed in a string in the following form:

Sun Aug 31 16:06:14 PDT 1986

If a *format* is specified, it normally consists of a string enclosed in single quotes. The quotes make the string a single argument and avoid confusing the shell. Characters within the quotes are printed literally, except that particular fields within the date are represented by a percent sign (%) followed by a code letter. For example, the expression %m represents the month number, and the command **date '+month = %m'** displays output in the form **month = 11**. Here is a list of the special field descriptors recognized by **date**:

DESCRIPTOR	MEANING
%n	Inserts a newline character.
%t	Inserts a tab character.
%m	The month number (1–12).
%d	The day number (1–31).
%y	The last two digits of the year (00–99).
%D	The date in the format *mm/dd/yy.*
%H	The hour (00–23).
%M	The minute (00–59).
%S	The second (00–59).
%T	The time in the format *HH:MM:SS.*

DESCRIPTOR	MEANING
%j	The day of the year (001–366).
%w	The day of the week (0–6; Sunday is 0).
%a	The day's name (Sunday–Saturday).
%h	The month's name (January–December).
%r	The time in AM/PM notation.
%%	Prints a single % symbol.

DATE/TIME FORMAT Here are the fields used in the second form of **date**, which the superuser uses to set the system clock:

FIELD	MEANING
mm	Two-digit month number (01–12).
dd	Two-digit day number (00–31).
hh	Two-digit hour number (00–23).
mm	Two-digit minute value (00–59).
yy	(Optional.) The last two digits of the year. The current year is assumed if the *yy* argument is omitted.

COMMENTS The system uses Greenwich Mean Time internally, but **date** makes the necessary conversions between GMT and local time, including the effects of daylight savings. The superuser preferably should change the date setting only when the system is in the single-user mode.

SEE ALSO UNIX Features: The Superuser

EXAMPLES

1. Display the current time and date.

```
$ date
Tue Sep 2  09:30:00 PDT 1986
```

2. Log when a certain shell script is used.

```
date >> /usr/hortence/pooh.log
```

If this line is contained in the script, it causes the time and date to be redirected and appended to the **pooh.log** file each time the script is run.

3. Display the time in a modified form.

```
$ date '+Date = %d/%m/%y'
Date = 28/10/88
```

This displays the date in European form: *day/month/year.*

4. Set the date.

```
date 04072210
```

This sets the date to April 7 of the current year, and sets the time to 22:10, or 10:10 pm.

PURPOSE Use the **dd** command to convert and copy files. It can convert character formats and copy from one device to another.

FORMAT **dd** [*option*=*value*] ...

DESCRIPTION The **dd** command copies the indicated input file to the indicated output file while making conversions (such as EBCDIC to ASCII) as indicated by the options. The standard input and output are used by default, but files, including files representing devices, can be specified. The **dd** command reads and writes data in blocks whose sizes can be matched to those required by the devices used. When finished, **dd** reports the number of whole and partial input and output blocks handled.

COMMON USES You can use **dd** to read a tape encoded in IBM mainframe EBCDIC code and copy it to a UNIX file using the ASCII code.

OPTIONS Each option is of the form *option*=*value*.

OPTION	ACTION
if=*file*	Uses *file* for the input file; this can be a device.
of=*file*	Uses *file* for output; this can be a device.
ibs=*n*	Reads the input in blocks of *n* bytes; the default is 512.
obs=*n*	Writes the output in blocks of *n* bytes; the default is 512.
bs=*n*	Sets both input and output block size to *n*. This supersedes **obs** and **ibs**.
cbs=*n*	Sets the conversion buffer size to *n* (see below for details).
skip=*n*	Skips *n* input blocks before starting to copy.
seek=*n*	Seeks *n* blocks from the start of the output file before copying. This means the output data begins *n* blocks into the output file.
count=*n*	Copies only *n* input blocks.
conv=**ascii**	Converts EBCDIC to ASCII.
conv=**ebcdic**	Converts ASCII to EBCDIC.
conv=**ibm**	Converts ASCII to EBCDIC (uses an alternative, less common mapping of characters).
conv=**lcase**	Converts uppercase to lowercase.
conv=**ucase**	Converts lowercase to uppercase.

(continued)

91

OPTION	ACTION	*(continued)*
conv=swab	Swaps the bytes in each pair of bytes. (Some machines store two-byte words with the high byte first and others with the low byte first.)	
conv=noerror	Keeps processing if errors occur.	
conv=sync	Pads every input block to the **ibs** value.	

A comma can be used to indicate more than one conversion. For example, **conv=ascii,lcase** specifies conversion to lowercase ASCII form.

The **cbs** option applies to **ascii** and **ebcdic** conversions only. When converting to ASCII, the number of bytes specified by **cbs** are read into a conversion buffer. Trailing blanks are omitted, a newline is added, and the resulting line is placed in the output file. When converting to EBCDIC, an ASCII line is placed in the buffer. The newline is omitted, and trailing blanks are added to produce a block of the length specified by **cbs**. EBCDIC data often consists of images of 80-column punched cards, so a **cbs** value of 80 is used for such cases, making each ASCII file line correspond to one 80-column card.

Block sizes can include the suffixes **k**, **b**, and **w** to indicate units of 1024, 512, and 2 bytes, respectively. Thus a block size of **2k** is 2048 bytes. Also, an **x** can be used to indicate multiplication; for example, **10x80** indicates 800 bytes. The 512- and 1024-byte units are common data transfer and storage block sizes for magnetic media.

COMMENTS While most of the computer industry uses the ASCII code to represent text, IBM mainframes use IBM's EBCDIC code. The **dd** command is particularly useful for transferring text from EBCDIC systems to ASCII systems.

SEE ALSO UNIX Commands: **tr**
UNIX Features: Standard I/O, Redirection, and Pipes; Filters; The Machine Collating Sequence

EXAMPLES

1. Convert a file to lowercase.

   ```
   dd if=mixed of=simple conv=lcase
   ```

   Here **mixed** is the input file, and **simple** is the output file.

2. Convert an EBCDIC tape to an ASCII file.

   ```
   dd if=/dev/rmt0 of=chomp.f ibs=800 cbs=80\
   conv=ascii,lcase
   ```

   Here **/dev/rmt0** indicates a tape device (we've used a backslash at the end of the first line to continue the command to the following line). The exact notation differs from machine to machine, but the **r** indicates a "raw" device; that is, a device without a standard buffer interposed. For raw devices, you can specify the block size in which data is to be read or written. In this case, the block size is **800**, corresponding to blocks representing ten 80-character cards.

df

PURPOSE Use the **df** command to find out how much file system space is still available.

FORMAT df [–t] [*filesystem(s)*]

DESCRIPTION The **df** command reports the amount of free space (in 512-byte blocks) and the number of free "i-nodes," or information nodes, available on the indicated file system. (An i-node is a table that stores information about a file, such as its location on the disk, its size, and so on. A file system is a set of files and directories stored as a unit on a particular device or portion of a device.) The file system can be identified by the hardware device or by the name of the directory on which the device is "mounted." If you don't identify a particular file system when giving the **df** command, the free space for all mounted file systems is given.

COMMON USES You can use **df** to see if you are running out of disk space.

OPTIONS The **df** command has only one option:

OPTION	ACTION
–t	In addition to reporting the free space, also reports the total space (free and used).

COMMENTS The number of files that can be stored on a file system depends on two things. First, it depends on the total amount of storage space available. Second, it depends on how much space has been set aside for i-nodes. Each file stored on a UNIX system must have an i-node set up for it. Thus there has to be room for the files themselves and room for the i-nodes.

File systems are set up using administrative commands not discussed in this book.

For system administrators, a good rule of thumb is that when an active file system, such as one used for databases or login directories, is more than 90 percent full, it's time to start deleting files that are not used (or to reorganize, moving applications or login IDs to other file systems). Using **df -t** displays this ratio and on some systems also computes the percentage.

SEE ALSO UNIX Features: Files and Directories; File Systems; Special Files

EXAMPLES

1. Find the total amount of disk space available.

```
$ df
/         (/dev/hp0a ):       2392  blocks      427 i-nodes
/u        (/dev/hp0g ):       8476  blocks    17311 i-nodes
/tmp      (/dev/hp1a ):       6669  blocks     3644 i-nodes
/usr      (/dev/hp1g ):      11628  blocks    12334 i-nodes
```

This system has four file systems. The device names suggest that there are two hard disks (**hp0** and **hp1**), each partitioned into two parts. (The device names depend on the system.) The root file system (/) is located on the **hp0a** disk partition, or, in UNIX terminology, the **/dev/hp0a** file system is mounted on the / directory. Similarly, the **/dev/hp1g** file system is mounted on the **/usr** directory. The root file system here has 2392 blocks of 512 bytes each open for use; up to 427 more files (the number of i-nodes left) can be accommodated.

2. Find the total capacity of a particular file system.

```
$ df -t    /dev/root
/    (/dev/root ):     16488 blocks    3361 i-nodes
           ( 36446 total blocks,  574 for i-nodes)
```

The total capacity of the root disk system is 36,446 blocks, or about 18MB of memory, of which 574 blocks are set aside for i-node information. Each block can hold several i-nodes, which is why 3361 (the number of i-nodes used) can be larger than 574 (the total number of blocks of i-nodes). This system uses a different device name from that of the first example.

diff

PURPOSE Use the **diff** command to compare two files; **diff** determines which lines in two text files must be changed to make the files identical.

FORMAT diff [–efbh] *file1 file2*

Here *file1* and *file2* are the two files to be compared.

DESCRIPTION The **diff** command looks at two text files whose names are provided as the *file1* and *file2* arguments, and indicates the editing changes (additions, deletions, and line replacements) necessary to make the first file identical to the second. The affected lines of each file are listed after each suggested change. The changes alone can be saved as a script usable by the **ed** editor.

If *file1* or *file2* is –, then the standard input is used for that file. If *file1* is a directory and *file2* is a regular file, then *file2* is compared with a file by the same name in the *file1* directory; that is, with *file1/file2*. A similar rule applies if *file2* is a directory and *file1* is a regular file.

COMMON USES You can use **diff** to find the differences between two files. To save space, you can erase one of two similar files and just retain the differences. This allows you to reconstruct, say, an earlier version if necessary without keeping the entire old file.

OUTPUT FORMAT The output uses the following formats to list any appends, deletions, or changes. In the following sections, *n* represents a line number and *line* represents a line of text.

FORMAT	DESCRIPTION
Appending	
*n1*a*n2,n3*	Appends lines *n2* through *n3* of the second file to the first file,
>*line n1*	following line *n1* of the first file. The line of text following the
<*line n2*	> (*line n1*) is the affected line from the first file. The lines of text
...	following the < are the affected lines from the second file; each
<*line n3*	line from *n2* through *n3* is displayed in this fashion.
Deleting	
n1,*n2*d*n3*	Deletes lines *n1* through *n2* in the first file; again, the affected
>*line n1*	lines of text are displayed. This brings the two files into agree-
...	ment up to (but not including) line *n3* of the second file.
>*line n2*	

FORMAT	DESCRIPTION
Changing	
n1,n2cn3,n4 **>***line n1* ... **>***line n2* — — — **<***line n3* ... **<***line n4*	Replaces lines *n1* through *n2* in the first file with lines *n3* through *n4* of the second file, and displays the affected lines.

Reversing the instructions and interchanging **a**'s with **d**'s produces instructions that convert the second file to the first (of course, it is simpler to reverse the order in which the files are listed in the **diff** command line).

In all cases, addresses of the form *n1,n2* can be replaced with a single number if just one line is affected.

OPTIONS The **diff** command has four options:

OPTION	ACTION
-b	Ignores trailing blanks (spaces and tabs) in a line and considers other strings of blanks to be identical, even if of different lengths.
-e	Produces a script of **a**, **c**, and **d** commands allowing **ed** to re-create *file2* from *file1*.
-f	Produces a similar script, but in the opposite order. The script, however, is not usable with **ed**.
-h	Does a fast, half-hearted job, without attempting to find the most efficient set of editing changes. Changes must be limited to short, well-separated stretches. The **-e** and **-f** options don't work with this option.

EXIT STATUS The command produces these exit values, which are usable by shell scripts:

VALUE	MEANING
0	No differences.
1	Differences.
2	Errors.

COMMENTS The **comm**, **diff**, and **cmp** commands all compare files. However, **comm** is limited to sorted text files, and **diff** is limited to text files. The **cmp** command can be used with both text and non-text files, including compiled programs, but its output is less informative.

The **–f** option of the **diff** command is not usable by **ed** because it uses notations like **d2** instead of **2d** (this notation reminds the user that the changes apply to the second file rather than to the first). Such a script can, however, be edited to fit the **ed** command format.

SEE ALSO UNIX Commands: **cmp**; **comm**; **ed**
UNIX Features: Exit Values; Standard I/O, Redirection, and Pipes

EXAMPLES

These examples use the following two files:

```
$ cat aha
The purpose of this file is to provide text that can be
used to test various features and commands of UNIX System V.
If necessary, more text will be added.

$ cat bah
The purpose of this file is to provide text that can be,
when necessary,
used to test various features and commands of UNIX System V.
```

1. Find the differences between two files.

```
$ diff aha bah
1c1,2
< The purpose of this file is to provide text that can be
---
> The purpose of this file is to provide text that can be,
> when necessary,
3d3
< If necessary, more text will be added.
```

Paraphrasing these commands and UNIX's responses: To change file **aha** so that it is the same as file **bah**, change line 1 of **aha** to lines 1 through 2 of **bah**, then delete line 3 of **aha**. The lines preceded by **<** are from **aha**, and the lines preceded by **>** are from **bah**.

---

2. Produce an **ed** script for making one file duplicate another.

```
$ diff -e aha bah
3d
1c
The purpose of this file is to provide text that can be,
when necessary,
.
```

This says to delete the third line and to change the first line to the text that follows. The period at the beginning of the last line indicates the end of the text. Note that the deletion is done first. If the change were done first, the subsequent line numbering would have been changed, and the line to be deleted no longer would have been number **3**.

3. Save and use an **ed** script.

```
$ diff -e aha bah > changes
$ echo w >> changes
$ echo q >> changes
$ ed aha < changes
```

This saves the script produced by **diff** (which we showed in Example 2) in the **changes** file. To complete the script, we add the **w** (write) command and the **q** (quit) command to the script by using **echo** and redirection. (Or you can use an editor to make these additions to the **changes** file.) Then redirection is used to feed the editing commands in **changes** to the **ed** command.

dircmp

PURPOSE Use the **dircmp** command to compare files in two directories.

FORMAT dircmp [–d] [–s] *dir1 dir2*

DESCRIPTION The **dircmp** command examines two specified directories. It generates lists of files that are unique to each directory. In addition, if no option is given, **dircmp** displays a list indicating whether files of the same name have the same contents.

COMMON USES You can use **dircmp** to help you clean up your directory system by locating duplicate files. Or you can use it to help update a backup directory.

OPTIONS This command had two options until Release 3, which added one more:

OPTION	ACTION
–d	If the same name occurs in both directories, compares the two files as described under **diff** (no options).
–s	Suppresses messages about identical files.
–w*n*	Changes the width of the output lines to *n* characters (the default width is 72 characters). New with Release 3.

SEE ALSO UNIX Commands: **diff**

EXAMPLES

1. Compare two directories.

```
$ dircmp Dir1 Dir2
Sep  1 10:57 1986  Dir1 only and Dir2 only Page 1

./col1
./colesc
./collect
./colt
./coltext

Sep  1 10:57 1986  Comparison of Dir1 Dir2 Page 1
directory .
same        ./filey
different ./oddy
```

(Several blank lines have been omitted from the output.) The output shows four files found in only one or the other directory, and two filenames found in both. Of the latter, the **filey** file is the same in each, but the two **oddy** files differ.

If the –s option had been used, the **filey** files would not have been mentioned. If the –d option had been used, the result of running **diff** on the two **oddy** files would have been displayed.

dirname

PURPOSE Use the **dirname** command to obtain the directory string portion of a complete pathname; for example, to obtain **/usr/biffo** from the pathname **/usr/biffo/socks**.

FORMAT dirname *pathname*

DESCRIPTION The **dirname** command takes a full pathname as an argument and prints everything before the final / in the name.

COMMON USES You can use **dirname** in shell scripts that create a new file in the same directory as a given file.

COMMENTS The **basename** command returns the basename that follows the final slash in a full pathname, while **dirname** returns the part before the final slash.

SEE ALSO UNIX Commands: **basename**
UNIX Features: Pathnames and the Directory Tree; Command Substitution; Shell Variables

EXAMPLES

Here is how **dirname** works:

```
$ dirname /usr/goethe/werther
/usr/goethe
```

Just the pathname up to the final component is displayed.

1. Save the directory path of a particular file.

```
DIR=`dirname $SOURCEFILE`
```

Here **SOURCEFILE** is a shell variable that previously was assigned a full pathname. The backquotes mechanism (command substitution) assigns the directory pathname to the shell variable **DIR**.

PURPOSE Use the **du** (disk usage) command to estimate the space used by a set of files or a directory.

FORMAT **du** [-ars] [*name(s)*]

Here *name(s)* are directory names and, in case of the **-a** option, possibly filenames.

DESCRIPTION The **du** command estimates, in blocks of 512 bytes, the file space occupied by the files in the indicated directories. The current directory is used if none is provided in the command line. All files in a directory, including those in all its subdirectories, are included. Files with two or more links are counted just once, and files that cannot be read or opened by the invoker of the command are not counted at all.

COMMON USES You can use **du** to determine which of your directories uses the most space. This can be helpful when it's time to trim back your files or to rearrange your directories.

OPTIONS The **du** command has three options:

OPTION	ACTION
-a	Accepts filenames as well as directory names as arguments.
-r	Gives messages about files that cannot be read or opened. The **du** command does not estimate sizes for such files, and normally it does not mention them.
-s	Gives only the grand total for the specified directories and (with -a) files (by default, a size is printed for each file in a directory).

SEE ALSO UNIX Commands: **df**
UNIX Features: Files and Directories; Pathnames and the Directory Tree

EXAMPLES

1. Find disk usage for the current directory and its subdirectories.

```
$ du
26      ./C
4       ./Doodahs/Glint/Rocks
26      ./Doodahs/Glint
2       ./Doodahs/Glow
262     ./Doodahs
4       ./bin
140     ./Ctrain
450     .
```

Here the /C subdirectory occupies 56 blocks, and so on. Note that the **Doodahs** total includes all its subdirectories as well as space used in the **Doodah** directory itself. Note, too, that the final listing is for ., the current directory.

2. Find the total space for a given directory without listing subdirectories.

```
$ du -s Doodahs
262     ./Doodahs
```

3. Find the space used by a given directory, listing each file.

```
$ du -a C
2       ./C/usaf.c
2       ./C/usaf.o
18      ./C/a.out
2       ./C/show.c
2       ./C/show.o
26      ./C
```

PURPOSE   Use the **echo** command to display messages.

FORMAT   **echo** [*argument(s)*]

DESCRIPTION   The **echo** command displays its arguments on the standard output (by default, the terminal). Each argument is separated from the next by a space when displayed, and the entire output is terminated with a newline. The **echo** command recognizes several special notations (see below).

COMMON USES   You can use **echo** to generate messages in shell scripts or in your **.profile** file, and to examine values of shell variables and shell parameters. You also can use **echo** with redirection to append messages to a file.

SPECIAL NOTATIONS   The **echo** command recognizes the following notations (note that, when used with these notations, the backslash is a shell metacharacter and must be quoted or preceded by another backslash; see the examples):

NOTATION	MEANING
\b	The backspace character.
\c	Prints arguments up to that point, omitting the newline and ignoring the remaining arguments.
\f	The form-feed character.
\n	The newline character (go to the beginning of the next line).
\r	The carriage-return character (go to the beginning of the current line).
\t	The tab character.
\v	The vertical tab character.
\\	The backslash character.
\0*n*	*n* is a one- to three-digit octal number giving the ASCII code for the desired character.

SEE ALSO   UNIX Commands: **sh**
UNIX Features: Standard I/O, Redirection, and Pipes; Shell Scripts; Shell Variables; Command Substitution; Quoting; Extending Commands over More than One Line

EXAMPLES

1. Display a message.

```
$ echo Be      a        good programmer.
Be a good programmer.
$ echo 'Be      a        good programmer.'
Be      a        good programmer.
```

In the first use, **echo** has four command-line arguments, and each argument is separated by a space in the output. In the second use, the single quotes make the entire phrase, including the spaces, a single argument, so it is printed as it originally appeared.

2. Use special characters.

```
$ echo Only some of this\\c line will be printed.
Only some of this$ echo bob'\t\t'cat
bob             cat
$ echo "\t\t"bob\\rcat
cat             bob
```

Note the different ways the special characters are represented. The backslash can be doubled to represent a single backslash, or the characters can be contained in single or double quotes. When **\c** is used, the rest of the input line is truncated. Since no newline is used, the shell prompt ($) is on the same line as the preceding output. The next **echo** statement uses tabs (**\t**) to put space between **bob** and **cat**. The last part of this example uses tabs to move **bob** to the right, and then it uses a carriage return (**\r**) to place the following text at the beginning of the output line.

3. Customize a **.profile** file.

```
echo Welcome back to Grandma\'s computer.
```

Including this line in **.profile** causes it to be printed each time you log in. The **\'** prevents the shell from interpreting the single quote as a metacharacter.

4. Find the value of a particular shell variable.

```
$ echo The value of LPDEST is $LPDEST
The value of LPDEST is printer1
```

LPDEST is an environmental shell variable used by the **lp** command, and **$LPDEST** represents the value (here **printer1**) of the variable.

5. Create error messages for a shell script.

```
case $# in
    0) echo Usage: $0 file(s) 1>2 ; exit 1 ;;
esac
```

This **case** statement checks to see if the number of command-line arguments (**$#**) is 0; if it is, **echo** displays an error message that is redirected (**1>$2**) to the standard error.

6. Put a message in a log file.

```
echo $0 used `date` >> $HOME/Logdir/logfile
```

This line would be used in a shell script. The $0 represents the name of the script, and command substitution replaces `date` with its output. The resulting line is appended to a log file.

ed

PURPOSE Use the **ed** command to create and edit text files.

FORMAT ed [–] [–p *string*] [–s] [*file*]

Here *file* is the file to be edited. If omitted when the editor is invoked, the filename can be provided from within the **ed** program.

DESCRIPTION The **ed** command is a two-mode, line-oriented text editor. The two modes are the command mode, in which keystrokes are interpreted as commands, and the text mode, in which keystrokes are entered as text. In general, a command has two parts: an address or range of addresses indicating which lines are to be affected, and an instruction to be performed on those lines. In the text mode, once a line of text has been entered, you cannot simply back up to modify it. Instead, you must switch to the command mode and then specify the lines and the changes that you wish to make; hence the term "line-oriented."

Both addresses and instructions may make use of patterns known as "limited regular expressions."

The editor does not work on a file directly. Instead, it copies the file into a work area called a "buffer." The edited copy eventually is saved by "writing" it to a file.

COMMON USES You can use **ed** to create and edit programs, documents, tables, and any other form of text file.

OPTIONS In versions of System V prior to Release 3, the **ed** command has two options (– and **–p**). Release 3 adds one option (**–s**).

OPTION	ACTION
–	Suppresses the character counts normally printed by the **e**, **r**, and **w** commands; suppresses the diagnostics produced by the **e** and **q** commands; and suppresses the ! prompt that follows a !*command* instruction. Note: This option will not be supported by versions following Release 3; these later versions will recognize only the **–s** notation (see below).
–p *string*	Uses *string* as the prompt when in the command mode. (By default, there is no prompt string, so unless you use this option, it may not be obvious which mode you are in.)
–s	Suppresses output as described under – above. This notation is being provided to make the option notation more consistent with standard UNIX usage. New with Release 3.

USING ed To use **ed** effectively, you need to be able to invoke the editor, select the text and command modes, give the appropriate **ed** commands, and use "regular expressions." These just happen to be the topics coming up next.

Invoking the editor

To create a new file called **peye**, use that name as an argument:

```
$ ed peye
?peye
```

The **ed** command normally reports back the size of the file. In this case, because the file is new, **ed** prints the filename preceded by a question mark. The purpose of the question mark is to warn you that you are not opening an existing file and that you may have mistyped a filename. The program comes up in the command mode, so the next line you type is interpreted as a command. By default, there is no prompt, so the cursor sits below the **?peye** line until you start typing.

To create a command-mode prompt, use the **-p** option:

```
$ ed -p 'cmd> ' peye
0
cmd>
```

Then you can see that you are in the command mode and that the editor is waiting for your input. Here we've assumed that the **peye** file has already been created, but is empty; hence it has a size of 0.

The same forms can be used to call up an existing file; in that case, the size most likely is not 0.

The **ed** command can be invoked without specifying a file. You can then use the **e** command from within **ed** to specify the file to be edited. Or, if it is a new file, you can specify the name when you use the **w** command to write to (save) the file.

When you use **ed** to edit a file, it first copies the file into a temporary work area called a buffer, where all changes take place. Then, when you give the **w** command, the buffer is copied into the original file, thus saving the changes.

Selecting modes

When you give the **ed** command to invoke the editor, you start up in the command mode and you are positioned at the last line of the file. (The file contents, however, are not displayed until you give a command to that effect.) Giving any one of three commands (**a** for append, **i** for insert, and **c** for change) moves you out of the command mode and places you in the text mode. The **a** command causes the text you enter to be inserted after the current line, the **i** command inserts it before the current line, and the **c** command uses it to replace the current line. Once you are in the text mode, every time you strike the <enter> key you start a new line of text. To return to the command mode, type a period at the beginning of a line and strike <enter>.

Here, for example, we open a file, enter two lines of text, and return to the command mode:

```
$ ed -p 'cmd> ' peye
0
cmd> a
Mike Jug didn't like the way his client was
looking. The word "dead" came to mind.
.
cmd>
```

Because the file is new, the appended lines become the first lines of the file.

ed COMMANDS Commands, in general, consist of an address specifier and an instruction. The address specifier can indicate a single line or a range of lines, and it can use line numbers and search patterns to indicate which lines are to be affected. The instructions allow you to insert, append, change, delete, and move whole lines. They also allow you to make substitutions within a line. Regular expressions, discussed later, can be used to specify lines and as part of substitution commands.

The **ed** program maintains the concept of the "current line," which generally is the last line affected by a command. A line can be identified by its line number, by its position relative to the current line, by patterns based on regular expressions, by a "mark," and by special symbols. Here are the details:

LINE SPECIFIER	MEANING
.	The current line.
$	The last line of the buffer.
n	The nth line, where n is an integer.
'$_c$	The line marked, through the **k** command (discussed later), with the character c, which must be a lowercase letter.
/expr/	The first line after the current line matching the regular expression *expr*. If no matching line is found by the time the end of the buffer is reached, the search wraps around to the beginning and continues until the expression is found or until the original current line is again reached. Empty slashes (//) repeat the last pattern used.

LINE SPECIFIER	MEANING
?expr?	Like the preceding specifier, except the search proceeds backward from the current line. Empty question marks (??) repeat the last pattern used.
+*n*	*n* lines forward from the current address.
+	One line forward from the current address; similarly, **++** is two lines forward, and so on.
-	One line backward from the current address; similarly, **--** is two lines backward, and so on.
-n	*n* lines backward from the current address.
*addr***+***n*	*n* lines forward from the address given in *addr*. The plus sign may be omitted if the address is not numeric.
addr–*n*	*n* lines backward from the address given in *addr*.
*addr***+**	One line forward from the address given in *addr*; similarly, *addr***++** is two lines forward, and so on.
addr–	One line backward from the address given in *addr*; similarly, *addr*–– is two lines backward, and so on.

Address ranges are indicated by two comma-separated addresses. For example, **1,10** represents lines 1 through 10, and **.,/popsicle/** represents the current line through the next line containing **popsicle**.

Using a semicolon instead of a comma causes the current line to be reset to the first address before the second address is evaluated. Thus **/fudge/;+5** represents the next line containing **fudge** and the following five lines. For convenience, a single comma (,) represents the range **1,$**, and a single semicolon (;) represents the range **.,$**.

An **ed** command may require no address, one address, an address range, or an address range and an address. Many commands assume a default address or address range if none is given. In the following list of commands, the default address is enclosed in square brackets ([]). The number of addresses within the brackets indicates whether a single address or a range is required. For instance, a default address of [.] means the default value is the current line and that the command requires only one address. The notation [.,.] means the default value is the current line and that the command normally requires a range. In general, if a range is needed, you can use just *addr* instead of *addr,addr* to indicate a single line.

Here are the command forms and their actions:

COMMAND	ACTION
[.]a *<appended text>* .	The append command places you in the text mode. Text you subsequently type is appended after the indicated line, which is, by default, the current line. A lone period at the beginning of a line returns you to the command mode; the period does not become part of the text. The last appended line becomes the new current line. An address of 0 can be used to place lines at the beginning of the buffer. The maximum number of characters per line (including the newline generated by the <enter> key) is 256.
[.]c *<replacement text>* .	The change command places you in the text mode. Text you subsequently type replaces the indicated line; the replacement text can be more than one line long. A lone period at the beginning of a line returns you to the command mode. The new current line is the last line of new input or, if there is no input, the preceding line.
[.,.]d	Deletes the addressed lines from the buffer. The line following the last deleted line becomes the new current line; if the deleted lines come at the end of the buffer, the new last line becomes the current line.
e *file*	Edits the *file* file. The entire contents of the buffer are deleted and replaced with a copy of *file*. The editor warns you by displaying a **?** if changes have been made to the buffer since the last write command. In that case, you can resume editing the buffer or else type a second **e** command to override the warning. The current line is set to the last line of the buffer. The name *file* becomes the "currently remembered filename," which is used by default by the **w** (write), **r** (read), and subsequent **e** commands; that is, if the filename is omitted in these commands, the currently remembered filename is used. (This assumes that a name was provided by a prior **e** command or an **f** command, or that a command-line filename was used when **ed** was invoked.)
E *file*	Like **e**, except that **ed** does not check to see if any changes have been made since the last **w** (write) command. For instance, if you wanted to scrap your current editing of a file, you could give the **E** command to clear the buffer and reload it with the original, unedited file.

COMMAND	ACTION
f *file*	Changes the currently remembered filename to *file*. If *file* is omitted, displays the currently remembered filename.

[1,$]g/*expr*/*command-list*	This **global** command first finds all lines in the indicated range (by default, the whole file) that match the regular expression *expr*. Each matching line in turn becomes the current line and has the *command-list* applied to it. For instance, **g**/**Boobelbub**/**d** deletes all lines containing the string **Boobelbub**. If you give no *command-list*, **ed** assumes a **p** (print) command. **g**, **G**, **v**, and **V** commands may not be used in the *command-list*.
	
	Multiple commands can be given by placing each command on a new line and terminating each line except the last with a backslash (\). Here is an example:
	
	`g/Lodi/s/Lodi/Reno/\`
	`a\`
	`Gambling is at your own risk.\`
	`.`
	
	For each line containing **Lodi**, **Reno** is substituted for **Lodi** and a line is appended after the edited line. If the very last command is a **.** to terminate input, as in this case, it can be omitted. The first line also could be typed
	
	`g/Lodi/s//Reno/\`
	
	because the empty slashes (//) are interpreted as duplicating the preceding pattern (/**Lodi**/).

[1,$]G/*expr*/	This interactive **Global** command first finds all lines matching the regular expression *expr*. Each of these lines becomes, in turn, the current line, and you then may type *one* command (other than an **a**, **c**, **i**, **g**, **G**, **v**, or **V** command) for each located line. After these interactive commands are executed, the next affected line is printed. To do nothing and skip to the next marked line, hit the <enter> key. To repeat the most recently executed command, type **&**. Since the interactive command may include an address, the command may be used to act on lines other than the marked lines. To terminate the **G** command before all marked lines are processed, type an interrupt (ASCII DEL or BREAK).
h	Helps by displaying a short error message explaining the reason for the most recent error response, which is the **?** symbol.
H	Toggles on and off the help feature, which prints error messages for the most recent error, if any, and for subsequent errors. By default, help is turned off.

(continued)

COMMAND	ACTION *(continued)*
[.]i *<inserted text>*	The insert command is similar to the **a** command, except that text is inserted before the indicated line instead of after it. The last inserted line, if any, becomes the current line; otherwise, the addressed line does. With the **i** command, 0 is an improper address.
[.,+1]j	Joins contiguous lines, as indicated by the address range, into one line. The lines are joined by removing the intervening newline character. If exactly one address instead of a range is used, there is no effect.
[.]k*c*	Marks the addressed line with the lowercase letter *c*, so that the address '*c* refers to that line. This provides a convenient way to move through text without remembering line numbers, and it is useful with the **m** (move) and **t** (copy) commands. Note that up to 26 lines can be marked.
[.,.]l	Lists the indicated lines. This command differs from the **p** (print) command in that it uses special representations of certain non-printing characters, such as tab and backspace, and provides ASCII code representations (in octal) of other nonprinting characters. The **l** command can be appended to other commands, excluding **e**, **E**, **f**, **r**, and **w**. For instance, **g/wimp/s//gentleman/l** lists all lines affected by this global substitution command.
[.,.]m*addr*	Moves the specified lines to just after the line whose address is *addr*. The *addr* address must be outside the initial specified range. Also, *addr* can be 0, in which case the text is moved to the beginning of the buffer. The new location of the last moved line becomes the current line.
[.,.]n	Prints the indicated lines, preceding each line with its line number and a tab character. The numbering is for information only; it does not become part of the buffer. Otherwise, the **n** command behaves like **p**.
[.,.]p	Prints the indicated lines. The last line displayed becomes the current line. The **p** command can be appended to any command except **e**, **E**, **f**, **r**, or **w**. For example, **s/Red/Rod/p** prints the affected line after the substitution has been made.
P	Toggles on and off a command-mode prompt. The initial setting is off. By default, the prompt is an *, but the **-p** command-line option enables you to define your own prompt string, and brings up the editor with the prompt toggled on.

COMMAND	ACTION
q	Quits **ed**. If you have made changes since last writing to a file (using **w**), the editor warns you by printing a **?**. In that case, you can resume editing or else type a second **q** to quit. To save your work and quit, give the **w** command, then the **q** command.
Q	Quits **ed** without checking to see if any changes have been made since the last **w** command.
[$]r *file*	The read command appends the contents of *file* after the indicated line. To place the contents at the beginning of the buffer, use an address of 0. If *file* is read successfully, the number of characters copied is displayed, and the current line is set to the last line read in. If no filename is provided, the currently remembered filename (as set by the **e** or **f** command, for example) is used. The **r** command does not reset the currently remembered filename unless *file* is the first filename mentioned since the editor was invoked.
[$]r *!command*	Like the preceding command, except that the output of *command* is read into the buffer. For instance, **r !ls** reads in the output of the **ls** command.
[.,.]s/*expr*/*rstring*/ [.,.]s/*expr*/*rstring*/**g** [.,.]s/*expr*/*rstring*/**n**	*The* substitute command searches each indicated line for an occurrence of the regular expression *expr*. In the absence of a **g** or *n* suffix, the first occurrence of *expr* in the line is replaced with the replacement string (*rstring*). The **g** suffix causes all occurrences on a given line to be replaced. An *n* suffix causes just the *n*th occurrence on a given line to be replaced; *n* must be an integer in the range 1–512. The last line in which a substitution was made becomes the current line. Characters other than a space or a newline can be used to delimit the regular expression and replacement string. For example, **s#USC#UCLA#g** is the same as **s/USC/UCLA/g**. This is convenient when the expression or string involves slashes. The **&** symbol can be used in *rstring* to represent the entire preceding regular expression *expr*. Thus **s/RETURN/[&]/g** replaces **RETURN** with **[RETURN]**. If you require a regular **&** in *rstring*, use **\&**. Thus **s/AND/\&/** replaces **AND** with **&**. *(continued)*

COMMAND	ACTION	*(continued)*

The construction *n* can be used in *rstring* to indicate the *n*th subexpression, as delimited by \\(and \\), of *expr*. For instance, the command s/\\(Donald\\) \\(Duck\\)/\\2, \\1/ replaces **Donald Duck** with **Duck, Donald**. Subexpressions are counted from left to right in order of the initial \\(. Subexpressions can be nested.

If the replacement string consists solely of the character %, the replacement string from the most recent substitution command is used. Use \\% to avoid this special interpretation.

To split a line, you can replace a character in the middle of the line with a newline character. Use **<enter>** to represent a newline in a replacement string, as in:

```
s/apple/apple\<enter>
/<enter>
```

This means "replace **apple** with **apple** followed by a newline," and the effect is to split the line following the word **apple**. This feature cannot be used as part of a **g** or **v** command, but it can be used with the **g** suffix.

[.,.]t *addr*

Appends a copy of the addressed lines after the *addr* address and leaves the original lines in place. To place the copy at the beginning of the buffer, use an address of 0. The *addr* address must be outside the specified address range. The current line becomes the last line of the copy.

u

The undo command undoes the most recent command that modified the buffer.

[1,$]v//*expr*/*command-list*

Like the global **g** command, except that every line *not* matching the regular expression *expr* is affected by the command list.

[1,$]V/*expr*/

Like the interactive global **G** command, except that those lines *not* matching the regular expression *expr* are affected.

[1,$]w *file*

The write command copies the indicated lines of the buffer onto *file*. If the command is successful, the number of characters written is displayed. The current line is unchanged. If no filename is specified, the currently remembered filename (as set by **e** or **f**, for example) is used. The **w** command does not reset the currently remembered filename unless *file* is the first filename used since **ed** was invoked.

[1,$]w !*command*

Like **w**, except that the specified lines become the standard input of the indicated command. For example, **w !wc** sends the buffer contents to the **wc** command, producing a word count.

COMMAND	ACTION
[$]=	Displays the line number of the indicated line; the current line is unchanged. This is commonly used to determine the file length in lines (the default use) or to find the current line number using the .= command.
!*command*	Sends the *command* to the shell to be interpreted (this is called a "shell escape"). For example, **!cat jokes** displays the contents of the **jokes** file. The output of the command is displayed on the screen, and its end is marked with a !. This output is not read into the buffer; use the **!rcommmand** for that purpose. The % symbol can be used to represent the currently remembered file-name. For example, **!wc %** produces a word count for the current file. Note that this command uses the original file, not the possibly edited version currently in the **ed** buffer. If ! is the first character of *command*, it is replaced by the text of the preceding command. For example, !! repeats the preceding command. The current line is unaffected.
[.+1]	An address alone on a line causes the line to be printed. Hitting <enter> is, by default, the same as .+1, so it causes the next line to be printed. You can use this feature to step through the buffer.

Here are some more pointers about **ed** commands:

For the most part, it is improper to have more than one **ed** command per line. However, the **l**, **p**, and **n** commands (list, print, and number) can be appended to all commands except **e**, **E**, **f**, **r**, and **w**. The **ed** command responds by printing a question mark (?) if it objects to a proposed command.

Sending an interrupt signal (typically <del> or <break>) causes **ed** to print a **?** and to return to its command mode; however, it does not return you to the shell.

If you omit the closing delimiter (typically /) in a replacement string, and if the next character is the newline, the addressed line is printed. For example, the following two lines are equivalent:

```
s/scool/school/p
s/scool/school
```

Unless help is requested through **h** or **H**, the error messages consist of **?** for command errors and of **?***file* if the *file* file is inaccessible.

LIMITED REGULAR EXPRESSIONS Regular expressions can be used in addresses and with several of the editing commands. A regular expression is a pattern that specifies a particular string or family of strings. It is constructed from ordinary characters, which represent themselves, and from special characters (metacharacters), which have more general interpretations. The regular expressions recognized by **ed** are called "limited regular expressions" to contrast them with the more extensive set of regular expressions recognized by **egrep** and **awk**.

One-Character Patterns

Some of the regular expressions recognized by **ed** match only one character:

PATTERN	MATCHES
c	Matches the character *c*, which is, in this case, any ordinary character (that is, not one of the special characters described next) that stands for itself.
c	Matches the character *c*, which is, again, any character. If it is a special character, its special nature is ignored. Thus \\o is the same as **o**, and * is just the character * and does not have the special meaning assigned to * below.
.	Matches any single character other than the newline. Thus **m.d** matches **mud** and **mad**, but not **maid**.
[*list*]	Matches any one character in *list*. Characters can be listed individually, as in [aeiou], or by range, as in [m-z]. Thus m[ai]d matches **mad** and **mid**, but not **mud** (there is no **u** in *list*) nor **maid** (which has two letters, not one, between m and d). To include a hyphen, make it first or last in *list*, as in [a-q-], which represents the letters **a** through **q** and a hyphen. To match a right bracket, make it first in *list*, as in []!.#]. Note that most special characters are not special when in a list. Only ^ (see below) and - may have a special meaning, depending on location.
[^*list*]	Matches any one character not in *list*. Thus m[^ai]d matches **mud** but not **mad**. The caret (^) has this special meaning only when it is the first character in *list*.

Multi-Character Patterns

The simplest multi-character patterns are formed by stringing together the single-character patterns just discussed, as in **house**, **Mr\\.**, and **[yY]ou**. In addition, there are the following constructions.

PATTERN	MATCHES
$c*$	Matches zero or more occurrences of the character c. For example, **mo*d** matches **md**, **mod**, **mood**, **moood**, and so on.
$c\backslash\{m\backslash\}$	Matches exactly m occurrences of the character c. For example, **mo\{2\}d** matches **mood** but not **mod** or **moood**. The integer m should be in the range 0–255.
$c\backslash\{m,\backslash\}$	Matches at least m occurrences of the character c. For example, **mo\{2,\}d** matches **mood**, **moood**, and so on. The range for m is 0–255.
$c\backslash\{m,n\backslash\}$	Matches from m through n occurrences of the character c. For example, **mo\{1,2\}d** matches **mod** and **mood**, but not **md** or **moood**. The range for m and n is 0–255.
$\backslash(expr\backslash)$	Matches *expr*, which is, in this case, a regular expression. Thus **\(hope\)** matches **hope**. The "escaped parentheses" create sub-patterns that can be referred to by the mechanism described next.
$\backslash n$	Matches the nth **\(***expr***\)** subexpression from the pattern. For instance, **\(Oliver\).*\1** represents two occurrences on the line of **Oliver** separated by zero or more characters; the **\1** represents **Oliver**. For instance, **\(Ho\)\1\1** represents **HoHoHo**; each **\1** represents the **Ho** pattern in escaped parentheses. Similarly, **\(Hi\)\(Ho\)\2\1** represents **HiHoHoHi**, with **\1** representing **Hi** and **\2** representing **\Ho**.

Anchoring Patterns

Normally, a pattern matches a line if the pattern is found anywhere within the line. For example, the pattern **stat** matches the line **All about estate planning**. Two special characters can be used to specify that a line should only be matched if the pattern, called an anchoring pattern, occurs in a particular place in the line.

PATTERN	MATCHES
$^\wedge expr$	A ^ at the beginning of a regular expression *expr* means that *expr* must match the beginning of a line.
$expr\$$	A $ at the end of a regular expression *expr* means that *expr* must match the end of a line.
$^\wedge expr\$$	This combination means that *expr* must match the line in its entirety.

COMMAND FILES The **ed** command can read command input from a file. Suppose, for example, that the file **edabit** contains a set of editing commands. They can be applied to the file **rawstuff** by using redirection:

```
ed rawstuff < edabit
```

Normally, the command file ends with the lines

```
w
q
```

and the editing process ends when those lines are reached. However, the editor also quits if a particular command fails.

COMMENTS Currently, UNIX System V supports three text editors: **ed**, **ex**, and **vi**. The **ed** editor is the oldest, simplest, and most compact of the three. The **ex** editor, like **ed**, is a line editor, but is more powerful. The **vi** editor (actually part of **ex**) is a screen editor, meaning that it allows you to move the cursor back and forth through the text, effecting changes at the cursor position. A screen editor is more convenient for detailed editing, while a line editor is better suited for wholesale changes, like global substitutions. (The **vi** editor does have an **ex** mode for making those sorts of changes.)

The **ed** editor also is available in a restricted version called **red**, which permits the editing only of files in the current directory and prohibits the use of the !*command* mechanism.

The **ed** editor often was criticized for its cryptic diagnostics (?) and its failure to indicate what mode it was in. The **h** and **H** commands for providing help and the **-p** option and the **P** command for establishing a command-mode prompt counter those criticisms. Beginning UNIX users who choose to use **ed** should use those features until they become familiar with **ed**.

SEE ALSO UNIX Commands: **red**; **ex**; **vi**; **sed**; **grep**
UNIX Features: Regular Expressions

1. Create a file.

```
$ ed fame
?fame
a
Ed Bonesmith was quite surprised
at the fame he achieved.
.
w
58
q
$
```

The **?fame** line indicates that **fame** is a new file.

2. Modify an existing file.

```
$ ed fame
58
P
*1,$p
Ed Bonesmith was quite surprised
at the fame he achieved.
*s/he/he had/p
at the fame he had achieved.
*w
62
*q
$
```

First, the editor reports that **fame** contains 58 characters. Then the **P** command is used to toggle on a default command-mode prompt: *. Next, the **p** command is used to display the file; after this command is executed, the current line is the last line printed. The **s** command then adds a word to the current line (line 2), and the **p** suffix displays the altered line.

(continued)

3. Read in text from a second file and save the result in a third file.

```
$ ed -p 'cmd> ' fame
62
cmd> r bio
112
cmd> w fameplus
174
cmd> q
$
```

Here the **-p** option is used to define **cmd>** as a command-mode prompt. The **r** command reads in the 112 characters of the **bio** file. Because no line is specified, the material is appended after the last line in the buffer. Next, the **w** command writes the contents of the buffer, now 174 bytes, to a file called **fameplus**. The **q** command quits the editor; since nothing was written to **fame**, the original file is unaltered.

4. Give a variety of commands. (The command-line prompt (*) is assumed to be turned on, so that you can distinguish between commands and the results of commands).

`*1,$s/^/     /`	*Inserts five spaces at the beginning of each line (you can use , as an abbreviation for 1,$)*
`*g/Tom/s//Tim/g`	*Replaces all occurrences of **Tom** with **Tim** (if the final g is omitted, only the first occurrence of **Tom** on each line is replaced)*
`*kb`	*Marks the current line with the letter **b***
`*/Pogo/`	*Moves to the next line containing the string **Pogo***
`*.,.+5m'b`	*Moves the current and the following five lines to just after the line earlier marked with the letter **b***
`*v/^Part Number/s/^/     /`	*Inserts five spaces at the beginning of each line that does not begin with **Part Number***
`*!date`	*Checks the time*
`Tue Sep 16 10:23:18 PDT 1986`	
`!`	*End of output*
`*.r !date`	*Appends the date after the current line*
`29`	*Twenty-nine characters appended*

PURPOSE Use the **egrep** command to search files for lines containing a given pattern or patterns.

FORMAT **egrep** [*option(s)*] [*pattern(s)*] [*file(s)*]

DESCRIPTION The **egrep** command normally displays those lines in a file that match the given search pattern or patterns. If more than one file is searched, the filename also is displayed with a matching line. A pattern may include special pattern-specifying characters. Patterns can be specified in the command line or in a separate file.

If you don't specify a file to be searched, **egrep** reads the standard input; in that case, you can use a pipe or redirection to provide input.

The output of **egrep** is sent to the standard output, which is, by default, the terminal. Redirection and pipes can be used to route the output to a file or to other commands.

COMMON USES You can use **egrep** to find lines containing a particular word, a particular pattern, or one of several of patterns. You can use matching patterns from a file instead of typing them as part of the command line.

OPTIONS The **egrep** command has eight options:

OPTION	ACTION
-v	Displays all but matching lines.
-c	Displays just a count of matching lines; multiple files are reported individually.
-l	Displays only the names of files with matching lines.
-n	Displays the line number before each line.
-b	Precedes each line displayed with the number of the block in which it is found. The first block is number 0, and blocks typically are 512 characters in size.
-e *pattern*	Like the *pattern(s)* option, except that this can be used with patterns beginning with hyphens or with the -f option.
-f *file*	Takes a pattern list from *file*.
-i	Ignores the distinction between upper- and lowercase when making comparisons.

PATTERNS The **egrep** command can use "full regular expressions" for creating patterns. These offer a wider range of patterns than can be used with **grep** or **sed**. Full regular expressions use the following notations:

NOTATION	MEANING
.	Matches any one character.
\	Turns off special meanings; for instance, \. matches an ordinary period.
[...]	Matches any one character from the enclosed list of characters; use a hyphen to show a range: **[a–z]**.
[^...]	Matches any one character not in the enclosed list.
*	Matches zero or more occurrences of the preceding expression.
+	Matches one or more occurrences of the preceding expression.
?	Matches zero or one occurrence of the preceding expression.
¦	The OR operator, used to separate elements in a list of patterns.
( )	Groups patterns.
^	Matches the beginning of a line.
$	Matches the end of line.

The *****, **+**, and **?** operators apply to the preceding character unless parentheses are used to show that the operator applies to a longer expression. To match ordinary parentheses, use **\(** and **\)**. A newline also can be used to separate elements in a list of patterns.

COMMENTS The **egrep**, **fgrep**, and **grep** commands perform similar functions. **egrep** increases **grep**'s pattern-making capabilities, allows you to specify several patterns, and permits pattern input from a file. **fgrep** allows multiple patterns and file pattern input, but it does away with metacharacters and only matches simple strings. **egrep** is the most powerful, but the **egrep** algorithm may, in some cases, require large amounts of working memory.

SEE ALSO UNIX Commands: **grep**; **fgrep**
UNIX Features: Regular Expressions; Standard I/O, Redirection, and Pipes; Extending Commands over More than One Line; Filename Generation; Filters

EXAMPLES

1. Find lines containing a particular word.

```
$ egrep overdue booklist
Grey Lensman:Smith:W.Buckley:6/30/86:overdue
Advanced UNIX:Prata:Waite:4/3/86:overdue
$
```

This finds and prints those lines in the **booklist** file that contain the word **overdue**. Actually, **egrep** searches for the string **overdue**, so it would, for example, find a line containing **Roverduel**.

2. Find lines containing a particular pattern.

```
$ egrep 'A[0-9]+Q' partnums
9399111    A2Q39210   farklenut    $000.23
9471393    13A0282Q   norfring     $009.42
$
```

This searches the **partnums** file for all lines containing an **A** and a **Q** separated by one or more digits. The single quotes keep the shell from trying to interpret the bracket meta-characters before they are passed on to **egrep**.

3. Find lines containing one of a choice of patterns.

```
egrep '[Bb]ob | [Dd]on' /etc/passwd
egrep '[Bb]ob
       [Dd]on' /etc/passwd
```

Either command searches the **/etc/passwd** file for lines containing **Bob**, **bob**, **Don**, or **don**. The single quotes prevent the shell from misinterpreting the ¦ symbol as a pipe and, in the second version, from misinterpreting the first newline as the end of the command line.

4. Find lines matching patterns taken from a file.

```
egrep -f partpatterns partlist
```

This searches the **partlist** file for patterns found in the **partpatterns** file. Note that **-f partpatterns** comes first; options (**-f partpatterns** is an option) always come before normal filename arguments.

(continued)

125

5. Find lines matching patterns from a file and from the command line.

```
egrep -f partpatterns -e 'A[0-9]+Q' partlist
```

This searches the **partlist** file both for patterns from the **partpatterns** file and for the **A[0-9]+q** pattern.

6. Find the number of lines containing a particular pattern that occur in a set of files.

```
$ egrep -c '[rR]ubenstein ! [sS]erkin' rec*
recs1:5
recs2:8
recs3:0
$
```

This reports that lines containing the names **Rubenstein**, **rubenstein**, **Serkin**, and **serkin** occur five times in the **recs1** file, eight time in **recs2**, and so on.

7. Use **egrep** with a pipe.

```
$ who ! egrep tty1?
tiger           tty12       May 21      12:13
ghoul           tty19       May 21      11:56
$
```

This reports who currently is using terminals **tty10** through **tty19**.

PURPOSE Use the **ex** command to create and edit text files.

FORMAT **ex** [*option(s)*] [**+***command*] [*file(s)*]

The **+***command* option causes the editing to begin with the indicated **ex** search or positioning *command*.

The files are edited in the order in which they are listed.

DESCRIPTION The **ex** command, like the less powerful **ed**, is a two-mode, line-oriented text editor. The first mode is the command mode, in which keystrokes are interpreted as commands. The second mode is the text, or input, mode, in which keystrokes are entered as text. In general, a command has two parts: an address or range of addresses indicating which lines are to be affected, and an instruction to be executed upon those lines. In the text mode, once a line of text has been entered, you cannot back up to modify it. Instead, you must switch to the command mode and then specify the lines and changes you wish to make.

Both addresses and instructions may make use of regular expressions.

The editor does not work on files directly. Instead, it copies a file into a work area known as a "buffer." The edited buffer eventually is saved by "writing" to a file. The **ex** editor also provides several auxiliary buffers that can be used for temporary storage of blocks of text.

The **ex** editor maintains a list of parameters whose settings modify the editor's behavior. These parameters may be set in the command mode, and default values can be provided by the **EXINIT** environmental variable or by a **.exrc** initialization file.

The **vi** editor is part of the **ex** program and can be invoked from the command line and from the command mode.

COMMON USES You can use **ex** to create and edit programs, documents, tables, and any other form of text file. The **ex** editor can accept commands from a script file as well as interactively.

OPTIONS Five options are available with **ex**.

OPTION	ACTION
-	Suppresses all interactive feedback; used with editing scripts.
-v	Invokes the **visual** mode of the editor (see **vi** for a description of this mode).
-r [*file(s)*]	Recovers the named files after a crash. If no file list is given, a list of all saved files is printed.
-R	Sets the **readonly** mode; this keeps the original file from being overwritten.
-l	Sets the **lisp** mode. Text is indented as appropriate for the LISP language. In **vi**, the meanings of the (,), {, }, [[, and]] commands are modified.

OVERVIEW When **ex** is invoked, it creates a temporary work area, or buffer. If **ex** is invoked with the name of an existing file, the file is copied into the buffer, and the editor is positioned at the last line of the file. The file contents are not, however, displayed on the screen. If no filename is given, or if the name does not yet belong to a file, the buffer is empty.

The editor comes up in the command mode; this is indicated by the presence of the : prompt. The **a** (append), **i** (insert), and **c** (change) commands can be used to enter the text mode. They cause the cursor to appear at the beginning of the next screen line, and subsequent keyboard input becomes part of the text. To return to the command mode, you must type a period at the beginning of a line, then hit <enter>; the period does not become part of the text.

To save text, use the **w** command to write the text to a file. If you provided a filename when invoking the editor, the **w** command writes to that file by default. Or you can provide a filename explicitly; this is necessary if you invoked **ex** without providing a filename. You can quit the editor after saving a file by giving the **q** command. To quit without saving the file, use the **q!** command.

The editor maintains a concept of the "current file," which is the name of the file currently being edited. The current file changes if you use the **n** (next) command to step through a list of files to be edited or if you change files using the **e** command.

The editor also maintains a concept of the "alternate file," which usually is the file most recently mentioned in an editing command. But if the last file mentioned became the current file, then the alternate file is the previous current file. The current file can be represented by **%** and the alternate file by **#**

in editing instructions, providing a simple notation for switching back and forth between files.

To use **ex**, you need to know how to specify addresses and what the **ex** commands are, you may need to know how to use regular expressions, and you should know about the various editor options available through **ex**'s **set** command. We'll look at these topics in turn.

ADDRESSING Lines of text can be specified by number, by relative offset, by pattern, by a "mark," and by some special symbols.

Basic Addresses

Here is a rundown of options for specifying a particular line to be used by an **ex** command:

ADDRESS	MEANING
.	The dot (.) refers to the current line. By default, when **ex** is invoked, the last line becomes the current line. Various positioning commands change the current line. When a command affects multiple lines, the current line usually becomes the last line that was affected.
n	Refers to the *n*th line in the buffer, where *n* is an integer; numbering begins with 1.
$	Refers to the last line in the buffer.
%	Refers to all lines in the buffer.
+*n*	Refers to *n* lines forward from the current line. The form .**+***n* is equivalent. Also, **++++** is the same as **+4**.
-*n*	Refers to *n* lines backward from the current line; otherwise, like **+***n*.
/*pat*/	Refers to the next line forward that contains the *pat* pattern. The pattern can be a regular expression. If no instructions follow this address, the final / can be omitted. Searches wrap around to the beginning of the buffer if no match is found before the buffer's end.
//	Searches forward, using the last pattern specified.
?*pat*?	Like /*pat*/, except that it searches backward for the previous line containing the pattern.
??	Searches backward, using the last pattern specified.
'*x*	Goes to the line that was previously marked with the lowercase letter *x* by the **mark** command.
''	Goes to the line that was current before the last nonrelative motion.

Address Ranges

Some commands accept an address range, which consists of two addresses separated by a comma or a colon. When a semicolon is used, the current line is set to the first address before the second address is interpreted. Thus

    +2,+3

means the second and third lines from the current line, but

    +2;+3

means the second through fifth lines from the original current line. In the second case, the second line becomes the current line, so the **+3** is measured from it.

The line described by the second address in a range must come after the line described by the first; **4,2** is an invalid range.

Addresses and Commands

Some commands require no address, some accept one address, some accept a range. If more addresses are provided than can be used, then all but the last one or two are ignored. A null address is interpreted to be the current line. For example, **3d** means "delete line 3," but **d** (no address) means "delete the current line."

COMMANDS The **ex** editor provides a wide range of commands. We'll first give you an overview of what is available, then we'll look at the details.

Overview

The commands can be typed in full or can be abbreviated, as indicated:

ABBREVIATION	NAME
Commands to enter text mode:	
a	append
i	insert
c	change

ABBREVIATION	NAME
Commands to manipulate text lines:	
c	copy
d	delete
j	join
m	move
pu	put
y	yank
<	leftshift
>	rightshift
File-related commands:	
ar	args
e	edit
f	file
n	next
pre	preserve
r	read
re	recover
rew	rewind
w	write
Editor-control commands:	
q	quit
se	set
sh	shell
so	source
vi	visual
x	xit

(continued)

ABBREVIATION	NAME	(continued)
Position and display commands:		
l	list	
k or ma	mark	
nu or #	number	
p	print	
z	(move window)	
^D	(scroll text)	
=	(show line number)	
Other commands:		
ab	abbrev	
g and v	global	
(none)	map	
r !	(read shell input)	
s	substitute	
una	unabbrev	
u	undo	
unm	unmap	
ve	version	
!	(shell escape)	
& or s	(resubstitute)	

Command Formats

In general, an **ex** editing instruction has the form

   address command count flags

The *address* indicates which lines are to be affected. It may be a line or a range of lines. In the Command Summaries section below, we use *line* for commands that require at most one address and *range* for commands that accept a range. If no address is given for commands expecting an address, the current line is used. If only one address is provided for a command that accepts a range, the effect of the command is confined to that one line, except as modified by *count*.

A *count* indicates how many lines are to be affected, starting with the line given by a *line* address. For example, **2d5** means "delete 5 lines, beginning with line 2." If a range is provided, the first address is ignored. Thus **2,5d3** deletes **3** lines beginning with line **5**. If *count* is omitted, the default value is 1.

The **flag** component instructs the editor to print the affected lines after execution. The *flag* can be **#**, **l**, or **p**, depending on the type of display desired (see the descriptions of these commands below). The **flag** also can contain any number of **+** or **−** signs. Each **+** advances the current line by one line, and each **−** moves it back one line. For example, the command

```
5s/dog/mutt/+++
```

replaces **dog** with **mutt** on line **5** and advances the current line to **8**.

Command Summaries

Not all commands allow all four components, so the following summaries indicate which components each command can use. A few commands have additional components; they, too, are discussed in these summaries. Here, we use the standard command abbreviations, as given in the Overview section above.

COMMAND	ACTION
line or *range*	If an address or address range is given without a command, the **print** command is understood.
(null)	Striking <enter> without giving an address or command causes the next line in the buffer to be printed. This provides a convenient way to step through the text.
ab *word str*	Makes *word* an abbreviation for the string *str*. If the editor is in the text, or input, mode of the visual mode (as described under **vi**) and *word* is typed, the editor replaces it with *str*. For example, `ab OGO O Great One` makes the word **OGO** an abbreviation for the string **O Great One**. It has to be typed as a distinct word; no substitution takes place if, say, **TOGO** is typed.
line **a**	Enters the text, or input, mode, placing new text after the current line. Use a *line* value of 0 to put a line at the beginning of the buffer. The last line of new input becomes the new current line. If there is no new input, the current line becomes *line*.
ar	Prints the current argument list; this is the list of files typed on the command line when **ex** is invoked. The current file has its names enclosed in brackets ([]).

(continued)

COMMAND	ACTION	(continued)
range **c** *count*	Enters the text, or input, mode and causes the new input to replace the lines indicated by *range* (or by *count*). The last line of new input becomes the current line. If there is no input, the effect is the same as for the **delete** command.	
range **co** *line flags*	Copies the lines specified by *range* to just after *line*. To copy text to the beginning of the buffer, use a *line* value of 0.	
range **d** *buffer count*	Deletes the lines specified by *range* or by *count*. Here *buffer* is a "named" auxiliary buffer into which the deleted material is copied. Each name is a single lowercase letter in the range **a** through **z**. If no *buffer* is given, the "unnamed" buffer is used (see the discussion of buffers below). The first line following the deleted material becomes the new current line, unless the deletion includes the last line of the buffer. In that case, the last remaining line becomes the current line.	
e **+***line file*	Begins editing *file*. If the current buffer has been altered since the last **w** (write) command, **ex** warns you and aborts the command. To continue, either save the current file with a **w** command or use **e!** instead of **e** to override the default response. This causes the editor to move to the new file without saving the alterations you have made; the old contents of the editing buffer are replaced by a copy of the new file. By default, the current line for the new buffer contents is the last line. However, if the command is given from the visual mode, the current line becomes the first line of the buffer. The **+***line* option causes *line* to become the current line. In this case, *line* can be a line number, the $ symbol (last line), /*pat*, or ?*pat*.	
f	Prints the current filename, the number of lines in the buffer, the current line, and other information.	
range **g** /*pat*/ *cmds*	First, marks all lines in *range* that match the *pat* pattern (the **g** stands for "global"). Then applies the *cmds* to the marked lines, with each marked line becoming the current line while it is being edited.	

COMMAND	ACTION

To extend the list of *cmds* over more than one line, terminate an intermediate line with a \–<enter> combination. Here is an example:

```
1,100g/test/s/test/TEST/\<enter>
a\<enter>
March 5, 1988\<enter>
.
```

This finds those lines in the range 1 through 100 containing the word **test**. On these lines, **TEST** is substituted for **test**. Then a date is appended following each modified line. (When the final command of a sequence is the . dot command, as in this example, it can be omitted.

Incidentally, the first line could be written this way:

```
1,100g/test/s//TEST/\
```

The editor interprets the empty slashes (//) to duplicate the preceding pattern (/**test**/).

If the *cmds* list is omitted, each matching line is printed. The **g** (global) and **u** (undo) commands cannot be used in the *cmds* list, and the edit parameters **autoprint**, **autoindent**, and **report** are ignored if set.

range **v** /*pat*/ *cmds*	Like the **g** command just described, except that the list of *cmds* is applied to those lines that do not match the *pat* pattern.
line **i**	Enters the text, or input, mode. Input text is placed before the indicated line. The last line inserted becomes the current line, but if no text is inserted, the line before *line* becomes the current line.
range **j** *count flags*	Joins the text from the indicated lines together into one line. See the Command Formats section below for the use of *range* versus *count*. The command inserts spaces between joined lines depending on context. If a line ends with a period, two spaces are provided. If a following line begins with a), no spaces are inserted between the joined lines. In other cases, at least one space is provided.
range **j!** *count flags*	Like **j!**, except that this command makes no space adjustments; lines are joined "as is."
line **k** *x*	See **ma**.
range **l** *count flags*	Displays ("lists") the indicated lines, using **^I** to indicate tab characters and $ to indicate the end of the line.

(continued)

135

COMMAND	ACTION	*(continued)*

map *c macro*

Works only in the visual mode (as described under **vi**). Sets up a "macro" definition with a single character *c* representing the *macro* sequence of commands. Then, when in the command mode of the visual mode, striking *c* has the same effect as typing the command sequence. For example, the definition

    map b d10

means that you can strike the **b** key to delete 10 lines. The <control-v> character must precede special characters, spaces, and newlines that are part of the macro. For example,

    map v $a:20:^V^]

maps **v** to the **vi** commands $ (go to end of line), **a** (enter **vi** append mode), :20: (append this sequence), and <escape> (return to the command mode). The <escape> key is a special character that is represented on screen by the pattern ^] and is preceded by a <control-v>.

To map a function key, use the combination **#**n, where *n* is the number of the function key.

Also, you can create a file of macros and activate them with the **so** command, which is discussed later.

map! *c macro*

Like **map**, except the macro works when the user is in the **vi** text mode instead of in the **vi** command mode.

line **ma** *x*

Marks the specified line with the character *x*, which should be a lowercase letter. Then the '*x* combination can be used to move to that line. The **ma** command (or its equivalent, **k**) does not change the current line position.

n [*newargs*]

Goes to edit the next file named in the command-line argument list. (The **ar** command displays that list, indicating the current file.) Here the optional *newargs* provides a new file list to replace the current argument list.

When this command is given, the current contents of the editing buffer are replaced with material from the next file. The editor balks at this unless you have not modified the current file since the last **w** (write) command, or unless you use **n!** to override this protection.

range **nu** *count flags*

(**#** can be used instead of **nu**.) Displays the indicated lines, preceding each line with its line number. The last line displayed becomes the current line.

COMMAND	ACTION
pre	Saves ("preserves") the current buffer contents as if the system had crashed. The **rec** (recover) command can be used to recall such a file. Use the **pre** command for emergencies—for example, when some quirk, such as running out of disk space, prevents you from saving the file by normal means.
range **p** *count*	Displays the specified lines. Nonprinting control characters, such as <control-g>, are represented as **^G**. The **DEL** character is represented as **^?**. The last line displayed becomes the current line.
q	Quits the current editing job. If the buffer has been modified since the last write, the editor balks unless you use the **q!** form to override this protection.
line **r** *file*	Reads the indicated file and copies it into the editing buffer after location *line*. Use a *line* value of 0 to place the text at the beginning of the buffer. If *file* is omitted, the current file is used. If *file* is used and there is no current file, then *file* becomes the current file. In the **ex** mode, the last line read becomes the current line. In the **vi** mode, the first line read becomes the current line.
line **r** *!cmd*	Goes to the command interpreter (the shell), executes the **cmd** system command, and places the output after the indicated line. A space or tab is needed in front of the !. For example, `r !date` places the output of the **date** command after the current line.
rec *file*	Recovers *file* from a save area. A file being edited is saved in this area when there is a system crash, an editor hangup, or when the **pre** command is used.
rew	Resets the command-line argument list of files to the first file in the list. The editor balks if the current contents of the buffer have been altered since the last write. This protection can be overridden by the **rew!** command.

(continued)

COMMAND	ACTION	*(continued)*

set *parameter*

The **ex** editor uses several settable parameters to control its behavior. If the **set** (or **se**, for short) command is used with no parameters, the editor displays those parameters that have been changed from the default settings. If *parameter* is the word **all**, all parameter settings are displayed.

Some parameters are "Boolean"; that is, on or off. To turn on a Boolean parameter, such as **autoindent** (**ai**, for short), use this form:

```
set ai
```

To turn off a Boolean parameter, use a **no** prefix with the parameter name:

```
set noai
```

Other parameters can be assigned values. Value parameters, such as **wrapmargin** (**wm**, for short), use the = sign to set values:

```
set wm=10
```

Note that there are no spaces around the = sign.

To find the current setting of a parameter, use a ? suffix with the parameter name:

```
set ai?
autointent
```

If the parameter has a value, the question mark can be omitted.

See the section on Edit Parameters below for a description of the built-in parameters.

sh

Calls up the command-line interpreter, typically the **sh** shell program. You remain in the shell until you exit it, usually by typing <control-d>, at which point you are returned to the editing process. (Note that a new shell is created by this command; the original shell still is waiting for **ex** to finish.)

so *file*

Reads and executes editing commands from the specified file. Typically, the file contains a package of macros (**map**), edit parameter settings, or both. For example, one file might configure the editor for C programs, and another might configure the editor for writing letters.

range **s**/*pat*/*repl*/ *options count flags*

For each line specified by *range* or by *count*, replaces the first occurrence of the *pat* pattern with the sequence *repl*. The pattern may be a regular expression, as described later. The *repl* replacement string also may use special notations discussed in the Replacement String section below.

COMMAND	ACTION
	Two options are available. The **g** option causes every instance of *pat* on the line to be replaced by *repl*; otherwise, just the first instance is replaced. The **c** option invokes the "confirm" mode. In this mode, each line subject to substitution is displayed with the proposed target marked by **^** characters beneath it. If you want the substitution to occur, respond with the letter **y**; all other responses prevent the substitution. The last line that contains a substitution becomes the current line.
una *word*	Deletes *word* from the list of abbreviations set up by the **ab** command.
u	Reverses ("undoes") the changes made by the previous editing command; positioning commands and display commands are not included. Commands that affect the external environment, like **e** or **w**, cannot be undone, but the **u** command itself can be reversed by a follow-up **u**.
unm *x*	Removes the macro definition previously created by **map** for *x*.
ve	Displays the current version identification of the editor.
line **vi** *type count*	Enters the visual mode (as described under the **vi** command entry) at the indicated line. The optional *type* parameter specifies where the line appears on the screen. A **-** indicates that the line should be placed at the bottom, and a **.** indicates that it is to be placed in the middle. If no *type* is given, the line appears at the top of the display. The *count* parameter sets the initial window size in lines. If it is omitted, the editor uses the current value of the edit parameter **window**. To return from the visual mode to the regular **ex** mode, use the **Q** command.
range **w** *file*	Writes the specified lines to the named file, and displays the number of lines and characters written. If *range* is omitted, the whole edit buffer is copied to the file. If *file* is omitted, the current filename is used. If there is no current file and if you omit *file*, the editor complains. If *file* exists and is not the current file, **ex** warns you that the file exists and refuses to write. To override this reluctance and overwrite the existing file, use **w!** instead of **w**. To append to a file, use the form **w >>** *file*. You can use **wq** instead of giving the **w** command and **q** command separately; **wq!** is equivalent to **w!** followed by **q**.

(continued)

COMMAND	ACTION	*(continued)*

range **w** *!cmd*
Like the **w** command, except the indicated lines are provided as input to the *cmd* shell command. For example,

```
20,50 w !mail ted
```

mails lines **20** through **50** to **ted**.

x
Copies the buffer, if altered, to the current file, and quits.

range **ya** *buffer count*
Copies, or "yanks," the lines specified by *range* or by *count* to the indicated *buffer*. (The original lines are not deleted.) The possible buffers are named by the lowercase letters **a** through **z**. If no *buffer* is given, yanked text is placed in the "unnamed" buffer. The **pu** command can be used to recover such text. See the Buffers section below.

line **z** *type count*
Displays *count* **lines** on the screen; the default value is provided by the edit parameter **window**. If *type* is omitted, the indicated *line* is placed at the top of the display; if *type* is **-**, *line* is placed at the bottom of the display; and if *type* is **.**, *line* is placed in the middle. The last line printed becomes the current line.

! *cmd*
Causes the command interpreter (typically the **sh** shell) to execute the indicated command, then returns control to the editor. The editor warns you if the buffer has been changed since the last write. When the command completes, the editor displays a single **!**. The current line is not affected.

Within *cmd*, **%** can be used to represent the current filename, and **#** the alternate filename, as described in the Overview section above. Also, **!** can be used in *cmd* to represent the preceding command given in this fashion. Thus **!!** means "repeat the preceding command." The editor echoes all such substitutions so that you can see how it has interpreted them.

*range***!** *cmd*
Passes the indicated lines to the *cmd* shell command and replaces those lines with the output of the command (see Example 7). Note that *range* cannot be omitted; leaving it out reduces this command to the somewhat different **!** *cmd* command just discussed. For example,

```
1,$! sort
```

sorts the file and replaces the current buffer with the output of **sort**; that is, with a sorted buffer.

range **<** *count*
Shifts the lines indicated by *range* or *count* to the left by the number of spaces specified by the **shiftwidth** edit parameter. Only blanks and tabs can be deleted by this shift process; text is not discarded. The last line changed becomes the current line.

COMMAND	ACTION
range **>** *count*	Shifts the lines indicated by *range* or *count* to the right by the number of spaces specified by the **shiftwidth** edit parameter. Characters other than spaces or tabs are not lost.
range **&** *options count flags*	Here **&** is replaced with the **s**/*pat*/*repl*/ used in the preceding **s** (substitute) command. Equivalently, you can use **s** instead of **&**. The options and flags are as described for the **s** command.
^D	(<control-d>.) Displays the next *n* lines, where *n* is the current value of the **scroll** edit parameter.
line=	Displays the line number of the specified line. If *line* is omitted, the line number of the last line is displayed. Another common usage is **.=** to get the current line number. This command does not reset the current line.

BUFFERS IN ex The **ex** editor uses several buffers, or areas of memory used for temporary storage. First, there is the edit buffer, which holds the material currently being edited. When the buffer is written, it is copied to a permanent file.

Then there is the "unnamed" buffer. When material is deleted or copied ("yanked") from the edit buffer, it is placed in the unnamed buffer. Each new deletion or yank replaces the previous contents of the unnamed buffer. You can use the **put** command to copy the contents of the unnamed buffer after the current line, so material accidentally deleted can be restored if no subsequent deletions or yanks have been made. Also, the **delete-put** command combination allows you to move text, and the **yank-put** combination allows you to copy text. The **put** command does not empty the buffer, so the same text can be moved or copied to several locations.

Finally, there are the named buffers. There are 26 of them, named **a** through **z**. They also can be used with the **delete**, **yank**, and **put** commands by specifying their names explicitly as described in the Command Summaries section above. If you change files without leaving the editor, the named buffers can be used to transfer text from one file to another.

REGULAR EXPRESSIONS The patterns that **ex** uses for addresses, for searching, and for the **s** (substitute) command are called "regular expressions." A regular expression can be a string of ordinary characters, such as **cake**, or it can contain various special characters to limit the context of the string or to provide a more general pattern. The **ex** editor has two levels of regular expressions. The normal level applies when the **magic** edit parameter is set; we'll describe it first. A more restrictive level applies when **nomagic** is set; we'll discuss that later.

A regular expression is constructed from a series of characters. In general, a regular expression defines a pattern, and the editor looks for strings in the buffer that "match" the pattern. Here is what various characters and character combinations signify:

CHARACTER	MEANING
c	Here c is any ordinary character, and it matches itself. Thus the address /G/ matches the next line containing the character **G**. Some characters are not ordinary and must be "escaped" if they are to be matched explicitly; this means they must be preceded by a backslash (\). The characters that must be escaped are ^ at the beginning of a pattern, $ at the end of a pattern, * anywhere other than at the beginning of a pattern, and ., \, [, and ~ anywhere in a pattern. Thus the address /\./ matches the first line containing a period.
^	Matches the beginning of a line when it is the first character in a pattern. Thus the address /^**Quiz**/ matches the first line beginning with the string **Quiz**.
$	Matches the end of a line when used as the last character in a pattern. Thus the address /1988$/ matches the next line ending with **1988**.
.	Matches a single character in a line. Thus the address /**k**.**t**/ matches the next line containing a **k** and a **t** separated by a single character. The intervening character need not be a letter, so both **kit** and **track team** are matched, with the space character being the intervening character in the second case.
\<	Matches the beginning of a "word." This means the matched string must begin with a "word-type" character, which in UNIX is a letter, digit, or underline character. Furthermore, the word must be at the beginning of a line or else be preceded by a character other than a word-type character; for example, a space or a parenthesis. Thus the address /\<**the**/ matches the sequence **in their faces** but does not match **weather**.
\>	Matches the end of a "word," as described above. Thus the address /\<**the**\>/ matches **the** but not **their**.

CHARACTER	MEANING

[list] Matches any *one* character from those in *list*. Thus the address /s[ea]t/ matches **set** and **sat**, but not **sit** (**i** is not in *list*) or **seat** (which has two characters, not one, between **s** and **t**). If the first character in *list* is a caret (**^**), then any one character *not* in *list* is matched. Thus, the address /s[^ea]t/ matches **sit** and **s#t**, but not **set**. A hyphen can be used to indicate a range. Thus the address /[A-Z]/ matches a line containing an uppercase letter. The special meanings for **^** and **-** can be removed by escaping them with a backslash.

* Matches zero or more occurrences of the preceding regular expression. For example, the address /fo*d/ matches **fd**, **fod**, **food**, and so on. A pattern like /f.*d/ (**f** separated from **d** by zero or more characters of any kind) matches the longest corresponding text string. For instance, if the text contains the line **food for good**, the command s/f.*d// deletes the whole phrase, not just **food**.

~ Matches the replacement string used in the last **s** (substitute) command. Consider this sequence of commands:

```
%g/good/s//well/g
%g/well/s/~wife/goodwife/g
```

The first command replaces all occurrences of **good** with **well** (// is short for the preceding pattern, /**good**/), and the second replaces **wellwife** with **goodwife**. The % address, recall, is short for **1,$**.

\(*expr*\) Groups the enclosed regular expression. The grouped expression then can be represented as \1, \2, and so on, in the replacement string of a substitution command (see Replacement Strings below).

As has been implicit in our examples, concatenating two regular expressions produces a new regular expression. For example, the regular expression **gal** is a concatenation of the expressions **g**, **a**, and **l**.

When the **nomagic** edit parameter is set, the only special characters recognized are **^** at the beginning of a pattern, **$** at the end, and ****. However, the other special characters can be turned on by escaping them. Thus * in the **nomagic** mode works the same as * in the **magic** mode.

You might use the **nomagic** mode if you need to edit a text heavily laced with special characters; for example, if you have to convert a bunch of asterisks to periods.

REPLACEMENT
STRINGS
The **ex** editor allows some special notations to be used for the replacement strings in the **s** (substitute) command. We'll look first at the notations used when the **magic** edit parameter is set.

NOTATION	MEANING

&	Stands for the text matched by the search string. Here are some examples:
	`s/equivocal/un&/`
	`s/[Jj]ohn/&son/g`
	The first replaces **equivocal** with **unequivocal**. The second replaces **john** with **johnson** and **John** with **Johnson**.

~	Stands for the replacement string used in the previous **s** (substitute) command. For instance,
	`1,$s/Smith/Jones/g`
	`%s/Brown/~/g`
	replaces all occurrences of **Smith** with **Jones**, then replaces all occurrences of **Brown** with **Jones**. (Note that **1,$** and **%** both specify all lines in the buffer.)

\n	Is replaced by the text represented by the *n*th pattern enclosed in a \(\) pair and in the search string, as described in Regular Expressions above. For example, `s/\(Pig\) and \(Whistle\)/\2 and \1/` replaces **Pig and Whistle** with **Whistle and Pig**.
\u	Converts the following character in the replacement string to uppercase if it is lowercase. For example, `s/[Tt]ed/\u&die/` converts **ted** and **Ted** to **Teddie**.
\l	Like **\u**, but converts the following uppercase character to lowercase.
\U	Turns on uppercase conversion until **\e**, **\E**, or the end of the replacement string is encountered. For example, `s/[Tt]ed/\U&DIE/` converts **ted** or **Ted** to **TEDDIE**.
\L	Like **\U**, except that conversion to lowercase is toggled on. If **nomagic** is set, you can use **\&** and **\~** to activate the special meanings of **&** and **~**.

EDIT PARAMETERS The **ex** editor features a variety of parameters that you can set to govern the behavior of the editor. The parameters have default settings, but there are several ways to set them to other values:

☐ While in the editor, you can use the **se** (set) command.

☐ While in the editor, you can use the **so** command to institute settings stored in a file.

☐ You can use the environmental variable **EXINIT** to hold settings that are to be **put** into effect when the editor starts up.

☐ You can store settings in a **.exrc** file in your home directory or current working directory to be used by **ex** when it starts up.

We will look further at these methods after examining the edit parameters themselves.

The edit parameters fall into two groups: Boolean and numeric. An example of a Boolean parameter is **magic**, which controls the interpretation of regular expressions. The command for turning on this parameter is

```
set magic
```

and the command to turn off **magic** is

```
set nomagic
```

In general, the **no** prefix is used to indicate an "off" setting for a Boolean parameter.

An example of a numeric parameter is **window**, which is set to the number of lines used for a text window in the visual mode. Numeric parameters are set in this fashion:

```
set window=24
```

No spaces are allowed around the equal sign.

The default settings for the edit parameters depend on the installation. The **set all** command displays all current settings.

Here is a list of edit parameters and their meanings. When an abbreviation is allowed, it is also listed. The parameters are Boolean unless otherwise indicated.

PARAMETER	ACTION
autoindent	(**ai**.) Aligns each new line you type in text mode with the beginning of the previous line; both tabs and spaces are used to achieve the alignment. The first line you type is aligned with the line it is appended after (if you are using the **a** command), the line it is inserted before (if you are using the **i** command), or the first line to be changed (if you are using the **c** command). Each time you indent further, the next text line is indented the same amount. Type **<control-d>** to back up over indentations. Each <control-d> backs up the number of columns specified by the **shiftwidth** parameter. To temporarily remove all indentation for the current line, type **^<control-d>** (a caret followed by a <control-d>). To remove all indentation for all subsequent lines, type **0<control-d>**.
autoprint	(**ap**.) Displays ("prints") the current line after the execution of any command that changes text in the buffer. This is suppressed for the global commands (**g** and **v**).
autowrite	(**aw**.) Writes the buffer to the current file if the buffer has been modified and if a **next**, **rewind**, or **!** command has been given.
beautify	(**bf**.) Discards all control characters, other than tab, newline, and form-feed characters, from the input text.
directory	(**dir**.) Sets the name of the directory used to hold the edit buffer. The editor quits if this is not a directory it can write in.
edcompatible	(**ed**.) Causes the editor to remember the presence of **g** and **c** suffixes in **s** (substitute) commands and to use the suffixes as toggles; that is, the first use of **g** causes all subsequent substitutions to be global until the **g** suffix is used again. (Despite what the name may suggest, the **ed** editor does not act this way.)
ignorecase	(**ic**.) When matching regular expressions, maps uppercase characters in the text to lowercase.
lisp	Modifies the **autoindent** mode and the **vi** commands (,), {, }, [[, and]] to conform to usage for the Lisp programming language.
magic	Changes the interpretation of special characters in regular expressions and in replacement strings (see the sections describing those topics for details).

PARAMETER	ACTION
number	(**nu.**) Shows line numbers when lines are displayed.
paragraphs	(**para.**) The value of this parameter is a string in which successive pairs of characters are names of text-processing macros (such as those used by **nroff**) that mark the beginnings of paragraphs. These macros have the form .*XY*, where the period is the first character of a line. For example, .**PP** is a common macro used to indicate a paragraph beginning, and it would be represented by the character pair **PP**. Note that the two-letter code without the period is used. The **para** parameter is used, for example, by **vi** commands that seek the beginning of a paragraph.
prompt	When **prompt** is set, the command mode is indicated by a : prompt; when **noprompt** is set, there is no command-mode prompt.
redraw	Simulates an intelligent terminal on a dumb terminal. For example, when this mode is set in the **vi** mode, deleting a line causes the text to close up. In the **noredraw** mode, however, the deleted line is replaced with an **@** marker on screen. The **redraw** mode increases the required data transfer between the computer and the terminal and thus does not work well with slow transmission speeds.
remap	Allows macros defined by the **map** command to use other defined macros. Only one step of translation is performed if **noremap** is set.
report	This parameter is set to the number of lines that must be altered before the editor displays on-screen a report of the number of lines affected. For example, if **report** is set to 10, then a large-scale deletion that affects 12 lines produces a report to that effect. A deletion that affects just 5 lines doesn't produce a report.
scroll	This parameter is set to the number of lines that the screen will scroll when the **<control-d>** command is given. Also, the **z** command displays twice the number of lines given by **scroll**.
sections	This parameter is set to a string in which each successive pair of characters represents a macro used to indicate sections of text (see **paragraph**).
shiftwidth	(**sw.**) The value of this parameter is used for the spacing of the tab stops used by the tab key, by the **autoindent** parameter, and by the **<** and **>** (shift) commands.

(continued)

PARAMETER	ACTION	*(continued)*
showmatch	(**sm.**) When the visual mode of the editor is used, causes the cursor to move briefly to the matching (or { when a) or } is typed, providing the matching character is still on the screen. This is very useful in text, such as C or Lisp programs, that may nest many such pairs.	
slowopen	(**slow.**) When the editor is in the visual mode, prevents the screen of an unintelligent terminal from updating during the input mode. This can speed up input when text is being inserted.	
tabstop	(**ts.**) The value of this parameter indicates the tab-stop spacing to be used for text from an input file. Note that this can be different from the **shiftwidth** value.	
terse	Results in shorter error messages.	
window	This parameter is set to the number of lines of text displayed in the visual mode.	
wrapscan	(**ws.**) Causes searches begun by the // or ?? command to go from the end to the beginning of a file (or vice versa) so that the entire file is searched. When this option is not set, the search runs from the start of the search to the end of the file (for //) or to the beginning (for ??).	
wrapmargin	(**wm.**) When the editor is in the visual mode and this option is set to a numeric value, say *n*, that is greater than 0, adds a newline to each input line when it reaches *n* spaces from the right margin. The break is made at a word boundary, so if the *n* space limit is reached in the middle of a word, the whole word is shifted to the next line. This is useful for speed typists who prefer not to have to worry about when to hit <enter> while typing a lot of text.	
writeany	(**wa.**) Inhibits the overwrite protection normally provided to **w** (write) commands.	

SETTING UP THE ex ENVIRONMENT The behavior of the **ex** editor can be modified by setting the edit parameters to new values. Earlier we mentioned four methods for doing this. We'll look at them in more detail now. All but the first also can be used to set up macros and abbreviations using the **map** and **ab** commands.

Using the set Command

The most direct method of setting up the **ex** environment is to use the **ex set** command to set the edit parameters as desired. This method is described in the Command Summaries section and in the previous section. One further point to note is that more than one parameter can be set at a time. For example,

```
set ai wm=5
```

sets the **autoindent** mode and sets the **wrapmargin** parameter to **5**.

Using the so Command

The **so** command causes the **ex** commands in a specified file to be executed. You could, for example, place this line in a file called **cprep**:

```
set ai wm=5 sw=4 ts=4
```

Then, when editing a file that uses these settings, you can give the following **ex** command:

```
so cprep
```

Using the EXINIT Environmental Variable

When **ex** (or **vi**) is invoked, it checks the current value of the **EXINIT** shell variable for editor initialization instructions. For example, you could place this line in your **.profile** file:

```
EXINIT='set noai wm=15' ; export EXINIT
```

When you log in, **EXINIT** is assigned the indicated string. (The quotes are necessary because the string contains spaces.) Then, when **ex** is invoked, the indicated instructions are executed.

Using the .exrc File

A fourth approach is to place **ex** instructions in a file called **.exrc**. When the editor is invoked, it automatically checks for this file and executes its contents. It first looks for a file by this name in the current directory. If it fails to find it there, it looks in your home directory. Thus you can set up a general **.exrc** file in your home directory and more specific **.exrc** files in particular directories. For example, your home directory could contain a **.exrc** file that you have set up for general text work, while the directory you use for C programs could contain a **.exrc** file with settings and macros that are suitable for C programming.

EXINIT and .exrc

What happens if you use both **EXINIT** and a **.exrc** file? The **EXINIT** settings are performed first, then the settings from the file are performed. Thus if any parameter is defined in both, the **.exrc** definition holds, since it is implemented later.

COMMENTS The **ex** editor is a more powerful editor than the older **ed**. Also, its set of edit parameters allows you to customize **ex** to meet particular needs. Most users find the visual mode of **ex** (also invokable as **vi**) preferable to **ed** or to the line-editing mode of **ex**; in particular, making modification within a line is much easier with **ex**.

The **vi** editor is particularly well-suited for writing programs, since it can provide autoindentation and check for matching parentheses and braces.

However, none of the editors is designed as a text formatter. The usual UNIX method of text formatting is to use an editor to create text with embedded commands that subsequently are interpreted by the **nroff** or **troff** text formatters.

SEE ALSO UNIX Commands: **vi**; **ed**
UNIX Features: Regular Expressions

EXAMPLES

1. Create a new file.

```
$ ex outwest
"outwest" [New File]
:a                                     Give append command to get to text mode
"What'll you have, stranger?" the
bartender asked, wiping a
glass on his soiled apron.
"Whiskey'll suit me just fine."
.                                      Return to command mode
:wq                                    Write and quit
outwest [New File] 3 lines, 119 characters
```

The editor repeats the filename and identifies it as a new file. Then **ex** provides a : prompt to indicate the command mode. The **a** command moves the cursor to the next line, where text is entered. An initial period terminates the text mode, the **w** command saves the file, and the **q** command quits the editor; these two commands can be combined, as here, or be given as separate commands. Finally, the editor reports data about the saved file.

2. Edit an existing file.

```
$ ex outwest
"outwest" 3 lines, 119 characters
:a                                          Append to the end of the file
An unshaven bear of a man at the end of
the bar turned and
grinned at me. It
wasn't a friendly grin.
.
:wq
"outwest" 5 lines, 220 characters
```

This time, **ex** reports data about the file. The file contents are not shown. The current line becomes the last line in the file, and the new text is appended to that.

3. Edit a sequence of files.

```
$ ex outwest downsouth upnorth
"outwest" 5 lines, 220 characters
:ar
[outwest] downsouth upnorth
:n
"downsouth" 6 lines, 245 characters
:ar
outwest [downsouth] upnorth
:rew
"outwest" 5 lines, 220 characters
```

The **ar** command lists the command-line arguments, here the three filenames; the current file is shown in brackets. The **n** command moves to the next file, and the **rew** command moves to the first file on the list. If changes are made in a file, you normally have to write the file before changing files or else use **n!** to override the protection.

4. Use **ex** with an editing script.

```
$ cat text
A jar is but a jar, but
a door can be ajar.
$ cat escript
%s/jar/can/g
:wq
$ ex - text < escript
$ cat text
A can is but a can, but
a door can be acan.
```

Here we show a file of text, an editing file, the editing command line, and the results of

(continued)

the editing. Note that redirection is used so that editing input is taken from the **escript** file instead of from the keyboard. Note, too, that the – option is used to inhibit **ex** messages. The editing script should incorporate all necessary instructions, including the **w** (write) and **q** (quit) instructions. The % address is short for **1,$** (all lines).

5. Use an editing script from within **ex**.

```
$ cat text
A jar is but a jar, but
a door can be ajar.
$ cat escript
%s/jar/can/g
$ ex text
"text" 2 lines, 44 characters
:so escript
:%
A can is but a can, but
a door can be acan.
:
```

Here **text** and **escript** are set up as before (except the **wq** command is omitted), but this time **escript** is invoked through the **so** command from within **ex**. The % symbol indicates the range **1,$**.

6. Set up a *.exrc* file.

```
$ cat .exrc
set ai sm wm=0 sw=4 ts=4
ab m main()
ab ma main(ac,ar)
ab pf printf
$
```

Suppose this file is in the **Cdir** directory. Then, when you use **ex** or **vi** in that directory, the indicated settings and abbreviations hold.

PURPOSE Use the **expr** command to evaluate and compare expressions.

FORMAT **expr** *expression*

Here *expression* is constructed using strings, integers, and the operators recognized by **expr**.

DESCRIPTION The **expr** command evaluates an expression and displays the result. The expression can be a string (a sequence of characters), an integer, or a more elaborate construction having a string or integer value. Several operators allow **expr** to perform arithmetic, do comparisons, and make simple choices.

COMMON USES You can use the **expr** command in shell scripts to perform calculations, count characters, and make comparisons. It is one of the few numerically oriented UNIX commands.

OPERATORS The **expr** operators operate on arguments that can be integers (such as **234** or **7**), strings (such as **baloney** or **/usr/boon/token**), shell variables, or other expressions that have a numeric or string value. These operators are listed below in groups in order of decreasing precedence. Note that arguments (*arg*) are separated by a space from the operators, and that certain operators use the backslash to avoid shell misinterpretation.

EXPRESSION	MEANING
arg1 : *arg2*	Checks whether the characters in *arg1* match those in *arg2*. The : operator compares the two arguments and normally returns the number of characters in *arg1* matched by *arg2*. Here *arg1* should be a string, while *arg2* should be a regular expression of the type recognized by **ed**. (One exception: Here the ^ character is not a special character, because the comparisons automatically start at the beginning of *arg1*.) Here are some examples:

```
$ expr catch : cat
3
$ expr catch : 'c.*c'
4
$ expr catch : '.*'
5
$ expr catch : cats
0
$ expr catch : at
0
```

The first example shows that **cat** matches the first three characters in **cat**. The next example uses the regular expression **c.*c**, which means two **c**'s separated by zero or more other characters; this matches **catc**, so the value is **4**. Similarly, **.*** means zero or

(continued)

153

EXPRESSION	MEANING	*(continued)*

more occurrences of any character, so all five characters are matched. The single quotes are used to prevent the shell from attempting to interpret the *. Next, note that the whole *arg2* must match; since **cats** is not contained in **catch**, there are no characters matched. Also, the comparison starts at the beginning of *arg1*, so **at** fails to match.

You can use the \(...\) notation in the regular expression to return the matching portion of a string instead of a count; that is, if the regular expression matches the first argument, the part corresponding to the portion of the *arg2* in escaped parentheses is displayed:

```
$ expr catch : '\(c.*t\)c'
cat
$ expr catch : '\(c.*t\)s'

$
```

In the first case, the pattern matches **catc**, and the portion matching '\(c.*t\)' is displayed. In the second case, the pattern as a whole does not match, so the null string (no characters) is displayed.

arg1 * *arg2*	Multiplies *arg1* by *arg2*.
arg1 / *arg2*	Performs integer division.
arg1 % *arg2*	Displays the remainder (modulus) of *arg1* divided by *arg2*.

These operators perform integer arithmetic. For division, the result is truncated to the largest integer. Note that the * for multiplication is preceded by a \ so that it will not be interpreted as a shell metacharacter. Here are some examples:

```
$ expr 80 \* 66
5280
$ expr 19 / 5
3
$ expr 19 % 5
4
```

The division and remaindering results reflect that 5 goes into 19 3 times with a remainder of 4. Note that the correct division result of 3.8 is truncated to 3, not rounded to 4.

EXPRESSION	MEANING
arg1 **+** *arg2*	Adds the two arguments.
arg1 **-** *arg2*	Subtracts *arg2* from *arg1*.

These operations are of lower precedence than the preceding ones. The arguments must be integers. Here are some examples:

```
$ expr 10 + 5
15
$ VAL=22
$ expr $VAL - 17
5
```

Here a shell variable (**VAL**) has been set to **22**, and its value (**$VAL**) is used as an argument.

EXPRESSION	MEANING
arg1 **=** *arg2*	Checks whether the arguments are equal.
arg1 **\>** *arg2*	Checks whether *arg1* is greater than *arg2*.
arg1 **\>=** *arg2*	Checks whether *arg1* is greater than or equal to *arg2*.
arg1 **\<** *arg2*	Checks whether *arg1* is less than *arg2*.
arg1 **\<=** *arg2*	Checks whether *arg1* is less than or equal to *arg2*.
arg1 **!=** *arg2*	Checks whether *arg1* is not equal to *arg2*.

With these operators, the comparison is made numerically if the arguments are integers and lexicographically (by extended alphabetic sequence) if the arguments are strings. A "true" result is represented by the value 1, and a "false" result is represented by the value 0. Note that **>** and **<** are prefixed with a \ to avoid confusion with the shell redirection symbols. Here are some examples:

```
$ VAL=27
$ expr $VAL = 27
1
$ expr animal \> house
0
```

The value of **VAL** is 27, so **expr** displays a **1**, or "true." The string **animal** is not greater than (does not come alphabetically after) **house**, so **0**, or "false," is displayed.

EXPRESSION	MEANING
arg1 **\&** *arg2*	Checks whether neither *arg1* nor *arg2* is zero, or "null." If neither argument is zero, *arg1* is displayed; otherwise 0 is displayed. The term "null" denotes a string with no characters, such as ' ' or " ".

(continued)

155

EXPRESSION	MEANING	*(continued)*

An undefined shell variable, for instance, has a null value. Here is an example:

```
$ NAME=phil
$ expr "$NAME" \& coot
phil
$ expr "$POO" \& coot
0
```

$NAME is defined and **coot** is a non-null string, but $POO is undefined and hence is also null. Note the use of quotes. In each case, the shell variable is replaced by its value. If the quotes are omitted, the first expression is

```
expr phil \& coot
```

which is fine. But without quotes, the second expression is

```
expr \& coot
```

because the null string is substituted for $POO. This produces a syntax error, since there is just one argument. With quotes, both expressions are okay after substitution:

```
expr "phil" \& coot
expr " " \& coot
```

arg1 \¦ *arg2*   Checks whether *arg1* is zero. This combination results in the first argument being displayed if it is non-zero and non-null; otherwise, the second argument is displayed. Suppose, for instance, you wish to set a shell variable equal to a second variable if the variable is defined and to a default value if it is not defined:

```
$ PRINTER=`expr $LPDEST \¦ printer2`
```

The backquote mechanism assigns the output of **expr** to the shell variable **PRINTER**. This output is the value of **LPDEST** if it is defined, and the string **printer2** if it is not defined.

EXIT VALUES   As well as displaying the result of its evaluation, **expr** also has an exit value.

EXIT STATUS	MEANING
0	The expression is not 0 or null.
1	The expression is 0 or null.
2	The expression is invalid.

A null string has a length of zero. Note that a 0 exit status implies a non-zero value. The exit value typically would be used in a shell script.

COMMENTS Although **expr** makes arithmetic possible, it does not make it simple to express, and it performs arithmetic quite slowly.

SEE ALSO UNIX Features: Command Substitution; Command Lines; Exit Values

EXAMPLES

---

1. Update a counter in a shell script.

```
CT=0
for file in $*
do
    ...
    CT=`expr $CT + 1`
done
echo $CT files were processed
```

Here **CT** keeps track of the number of iterations. Each time the **for** loop is traversed, **CT** is increased by one. The backquote mechanism, which replaces an expression with its outputs, is often used with **expr**. (The **for file in $*** construction means "for each command-line argument, set **file** equal to the argument and execute the following instructions.")

2. Write a shell script that sums its arguments.

```
SUM=0
for number in $*
do
    SUM=`expr $SUM + $number`
done
echo The sum is $SUM
```

Here **SUM** is the running total and **number** is a number from the command-line argument list for the script. The **expr** command evaluates the sum, and the backquote mechanism updates **SUM** to the new total.

3. Assign the number of characters in one shell variable to another.

```
NLETS=`expr "$LOGNAME" : '.*'`
```

This combines the backquote mechanism with the counting algorithm described in the section on the : operator.

---

false

PURPOSE Use the **false** command in shell scripts to return a non-zero exit value. Such a value normally is returned by UNIX commands that have failed.

FORMAT false

DESCRIPTION The **false** command does nothing other than return a non-zero exit value.

COMMON USES You can use **false** in constructing and testing shell scripts. For instance, in testing an **if** statement, you can temporarily use it with the **false** statement so that you will know for certain what the behavior of the command should be.

COMMENTS The companion **true** command does nothing except return a zero exit value. UNIX commands commonly have a zero exit status if they run error free and a non-zero exit status if they experience an error. This conflicts with the C representation (shared by the **awk** and **expr** commands) of true by non-zero and false by zero.

SEE ALSO UNIX Commands: **true**
UNIX Features: Exit Values; Shell Scripts

EXAMPLES

---

1. Illustrate the fact that the **false** command does nothing but has an exit value.

```
$ false
$ echo $?
1
```

The $? shell parameter represents the exit status of the preceding command. Here the **false** command has no visible effect, but echoing $? shows that the exit value is **1**.

2. Check part of a shell script.

```
if false
then
    echo Bye bye
    exit 1
else
    echo Going on
fi
```

You can use this technique to check that the program exits properly for a false condition, then replace **false** with the actual test condition.

PURPOSE Use the **fgrep** command to search files for lines containing given strings.

FORMAT **fgrep** [*option(s)*] [*string(s)*] [*file(s)*]

DESCRIPTION The **fgrep** command normally displays those lines in a file (or files) that match a given string (series of characters) or set of strings. If more than one file is searched, the filename is displayed, too. More than one string can be searched for, and the list of search strings can be stored in a file. If no filenames are given in the command line, the standard input is used. Thus a pipe or redirection can be used in place of an input file. Unlike **grep**, **fgrep** does not recognize regular-expression special characters.

COMMON USES You can use **fgrep** to find lines containing a particular word, files containing a particular word, or lines containing one of a list of words.

OPTIONS The **fgrep** command has seven options:

OPTION	ACTION
-v	Displays all but the matching lines.
-x	Displays just the lines matched in their entirety.
-c	Displays just a count of matching lines; multiple files are reported individually.
-l	Displays just the names of files with matching lines.
-n	Displays the line number before each line.
-b	Displays the block number for each line.
-f *file*	Takes the string from *file* instead of from the command line.

STRINGS A string is series of characters. If you wish **fgrep** to search for more than one string, separate the strings with a newline. If the entire search pattern is enclosed in quotes, you can generate a newline with the <enter> key. Or, if you don't use quotes, you can type a backslash (\) just before an <enter>.

COMMENTS The **fgrep** command is line oriented, so a phrase spread over more than one line is not found. **fgrep**, along with **egrep**, belongs to the **grep** family. **grep** provides a pattern-matching scheme termed "limited regular expressions," but can search for only one pattern at a time. **egrep** uses "full regular expressions" and, like **fgrep**, can search for multiple patterns. However, **egrep** uses an algorithm that may require more memory than **fgrep** requires.

SEE ALSO

UNIX Commands: **grep**; **egrep**

UNIX Features: Standard I/O, Redirection, and Pipes; Extending Commands over More than One Line; Filename Generation; Filters

EXAMPLES

1. Find lines containing a particular word.

```
$ fgrep overdue booklist
The Golden Bough:Frazer:M.Stooge:2/22/56:overdue
Where's the Rest of Me?:Reagan:G.Bush:1/1/84:overdue
$
```

This finds and prints those lines in the **booklist** file that contain the word **overdue**.

2. Find files containing a particular word.

```
$ fgrep -l Carruthers report*
report2
report7
report91
$
```

This looks for the word **Carruthers** in all files in the current directory that have names beginning with **report**. The –l option causes just the names of the matching files to be displayed.

3. Find lines containing one of a list of words.

```
$ fgrep 'Sue
        Samuel
        Sandra
        Stuart'   phonelist
Adams, Samuel 444-4444
Grep, Bobbie Sue 939-9919
Stuart, Nick 839-9618
Zipf, Stuart 222-1122
$
```

This searches the **phonelist** file for all lines containing any of the four names listed. Note the use of single quotes to bind the four names into a single list.

4. Find lines containing one or more strings from a file.

```
$ cat birdlist
eagle
chicken
swallow
finch
seagull
...
$ fgrep -f birdlist chapter1
scored an eagle on the eleventh hole to increase his lead to
a chicken from his hat. The other diners grimaced at the
in the candlelight. Felicia swallowed her pride and asked
$
```

This command finds all lines in the **chapter1** file that contain any string listed in the **birdlist** file. That file includes **eagle**, **chicken**, and **swallow**.

5. Find which users in a certain list are currently logged in.

```
$ who | fgrep -f committee
piff      tty04          Feb 29      9:23
dribble   tty08          Feb 29     10:15
babble    tty12          Feb 29      8:54
$
```

The output of **who** is piped to **fgrep**, which finds those current users who also are listed in the **committee** file.

file

PURPOSE Use the **file** command to determine file types.

FORMAT **file** [−c] [−f *lfile*] [−m *mfile*] [*file(s)*]

Here *file(s)* is the list of files to be classified, and *lfile* is a file containing such a list. You should use at least one of these two ways to indicate which files should be classified. Also, *mfile* is the name of an alternative file of "magic numbers."

DESCRIPTION The **file** command takes a list of one or more files and classifies each file. It attempts to guess the type of text file; that is, ASCII text, C program source code, FORTRAN program source code, and so on. This command uses the **/etc/magic** file to help guess the file type. The **/etc/magic** file lists "magic numbers," which are specific numeric or string constants included in a file to indicate its type.

COMMON USES You can use **file** to help classify files in a directory without having to read the files directly.

OPTIONS Of the three options that follow, the first is part of System V Release 2. The second and third first appeared in a pre–Release 2 manual and have now shown up again in the Release 3 manual.

OPTION	ACTION
−f *lfile*	Tests the files whose names are found in the *lfile* file.
−c	Checks the magic file for format errors; no file typing is done.
−m *mfile*	Uses *mfile* instead of **/etc/magic** as the magic file.

SEE ALSO UNIX Commands: **find**
UNIX Features: Files and Directories; Standard I/O, Redirection, and Pipes; Filters

1. Classify the files in the current directory.

```
$ file *
a.out:      executable not stripped
arcp:       cpio archive
arv0:       archive
asamp:      English text
awk1:       ascii text
file2:      empty
show.o:     8086 relocatable, Small model
show.c:     c program text
top.sh:     commands text
```

Here **arv0** is an archive produced by **ar**.

2. Find the text files in the current directory.

```
$ file * ! grep text
asamp:      English text
awk1:       ascii text
show.c:     c program text
top.sh:     commands text
```

The output produced in Example 1 is piped through the **grep** command, which selects just those lines containing the string **text**.

3. Find file types for files larger than a certain size.

```
$ find . -size +100 -print > sizable
$ file -f sizable
```

Here the **find** command is used to produce a file containing the names of files larger than 100 blocks (512 bytes per block) in the current working directory and its subdirectories. Then the file (**sizable**) is used to provide the **file** command with a list of files to check.

find

PURPOSE Use the **find** command to locate and perhaps run selected commands on particular files.

FORMAT find *pathname-list search-expression*

Here *pathname-list* describes the directory or directories to be searched, and *search-expression* indicates which files are sought and what, if anything, should be done with them.

DESCRIPTION The **find** command searches through the indicated directories and all their subdirectories for files that match a search criterion. This criterion may be a particular filename, a general pattern for filenames, a property of the file (such as size or time of last modification), or a combination. The command can specify that the names of matching files be displayed or that some other command, such as **rm** (remove), be performed on the matching files.

COMMON USES You can use **find** to locate a particular file in a hierarchy of directories, to find all files larger than a given size, or to remove all files that have not been accessed within a given time period. You can require confirmation for each file before it is removed.

THE LIST OF PATHNAMES The *pathname-list* argument is a list of one or more directory names. The names are separated by spaces, as in the following:

```
/usr/bootes . orion
```

Each directory in the list, as well as all its subdirectories, is searched. You can use shell directory abbreviations such as the dot for the current directory.

THE SEARCH EXPRESSION The *search-expression* argument consists of one or more "primary" expressions, like the following:

```
-print
-name flossy
```

Each primary is considered to be a "Boolean expression"; that is, to be an expression whose value is "true" or "false." Most of the primaries describe properties of a file, but some, like **-print**, prescribe actions to be taken. For logical consistency, these action primaries also have true or false values associated with them. Three "operators" are used to modify and to join primaries. Expressions with more than one primary are evaluated from left to right. As soon as **find** detects a condition that makes the entire expression false, it stops and moves on to the next file. This means that the position of a primary may be important.

Primaries

In the following expressions, *n* represents a decimal integer. The combination **+***n* means "more than *n*," **–***n* means "less than *n*," and *n* means "exactly *n*." Each occurrence of *n* in the following can be replaced by **+***n* or **–***n* with a corresponding change in interpretation. For example,

    -mtime +5

means "files last modified more than **5** days ago," and

    -mtime -5

means "files modified within the last **5** days."

The term "current file" means the particular file being examined by **find** as it searches through directories. Thus the current file becomes, in turn, each of the files being examined.

EXPRESSION	VALUE
–name *file*	True if *file* matches the current filename. The shell's wildcard notation can be used if quoted; for example, **–name '*.c'**.
–perm *onum*	True if the file permission flags match the octal number *onum*, which describes permissions in the format discussed under **chmod**. Prefixing *onum* with a minus sign causes additional bits to be compared, matching the format used by the **stat( )** system call.
–type *c*	True if the file is of type *c*, where *c* is a **b** (block special), **c** (character special), **d** (directory), **p** (pipe, or fifo), or **f** (regular) file. See **ls**.
–links *n*	True if the current file has exactly *n* links.
–user *name*	True if the file belongs to the user *name*. If *name* is a number and if that number is not a login name, then *name* is taken to be a user ID number from the **/etc/passwd** file.
–group *name*	True if the file belongs to the group *name*. If *name* is a number and if that number is not a group name, then *name* is taken to be a group ID number from the **/etc/group** file.
–size *n*[**c**]	True if the file is *n* blocks long, where one block is 512 bytes. If *n* is followed by a **c**, *n* is taken to be the number of characters. (One character is one byte.)
–atime *n*	True if the file has been accessed *n* days ago. Note: The directories in the pathname list have their access times changed by **find**.
–mtime *n*	True if the file was modified *n* days ago.
–ctime *n*	True if the file i-node was modified *n* days ago.

(continued)

EXPRESSION	VIEW	(continued)
-newer *file*	True if the current file has been modified more recently than *file*.	
-print	True if present; it causes the current pathname to be displayed.	
-exec *cmd*	True if the executed command (*cmd*) returns a zero exit status (successful execution). A set of open and close braces (**{}**) can be used to represent the current pathname. The end of *cmd* must be marked with an escaped semicolon (**\;**). For example, `-exec ls -l {} \;` means "list the status information on each file found."	
-ok *cmd*	Like **-exec**, except that the desired command line is displayed first with a question mark. The command is executed only if the user responds by typing **y**.	
-depth	True if present. This primary causes the directory hierarchy to be processed so that all entries in a directory are acted upon before the directory itself is.	
-mount	True if present. This restricts the search to the file system containing the specified directory. If no directory is specified, the current directory is assumed. New with Release 3.	
-local	True if the found file physically resides on the local system. New with Release 3.	

Combinations

Primaries can be combined with Boolean operators to produce a larger range of expressions:

OPERATOR	ACTION
Logical NOT	Uses the **!** operator to negate an expression. Thus `! -name '*.c'` means "all filenames not ending in .c."
Logical AND	Is implied by following one primary with another. Thus `-size +10 -links 3` means "all files having both a size in excess of 10 blocks and exactly 3 links."
Logical OR	Represented by the **-o** operator between two primaries. Thus `-size +10 -o -links 3` means "all files having either a size greater than 10 blocks or exactly 3 links."

These operators are listed in order of decreasing precedence. Thus

```
! -name oye -size -5
```

means "a file whose name is not **oye** and whose size is less than **5** blocks; that is, the NOT is applied to just the first primary.

Parentheses can be used to group primaries. To avoid confusing the shell, use escaped parentheses; that is, \(and \). For example,

```
! \( -name oye -size -5 \)
```

causes the whole expression within the parentheses to be negated.

COMMENTS The **find** utility is unique among UNIX commands in its syntax. It often is used in shell scripts to produce a list of files to be processed by the rest of the script.

SEE ALSO UNIX Features: Files and Directories; Extending Commands over More than One Line; Quoting; Pathnames and the Directory Tree

EXAMPLES

1. Find a particular **file** in a hierarchy of directories.

```
find . -name brahms -print
```

This searches the current directory and subdirectories for files named **brahms** and prints out the pathnames of matching files. Be careful not to do this:

```
find . -print -name brahms        Bad command
```

Because primaries are tested from left to right, this version prints the name of each file, then checks to see if there is a file named **brahms**. The original version only gets to **-print** if one of the files already passed the **brahms** test.

2. Find all files larger than a given size.

```
find ./reports -size +20 -print
```

This command searches the **reports** subdirectory of the current directory as well as subdirectories of **reports** for files larger than 20 blocks. It prints the names of those files it finds.

(continued)

3. Remove all files that have not been accessed within a given time period.

```
find . -atime +20 -exec rm {} \;
```

This finds all files in the current directory and its subdirectories that were last accessed over 20 days ago and removes them.

4. Remove upon confirmation all files that have not been accessed within a given period.

```
find . -atime +20 -ok rm {} \;
```

This finds all files in the current directory and its subdirectories that were last accessed over 20 days ago. For each file found, you are asked if you wish to remove the file. If you do, type y.

5. Display names and contents of files meeting certain specifications.

```
find . \( -name '*.[cf]' -o -name '*.old' \) -atime -5 \
-print -exec cat {} \;
```

This command (typed as one command line) finds files whose names end in .c, .f, or **.old** that were last accessed less than **5** days ago and displays their names and contents on the screen. The \ after **-5** is the standard Bourne shell method for extending a command over more than one line of the screen.

PURPOSE Use the **getopts** command in shell procedures to read command lines and check for valid options.

FORMAT **getopts** *optstring name* [*arg(s)*]

DESCRIPTION Release 3 of UNIX has adopted a uniform set of rules for representing options. Not all UNIX commands have been converted to that standard, but **getopts** allows you to write conforming shell scripts.

The command-line arguments to a shell script are passed to it as positional parameters, with **$1** being the first argument, **$2** being the second argument, and so on. By default, **getenv** parses (reads and analyzes) the positional parameters to a shell script. It expects all options to begin with a hyphen (-) and that all options precede other arguments on the command line. See Command-Line Syntax in the "UNIX Features" section for a full description of option syntax. Each time **getenv** is invoked in a shell script, it obtains the next option in the command line and assigns the option letter, if it is valid, to the *name* shell variable (see the Format section). The string *optstring* consists of the valid option letters. If an option takes an argument, as in **-o** *filename*, the option letter should be followed by a colon in *optstring*. Thus an *optstring* of **bhl:** indicates that valid options are **-b**, **-h**, and **-l**, with the **-l** option requiring a further argument. If an option requiring an argument is detected, the argument is assigned to a shell variable called **OPTARG**. If an invalid option letter is found, the character **?** is assigned to *name*. The shell variable **OPTIND**, which is initialized to 1 when the shell script is invoked, is set to the index (positional parameter number) of the next option to be read.

When **getopts** finds no further options to read or when it encounters the **--** special argument, **getopts** exits with a non-zero status. This allows it to be used to control a **while** loop.

If the optional *arg(s)* argument is provided, it is parsed instead of the shell script command line.

COMMON USES You can use **getopts** to simplify option-processing in a shell script.

COMMENTS The **getopts** command actually is built into the Release 3 **sh** shell. Some older UNIX versions have a **getopt** command; in the future, this command will no longer be supported.

Note that **OPTIND** keeps track of the positional parameter index, rather than the number of options read. For example, consider the following two command lines:

```
bash -a -q -d doors
bash -aq -d doors
```

In the first case, after the **a** option is processed, **OPTIND** is set to **3**, since the next option name (q) is found in $3, the third positional parameter. In the second case, after **a** is processed, **OPTIND** is set to 2, since the next option name (q) is found in $2.

SEE ALSO   UNIX Commands: **sh**
UNIX Features: Command Lines (the Command-Line Syntax discussion)

EXAMPLES

1. Set up a **getopts** call to recognize three options.

```
getopts bhl: opt
```

This single call to **getopts** reads the next option, if any, from the list of positional parameters ($1, $2, and so on) passed to the shell script containing this call. If the option is a –b, –h, or –l, then –b, –h, or –l is assigned to the **opt** shell variable. If the would-be option uses some other letter, as in –d, a ? is assigned to **opt**. The : following the l indicates that l should be followed by an argument, as in –l 20. The argument is assigned to a shell variable called **OPTARG**.

2. Process a list of options in a shell script.

```
MESSAGE="$0: -$opt is not a valid option and is ignored"
...
while getopts bhl: opt
do
      case $opt in
            b) FLAGB=YES ;;
            h) FLAGH=YES ;;
            l) FLAGL=YES ; LINES=$OPTARG ;;
            \?) echo $MESSAGE ;;
      esac
done
shift `expr $OPTIND - 1`
...
```

The **while** loop causes **getopts** to process options until it returns a non-zero status, which occurs when no more options are left or when –– is encountered. The **case** statement uses the value of **opt** to determine what actions are taken during each loop cycle. The **OPTIND** variable is incremented each time a new positional parameter is due to be processed, thus keeping track of how many have been read. The **shift** expression then readjusts the positional parameters so that $1 refers to the first post-option argument in the original command line.

PURPOSE Use the **grep** command to search files for lines containing a given pattern.

FORMAT **grep** [*option(s)*] *pattern* [*file(s)*]

DESCRIPTION The **grep** command normally displays those lines in a file that match a given search pattern. The pattern may be a word or, more generally, a string (a sequence of characters). The pattern may include special pattern-specifying characters. If more than one file is searched, **grep** displays the filename along with the matching lines.

The **grep** command processes those files listed in the **grep** command line. If no filename arguments are given, **grep** reads the standard input. This allows **grep** to accept input from a pipe.

COMMON USES You can use **grep** to find lines containing a particular word or string, to find files containing a particular word or string, to count lines containing a particular word or string, and to find lines containing a particular pattern.

OPTIONS You can use six options to specify the kind of information you want **grep** to display:

OPTION	ACTION
–v	Displays only those lines *not* matching the pattern.
–c	Displays just a count of matching lines; multiple files are reported individually.
–l	Displays only the names of files with matching lines, not the lines themselves.
–n	Displays the line number before each matched line.
–b	Precedes each line displayed with the number of the block in which it is found. The first block number is 0, and blocks typically are 512 characters in size.
–s	Suppresses the display of error messages for nonexistent or nonreadable files.

PATTERNS The **grep** command can use "limited regular expressions" for creating patterns. These expressions, adapted from those used by the **ed** command, use the following notations:

EXPRESSION	ACTION
.	Matches any one character.
\	Turns off special meanings; for instance, \. matches an ordinary period.
[...]	Matches any one character from the enclosed list of characters.
[^...]	Matches any one character *not* in the enclosed list.
*	Matches zero or more occurrences of the preceding character.
^	Matches the beginning of a line.
$	Matches the end of a line.
c\{m\}	Matches exactly m occurrences of the character c. The integer m has to be in the range 0–255.
c\{m,\}	Matches at least m occurrences of the character c. The range for m is 0–255.
c\{m,n\}	Matches from m through n occurrences of the character c. The range for m and n is 0–255.
\(*expr*\)	Matches *expr*, where *expr* is a regular expression. Thus \(**hope**\) matches **hope**. These "escaped parentheses" create subpatterns called "tagged expressions" that can be referred to by the mechanism described next.
\n	Matches the nth \(*expr*\) subexpression from the pattern. For instance, \(**Oliver**\).*\1 is the same as **Oliver.*Oliver**, since the \1 represents **Oliver**.

The **ed** entry and the Regular Expressions section in "UNIX Features" describe regular expressions more fully.

COMMENTS The **grep** command is line oriented, so a phrase spread over more than one line is not found.

The **grep** family also includes **egrep** and **fgrep**. **egrep** uses a more extensive pattern-matching scheme called "full regular expressions," and it can search for several patterns simultaneously. **fgrep** uses ordinary strings with no pattern-matching symbols, and it also can search for several patterns simultaneously. Someday all three of these commands will be subsumed in a new **grep**.

SEE ALSO

UNIX Commands: **ed**; **egrep**; **fgrep**
UNIX Features: Standard I/O, Redirection, and Pipes; Regular Expressions; Quoting; Extending Commands over More than One Line; Filename Generation; Filters

EXAMPLES

1. Find lines containing a particular string.

```
$ grep overdue booklist
Magister Ludi:Hesse:Y.Berra:overdue
```

This finds and displays those lines in the **booklist** file that contain the string **overdue**. Note that **grep** finds the string even if it is embedded in a longer string. For instance, the above command matches a line containing **loverduet**.

2. Find files containing a particular string.

```
$ grep -l Zorba report*
report3
report5
```

This looks for the word **Zorba** in all files in the current directory having names beginning with **report**. The -l option causes just the names of the matching files to be displayed.

3. Count lines containing a particular word or pattern.

```
$ grep -c schlock inventory
23
```

This counts the number of lines in the **inventory** file containing the word **schlock**.

4. Find lines containing a particular pattern.

```
$ grep '^[zZ]orro' guestlist
Zorro Lei
zorro mcdougal
Zorro Vandermint
```

This finds all lines beginning (because of the ^) with either **Zorro** or **zorro** in the **guestlist** file. The brackets have a special meaning to the shell as well as to **grep**; the single quotes cause the pattern to be passed to **grep** intact without any shell fiddling.

(continued)

5. Find lines containing a phrase.

```
grep 'O Great One' letterheads
```

This searches the **letterheads** file for the phrase **O Great One**. The quotes are used to pass all three words of the phrase as a unit to **grep**. Without them, **O** would be considered the search pattern, and **Great**, **One**, and **letterheads** would be considered filenames.

6. Use a tagged expression.

```
grep '\([Cc]osts\).*area.*\1' duddly
```

This finds all lines in the **duddly** file that contain the strings **costs** or **Costs** with the string **area** somewhere in between. The **\1** duplicates the tagged expression in the escaped parentheses.

7. Use **grep** with a pipe.

```
who | grep '06e'
```

Because no file is specified, **grep** uses standard input. The pipe causes the standard input to be the output of the **who** command, so **grep** scans the output of **who** for lines containing the pattern **06e**. If, for example, all students enrolled in a certain course have been assigned login names ending with **06e**, this command lists those students who are both enrolled in the course and currently logged in.

PURPOSE Use the **id** command to obtain your user ID number and your group ID number.

FORMAT **id**

DESCRIPTION Each official user of a UNIX system is assigned a user ID number (UID) and a group ID number (GID), which identify the user and his or her group. The **id** command displays these ID values along with the corresponding names. If you use a program that has its "set-user-ID" bit or "set-group-ID" bit set (see **chmod**), you temporarily are assigned an "effective ID" corresponding to the program's owner or owner's group. The **id** command reports both real and effective IDs when they differ.

COMMON USES You can use **id** to see who you are and to keep records of who uses certain programs. If you have been using **newgrp** to change your group, you can use **id** to check your current group.

SEE ALSO UNIX Commands: **logname**; **chmod**; **newgrp**
UNIX Features: Groups

EXAMPLES

1. Check your IDs.

   ```
   $ id
   uid=252(starfeld) gid=55(sales)
   ```

   Here **uid** is the user ID, and **gid** is the group ID. The associated login name and group name also are shown.

2. Check who uses a shell script.

   ```
   echo `id` : `date` >> /usr/hal/donkey.use
   ```

   For this to work, whoever uses the script containing this line (call it **donkey**) must have write permission for the **donkey.use** log file. One method to ensure this is to make **donkey.use** writable by everyone:

   ```
   chmod ugo+w donkey.use
   ```

   However, this leaves the file open to tampering. If **donkey.use** is written as a C program instead of as a shell script, we can use a better approach: setting the set–owner–ID bit in the permission mode of the script, as in

   ```
   chmod u+s donkey
   ```

   This temporarily grants the user of **donkey** the same file permissions as the owner of **donkey** while the **donkey** program is running. In this case, **donkey.use** can have just the owner write permission set.

PURPOSE   Use the **join** command to join corresponding lines in two files. To be "corresponding," the two lines must have a "join field" in common.

FORMAT   **join** [*option(s)*] *file1 file2*

Using - for *file1* causes the standard input to be used.

DESCRIPTION   The **join** command takes two files as arguments. Normally, the first field in each file is considered a "join field." The **join** command displays the join field followed by the rest of the line from the first file and then by the rest of the line from the second file. For instance, if the first file contains the line

```
john pickles chips
```

and the second file contains the line

```
john dip pretzels
```

then the join field is **john** and the output line is

```
john pickles chips dip pretzels
```

The standard output (by default, the terminal) is used. Fields are marked off, or delimited, by field separators; the default separators are the space, tab, and newline characters. In the output, a blank is used when displaying the fields. Options allow you to select a different field separator, a different join field, and a different output format.

Each file should be sorted so that the join fields are in ASCII collating sequence. This is alphabetic order expanded to include upper- and lowercase letters, as well as other characters (the **sort** command can be used to achieve this ordering).

Normally, if a join field is found only in one file, no line is output.

COMMON USES   You can use **join** to combine two related data files on a line-by-line basis.

OPTIONS When *n* is used in the options below, it can be a **1** and refer to *file1* or it can be a **2** and refer to *file2*.

OPTION	ACTION
-a*n*	If an unpaired join field is found in file *n*, outputs that line.
-e *str*	Replaces empty output fields (as produced by the **-o** option) with the string *str*.
-j*n m*	Uses the *m*th field of the *n*th file as the join field. If *n* is omitted, uses the *m*th field of each file. Fields are numbered from left to right, starting with number 1. Files must be sorted by the join field.
-o *list*	Here *list* specifies the fields to be displayed. Each element of the list has the form *n.m*, with *n* specifying the file and *m* indicating the field. Uses a space to separate elements of the list.
-t*c*	Uses the character *c* as the field separator instead of the default space, tab, or newline. This character also is used as the field separator in the output.

COMMENTS The **join** command is useful for merging line-oriented data files, such as files in which each line contains a name and a list of grades, sales, or something similar. The **paste** command also provides horizontal merging, but it is not field sensitive.

SEE ALSO UNIX Commands: **sort; paste**
UNIX Features: Standard I/O, Redirection, and Pipes; The Machine Collating Sequence; Filters

EXAMPLES

The first two examples assume that you have two files, one called **benlist** containing the following data:

```
animal pig horse frog
art big cheap
dog tana fifi
```

and the other called **didilist** containing this data:

```
animal horse donkey
bird eagle swift
dog lassie rex
```

1. Join two files line by line on a join field.

   ```
   $ join benlist didilist
   animal pig horse frog horse donkey
   dog tana fifi lassie rex
   ```

   By default, the join field is the first word in each line. The only join fields found in both files are **animal** and **dog**. Note that the join field is displayed just once. The **-a1** option would cause the non-matched line (the one beginning with **art**) to be displayed, too.

2. Display only certain fields from the input files.

   ```
   join -o 1.2 2.2 benlist didilist
   pig horse
   tana lassie
   ```

   Here we display the second fields from each file. Note that the join field is not displayed; to display it, use **1.1** or **2.1** in the list.

   (continued)

The next two examples assume that you have a file called **data1** containing

```
Crad, Nat:Dejet, Belle:Boston:MA
Barr, Tex:Tonker, Honey:Denver:CO
```

and a file called **data2** containing

```
Potts, Rose:O'Toole, Hank:Boston:MA
Zot, Retina::Denver:CO
```

3. Use a different join field and field separator.

```
$ join -t: -j1 3 -j2 3 data1 data2
Boston:Crad, Nat:Dejet, Belle:MA:Potts, Rose:O'Toole, Hank:MA
Denver:Barr, Tex:Tonker, Honey:CO:Zot, Retina::CO
```

This says to use the colon as a field separator and to use the third field in each file as the join field. Since the same join field is used for each file, we could have used **-j 3** instead of **-j1 3 -j2 3**. Note that the join field is listed first and that the colon is used as the output separator, too.

4. Replace empty fields with a string.

```
$ join -t: -j 3 -o 1.3 1.4 1.1 2.2 -e MISSING data1 data2
Boston:MA:Crad, Nat:O'Toole, Hank
Denver:CO:Barr, Tex:MISSING
```

Again, we specify the colon to be the field separator and the third field of each file to be the join field. Only certain fields are displayed, and the second field of the second line of the second file is empty (::); it is replaced with the text supplied by the **-e** option.

5. Use **join** in a pipe.

```
$ sort newgrades ¦ join grades -> allgrades
```

First, the **sort newgrades** command outputs the contents of **newgrades** in sorted order. Then the pipe (¦) makes that output the standard input to **join**. The – indicates that the standard input (the sorted output of **newgrades**) is to be treated as *file2* and is to be joined with the **grades** file, which is *file1*. The resulting output is redirected to the **allgrades** file.

PURPOSE   Use the **kill** command to send a signal, such as a demand to terminate, to a program.

FORMAT   kill [-*signal*] *PID(s)*

Here *signal* is an implementation-dependent numeric value, and *PID* is the process ID number, as provided by the **ps** command.

DESCRIPTION   The **kill** command sends a specified signal to the indicated "process." (A process is a program that is being run.) The signal is indicated by an integer and the process by a PID number. The signals are implementation-dependent: typically, they are listed in the **/usr/include/signal.h** file. The PID can be found by using the **ps** command. The terminate signal (**SIGTERM**, in symbolic form) is sent if no signal is specified. Only the superuser can send signals for processes other than his or her own.

The PID value 0 has a special meaning; it means "signal all processes in the process group." An example of a process group is all the processes run by your login shell, so using a PID of 0 sends a terminate signal to your login shell and to all processes it has started up. (The shell happens to be immune to the terminate signal, but the other processes, by default, are not, so this command kills all normal background jobs.)

COMMON USES   You can use **kill** to terminate a background job that has gotten stuck (it might be in an infinite loop or be waiting for input that it can't get).

SIGNALS   The exact set of signals depends on the implementation, but here we'll list some typical values. The symbolic forms shown below are used by some of the UNIX system calls; eventually **kill** will be converted to use them, too.

VALUE	SYMBOLIC NAME	MEANING
1	**SIGHUP**	Halt if the user hangs up.
2	**SIGINT**	Interrupt the program (like a keyboard \<del\>, \<break\>, or \<control-c\>).
3	**SIGQUIT**	Quit, providing a core dump (like a keyboard \<control-\\>).
9	**SIGKILL**	Kill (cannot be ignored).
15	**SIGTERM**	Software terminate signal.

Both C programs and shell scripts can include instructions to ignore certain signals, such as **SIGINT** and **SIGQUIT**, but **SIGKILL** is a "sure kill."

181

COMMENTS If you make a mistake when writing a program so that it misbehaves and "locks up" the keyboard, you can log in on another terminal and give your **kill** instructions from there. Use the **-u** (user) option of **ps** to obtain PIDs for your own processes on all terminals. (The standard **ps** format just lists those of your processes that are generated from your current terminal.)

SEE ALSO UNIX Commands: **ps; sh**
UNIX Features: Processes

EXAMPLES

---

1. Kill a background process.

```
$ big_n_slow > bnsout &
3712
$ ps
   PID TTY TIME COMMAND
  3699 02  0:04 sh
  3712 02  1:03 big_n_slow
  3713 02  0:05 ps
$ kill 3712
big_n_slow: 3712 terminated
```

The & causes the preceding command to be run in the background; the system prints out the PID of the background process. The **ps** command prints out PID values and other information about processes belonging to the user. Note that it shows the new background process, reporting the same PID displayed after the original command. Because the job is in the background, the user can't abort it by hitting the <del> key, but he or she can use **kill** to send the terminate signal (SIGTERM), which is the default signal sent if no other signal is mentioned.

---

2. Kill a background job that is immune to the normal termination signal.

```
$ tuf_n_slow > tnsout &
3756
$ kill 3756
$ ps
   PID TTY TIME COMMAND
   3699 02  0:04 sh
   3756 02  1:03 tuf_n_slow
   3757 02  0:05 ps
$ kill -9 3756
tuf_n_slow: 3756 terminated
```

A program can be made immune to the interrupt signal. This can be done with the **signal( )** system call for C programs and with **sh's trap** command for shell scripts. Apparently **tuf_n_slow** falls in this category, since the ordinary **kill** failed to stop it. But the "sure kill" **-9** signal cannot be ignored.

3. Kill all background jobs.

```
$ spell encyclo > encyclo.sp &
4032
$ kill 0
terminated
```

Some commands, when run in the background, initiate more than one process, and tracking down all the PID numbers can be tedious. The **kill 0** command sends an interrupt signal to all processes started by the login shell, thus terminating all of them. The login shell itself is signaled, but it ignores the terminate signal.

4. Create a shell script for logging out.

```
$ cat logout
banner BYE!
kill -9 0
```

This displays a large **BYE!** on the screen (see **banner**) and then logs out. The 0 ID causes a signal to be sent to the login shell and any processes started by it, and the **-9** specifies a signal to terminate that cannot be ignored. Thus running this **logout** command kills the login shell, logging you out.

line

PURPOSE Use the **line** command to read a line of input. Most typically, you would use **line** in a shell script.

FORMAT line

DESCRIPTION The **line** command copies a line from the standard input (by default, the keyboard) to the standard output (by default, the screen). It has an exit status of 1 if it encounters the end-of-file signal.

COMMON USES You can use **line** in a shell script to obtain keyboard input.

SEE ALSO UNIX Commands: **read** (part of **sh**)
UNIX Features: Standard I/O, Redirection, and Pipes; Shell Scripts; Command Substitution

EXAMPLES

1. Obtain keyboard input in a shell script.

```
echo What is your name/?
NAME=`line`
echo Hello, $NAME.
```

This script prompts the user to type his or her name. (The \ turns off the wildcard special meaning of ?.) The **line** command alone would display the response, but the command-substitution mechanism (` `` `) assigns the response to the shell variable **NAME** instead. The net effect in this case is the same as if we had used the built-in shell command **read**:

```
echo What is your name/?
read NAME
echo Hello, $NAME.
```

2. Use **line** in a script with redirection from a file.

```
echo Here is the first line of the file $FILE:
line < $FILE
```

This assumes that **FILE** is a shell variable that has been set to the name of some file. The redirection makes **line** read input from the file instead of from the keyboard. Note: Prior to Release 2, the **read** command could not be used with redirection in this way; that is, the command

```
read NAME < $FILE
```

was invalid.

PURPOSE   Use the **ln** command to link, or assign, an additional name to a file.

FORMAT   **ln** [−f] *name1 name2*

             ln [−f] *name(s) directory*

DESCRIPTION   UNIX identifies files internally by an "i-node number." The user, however, identifies files by name. When a file is created, a name is associated with, or linked to, its corresponding i-node value. The **ln** command allows you to link additional names to the same file. The command can be used to assign a new name to a given file or to link the file to the same name in a different directory. Normally, if the desired new name already exists and belongs to a write-protected file, the permission mode is displayed and you are asked if you wish to continue.

      On many UNIX systems, files and directories are organized into more than one file system, with each file system stored on a particular device or subsection of a device. The **ln** command will not link across such file systems, because i-node numbers are unique only within a given file system.

COMMON USES   You can use **ln** to create a more conveniently typed alias for a long filename. Or you can link a file to names in different directories so that the file can be accessed from those directories without using pathnames. You can use different names for a program file to indicate the mode in which the program is to be run. For example, **vi** and **ex** are links to the same program file. The program examines the command line, and if **vi** was used, it goes to the visual mode of **ex**.

USAGE   The **ln** command establishes new links to (names for) one or more files. Its general form is this:

      ln *file(s) target*

If *target* is not a directory, then there must be just one *file* argument. In that case, *target* is used as an additional link to the file. If *target* is the name of a write-protected file, the user is asked if he or she wishes to override the protection.

      If *target* is a directory, then the listed files are linked to that directory; that is, a new name is created using the basenames of the original files and the directory pathname of the target directory.

OPTIONS   The **ln** command has only one option:

OPTION	ACTION
-f	Asks no questions, even if the new name belongs to a write-protected file.

COMMENTS   The **ln** command establishes additional names for an existing file. The **mv** command replaces one name for a file with another. The **cp** command creates a new file along with a name for it.

SEE ALSO   UNIX Commands: **mv**; **cp**; **rm**
UNIX Features: Files and Directories; File Systems; Pathnames and the Directory Tree

EXAMPLES

---

1. Create a second name for a file.

```
$ ln reportSpring rs
$ ls -i r*
3721 reportSpring
3721 rs
```

Now both **reportSpring** (the original name) and **rs** can be used to refer to the same file. The **-i** option for the **ls** command causes the i-node number to be listed; here we see that both names have the same i-node.

2. Link files to another directory.

```
$ cd /usr/prabbit/Class_all
$ ln /usr/prabbit/Class236/*.recs .
```

This causes all files in the **Class236** directory that match the ***.recs** pattern to be linked to the current directory (**.**, or **/usr/prabbit/Class_all**). A file with the full pathname **/usr/prabbit/Class236/quiz.recs** can be referred to as **/usr/prabbit/Class_all/quiz.recs** as well, for example. More usefully, this file can be referred to as **quiz.recs** in either of the two directories.

PURPOSE   Use the **logname** command to display the user's login name.

FORMAT   **logname**

DESCRIPTION   The **logname** command returns the user's login name.

COMMON USES   You can use **logname** in shell scripts to print or record the name of the person using the script.

SEE ALSO   UNIX Commands: **chmod**
UNIX Features: Command Substitution; Shell Variables

EXAMPLES

---

1. Print your login name.

```
$ logname
falstaff
```

Typing this on an abandoned but still connected terminal would be one way of finding out who had been using it.

2. Print a user's name from a shell script.

```
echo Hello, `logname`
```

The backquote mechanism (command substitution) replaces a command with its output; in this case, the login name. Note that we also can use the shell variable **LOGNAME** if it has been defined:

```
echo Hello, $LOGNAME
```

But the **logname** command works even if **LOGNAME** has not been defined.

(continued)

---

3. Keep track of who has used a script.

```
echo `logname` : `date` >> /usr/falstaff/snurt.use
```

For this to work, whoever uses the script (let's call it **snurt**) must have write permission for the log file **snurt.use**. One method for ensuring this is to make **snurt.use** writable by everyone:

```
chmod ugo+w snurt.use
```

However, this leaves the file open to tampering. If we rewrite **snurt** using C, we can use the "set-owner-ID" feature to provide better protection. Just set the set-owner-ID bit in the permission mode of the script:

```
chmod u+s snurt
```

This temporarily grants the user of **snurt** the same file permissions as **snurt**'s owner while the **snurt** program is running. In this case, **snurt.use** can have just the owner write permission set.

PURPOSE   Use the **lp** command to send requests to a line printer.

FORMAT   **lp** [*option(s)*] *file(s)*

DESCRIPTION   The **lp** command arranges for the line printer to print a "request" (files and associated information). When several files are specified, they are printed in the order given. The **lp** command creates an identification string, called a request ID, and displays it on the screen by default. You can use the request ID to inquire about the status of your request (with **lpstat**) and to cancel a request (with **cancel**).

The printed files are preceded with a printed "banner" providing the user's login name and other information about the printing job.

If no files are named, the standard input is used to provide the text to be printed. A hyphen (-) can be used as a filename to stand for the standard input. Normally, in this context, a pipe is used to provide the standard input.

COMMON USES   You can use **lp** to produce hard copies of your files.

OPTIONS   The **lp** command's eight options allow you to give specific instructions about your printing request.

OPTION	ACTION
-c	Causes **lp** to make copies of the named files and to print the copies (normally, **lp** simply prints the contents of the named files). If you do not use this option, and if you change or remove a file between the time of your request and the time of the actual printing, the printing reflects the current state of the file.
-d *dest*	Specifies the particular printer or class of printer to be used. (The -c option of **lpstat** can be used to provide a list of printers and classes.) If *dest* is a particular printer, then that printer is used. If *dest* is a class, then the first available printer in that class is used. If for some reason the requested printer is not available, nothing is printed. When this option is omitted, **lp** uses the printer specified by the environmental variable **LPDEST** if it is set. If **LPDEST** is undefined, a default value for the computer system is used. You can set **LPDEST** whenever you like by giving a command of the form **LPDEST**=*printname* Placing this command in your **.profile** file causes **LPDEST** to be set automatically when you log in.

(continued)

OPTION	ACTION	*(continued)*
−m	Notifies the user by electronic mail (**mail**) when the files have been printed.	
−n *number*	Prints *number* copies; normally, just one copy is printed.	
−o*option*	Lets you specify a printer-dependent option, represented by *option*. To specify more than one such printer option, use the **−o***option* combination repeatedly.	
−s	Suppresses messages, such as the request ID report, from **lp**.	
−t *title*	Prints the *title* string on the banner.	
−w	Writes a message on the user's terminal when a printing job is finished. If the user is not logged in, uses **mail** instead.	

COMMENTS The **lp** command supersedes the **lpr** command present in earlier UNIX versions. One of its main improvements is that it is suitable for a multi-printer environment. Some systems link the **lpr** name to **lp** so that either name can be used to run the **lp** command.

SEE ALSO UNIX Commands: **cancel**; **lpstat**
UNIX Features: Standard I/O, Redirection, and Pipes; Shell Variables; The **.profile** File

EXAMPLES

1. Print the contents of a file.

```
$ lp rates
request id is printer1-302 (1 file)
```

   This prints the contents of the **rates** file. The request ID, usable by **cancel** and **lpstat**, is **printer1-302**. The actual string is implementation–dependent.

2. Print several files.

```
$ lp trig calculus algebra
request id is printer1-345 (3 fileso)
```

   Only one banner is printed for the request, and each file is printed beginning at the top of a page.

3. Use **lp** as part of a pipe.

```
$ cat trig calculus algebra ¦ lp
request id is printer1-365 (1 file)
```

   Here the three files are combined into one and sent on to **lp**. No page breaks are inserted between the files.

4. Print several copies on a particular printer.

```
lp -m -n10 -dlaserhp notice
```

   This causes **10** copies of **notice** to be printed using the printer labeled **laserhp**. The **–m** option causes **lp** to notify you by electronic mail when the job is done.

lpstat

PURPOSE   Use the **lpstat** command to obtain information about printing requests and about line printers.

FORMAT   **lpstat** [*option(s)*] [*request-id(s)*]

DESCRIPTION   The **lpstat** command, when used without arguments, displays the status of all the printing requests you have made via **lp**. To review specific requests, you supply the request IDs as arguments (these are displayed by **lp** when the original printing requests are made). Various options allow you to review other information about the line printers.

In general, each printer has a printer name and also belongs to a printer class. The class could depend on the location as well as on the type of printer. These details are installation-dependent.

COMMON USES   You can use **lp** to see if a printing request has been processed, how many requests are ahead of you, what printers are installed at your site, and what printers are available.

OPTIONS   Several of the options for **lpstat** have an optional *list* that can be used to limit its output to just those items mentioned in the list. A *list* consists of comma-separated names with no spaces; spaces can follow commas only if the whole list is in double quotes. When you use an option that can be limited by a list but you omit the list, all information of the indicated kind is displayed. For example, the **-u** option reports on all users, while either of the following reports just on the listed users:

```
-usarah,sue,sally
-u"sarah, sue, sally"
```

Note that there is no space between the **u** and the list.

192

OPTION	ACTION
-a[*list*]	Displays whether or not the listed devices are accepting printing requests. Here *list* consists of printer names, printer class names, or both.
-c[*list*]	Displays the names of each printer class and lists the printers in each class. Here *list* is a list of class names.
-d	Displays the name of the printer used as the system default.
-o[*list*]	Displays the status of output requests. Here *list* can contain printer names, class names, and request IDs.
-p[*list*]	Displays the status of printers. Here *list* is a list of printer names.
-r	Displays the status of the **lp** request scheduler. (The scheduler is a program that schedules the requests from **lp** for printing.)
-s	Displays a status summary consisting of the information provided by options **-c**, **-d**, **-r**, and **-v**.
-t	Displays all status information.
-u[*list*]	Displays the status of output requests from users. Here *list* is a list of user login names.
-v[*list*]	Displays the name of each printer and the pathname of the associated device. Here *list* consists of printer names.

SEE ALSO UNIX Commands: **cancel; lp**

EXAMPLES

1. Find out the status of your printing request.

```
$ lpstat
printer1-27    rebecca        892    Jan 13 17:05
```

The job is queued, but is not being printed (if it were being printed, this would be indicated in the status summary).

2. Find out all current printing requests.

```
$ lpstat -u
printer1-25    heidi          607    Jan 13 17:04 on printer1
printer1-26    heidi          766    Jan 13 17:04
printer1-27    rebecca        892    Jan 13 17:05
```

The user **heidi** has two jobs, one being printed on **printer1**. Typing **lpstat –uheidi** would list just **heidi**'s jobs.

3. Find which devices correspond to which printers.

```
$ lpstat -v
device for printer1: /dev/lp
device for hplaser: /dev/hplp
```

Here the **/dev/lp** special device file corresponds to the printer known to the system as **printer1**. Similarly, **hplaser** corresponds to the **/dev/hplp** special device file.

4. Find the system default printer.

```
$ lpstat -d
system default destination: printer1
```

PURPOSE   Use the **ls** command to list the names of files and directories. Options provide additional details, such as file sizes and creation times.

FORMAT   **ls** [*option(s)*] [*file(s)*] [*directory(s)*]

DESCRIPTION   The **ls** command by itself lists the files in the current directory. Options provide additional information about the files. You can list a single file or another directory by providing its name as an argument. Names are sorted alphabetically, with numbers coming before letters, and uppercase letters before lowercase letters. (The machine collating sequence is used.) Names beginning with a period are not listed unless you use the **-a** option. By default, filenames are displayed one per line, but you can change this format by specifying options.

COMMON USES   You can use **ls** to see which files exist in your current directory or another directory. By using options, you can display other items of information, such as the size of each file, file permissions (described below), time of creation, and type of file. Also, you can choose different display formats to emphasize various factors, such as time of last use.

OPTIONS   The options for **ls** can be strung together on one hyphen; for instance, **ls -a -x** is the same as **ls -ax**.

OPTION	ACTION
-C	Produces multi-column output with entries sorted down the columns. The number of columns depends on the screen width and on the lengths of the filenames. New with Release 2.
-F	If a file contains an executable program, places an asterisk (∗) after the filename. If the file is a directory, places a slash (/) after the name. New with Release 2.
-R	Recursively lists subdirectories; that is, lists all files and subdirectories in any subdirectory encountered.
-a	Lists all entries; otherwise, names beginning with a period (.), such as **.profile**, are not listed.
-b	Forces the display of non-graphic characters to be in octal notation, using the *ddd* format. New with Release 3.

(continued)

195

OPTION	ACTION	*(continued)*
–c	Uses the time of the last i-node modification, such as a mode change or the creation of new links, instead of the time of the last file modification. (The i-node is a table of file information maintained by the system.) Used to modify the –t and –l options.	
–d	If an argument is a directory, lists only its name and not its contents. This option is often used with –l to get the directory permission modes.	
–f	Forces each argument to be interpreted as a directory and then prints the name of each file listed in the directory. This option turns off –l, –t, –s, and –r, and turns on –a. The order in which filenames are displayed is the order in which entries appear in the directory file. (Note: A directory is a file formatted in a particular way that lists filenames and corresponding i-node numbers.) If an argument is, in fact, not a directory but a regular file, gibberish is displayed as **ls –f** attempts to interpret the file as if it were in directory format. New with Release 2.	
–g	Like –l below, except that the name of the owner of each file is not displayed.	
–i	Precedes each filename with its i-node number, the internal numbering system used to identify files.	
–l	Lists in the long format, giving the mode (see below), number of links, owner, group, size in bytes, and time of last modification of each file. If the file is a special file (that is, it describes a device), the size field contains the major and minor device numbers rather than the size.	
–m	Lists files across the page, separated by commas.	
–n	Like –l, except that the owner's UID (user identification) and group's GID (group identification) numbers are displayed instead of the actual names.	
–o	Like –l, except that the group is not displayed.	
–p	Places a slash (/) after directory names.	
–r	Reverses the sorting order.	
–s	Gives the file size in units of 512 bytes.	
–t	Sorts by time last modified (latest first).	
–u	Sorts using the time of last access instead of last modification. This option is used with –t and –l.	
–x	Displays multi-column output with entries sorted across instead of down the page.	

FILE MODES   The **–l** option includes an entry called the "file mode," which is a string of ten characters. The following is a typical example:

```
-rwxr-xr--
```

The first character indicates the type of file, and the remaining nine indicate various access "permissions" to the file. The following is a list of the file-type characters:

CHARACTER	FILE TYPE
d	The file is a directory.
b	The file is a block special file; that is, the file describes a device, such as a disk drive, that handles data in blocks.
c	The file is a character special file; that is, the file describes a device, such as a terminal, that handles data a character at a time.
p	The file is a FIFO (named pipe) special file. (A "named pipe" is used for interprocess communication; FIFO stands for "first-in/first-out.")
-	The file is an ordinary file.

The nine permission characters consist of three sets of three characters each. Each set details permission to read the file (**r**), permission to write in the file (**w**), and permission to execute a file (**x**), in that order. The first set indicates the file owner's permissions, the second indicates the permissions for users belonging to the file's group (each file is associated with a group), and the third indicates the permissions for the remaining users. Here are the codes used:

CODE	MEANING
r	Permission to read the file.
w	Permission to write in the file.
x	Permission to execute the file.
-	Permission is denied.
s or S	Set-owner-ID or set-group-ID mode (see below).
l	Mandatory locking is set for this file (see below).

As a simple example, the mode string **-rwxr-xr--** indicates an ordinary file (the initial **-**) for which the owner has read, write, and execute permissions (**rwx**), for which group members have read and execute permissions (**r-x**), and for which others have only read permission (**r--**).

If the file is a directory, execute permission means permission to search the directory for a particular file.

It is possible to set up executable files so that any user temporarily has the same permissions as the file's owner (see **chmod**). This set-owner-ID mode is indicated by an **s** in the owner execute permission position. Similary, an **s** in the group execute permission position means all other users temporarily have the same permissions as group members. These temporary positions last as long as the program contained in the file is executing. An **S** indicates that the corresponding execute permission is not set; that is, the program user has the same permissions as the program owner, but those permissions do not include execute permission. (Since the **s** or **S** occupies the position normally used for **x**, the **x** setting cannot be seen directly.)

System V Release 3 adds file locking to UNIX; that is, files temporarily are made unavailable to others while they are being used. An **l** in the group execute permission position indicates the file is locked.

ENVIRONMENTAL VARIABLES The formats for the **-C**, **-x**, and **-m** options depend upon the number of character columns available on one output line. **ls** uses the value of the **COLUMNS** environmental variable to determine that number. If this variable is not set, **ls** uses the **terminfo** database, relying on the **TERM** environmental variable to tell it which terminal is being used. If this fails, the command assumes a width of 80 columns.

If you want **ls** to use **COLUMN**, you can define the variable in your **.profile** file.

SEE ALSO UNIX Commands: **chmod; ln**
UNIX Features: Command Lines; Environmental Variables; Groups; File-name Generation

EXAMPLES

1. List the files in the current directory.

    ```
    $ ls
    Parks
    acorns
    berrytime
    bigfoot
    bottlebill
    lynx
    prigfoot
    rain
    snow
    wildrice
    ```

    Note that the files are listed one per line in ASCII collating sequence, with uppercase letters preceding lowercase.

2. List files sorted downward in columns.

    ```
    $ ls -C
    Parks        berrytime   bottlebill   prigfoot    snow
    acorns       bigfoot     lynx         rain        wildrice
    ```

    If all the filenames fit on one line, just one line is used. When more than one line is needed, the order is down the first column, then down the second, and so on.

3. List files sorted across in columns.

    ```
    $ ls -x
    Parks        acorns      berrytime    bigfoot     bottlebill   lynx
    prigfoot     rain        snow         wildrice
    ```

4. List files, showing the type.

    ```
    $ ls -CF
    Parks/       berrytime   bottlebill   prigfoot    snow
    acorns       bigfoot     lynx*        rain        wildrice
    ```

    The slash indicates that **Parks** is a directory, and the asterisk marks **lynx** as an executable file.

    (continued)

5. List files in another directory.

```
$ ls -x Parks
glacier        sequoia       yellowstone  yosemite
```

Here the files in the **Parks** subdirectory of the current directory are listed.

6. List files using wildcard metacharacters.

```
$ ls -x [pP]*
prigfoot

Parks:
glacier        sequoia       yellowstone  yosemite
```

The **[pP]*** notation matches **prigfoot** and **Parks**. When a regular file is given as an argument, the file is listed. When a directory is given as an argument, the contents of the directory are listed. Note that regular files are listed first, then directories and their contents.

7. List just directory names when a directory is an argument.

```
$ ls -xd [pP]*
Parks      prigfoot
```

Compare this to Example 6, in which the contents of the directory are displayed, too.

8. List files and file sizes.

```
$ ls -s
total 28       2 Parks        2 acorns       2 berrytime
    4 bigfoot  6 bottlebill   4 lynx         2 prigfoot
    2 rain     2 snow         2 wildrice
```

The sizes here are in units of 512 bytes. The example was generated on a system that uses blocks of 1024 bytes, so that the smallest non-zero count is 2, the number of 512-byte units in a 1024-byte block. Note that the total count for the directory is given. Also note that the count for **Parks** reflects the size of the directory file; it does not represent the sizes of the files in the **Parks** directory.

9. Produce a long listing providing file permission modes and other information.

```
$ ls -l
total 28
drwxr-xr-x   2 smokey   nps        96 Sep 13 10:04 Parks
-rw-r--r--   1 smokey   nps       695 Sep 23 08:08 acorns
-rw-r--r--   1 smokey   nps       695 Sep 24 11:08 berrytime
-rw-r--r--   1 smokey   nps      1390 Sep 25 12:09 bigfoot
-rw-r--r--   1 smokey   nps      2780 Sep 24 14:09 bottlebill
-rwxr--r--   1 smokey   nps      3874 Oct 11 10:10 lynx
-rw-r--r--   1 smokey   nps       695 Sep 21 09:09 prigfoot
-rw-r--r--   1 smokey   nps         9 Sep 30 15:09 rain
-rw-r--r--   1 smokey   nps        12 Oct 19 07:09 snow
-rw-r--r--   1 smokey   nps        21 Sep 18 12:10 wildrice
```

The first set of ten characters in each line is the file mode, which indicates the type of file and the file permissions (see the discussion of file permissions in the File Modes section). Next comes a number indicating the number of links to the file (see the **ln** entry). The next two columns are the owner of the file (**smokey**) and the group (**nps**). Then comes the size of the file in bytes, the date of the last modification, and the name of the file.

10. List the i-node values for each file.

```
$ ls -i
1150 Parks
1111 acorns
1294 berrytime
1410 bigfoot
1304 bottlebill
1777 lynx
1192 prigfoot
1518 rain
1849 snow
1241 wildrice
```

The initial number is the i-node number used by the system to identify the file.

11. Use **ls** with a pipe.

```
$ ls  /usr/snip | wc -l
23
```

The **wc -l** command counts the number of lines in its input, which is, in this case, the piped output of the **ls** command. Since **ls** displays one file per line, the number of lines equals the number of files.

mail
(Release 2)

PURPOSE Use the **mail** command to send electronic mail to other users.

FORMAT **mail** [**-t**] *name(s)*

mail [**-epqr**] [**-f** *file*]

The first form sends mail to users with the indicated login names. The second form reads mail sent to you.

DESCRIPTION The **mail** command is the basic UNIX electronic mail command. If invoked without arguments, it displays mail to you in last-in/first-out order. To send mail, you invoke **mail** with the login names of the recipients as arguments.

COMMON USES You can use **mail** to exchange information with other users.

OPTIONS The **mail** command has six options:

OPTION	ACTION
-t	Precedes the sent message with a list of the other recipients of the same message.
-e	Doesn't show the mail. You can use the exit status of **mail -e** (0 for mail, 1 for no mail) to check whether or not mail was sent.
-p	Displays all mail messages without prompting you to respond individually to each message.
-q	Causes **mail** to quit on an interrupt signal, such as <del>. Normally, an interrupt terminates the display of a particular message rather than terminating **mail** itself.
-r	Displays messages in the order in which they were sent.
-f *file*	Causes **mail** to read from *file* instead of from the default mail file ordinarily used.

OVERVIEW The electronic mail system uses a directory setup to contain a "mail file" for each user of **mail**. When you send a message to someone, the message is appended to his or her mail file. When you read your mail, the **mail** command normally scans your mail file for messages. After reading a message, you can leave it in your mail file, delete it, or save it in another file.

SENDING MAIL   To send mail, type **mail** and the login names of the persons to whom you are writing. After you hit <enter>, the cursor moves to the beginning of the next line; no prompt is displayed. Type your message, terminating it by typing an EOF (usually <control-d> at the beginning of a line) or by entering a line consisting solely of an initial period.

You can correct errors on your current line by backing up over and erasing text, but **mail** has no provision for correcting lines once they are entered. Also, you should hit <enter> to start a new line rather than typing through. If you don't hit <enter>, text wrapped around to the next screen line may be internally part of the original line, and you eventually may run into a maximum-characters-per-line limit.

Instead of typing your message, you also can use redirection to send input from a file, as in

```
mail toto < newinfo
```

When you send your message, it is preceded with a header identifying the sender and the time of sending.

If mail is undeliverable (due to an incorrect login name, for example), it is placed in your current directory in a file called **dead.letter**. New dead mail overwrites old in this file.

RECEIVING MAIL   The basic method for receiving mail is to type **mail** with no arguments. The last message received is displayed, followed by a **?** prompt. Type one of the following responses:

RESPONSE	ACTION
<enter>	**Goes to the next message.**
+	Goes to the next message.
d	Deletes the message just displayed and goes to the next message.
p	Displays the message again.
-	Goes to the preceding message.
s [*file*]	Saves the message in *file* and deletes it from the system mail file. If the *file* argument is omitted, saves the message in a file called **mbox** in your home directory.
w [*file*]	Like **s**, except that the header in the message is omitted.
m [*name(s)*]	Mails a message to the given login names. If no names are given, the message is sent to its author. You type the message the same way as in the usual send-mail mode.

(continued)

203

RESPONSE	ACTION	(continued)
q	Quits, leaving undeleted messages in the system mail file.	
x	Quits, leaving all messages unchanged in the system mail file.	
!*command*	Causes the shell to execute the indicated command.	
*	Displays a list of **mail** commands.	

REMOTE MAIL To send mail to someone on a remote system linked to yours, precede the login name with the name of the remote system and an exclamation mark; for example,

```
tedsvax!sally
```

Everything after the first exclamation mark is passed on to the remote system for interpretation. This feature can be used to send mail to systems not directly connected to yours but sharing a connection to a third system. Thus

```
tedsvax!honestbob!kent
```

sends mail from your system through the **tedsvax** system to the **honestbob** system and then to the user **kent**. This ! notation is used by systems connected using **uucp**; other systems may use different notations.

COMMENTS The **mail** command provides a basic mail service, while **mailx** provides a much more advanced service that offers editing facilities. Both commands use the same system mail files, so messages sent by **mail** can be read by **mailx** and vice versa.

SEE ALSO UNIX Commands: **mailx**
UNIX Features: Standard I/O, Redirection, and Pipes; Exit Values; The **.profile** File

EXAMPLES

1. Send mail to someone.

   ```
   $ mail trish
   Thank you for forwarding the proof of
   Gizzward's Theorem to me.
   .
   ```

   The lone period terminates the message.

2. Check your mail.

   ```
   $ mail
   > From trish Thu Sep 25 11:13:37 1986

   No problem.

   ? d
   > From starfish Thu Sep 25 09:28:14 1986

   The account number is 341223A912.

   ? s accts
   ? q
   ```

   Here the user deletes the first message, saves the second in a file called **accts**, and quits **mail**.

mail
(Release 3)

PURPOSE Use the **mail** command to send electronic mail to other users.

FORMAT mail [-oswt] *person(s)*

mail [ehpqr] [-f *file*] [-F *person(s)*]

The first form is for sending mail to *person(s)*; the second is for reading mail sent to you.

DESCRIPTION The **mail** command is the basic UNIX electronic mail command. If you invoke it without arguments, it displays mail sent to you in last-in/first-out order. To send mail to others, invoke **mail** with the login names of the recipients as arguments. Each mode has its own set of options.

COMMON USES You can use **mail** to exchange information with other users.

OPTIONS The following options are for use in sending mail:

OPTION	ACTION
-o	Suppresses the address optimization facility.
-s	Suppresses the addition of a newline at the top of the message you are sending.
-w	Causes a message to be sent to a remote user without waiting for the remote transfer program to complete.
-t	Adds a destination line to the message. This line consists of **To:** followed by a list of the intended recipients.

The following options are for use with mail sent to you:

OPTION	ACTION
-e	Doesn't show the mail. You can use the exit status of **mail -e** (0 for mail, 1 for no mail) to check whether there was mail.
-h	Displays a numbered list of messages. Each item of mail is described by a header indicating the sender, date, and message size. This display is followed by a ? prompt.
-p	Displays all mail messages without prompting you to respond individually to each message.
-q	Causes **mail** to quit on an interrupt signal, such as <del>. Normally, an interrupt terminates the printing of a particular message rather than of **mail** itself.

OPTION	ACTION
-r	Has **mail** display messages in the order in which they were sent.
-f *file*	Has **mail** read from *file* instead of from the default file that is ordinarily used.
-F *person(s)*	Modifies an empty mail file so that all incoming mail is forwarded to *person(s)*.

OVERVIEW The electronic mail system uses a directory containing an individual "mail file" for each user of **mail**. When you send mail to someone, the message is appended to his or her mail file. When you read your mail, the **mail** command normally scans your mail file for messages. Once you have read a message, you can leave it in your mail file, you can delete it, or you can save it in another file of your own. Typically, your mail file is **/usr/mail/**/user/, where *user* is your login name.

SENDING MAIL To send mail, type **mail** followed by the login names of those to whom you are writing. After you hit <enter>, the cursor moves to the beginning of the next line; no prompt shows. Type your message, terminating it by typing an EOF (usually <control-d> at the beginning of a line) or by entering a line consisting solely of an initial period.

You can correct errors on the current line by backing up over and erasing text, but **mail** has no provision for correcting lines once they are entered. Also, you should hit <enter> to start a new line rather than typing through. If you don't hit <enter>, text wrapped around to the next screen line can be part of the original line internally, and you eventually can run up against a maximum–characters-per-line limit.

You also can use redirection to send input from a file, as in

```
mail toto < newinfo
```

Each transmitted message is prefaced with a header, or "postmark," identifying the sender and the time of sending.

If mail is undeliverable (due, for example, to an incorrect login name), a copy is returned to you via **mail**. If **mail** is interrupted during input, a copy of the message is placed in your current directory in a file called **dead.letter**, giving you the opportunity to edit and resend the message. New dead mail overwrites this file.

RECEIVING MAIL The basic method for receiving mail is to type **mail** with no arguments. The last message received is displayed, followed by a **?** prompt. You can respond to the prompt with commands from the following list.

RESPONSE	ACTION
\<enter\>	Goes to the next message.
+	Goes to the next message.
-	Goes to the preceding message.
a	Displays a message that arrived during the **mail** session.
d or dp	Deletes the message just displayed and goes to the next message (messages actually are deleted when **mail** exits).
d *n*	Deletes message number *n*, and does not go to the next message.
dq	Deletes the current message and quits **mail**.
h	Displays a window of headers (numbered message descriptions), including that of the current message.
h *n*	Displays the header for message number *n*.
h a	Displays the headers for all messages.
h d	Displays the headers of those messages scheduled for deletion.
m [*person(s)*]	Mails a message to the given login names. If you omit the recipients' names, the message is sent to you. You type the message the same way as in the send-mail mode, and **mail** returns to the command mode afterwards.
n	Goes to the next message.
num	Displays message number *num*.
p	Displays the message again.
q	Puts undeleted mail back in your mail file and quits.
\<control-d\>	Same as **q**.
r [*person(s)*]	Replies to the sender of the current message and sends a copy to *person(s)*. The message then is marked for deletion.
s [*file*]	Saves the message in *file* and deletes it from the system mail file. If the *file* argument is omitted, saves the message in the **mbox** file in your home directory.
u [*num*]	Undeletes message number *num*. By default, the last message read is undeleted. This command must be given before you exit **mail**.
w [*file*]	Like **s**, except that the message header is omitted.

RESPONSE	ACTION
x	Quits, leaving all mail unchanged and in your mail file.
y	Same as **s**.
!command	Has the shell execute the indicated command.
?	Displays a list of **mail** commands.

REMOTE MAIL To send mail to someone on a remote system linked to yours, precede the login name with the remote system name and an exclamation mark; for example,

```
tedsvax!sally
```

Everything after the first exclamation mark is passed on to the remote system for interpretation. This feature can be used to send mail to systems not directly connected to yours but sharing a connection to a third system. Thus

```
tedsvax!honestbob!kent
```

sends mail from your system through the **tedsvax** system to the **honestbob** system and from there to the user **kent**. This ! notation is used by systems connected using **uucp**; other systems may use different notations.

MAIL FORWARDING You can arrange for mail delivered to your mail file to be delivered to another destination. This can be useful if you have more than one account on a system, or if you have accounts on two or more systems connected by remote mail. To arrange for mail forwarding, first empty your mail file by deleting or saving any mail in it. Then invoke **mail** using the **-F** option. The **F** should be followed with the login name to which mail is to be forwarded. For example,

```
mail -Ftosca
```

causes mail to be forwarded to the user **tosca**. For a remote system, use the appropriate system prefix. For example,

```
mail -Funifoo!mimi
```

forwards mail to the user **mimi** on the **unifoo** system. To forward to more than one user, use a list enclosed in double quotes. Items in the list can be separated by commas or by white spaces, as in

```
mail -F"tosca,unifoo!mimi,uniring!brunhilda"
mail -F"tosca unifoo!mimi uniring!brunhilda"
```

This list of names can be up to 1024 bytes long.

To cancel mail forwarding, use an empty string:

```
mail -F""
```

Using the **–F** option with a non–empty string places a line of the form

Forward to *person(s)*

at the beginning of the mail file. For forwarding to work properly, the mail file should have **mail** as its group ID, and the group permissions should be read and write.

COMMENTS The **mail** command provides a basic mail service, while **mailx** provides a much more advanced service that offers editing facilities and a means for organizing incoming mail. Both use the same system mail files, so mail sent by **mail** can be read by **mailx** and vice versa.

SEE ALSO UNIX Commands: **mailx**

UNIX Features: Standard I/O, Redirection, and Pipes; Exit Values

EXAMPLES

---

1. Send mail to someone.

```
$ mail trish
Thank you for forwarding the proof of
Gizzward's Theorem to me.
.
```

The lone period terminates the message.

2. Check your mail.

```
$ mail
> From trish Thu Sep 25 11:13:37 1986

No problem.

? d
> From starfish Thu Sep 25 09:28:14 1986

The account number is 341223A912.

? s accts
? q
```

Here we delete the first message, save the second in a file called **accts**, and quit **mail**.

PURPOSE   Use the **mailx** command to send and receive electronic mail.

FORMAT   **mailx** [*option(s)*] [*name(s)*]

Here the *name(s)* argument represents the login names of the recipients. The possible *option(s)* are discussed below.

DESCRIPTION   The **mailx** command allows you to exchange electronic mail with other users. It uses the same mail delivery system as the older **mail** command, but it provides a more flexible, powerful service. When receiving mail, you can use **mailx** commands to list, select, save, delete, or reply to mail. When sending mail, you can edit and review letters and perform other actions by using a set of "tilde escape" commands.

The **mailx** command recognizes a large set of environmental variables that can be used to customize the behavior of the command. These variables can be set in a file named (by default) **.mailrc**, which, if present in the home directory, is used to initialize **mailx**.

COMMON USES   You can use **mailx** to exchange memos, programs, data, and other forms of information with other users. If your system is linked to others, you can use remote mail to communicate with users on other systems.

OPTIONS   The **mailx** command has twelve options:

OPTION	ACTION
-e	Tests whether mail is present. Nothing is displayed, but **mailx** returns an exit value of zero (success) if there is mail. This option typically is used in a shell script.
-f [*filename*]	Reads messages from the *filename* file instead of from the system "mailbox." The **mbox** file is used if the *filename* argument is omitted.
-F	Records the outgoing message in a file named after the first recipient. This option overrides the **record** parameter (see Environmental Variables below), if set.
-h *number*	Passes on the "hop" count for mail forwarded to other systems. This option is used by mail-processing software and is not intended for human users.
-H	Displays only the header summaries of incoming mail.
-i	Ignores interrupts.
-n	Does not initialize **mailx** from the **.mailrc** file.
-N	Does not print the initial header summary.

(continued)

OPTION	ACTION	(continued)
-raddress	Passes *address* to network delivery software, and disables the tilde escape commands. This option is used by mail-processing software and is not intended for human users.	
-ssubject	Sets the **Subject** header field to the string *subject*. Use quotes if *subject* contains spaces. (The optional **Subject** header appears when mail is listed and can be used to inform the recipient what to expect.)	
-uuser	Reads the mailbox that the system maintains for *user*. This works only if *user*'s mailbox is not read-protected.	
-U	Converts **uucp** style addresses to internet standards.	

Note: The **-h**, **-r**, and **-U** options can be used only if the **mailx** mail-delivery program is a program other than the standard /**bin/mail**.

OVERVIEW In this section, we'll summarize the default behavior of **mailx**. Some of the behavior described here can be altered by resetting the **mailx** environmental variables, as discussed in the Environmental Variables section.

To send mail, invoke **mailx** followed by a list of the users to whom you wish to send a particular message. To receive mail, invoke **mailx** without a list of users.

When mail is sent, it is stored in a standard file called the "system mailbox" (here we'll just call it the "mailbox," for short). Each user has his or her own mailbox. Typically, the mailbox files are kept in a special mail directory. For example, a user whose login name is **binky** could have as his system mailbox /**usr/mail/binky.**

The **mailx** command adds a "header" to each message, identifying the sender, and providing the date of transmission along with other information. When **mailx** is invoked to read mail, it checks your mailbox for mail. If any is there, **mailx** prints a numbered list of messages, using the message header to identify the source. As you read each message item, you can choose to delete it or to save it in a specified file. If you read a message and then exit **mailx** without explicitly disposing of it, it is, by default, saved in a file called **mbox**. Normally, this file is placed in your home directory. You can change its name and location, as described later, so the actual name may not be **mbox**, but we will use **mbox** as a generic label for this file.

In summary, your mailbox contains any new mail you have been sent, while your **mbox** file contains mail you have read and not deleted or saved elsewhere.

The **mailx** command uses the same mailboxes as **mail**, and mail sent by either command can be read by the other.

SENDING MAIL To send mail to someone, use that person's login name as an argument to **mailx**:

```
mailx ted
```

If you provide more than one login name, the message is sent to each person in the list:

```
mailx ted dick marge
```

The default behavior of **mailx** is to prompt you for a **Subject** string. You can hit <enter> to ignore the prompt or else enter a description:

```
mailx botts
Subject: coffee breaks
```

After the subject, you type the text of the message, hitting the <enter> key to start a new line. The default editor is primitive; you can use the backspace key to erase text on the current line, then continue typing, but you can't return to a previous line. To end the message, you need to simulate an end-of-file signal, typically by typing <control-d> at the beginning of a line (see Example 1 below).

The Tilde Escape Commands section discusses other options you can use when sending mail, and the Environmental Variables section discusses possible changes in the default behavior.

READING MAIL To read mail, invoke **mailx** without a list of recipients:

```
mailx
```

If you have any mail, you are shown a numbered list of messages (see Example 2 below). This list contains information about the message status (new, old but unread, and so on), the sender of the message, the time of delivery, its size, and its subject.

You also are provided with the **mailx** command-mode prompt, which is, by default, a ?. To read a particular message, type the corresponding message number after the prompt. To quit **mailx**, type **q** after the prompt. As mentioned earlier, this normally causes mail that has been read, but not deleted or saved, to be transferred to your **mbox** file, while unread mail remains in your system mailbox. (We'll discuss the other commands you can use shortly.)

REMOTE MAIL You can use **mailx** to send mail to remote systems connected to yours by the **uucp** network. If your machine is linked directly to another, you can use an address of the form *host!name*, where *host* is the name of the recipient's machine and *name* is the recipient's login name. For instance,

```
mail unifoo!marge
```

initiates mail to **marge** on the **unifoo** system.

If the recipient is on a machine that is not linked to yours but that shares a link to a third machine, you can route material through the common link:

```
mail unifoo!vaxlax!ralph
```

This sends mail to the **unifoo** machine, which forwards it to **ralph** on the **vaxlax** machine.

Other networking systems use different mechanisms. For example, the form *name@host* can be used to reach *name* on the *host* machine on Arpanet.

HEADERS When **mailx** sends a message, it adds a header to the beginning of it (see Example 2 below). The header provides information about the message and its sender. When reading a mail file in the receive mode, **mailx** uses this information to construct listings of your messages; for example, when you use the command-mode **header** command to display a list of your messages.

The header consists of separate fields. For instance, here is the header from Example 2:

```
Date: Wed, 17 Dec 86 08:32:09 PST
From: gopman (Merle Gopman)
To: botts
Subject: coffee break
```

It has a **Date** field, a **From** field, a **To** field, and a **Subject** field. In general, the **To** field shows the complete list of people to whom the message was sent.

The **mailx** command offers some control over which fields are displayed. Some of this control is achieved by using environmental variables or tilde commands, both of which are discussed later. For example, the **asksub** variable, when set, causes the **Subject:** prompt to be displayed when you send mail. By default, it is set, but **asksub** can be turned off. Whether it is set or not, the **-s** command-line option can be used to generate a subject field, as can the **~s** command when you are in input mode for sending mail. (Note: Sending mail places you in the input mode, as do several commands available in the receiving mode.)

Another field, **Cc** (carbon copy), is not set by default like the others. It can be turned on by setting the **askcc** variable or by using the ~c or ~h tilde escape command. When this field is turned on, you can provide a list of the users who are to receive carbon copies of the message you are sending. The header for the message will include the **Cc** field so that all recipients know who received carbon copies of the message.

A second, similar field is **Bcc** (blank carbon copy). Other recipients are not told who received the blank carbon copies. Use the ~b or ~h command to turn on **Bcc**.

USING THE COMMAND MODE WHEN READING MAIL

Here we'll look at the complete list of **mailx** command-mode commands. To read mail, recall, you invoke **mailx** without supplying a list of mail recipients. This places **mailx** in its "command mode." If you have no mail, **mailx** tells you so and exits, but if you do have mail, it displays a numbered list of the messages currently in your mailbox (again, see Example 2). The "current message" is indicated by a **>**, and some messages are identified by subject. At this point, you can respond to the **mailx** prompt (?) by giving a **mailx** command.

In general, these commands have this form:

[*command*] [*msglist*] [*argument(s)*]

If the *command* portion is omitted, the **print** command is understood. Thus simply entering the number of a message is sufficient to display the message.

The optional *msglist* details which messages are to be acted upon by the command. If this list is omitted, **mailx** assumes you want *command* applied to the current message. Thus entering just **delete** (or **d**) deletes the current message. If you omit both *command* and *msglist* and simply strike the <enter> key, the current message is displayed. Hitting the <enter> key successively steps you through your messages.

Some commands may use additional *argument(s)*, which are discussed in the Command Summaries below.

The Message List

The **mailx** command offers several ways to specify messages, so let's run through them before summarizing the commands. Note that some (or all) of the message-list forms may not make sense with a particular command.

A *msglist* consists of one or more of the following message specifications separated by spaces:

SPECIFICATION	MEANING
n	Message number *n*, where *n* is an integer.
.	The current message.
^	The first undeleted message.
$	The last message.
*	All messages.
n–m	Messages *n* through *m*, where *n* and *m* are integer message numbers.
user	All messages from *user*.
/*str*	All messages with the string *str* in the subject line (case is ignored).
:d	All deleted messages.
:n	All new messages.
:o	All old messages.
:r	All read messages.
:u	All unread messages.

Some commands only operate on a single message. In the Command Summaries below, we'll use *message* instead of *msglist* when a single message must be specified.

Command Summaries

Now here are the commands, with their abbreviations given in parentheses. Some command discussions refer to environmental variables that we'll discuss later.

COMMAND	ACTION
!*cmd*	Escapes to the command interpreter (typically the **sh** shell) and has it run the *cmd* command. Returns to **mailx** when the command completes.
# *comment*	This is the format for placing comments in the **.mailrc** startup file.
=	Displays the current message number.

COMMAND	ACTION
?	Displays a summary of **mailx** commands.
alias *alias name(s)*	(**a**) Establishes *alias* as representing the list of *name(s)*. When *alias* is given as a message's recipient, the message is sent to all those in the *name(s)* list. This command typically is used in the **.mailrc** startup file.
alternates [*name(s)*]	(**alt**) This command is for those with accounts on several systems. If you have such accounts, mail forwarded to you might identify you by another login name. If you use the **reply** command (see below) to reply to a forwarded message, a copy is sent not only to the sender of the original message but to you under the other login name, since **mailx** thinks the name identifies another user. With the **alt** command, the listed *name(s)* are identified as your alternative login names, and those names are deleted from the list of users who will receive replies to forwarded messages. With no arguments, **alt** displays the current list of alternative names.
cd [*directory*]	Changes to the indicated directory; changes to $HOME if *directory* is omitted.
chdir [*directory*]	(**ch**) Same as **cd**.
copy [*filename*] **copy** [*msglist*] *filename*	(**co**) Copies the indicated messages to the indicated file, but doesn't mark the messages as "saved." Except for not marking the files, **copy** is like **save**. If *filename* is omitted, **mbox** is used by default, unless **MBOX** is set to another name.
Copy [*msglist*]	(**C**) Copies the indicated messages to a file whose name is derived from the message's sender. For instance, if the sender is **vaxlax!lazlo**, the file is named **lazlo**. This is like the **Save** command except that the message is not marked as "saved."
delete [*msglist*]	(**d**) Deletes the specified messages from the system mailbox. If **autoprint** is set, the message following the last deleted message is displayed.
discard [*header-field(s)*]	(**di**) Suppresses the indicated header fields when displaying messages on the screen. For example, `discard cc` suppresses the display of the **Cc** (carbon copy) field.

(continued)

COMMAND	ACTION	*(continued)*
dp [*msglist*]	Deletes the specified messages from the system mailbox and displays the message that follows the last deleted message.	
dt [*msglist*]	Same as **dp**.	
echo *string(s)*	(**ec**) Echoes the given strings, in the same manner as the shell **echo** command. This can be used, for example, in the **.mailrc** startup file.	
edit [*msglist*]	(**e**) Edits the given messages. The **EDITOR** variable specifies which editor to use; the default editor is **ed**. Editing takes place in a temporary file.	
exit	(**ex**) Exits from **mailx** without changing the system mailbox. No messages are saved in **mbox**.	
file [*filename*]	(**fi**) Quits the current file of messages and reads in the specified file. This could be, for example, **mbox** or some other file containing saved messages. If *filename* is omitted, the current system mailbox is used. The command also recognizes these special characters:	

CHARACTER	MEANING
%	The current system mailbox.
%*user*	The system mailbox for *user*.
#	The previous file.
&	The current **mbox** file.

The %*user* form requires that you have permission to access *user*'s mailbox.

COMMAND	ACTION
folder [*filename*]	(**fold**) Same as **file**.
folders	Displays the names of files in the user's mail directory. This directory is defined by the **folder** environmental variable.
followup [*message*]	(**fo**) Responds to the indicated message (like **reply**), and saves a copy of the response in a file named after the sender of the original message. The **record** variable, if set, is overridden.
Followup [*msglist*]	(**F**) Responds to the first message in *msglist*, and sends copies of the response to each sender of a message in *msglist*. The response uses the subject line of the first message, and a copy of the response is placed in a file named after the sender of the first message. Also see **Reply**.

COMMAND	ACTION
from [*msglist*]	(**f**) Displays the header summary for the indicated messages.
group *alias name(s)*	(**g**) Same as **alias**.
headers [*msglist*]	(**h**) Displays the "page" of headers that contains the specified messages. The number of headers per page is given by the **screen** variable.
help	(**hel**) Displays a summary of commands.
hold [*msglist*]	(**ho**) Holds the specified messages in the system mailbox. By default, they are copied to the **mbox** file.
if *mode* *mail-commands* **else** *mail-commands* **endif**	(**i el en**) Here *mode* is either **s** (send) or **r** (receive). If *mode* is **s**, the commands up to **else** or **endif** (whichever comes first) are executed if **mailx** is in the send mode, and the commands after **else**, if any, are executed if **mailx** is in the receive mode. If *mode* is **r**, the behavior is reversed. This command typically is used in the **.mailrc** startup file.
ignore *header-field(s)*	(**ig**) Same as **discard**.
list	(**l**) Lists all available commands without further explanation.
mail *name(s)*	(**m**) Mails a message to the indicated users.
mbox [*msglist*]	(**mb**) Has the listed messages copied to the standard **mbox** file upon normal termination of **mailx**. The **MBOX** variable can be used to provide a filename other than the default **mbox**.
next [*message*]	(**n**) Skips to the next matching message. This is useful when *message* is specified by *user* or */str*, for example (see the message specifiers discussed earlier).
pipe [*msglist*] [*command*]	(**pi**) Pipes the message through the given command. For example, `pipe 3 wc -w` produces a word count for message **3**. The default message is the current message, and the default command is the one specified by the **cmd** variable. A form-feed character is inserted after each message in the list if the **page** variable is set. Piping a message constitutes reading it, as far as **mailx**'s bookkeeping system is concerned.

(continued)

COMMAND	ACTION	(continued)

¦ [*msglist*] [*command*]
          Same as **pipe**.

preserve [*msglist*] (**pre**) Same as **hold**.

Print [*msglist*] (**P**) Displays the indicated messages on the screen. Like **print**, except that the header fields are displayed even if the **ignore** command directs otherwise.

print [*msglist*] (**p**) Displays the indicated messages on the screen. To keep long messages from scrolling past so rapidly that you cannot read them, set the **crt** mail variable to the number of lines you wish per "page" of display. Then that number of lines is paged through the command specified by the **PAGER** mail variable. By default, that command is **pg**.

quit (**q**) Quits the **mailx** program. Read messages are placed in **mbox**, and unread messages are returned to the system mailbox. If a message has been marked for deletion or has been saved (automatically or explicitly), it is deleted from the system mailbox.

Reply [*msglist*] (**R**) Sends a response to the sender of each message in *msglist*. These responses use as their subject the subject line of the first message on the list. If the **record** mail variable is set to the name of a file, then a copy of the response is saved in that file. **Reply** differs from **Followup** in that the latter saves the response in a file named after the sender, while **Reply** either doesn't save the response at all or else saves it in a general file used for all responses.

reply [*message*] (**r**) Replies to the indicated message. The subject line of the original message is used, and a reply is sent to all other recipients of that message. If the **record** mail variable is set to the name of a file, then a copy of the response is saved in that file.

Respond [*msglist*] (**R**) Same as **Reply**.

respond [*message*] (**r**) Same as **reply**.

COMMAND	ACTION
Save [*msglist*]	(**S**) Saves the indicated messages in a file named after the sender of the first message. (The filename is the sender's login name stripped of network addressing prefixes.) See the **outfolder** mail variable.
save [*filename*] **save** [*msglist*] *filename*	Saves the indicated messages in the indicated file. In the first form, the current message is saved, and **mbox** is the default file for saving. Saved messages are deleted from the system mailbox unless the **keepsave** mail variable is set.
set **set** *name* **set** *name*=*value*	(**se**) The **set** command with no arguments causes **mailx** to display all defined **mailx** environmental variables and their values (these variables are described later under Environmental Variables). The second form is used to set Boolean (true/false) variables, such as **hold**, and the third form is used to assign a string or numeric value to a variable. You can make up mail variables of your own, and then access them when sending mail by using the **~i** escape command. See Environmental Variables for a further discussion of mail variables. Also see **unset**.
shell	(**sh**) Invokes the interactive command interpreter, as specified by the **SHELL** variable. You can return to **mailx** by exiting the shell, typically by typing a <control-d> at the beginning of a line.
size [*msglist*]	(**si**) Displays the size, in characters, of the indicated messages.
source *filename*	(**so**) Reads **mailx** commands from the given file, returning to the **mailx** command mode when finished. This is useful if you modify **.mailrc** while in **mailx** and you want to make the changes take effect.
top [*msglist*]	(**to**) Displays the first few lines of the indicated messages. The default number of lines is five, but you can set the **toplines** variable to the number of lines you prefer.
touch [*msglist*]	(**tou**) "Touches" the specified messages. This causes any message in *msglist* that is not explicitly saved to be saved in **mbox**.
Type [*msglist*]	(**T**) Same as **Print**.
type [*msglist*]	(**t**) Same as **print**.

(continued)

COMMAND	ACTION	(continued)

undelete [*msglist*] (**u**) Restores the indicated messages. This works only for messages deleted during the current **mailx** session. If the **autoprint** variable is set, the last restored message is displayed.

unset *name(s)* (**uns**) Erases the indicated mail environmental variables.

version (**ve**) Displays the current version of **mailx** and its release date.

visual [*msglist*] (**vi**) Edits the indicated messages with the screen editor specified by the **VISUAL** mail variable. The default screen editor is **vi**.

write [*msglist*] *filename*

(**w**) Writes the indicated messages in the specified file. Like **save**, except that the header and trailing blank line of each message are not copied.

xit (**x**) Same as **exit**.

z[+] Scrolls the message list forward one screenful. The **screen** mail variable gives the number of lines displayed per screen. The **+** is optional.

z– Scrolls the message list backward one screenful. Otherwise, like **z**.

TILDE ESCAPE COMMANDS The commands just described normally are used in the **mailx** command mode. The tilde escape commands are used in the **mailx** input mode; that is, when you are typing a message. When in the input mode, **mailx** requires that you distinguish between normal input and commands by typing a tilde at the beginning of the line when you want to initiate a command, then typing one or more characters to specify the command. For example, typing **~v** calls up the visual editor (typically **vi**). This provides more powerful editing capabilities that you can use when writing the message.

You can use the **escape** mail environmental variable to redefine the "escape" character to be something other than the tilde.

You have two routes to the input mode of **mailx**. One is invoking **mailx** to send mail by providing a list of recipients. The second is invoking **mailx** in the read-mail mode and then using one of the **mailx** commands, say **reply** or **mail**, to send mail. Most tilde escapes can be used in either circumstance, but some escapes can be used only when **mailx** was originally invoked to read mail. These more restricted forms are identified in the following descriptions.

ESCAPE COMMAND	ACTION
~! *cmd*	Causes the command interpreter (typically **sh**) to run the *cmd* command, then return to input mode.
~.	Terminates the message.
~: *cmd* **~_** *cmd*	Executes the **mailx** command *cmd*. These can be used only when **mailx** was invoked to read mail.
~?	Displays a summary of tilde escapes.
~A	Inserts the value of the **mailx** variable **Sign** into the message. This variable could be set to a standard sign-off string or signature. The similar **~a** gives you an alternate choice for a message.
~a	Inserts the value of the **mailx** variable **sign** into the message. This variable could be set to a standard sign-off string or signature.
~b *name(s)*	Adds the indicated names to the blind carbon copy (**Bcc**) list. Recipients of the message are not told who received blind copies.
~c *name(s)*	Adds the indicated names to the carbon copy list.
~d	Reads the message into the **dead.letter** file (described under **DEAD** in the Environmental Variables section). You can then recover it from that file at a later time.
~e	Invokes an editor for editing the outgoing message. The mail variable **EDITOR** specifies which editor is to be used.
~f [*msglist*]	Inserts the indicated messages, without alteration, into the message text. This command can be used only when **mailx** was invoked in the read mode.
~h	Prompts for the **Subject**, **To**, **Cc**, and **Bcc** header fields.
~i *variable*	Inserts the value of the named variable into the text. The variable can be a mail variable or an exported shell variable.
m [*msglist*]	Inserts the indicated messages into the text, shifting each line one tab stop to the right. This command is useful for quoting other messages. It can be used only when **mailx** was invoked in the read mode.
~p	Displays the message being entered.

(continued)

223

ESCAPE COMMAND	ACTION	(continued)
~q	Quits input mode by simulating an interrupt. This aborts the message, but the partial message, if any, is saved in the **dead.letter** file (see **DEAD** under Environmental Variables).	
~r *filename*		
~< *filename*	Reads the specified file into the message.	
~<! *cmd*	Executes the system command *cmd* and places its output into the message.	
~s *str*	Sets the subject field of the header to the string *str*.	
~t *name(s)*	Adds the indicated names to the **To** field of the header.	
~v	Invokes the screen editor identified by the **VISUAL** mail variable. The default visual editor is **vi**.	
~w *filename*	Copies the partial outgoing message, without the header, to *filename*.	
~x	Exits, aborting the message without copying it into the **dead.letter** file.	
~¦ *cmd*	Pipes the current text (the text up to the time you give this command) of the message through the *cmd* command. If the command runs successfully, the current text is replaced by the output of the command.	

ENVIRONMENTAL VARIABLES

The **mailx** command recognizes several environmental variables whose values affect the behavior of **mailx**. Some are taken from the shell's list of environmental variables, and some are internal to **mailx**. The internal variables can be set from the **mailx** command mode with the **set** command, and they can be unset with the **unset** command. Also, when **mailx** is invoked, it reads the **mailx** startup file for instructions; these instructions can include **set** commands. You can create and modify this file (which is, by default, called $HOME/.mailrc) using a regular editor.

Many of the mail variables are "Boolean"; that is, they have two possible values, true and false. "Setting" a Boolean variable means setting it to true. An example of such a variable is **asksub**. When **asksub** is set, you are prompted to provide a **Subject** string. When it is not set, you are not prompted. Such variables are set using a command with the following form:

```
set asksub
```

This command can be given from the command mode or it can be placed in the startup file.

A second group of variables have values that can be numbers or strings. For example, the commands

```
set crt=20
set EDITOR=ex
```

set the **crt** variable to **20** and the **EDITOR** variable to **ex**.

The default settings for the variables are given below, but the system administrator may have modified the settings of those on your system. By giving the **mailx set** command with no arguments, you can display the current settings.

To set a variable to false, you can use the **unset** command, as in:

```
unset crt asksub EDITOR
```

which reverses the three settings we made previously.

Now let's look at the variables. Those that are Boolean are listed below just by name. Those that are assigned values are listed in this format:

name=*value*

Shell Variables
The following variables are regular shell variables (as discussed under **sh**). They are used by **mailx** but cannot be changed from within **mailx**.

VARIABLE	ACTION
HOME=*directory*	Defines the user's home directory, which normally is his or her login directory.
MAILRC=*filename*	Defines the startup file read by **mailx** each time it is invoked. If this variable is undefined, the default value of **$HOME/.mailrc** is used.

Internal Variables

These variables can be set in the startup file or be set internally from **mailx**. Also, they can be reversed using the **unset** command.

VARIABLE	ACTION
addsopt	When set, specifies that **/bin/mail** is to be used to deliver messages. Use **noaddsopt** if another program is to be used. This variable is enabled by default.
allnet	Treats all network names with the same login name as identical; that is, **unifoo!jake** and **xacto!jake** are treated as the same person. This causes **jake**, when used as part of a [*msglist*] specification, to select messages from both the **unifoo!** and **xacto!** systems. By default, this variable is not set.
append	When a **mailx** reading session terminates, appends messages to the end of the **mbox** file instead of the beginning. The default setting is off.
askcc	Prompts for the **Cc** (carbon copy) list after the message is entered. By default, this variable is not set.
asksub	Prompts for the **Subject** field when sending mail. If you already have used the command-line **-s** option to specify a subject, you won't be prompted. By default, **asksub** is set.
autoprint	Displays a message automatically after you have used the **delete** or **undelete** command (see these commands for more details). By default, this variable is not set.
bang	Treats exclamation points in escape command lines the same way that the **vi** command treats them. By default, this variable is not set.
cmd=*cmd*	Sets the default command used by pipe to the *cmd* system command. There is no default value for this variable.
conv=*conversion*	Converts **uucp** addresses such as **unifoo!dolt** to a style described by *conversion*. This variable is disabled by default. The only conversion available at this time is **internet**, which requires a mail delivery program conforming to the RFC822 standard for electronic mail addressing.
crt=*number*	Pipes messages having more than *number* lines through the command specified by the **PAGER** variable; **pg** is the default command. By default, this variable is not set.
DEAD=*filename*	Undeliverable letters and partial messages that were interrupted are placed in the *filename* dead-letter file. The default value is **$HOME/dead.letter**.

VARIABLE	ACTION
debug	Enables verbose diagnostics for debugging. Mail is not delivered if **debug** is set. This variable is not intended for general use. By default, it is not set.
dot	Causes a line consisting solely of a period to terminate input. By default, **dot** is not set.
EDITOR=*cmd*	Sets the editor invoked by the **edit** or **~e** command to *cmd*. The default value is **ed**.
escape=*c*	Makes the character *c* the escape character that is used for tilde escape commands; that is, **escape=@** means that you need to use **@v** instead of **~v** to invoke the visual editor.

folder=*directory*	Makes *directory* the standard directory for saving mail files. File-names with a **+** prefix are understood to be in this directory. For example, suppose **folder=Email** and that you give the mail command
	
	`s +junk`
	
	The current message is saved in the **$HOME/Email/junk** file. The directory name is assumed to branch from the home directory unless it is given as an absolute pathname; for example, as **/tmp**.
	
	   For the **+** construction to work with the **mailx** command line, as in this one:
	
	`mailx -f +junk`
	
	folder must be an exported environmental variable (see Example 6 below and the **sh** entry).
	
	   There is no default value for **folder**.

header	Causes the header summary to be displayed when **mailx** is invoked in the read mode. This variable is enabled by default.
hold	Saves read messages in the system mailbox instead of your **mbox** file. By default, **hold** is not set.
ignore	Ignores interrupts while in the input mode. This is used for noisy dial-up lines that may accidentally generate an interrupt signal. This variable is not set by default.
ignoreeof	Ignores the end-of-file signal during message input. If this is set, you must either set **dot** and use an initial period to end input or else use the **~.** command. This variable is not enabled by default.
keep	When your system mailbox is empty, truncates it to zero length and retains it in the mail directory. If **keep** is not set (the default), empty mailbox files are removed.

(continued)

VARIABLE	ACTION	*(continued)*
keepsave	If a message is saved in another file, still keeps it in the system mailbox instead of deleting it. By default, **keepsave** is not set.	
LISTER=*cmd*	The *cmd* command (including any options) is used to list files in the **folder** directory when the **folders** command is given. The default **LISTER** command is **ls**.	
MBOX=*filename*	Uses *filename* to save messages that have been read. Explicitly saving a message in another file or using the **xit** command disables this automatic saving. The default file is $HOME/mbox.	
metoo	If **metoo** is not set (the default), your name is deleted from the list of recipients when you use the **reply** command. If **metoo** is set, your name remains on the list so that you get sent a copy of your own reply.	
onehop	When set, improves the efficiency of the **reply** command in some networks. The usual behavior is this: Suppose **unifoo!joe** sends mail to **xacto!jane** and **bigtime!sal**. If **sal** uses the **reply** command, then the reply is sent both to **unifoo!joe** and to **unifoo!xacto!jane**; that is, mail addresses relative to the original sender's site are used. If **onehop** is set, then the second reply goes to **xacto!jane**. For this strategy to work, all the network sites involved must have direct access to one another.	
outfolder	Causes messages saved by the **Save**, **Copy**, **followup**, and **Followup** commands, and messages saved in response to the **record** variable being set, to be placed in the **folder** directory. However, an absolute pathname (one beginning with /) overrides this feature. By default, **outfolder** is not set.	
page	When set, causes a form feed to be inserted after each message routed through a **pipe** command. By default, **page** is not set.	
PAGER=*cmd*	Uses the *cmd* system command for paging output when **crt** is set. The command can include options. The default **PAGER** command is **pg**.	
prompt=*str*	Sets the command-mode prompt to the string *str*. The default prompt is **?** ; note the trailing blank.	
quiet	Doesn't display the opening message and version identifier when **mailx** is invoked to read mail. By default, **mailx** is not **quiet**.	
record=*filename*	Records all outgoing mail in the *filename* file. By default, this option is not set.	

VARIABLE	ACTION
save	Causes messages that suffer an interrupt or a delivery error to be placed in the dead-letter file specified by the **DEAD** variable. By default, **save** is set.
screen=*number*	Sets the number of lines considered to be one screenful by the **headers** command.
sendmail=*cmd*	Establishes an alternative command for delivering messages. This variable is not used by most users.
sentwait	Normally, **mailx** runs in the background so that you can continue with other work. Setting this option means control is not returned to you until the mailer finishes its work. By default, this variable is not set.
SHELL=*cmd*	Here *cmd* is the command interpreter used by the ! and ~! commands. The default value is **sh**.
showto	Displays the recipient's name instead of the sender's name in the header summary when the message is from the user. For instance, if you send yourself a carbon copy of a message to someone else, setting **showto** causes that person's name instead of yours to appear in the header list displayed on your screen.
sign=*str*	Inserts the string *str* into the text of a message when you give the ~a command. This is useful if you want to use a signature or sign-off string. The variable has no default value.
Sign=*str*	Inserts the string *str* into the text of a message when you give the ~A command. This is also useful for a signature or sign-off string, and also has no default value.
toplines=*number*	Sets the number of lines looked at by the **top** command. The default value is 5.
VISUAL=*cmd*	Establishes which screen editor is used when the **visual** or ~v command is given. The default is **vi**.

SPECIAL FEATURES The **mailx** command has several features not found in the simpler **mail** command. The preceding discussions of the **mailx** commands and the mail environmental variables detail many of these features, but because you may find it useful to have some of them summarized separately, we have used the Examples section to discuss the **.mailrc** file, the use of folders, and the use of **mailx** with mail files.

SEE ALSO UNIX Commands: **mail**; **pg**; **ed**; **vi**; **ls**
UNIX Features: Standard I/O, Redirection, and Pipes; Shell Variables

EXAMPLES

1. Send mail.

```
$ mailx botts
Subject: coffee breaks
Nettie,
     I've noticed that you have been working through
your assigned coffee breaks. This is not good
for you in the long run, and it is upsetting
the other employees. Please take your coffee breaks.
<control-d>
$
```

The sender has responded to the **Subject:** prompt by entering **coffee break**. The **<control-d>** at the beginning of the line serves to terminate the message.

2. Receive mail.

```
$ mailx
mailx version 2.14 8/01/84.  Type ? for help.
"/usr/mail/botts": 3 messages 3 unread
>N  1  gopman     Wed Dec 17 08:32  11/343 "coffee breaks"
 N  2  steade     Wed Dec 17 09:15  12/339
 N  3  gihon      Wed Dec 17 09:22  14/406 "gopman"
? 1

Message  1:
From gopman Wed Dec 17 08:32:08 1986
Date: Wed, 17 Dec 86 08:32:09 PST
From: gopman (Merle Gopman)
To: botts
Subject: coffee break

Nettie,
     I've noticed that you have been working through
your assigned coffee breaks. This is not good
for you in the long run, and it is upsetting
the other employees. Please take your coffee breaks.

?
```

Here **mailx** identifies **/usr/mail/botts** as being the system mailbox being used by the receiver. The mailbox contains three new messages, as indicated by the **N** in the first field of each message header. Message 1 is, as indicated by the **>**, the current message. The notation **11/343** means the message contains **11** lines and **343** characters. These counts include the header that **mailx** adds to the message.

The strings in double quotes are the message subjects, as provided by the sender. Note that message 2 lacks a subject; that happens if the user fails to enter the subject or suppresses that feature.

Typing **1** causes message 1 to be displayed.

3. Use **mailx** to send a file.

```
mail fergie < fall87
```

This sends the contents of the **fall87** file to user **fergie**. Since sending mail uses the standard input, you can use redirection to mail the contents of a file. Note that the usual mail header is added to the beginning of the file when it is mailed.

4. Set mail environmental variables.

```
set append LISTER='ls -s'
```

This sets the **append** variable, causing new messages to be placed at the end of **mbox** instead of at the beginning. It also changes the listing command from the default **ls** to **ls –s**, so that the size of the files will be shown. This command can be given from the **mailx** read mode, in which case it holds just for the current reading session, or it can be placed in the **.mailrc** file so that it comes into effect each time you invoke **mailx**.

5. Set up a **.mailrc** file.

```
$ vi .mailrc
alias biology mendel pasteur salk watson crick
alias rick ptsfa!bevax!CAE780!rgh
ignore date Cc
set keep hold dot crt=22 record=outgoing
```

When invoked, **mailx** executes commands found in the startup file in your home directory (by default, **.mailrc**; you can change this default by defining the **MAILRC** shell variable to be a different file and, typically, placing the new definition in your **.profile** file).

Not all **mailx** commands can be used in the startup file; **!**, **Copy**, **edit**, **followup**, **Followup**, **hold**, **mail**, **preserve**, **reply**, **Reply**, **shell**, and **visual** are prohibited. The commands most often used are those in the sample file above: **alias**, **ignore**, and **set**. The **alias** command lets a single name represent a group of recipients; it also is useful for letting short names represent long pathnames for remote correspondents. The **ignore** command controls what header fields are shown when a message is read, and the **set** command is used to set various **mailx** environmental variables.

(continued)

6. Use the folder feature.

The folder feature offers a convenient way to organize mail. You can devote one directory to mail, using separate files for separate topics or correspondents. Before you can use the folder feature, you need to define the **folder** variable. You can do this by including this command in the startup file:

```
set folder=Email
```

Unless you provide an absolute pathname, **mailx** assumes the pathname you provide originates from your home directory, so this example designates the **Email** subdirectory of your home directory. Note that this command does not create the directory but simply establishes its purpose. Use **mkdir** to create the directory.

How is the folder feature used? Well, if you use a **+** prefix with filenames, **mailx** understands that you want those files to be in the **Email** directory. For example, suppose you have a lot of mail on the subject of fees. While in the mail-reading mode, you can give the command

```
s /fees +fees
```

to save all messages that have the string **fees** in the subject field of their headers in the **fees** file in the **Email** directory. If the **+** is omitted, then **fees** is created in the current directory instead of the **Email** directory.

There is a hitch if you want to use the **+** notation in the command line, as in the following:

```
mail -f +fees
```

For this to work, **folder** has to be an exported environmental variable. To accomplish that, you can place these lines in your **.profile** file:

```
folder=Email
export folder
```

7. Use **mailx** with a mail file.

```
mail -f mbox
```

The **mbox** file is the default file for storing read, but undeleted, mail. Messages are stored just as they were delivered by **mailx**; that is, each has its own header. The **-f** option allows you to use all the facilities of **mailx** with the messages kept in the file; that is, you can read them, delete them, reply to them, store them elsewhere, and so on, just as you would when reading mail from the system mailbox.

8. Send mail over a network.

```
mail unifoo!roscoe
```

This sends mail to user **roscoe** on the **unifoo** system. This is the method used for communicating with systems that use the **uucp** program for networking.

9. Use a tilde command when sending mail.

```
$ mailx wimpler
Subject: neutrinos
Weather or not neutrinos have mass really hasn't
been settled yet. The data from the suppernova of
~v
```

At this point the writer notices some errors and uses **~v** to call up the **vi** editor. The text then shows up as a **vi** buffer:

```
Weather or not neutrinos have mass really hasn't
been settled yet. The data from the suppernova of
~
~
"/tmp/Re17676" 2/99
```

The sender can then edit the message and exit **vi** normally. He or she is still in the **mailx** sending mode, however, and must also terminate that by typing period at the beginning of a line.

```
Whether or not neutrinos have mass really hasn't
been settled yet. The data from the supernova of 1987
does provide an upper limit, and it may, according
to some, provide an actual value or two.
:wq
"/tmp/Re17676" 4/1950
(continue)
.
EOT
$
```

mesg

PURPOSE Use the **mesg** command to control whether or not others can send messages to your terminal screen.

FORMAT mesg [y] [n]

DESCRIPTION The **mesg** command, when used with an **n** argument, prevents another user from sending information to your screen (via **write**, for example, or by redirecting output to your terminal). A **y** argument restores write permission. **mesg** with no arguments causes the current permission to be displayed.

The exit value for this command is 0 if messages are receivable, 1 if they are not, and 2 if there is an error.

COMMON USES You can use **mesg** to shut off messages from others when you don't wish to be bothered. If you want such exclusivity to be your default state, you can place a **mesg n** command in your **.profile** file.

COMMENTS The **mesg** command essentially is a **chmod** command made friendlier and more specific. You can, for example, turn off write permission to your terminal with this command:

```
chmod go-w /dev/tty
```

Here **/dev/tty** is the special file representing your terminal. This is a generic term; that is, it works with all terminals. You can, of course, use your particular terminal number:

```
chmod go-w /dev/tty21
```

This command is more selective than **mesg**, since it still allows group members to communicate with you.

SEE ALSO UNIX Commands: **chmod**; **write**
UNIX Features: Permissions; Special Files

EXAMPLES

1. Turn off electronic chitchat.

   ```
   mesg n
   ```

   Note that this does not prevent people from sending you electronic mail; it affects only those processes that attempt to write directly to your terminal.

2. Restore write permission so that you can receive a reply when you **write** to someone.

   ```
   $ mesg y
   $ write jezabel
   ```

PURPOSE   Use the **mkdir** command to make a directory.

FORMAT   **mkdir** [**-mp**] [*directory-name(s)*]

DESCRIPTION   The **mkdir** command takes one or more names as arguments and creates directories that have those names. You must have write permission for a directory in order to create a new subdirectory in it.

Two standard entries are made in each new directory: . for the directory itself, and .. for the parent directory.

COMMON USES   You can use **mkdir** to set up a directory hierarchy to organize your files.

OPTIONS   The **mkdir** command had no options until Release 3 happened along; now it has two:

OPTION	ACTION
-m *mode*	Sets the mode for the new directories to *mode*, using the octal mode representation discussed under **chmod**. New with Release 3.
-p	Creates intermediate directories when a *directory-name* includes nonexistent directories in the pathname. New with Release 3.

COMMENTS   Making a directory entails creating a directory file. Internally, each file, including directory files, is described by a table called an i-node (information node), and each i-node has an identifying i-node number. A directory file contains the user name and the system i-node number for each file or directory added to the directory. The two standard entries, . and .., are followed by the i-node numbers for the directory file itself and for the parent directory.

SEE ALSO   UNIX Commands: **rmdir; rm**
UNIX Features: Files and Directories; File Systems; Pathnames and the Directory Tree; Permissions

EXAMPLES

1. Create a subdirectory in your current directory.

   ```
   mkdir Vantage
   ```

   Now you can **cd** to the **Vantage** directory and create files in it.

2. Create a subdirectory using a relative pathname.

   ```
   mkdir Vantage/Ads
   ```

   This command assumes you are in **Vantage**'s parent directory.

3. Create a directory using a full pathname.

   ```
   mkdir /usr/crone/Vantage/QC
   ```

   This command can be given from any directory, as long as you have write permission for the **Vantage** directory.

4. Create intermediate directories.

   ```
   mkdir -p crone/Recipes/Stews/Beef
   ```

   If there is no **Recipes** directory when this command is given, the **Recipes**, **Stews**, and **Beef** directories are all created.

PURPOSE Use the **mv** command to change the name of a file or directory, or to move a file from one directory to another.

FORMAT **mv** [**-f**] *name1 name2*

mv [**-f**] *name(s) directory*

DESCRIPTION The **mv** command changes the name of a file. Because a full pathname for a file identifies the directory the file is in, changing the pathname means changing the directory in which a file is found. The **mv** command is used in two forms, as shown in the Format section above. In the first form, *name1* can be the name of a directory or of a regular file, and *name2* is its new name. In the second form, *name(s)* represents the names of regular files and *directory* is the name of the directory into which the files will be placed. Note that if more than two arguments are provided, the final argument must be the name of an existing directory. In any case, if the final argument is a directory name, **mv** assumes the second form is to be used.

Normally, if the proposed new name for a file is that of an existing file, the existing file is overwritten with the new material. However, if that target file is write-protected, then **mv** asks you whether you wish to overwrite it.

When moving files to another directory, you need to have write permission in the target directory.

COMMON USES As you organize your files, you can use **mv** to shift files from one directory to another. You also can use **mv** to change default filenames, such as **a.out**, to something more suitable.

OPTIONS The **mv** command has only one option:

OPTION	ACTION
-f	Normally, if the final argument is a file whose mode prohibits writing, **mv** prints the mode and asks if the user wishes to proceed. With the **-f** option, **mv** asks no questions and proceeds if possible.

COMMENTS The **cp** command creates new files, while the **mv** command creates new names for existing files. The **ln** command creates additional names for existing files.

SEE ALSO UNIX Commands: **cp**; **ln**

UNIX Features: Files and Directories; Permissions; Pathnames and the Directory Tree

EXAMPLES

1. Change the name of a file in the current directory.

   `mv a.out sum_up`

   This changes the name of **a.out** to **sum_up**.

2. Move a file, retaining its basename.

   `mv pone Senate`

   This moves the **pone** file to the **Senate** subdirectory. The new name of the file, relative to the current directory, is **Senate/pone**.

3. Move a file, changing its basename.

   `mv bill2 Senate/bill8`

   This moves **bill2** to the **Senate** directory, changing its basename to **bill8**.

4. Move several files to another directory.

   `mv jay robin bird* Birds`

   This moves the **jay** and **robin** files and files matching the **bird*** pattern to the **Birds** directory. Each retains its original basename.

PURPOSE Use the **newgrp** command to temporarily switch among your group affiliations.

FORMAT newgrp [-] [*group*]

Here *group* is the group name (not the group ID number) as it is listed in the **/etc/group** file.

DESCRIPTION Each user is assigned to a particular group by the system administrator. The **/etc/group** file contains a list of group names for the system, the group ID number for each group, and the members of each group. You can be listed in more than one group in the **/etc/group** file, but it is your group entry in the **/etc/passwd** file that determines the group assignment you are given when you log in. The **newgrp** command lets you change this group assignment to any of those of which you are a member. Use the group name as an argument to the command. If you use **newgrp** without arguments, you are assigned to the group given in the **/etc/passwd** file.

Exported environmental variables retain their values after you change groups. Non-exported environmental variables are reset to their default values or, if they are not normally provided by the shell, they are not in the new shell at all.

COMMON USES You can use **newgrp** to gain access to files and programs restricted to a certain group, provided that you are listed as a group member in the **etc/group** file.

OPTIONS The **newgrp** command has only one option:

OPTION	ACTION
-	Resets environmental variables to the values they would have if you logged in again. Ordinarily, exported environmental variables are carried over, and non-exported variables are set to default values, if any, or else to null.

SEE ALSO UNIX Commands: **id**; **chgrp**
UNIX Features: Environmental Variables

EXAMPLES

1. Change from your login group to another group.

```
$ id
uid=234(vanmoose) gid=58(accounts)
$ newgrp xsales
$ id
uid=234(vanmoose) gid=56(xsales)
```

The **id** command lists user and group IDs. Note that the new group is specified by name in the command and that the user ID is unaffected.

2. Change back to your login group.

```
newgrp
```

If this were a continuation of Example 1, this command would change your group back to **accounts**. The – option causes the environmental variables to be set to the values they normally have when you log in.

PURPOSE   Use the **news** command to find out what news is available on the system.

FORMAT   news [-a] [-n] [-s] [*item(s)*]

Here *item(s)* represents the names of individual files in the news directory.

DESCRIPTION   The system has a news directory, typically **/usr/news**, into which "news" files can be placed. When used with no arguments, the **news** command checks to see which files are current; that is, which files have been added since you last used **news**. Each current news file is displayed along with a header, with the newest file being displayed first.

To halt the display of one news item and continue to the next, type an interrupt (typically, <del> or <control-c>). Type two interrupts within one second to terminate the **news** command.

Options let you see all news files (old and new), list just the filenames, or list the number of new files. To look at specific news files, you can supply their names as arguments.

The **news** command creates a file called **.news_time** in your home directory the first time you use it. Normally, **news** updates the access time of the file each time **news** is invoked. The **.news_time** file itself is empty, but its access time is used to determine the last time you gave the command.

COMMON USES   You can use **news** as a form of bulletin board. You can place the **news** command in your **.profile** file so that new news is displayed each time you log in.

OPTIONS   These three options are mutually exclusive. None of them updates the system's record of your last use of **news**.

OPTION	ACTION
-a	Displays all news files, current or not.
-n	Displays the names of the current items without displaying their contents.
-s	Displays the number of current items.

SEE ALSO   UNIX Features: The **.profile** File

241

EXAMPLES

1. Check the latest news.

```
$ news
pingpong (root) Wed Oct  1 15:10:03 1986

    Inform Megan if you want to compete in the
    company table tennis tournament in two weeks.

stats    (root) Wed Oct  1 10:49:44 1986

    See Eldric about the new statistics package.
```

The header for each news item gives the filename, the file owner, and the time the file was placed in the news directory.

2. List the current news items.

```
$ news -n
potatoes (root) Thu Oct  2 14:32:19 1986
theboss  (root) Thu Oct  2 12:06:51 1986
bakesale (root) Thu Oct  2 03:24:37 1986
```

Just the headers are displayed.

3. Check a particular news file.

```
$ news bakesale
bakesale (root) Thu Oct  2 03:24:37 1986

There will be a bake sale Fri Oct 10 in Room 245
to raise money for a new disk drive.
```

PURPOSE   Use the **nl** command to number the lines in a file.

FORMAT   **nl** [*option(s)*] [*file*]

DESCRIPTION   The **nl** command takes input from the *file* file (or from the standard input if no *file* argument is given), numbers the lines as instructed, and sends the numbered lines to the standard output (by default, the screen). Unless you specify otherwise, only lines with printable text are numbered.

     Special notations in the text cause it to be divided into "logical pages," with each logical page containing a header, a body, and a footer. By default, line numbering is reset for each logical page. In the absence of the special logical-page notation, the entire file is taken to be one logical page.

COMMON USES   You can use **nl** to add line numbering to text; for example, to a program listing.

LOGICAL PAGES   Text can be divided into logical pages by using the following notations. Each notation must be the sole entry on a line.

NOTATION	MEANING
\:\:\:	The beginning of the header.
\:\:	The beginning of the body.
\:	The beginning of the footer.

It is okay to have an empty section.

OPTIONS   The following options give specific line-numbering instructions:

OPTION	ACTION
-b*type*	Specifies which lines in the body are to be numbered. Here *type* is one of the following:

TYPE	MEANING
a	Number all the lines.
t	Number only the lines with printable text.
n	Don't number the lines.
p*str*	Number only the lines containing the regular expression *str*.

The default *type* is **t**.

(continued)

OPTION	ACTION	(continued)
-h *type*	Specifies which lines in the header are to be numbered. The types are the same as described for **-b**. The default *type* is **n**.	
-f *type*	Specifies which lines in the footer are to be numbered. The types are the same as described for **-b**. The default *type* is **n**.	
-p	Doesn't reset the line numbering for each new logical page.	
-v *nstart*	Uses the integer *nstart* to number the first line. The default value of *nstart* is 1.	
-i *ninc*	Increments line numbers by the integer *ninc*. The default value of *ninc* is 1.	
-s *str*	Uses the string *str* to separate the line number from the text line. The default value is a tab character.	
-w *nwid*	Uses a field *nwid* characters wide for the line number. The default value is 6.	
n *format*	Uses the *format* string to specify the format for displaying the line numbers. The possible values are these:	

FORMAT	MEANING
ln	Left justified, with leading zeros suppressed.
rn	Right justified, with leading zeros suppressed.
rz	Right justified, with leading zeros displayed.

The default value is **rn**.

OPTION	ACTION
-l *n*	Counts *n* blank lines as one line. The default value is 1. This option makes sense only if the **a** type has been specified for at least one of the **-h**, **-b**, or **-t** options; otherwise, blank lines aren't numbered at all.
-d *xy*	Changes the logical-page delimiter characters (by default, \:) to *xy*. If *y* is omitted, then just the first character is changed to *x* and the second character remains :. Note that there is no space between **d** and *xy*. To enter a backslash, type two backslashes, since a single backslash "quotes" the character that follows it.

COMMENTS The **nl** command takes at most one file as an argument. The **-n** option of the **pr** command also numbers lines, but without the capability of recognizing headers, footers, and logical pages.

SEE ALSO UNIX Commands: **pr**
UNIX Features: Regular Expressions

EXAMPLES

The following examples assume that this text is found in the **pretzel** file:

```
\:\:\:
PRETZEL FORMS
\:\:
Generally speaking, pretzels are twisted into

a pretzel shape, but a minority of pretzels
\:
THE PRETZEL MAKER'S HANDBOOK
\:\:\:
PRETZEL FORMS
\:\:
come in a straight form.
\:
THE PRETZEL MAKER'S HANDBOOK
```

This file consists of two logical pages, because it has two headers.

1. Number the lines in the file.

```
$ nl pretzel

      PRETZEL FORMS

   1     Generally speaking, preztels are twisted into

   2     a pretzel shape, but a minority of pretzels

     THE PRETZEL MAKER'S HANDBOOK

      PRETZEL FORMS

   1     come in a straight form.

     THE PRETZEL MAKER'S HANDBOOK
```

This illustrates the default numbering. Note that the header and the footer are not numbered and that the blank line on the first logical page is not numbered. Also note that the numbering is reset for the second page. Headers and footers are set off by blank lines.

(continued)

2. Number all text lines, headers, and footers.

```
$ nl -ba -ht -ft pretzel

    1    PRETZEL FORMS

    2    Generally speaking, preztels are twisted into
    3
    4    a pretzel shape, but a minority of pretzels

    5    THE PRETZEL MAKER'S HANDBOOK

    1    PRETZEL FORMS

    2    come in a straight form.

    3    THE PRETZEL MAKER'S HANDBOOK
```

The **–ba** option causes all text lines in the body, including blank lines, to be numbered. **–ht** and **–ft** cause the headers and footers to be numbered, too. Note that the numbering is not reset between header and body and between body and footer.

3. Vary the format.

```
$ nl -s'> ' -w2 -nln

   PRETZEL FORMS

1 > Generally speaking, preztels are twisted into

2 > a pretzel shape, but a minority of pretzels

   THE PRETZEL MAKER'S HANDBOOK

   PRETZEL FORMS

1 > come in a straight form.

   THE PRETZEL MAKER'S HANDBOOK
```

There are two reasons for using single quotes with the **–s** option. First, they keep the shell from interpreting **>** as redirection. Second, they are needed to make the space part of the string. The **–w2** option produces a field width of two for the line numbers, which is why there is a space between the one-digit line numbers and the **>**.

PURPOSE   Use the **nohup** command to allow a process to continue running after you log out of the system and to make the process immune to the quit signal.

FORMAT   **nohup** *command* [*command-argument(s)*]

DESCRIPTION   Logging out of the system causes a "hangup" signal to be sent to any of your processes that are still running; this signal normally terminates the process. The **nohup** command causes *command* to ignore the signal and to continue running. If the output and error messages from *command* are not redirected, they are sent to a file called **nohup.out**. This file is placed in the current directory if possible and in your home directory otherwise. The **nohup** command also causes *command* to ignore the "quit" signal, typically generated by typing <control-\>.

COMMON USES   You can use **nohup** to initiate a lengthy job in the background, then log out.

COMMENTS   Both the **nohup**-background combination and **batch** can be used to run programs in the background, even after the user logs out. The newer **batch** command is more convenient, especially if several commands are to be run. The **csh** shell, available on some installations, does not require **nohup**, since **csh** background jobs continue automatically when you log out.

SEE ALSO   UNIX Commands: **batch**
UNIX Features: Shell Scripts; Processes

EXAMPLES

---

1. Protect a command from hangups.

```
nohup spell warandpieces &
```

The command being run is **spell warandpieces**. The & causes it to be run in the background, and **nohup** prevents it from being terminated if you log out before the process is complete. Because no redirection is used, the output of **spell** is placed in the **nohup.out** file.

2. Run a pipeline or other sequence of commands.

```
$ cat cmds
spell warandpiece ! wc > wapcnt
$ nohup sh cmds &
```

The **nohup** command will not work directly with a pipe or list of commands, but the commands can be placed in a file and run as a shell script under **nohup**'s management.

---

od

PURPOSE Use the **od** command to view the contents of a file byte by byte or word by word.

FORMAT od [*option(s)*] [*file*] [[**+**]*offset*[.][**b**]]

Here *offset* specifies where in the file to start. Note that the optional offset argument has its own optional components. Note also that at most one file can be specified.

DESCRIPTION The **od** command displays the contents of a given file using an indicated format. By default, it displays the numeric value of each two-byte unit ("word") in octal form. If no file is named, the standard input is used. Various options select other formats. The filename can be followed by an offset argument that indicates which byte to start with.

COMMON USES You can use **od** to examine text files containing nonprinting characters and to examine non-text files, such as those containing machine code or data in binary form.

OPTIONS In the following list, a "word" is 16 bits, regardless of the actual word size of the machine.

OPTION	ACTION
-b	Displays each byte in octal.
-c	Displays each byte as an ASCII character. Certain nonprinting characters have special representations:

NOTATION	MEANING	ASCII LABEL
\0	Null	NUL
\b	Backspace	BS
\f	Form feed	FF
\n	Newline	NL
\r	Carriage return	CR
\t	Tab	HT

Other nonprinting characters are represented by their three-digit octal ASCII codes.

OPTION	ACTION
-d	Displays words in unsigned decimal.
-o	Displays words in octal (the default).
-s	Displays words in signed decimal.
-x	Displays words in hexadecimal.

THE OFFSET In its simplest form, the optional offset argument consists of an *offset* integer that represents the byte number, in octal, at which the display will begin. The optional . suffix means *offset* is taken to be in decimal form. The **b** suffix means the offset count is in blocks of 512 bytes rather than in single bytes. The optional **+** prefix is used when the standard input is used instead of a file-name. Without it, **od** would think that *offset* was a filename.

COMMENTS The **cat** command assumes that each byte in a file represents an ASCII code, but **od** lets you specify the interpretation you want, within limits. It is interesting to compare the results of **cat –v** and **od –c**.

SEE ALSO UNIX Commands: **cat**

EXAMPLES

The following examples assume the **odfile** file has these contents:

```
bell=^G
bye!
```

Here **^G** represents the <control-g> character.

1. Look at a file a word at a time.

```
$ od odfile
0000000 062542 066154 003475 061012 062571 005041
0000014
```

Here the initial letters **be** in the file occupy a full word of memory. The combined bytes give an octal value of **062542** for the word. The first column of numbers are byte counts. The display starts at byte 0000000 of the file, and there are 0000014 (octal), or 12 (decimal), bytes in the file. This default form is not particularly useful for text files.

2. Look at a file a byte at a time.

```
$ od -bc odfile
0000000    b   e   l   l   =  007  \n   b   y   e   !  \n
         142 145 154 154 075 007 012 142 171 145 041 012
0000014
```

Here each byte is displayed as a character and, immediately below, in octal form. Note that more than one display mode can be used simultaneously.

---

pack

PURPOSE Use the **pack** command to compress files.

FORMAT pack [-] [-f] *name(s)*

DESCRIPTION The **pack** command attempts to store in compressed form the files named in the command line. When a file called *name* is successfully compressed, it is replaced with a compressed version called *name*.**z**, and the original file is removed. A text file typically is reduced to 60 to 75 percent of its original size. The **pack** command has an exit value equal to the number of files it fails to pack; see Reasons for No Packing below for possible reasons for failure.

The command uses Huffman minimum redundancy code.

COMMON USES You can use **pack** to reduce the storage space required for your files.

OPTIONS The **pack** command has two options:

OPTION	ACTION
-	Acts as a toggle switch that controls whether or not the command displays information about the compression algorithm. It can be intermixed with filenames to activate and deactivate this feature for individual files. The first appearance of – turns on the feature, the second turns it off, and so on.
-f	Forces the packing to take place even if there is no saving of space. This is useful when you wish to pack the entire contents of a directory and not have a mixture of formats.

REASONS FOR NO PACKING There are several reasons **pack** may refuse to pack a file. They are:

- ☐ The file appears to be packed already.
- ☐ The filename is too long. Since two characters are added to the name, the original name must be at least two characters shorter than the maximum length.
- ☐ The file has links. If **pack** were to pack linked files, only one of the file's names would have the **.z** suffix added. (Use **rm** to remove links.)
- ☐ The file is a directory.
- ☐ The file cannot be opened.
- ☐ The file is empty.
- ☐ Packing does not save disk storage blocks. (Typically, a block is 512 or 1024 bytes, so cutting a file from 500 to 300 bytes saves no blocks.)

    ☐   A file called *name*.**z** already exists.

    ☐   The **.z** file cannot be created.

    ☐   An I/O error occurred during processing.

COMMENTS The **pcat** command can be used to view packed files, and the **unpack** command unpacks them. The packed file is not in text form.

SEE ALSO UNIX Commands: **pcat**; **unpack**
UNIX Features: Files and Directories; Exit Values

EXAMPLES

---

1. Pack a file.

```
$ ls -s f*
12 flights
$ pack flights
$ ls -s f*
9 flights.z
```

Here the **flights** file (which is **12** blocks in size) is replaced by the smaller **flights.z** file (which is **9** blocks in size). The **-s** option of **ls** displays the file size in blocks.

2. Get information about the packing.

```
$ pack bam
pack: bam: 44.7% Compression
      from 3474 to 1921 bytes
      Huffman tree has 12 levels below root
      68 distinct bytes in input
      dictionary overhead = 87 bytes
      effective  entropy  = 4.42 bits/byte
      asymptotic entropy  = 4.22 bits/byte
```

The most important fact is the **44.7** percent compression; **effective entropy** is a fancier way of saying the same thing. If **4.42** bits, on the average, are used to hold a byte (8 bits), then 3.58 bits are saved per byte; that's $3.58/8 \times 100 = 44.7$ percent. The **asymptotic entropy** figure indicates the efficiency of storing bytes not counting the dictionary overhead. The file contained 68 distinct characters.

---

passwd

PURPOSE Use the **passwd** command to add or change your password.

FORMAT passwd

DESCRIPTION The **passwd** command lets you create or change your password interactively. After you give the command, you are asked to type your current password; this step is skipped if you do not yet have one. Then you are asked to enter your new password. Next, you are asked to repeat the new password. Since none of the password entries shows up on the screen, the second typing verifies that you have typed what you thought you typed.

A password that is too short is rejected. Typically, six characters are sufficient, and fewer may serve if a variety of character types (uppercase, lowercase, punctuation, digits) is used. The system administrator can adjust the minimum requirements.

Some systems maintain "password aging," which prevents you from changing a password until it has been sufficiently "aged," as defined by the system.

COMMON USES You can use **passwd** to create and change passwords in order to prevent others from using your account.

COMMENTS Passwords are stored in the **/etc/passwd** file in encrypted form. If you forget your password, it cannot be recovered from the encrypted form, and the system administrator will have to use **passwd** to give you a new one.

EXAMPLES

---

1. Change a password.

```
$ passwd
Changing password for henry
Old password:
New password:
Retype new password:
$
```

The user's input is not echoed on the screen. If the prompt ($) returns without any complaints from **passwd**, the change was successful.

PURPOSE   Use the **paste** command to merge corresponding lines of separate files or to join successive lines in a single file.

FORMAT   **paste** [**-d***list*] *file(s)*

paste -s [**-d***list*] *file(s)*

DESCRIPTION   The **paste** command has two modes. The first mode (parallel merging) takes a list of input files as arguments, merges the corresponding lines of each file, and sends the result to the standard output (by default, the screen). The separate input lines are connected together with tab characters (by default) to form the output line.

   The second mode (serial merging) is invoked when the **-s** option is used. In this mode, each input line is added to the end of the preceding line, creating one long line. Again, the tab character, by default, is used to join the lines.

   A hyphen (-) can be used as a filename to represent the standard input.

COMMON USES   You can use **paste** to combine files "horizontally." For example, if one file contains the names of a sales team and a second file contains sales data for each person, **paste** can join the files so that the name and data for each person form one line.

OPTIONS   The **paste** command has two options:

OPTION	ACTION
-d*list*	Resets the characters used to join lines. If *list* includes more than one character, the first character is used for the first join on a line, the second character for the second join, and so on. If the list is exhausted before reaching the last join on the line, it is used again, starting with its first character. Characters with a special meaning to the shell, such as * or a space, must be quoted. The following special notations can be used:

NOTATION	MEANING
\n	A newline.
\t	A tab.
\\	A backslash.
\0	The empty string (no character at all).

Note that \0 does not have the same meaning as it does in C, where it means the character having an ASCII code value of 0.

(continued)

253

OPTION	ACTION	*(continued)*
–s	Uses serial instead of parallel merging. All the lines from one input file are merged, then all the lines from the next input file are merged.	

COMMENTS The **join** command also combines files horizontally, but it supplies a different and more varied output format than **paste**. The **pr** command can merge files horizontally, too; it supplies yet another output format. The **cut** command extracts particular columns or fields from each line of a file. It can be used with **paste** to rearrange columns in a file of data.

SEE ALSO UNIX Commands: **cut**; **join**; **pr**
UNIX Features: Standard I/O, Redirection, and Pipes

EXAMPLES

The following examples assume that you have three files with the following names and contents:

```
$ cat names
Dorrie Smeekle
Kirstin Flottle
Doug Deekdup
Tranie Vishicup
$ cat may
106
234
 90
157
$ cat july
116
 87
143
103
```

1. Paste three files together horizontally.

```
$ paste names may july
Dorrie Smeekle  106       116
Kirstin Flottle 234        87
Doug Deekdup     90       143
Tranie Vishicup 157       103
```

The first lines of each input file are joined into one output line. The default tab character separates **Smeekle** from **106** and **106** from **116**.

2. Use a different character to join lines.

```
$ paste -d:# names may july names
Dorrie Smeekle:106#116:Dorrie Smeekle
Kirstin Flottle:234# 87:Kirstin Flottle
Doug Deekdup: 90#143:Doug Deekdup
Tranie Vishicup:157#103:Tranie Vishicup
```

Note that first a : is used as a join, then a **#**. That exhausts the list, so : is used again.

3. Blend files with keyboard input.

```
$ paste names may - july
123<enter>
Dorrie Smeekle  106       123       116
211<enter>
Kirstin Flottle 234       211        87
143<enter>
Doug Deekdup     90       143       143
101<enter>
Tranie Vishicup 157       101       103
```

Once the number **123** is typed and the <enter> key struck, that line of input is merged as the third column of output because the hyphen is third in the list of names. More typically, **–** is used to collect input from a pipe.

(continued)

4. Merge lines serially.

```
$ paste -s names
Dorrie Smeekle  Kirstin Flottle  Doug Deekdup    Tranie Vishicup
```

The four lines of **names** are merged into one.

5. Merge lines in a file by pairs.

```
$ paste -s -d'\t\n' names
Dorrie Smeekle  Kirstin Flottle
Doug Deekdup    Tranie Vishicup
```

Here every other join character is a newline, so a new line is started after every second line. Note that the special characters in the join list have been quoted.

PURPOSE Use the **pcat** command to view files previously compacted with the **pack** command.

FORMAT pcat *file(s)*

DESCRIPTION The **pcat** command displays in uncompacted form the contents of the named compacted files. These are files created with the **pack** command, which gives them a **.z** suffix after packing them. When listing packed files as arguments for the **pcat** command, the **.z** suffix can be omitted.

COMMON USES You can use **pcat** to check the contents of a packed file.

COMMENTS The **pcat** command displays the unpacked version of a file. Use **unpack** to replace the packed file with an unpacked version.

SEE ALSO UNIX Commands: **pack**; **unpack**

EXAMPLES

---

1. Display in text form the contents of a packed file.

   ```
   pcat farms.z
   ```

   This command also could be typed **pcat farms**.

2. Display a long packed file.

   ```
   pcat booklist.z ¦ pg
   ```

   This pipes the output to the **pg** command, which lets you look at the material a page at a time.

---

pg

PURPOSE Use the **pg** command to view material one screenful at a time.

FORMAT **pg** [*option(s)*] [*file(s)*]

DESCRIPTION The **pg** command lets you examine a file or series of files a screen at a time. A prompt is displayed at the bottom of the screen. Striking <enter> in response to the prompt causes the next page to be displayed. Other responses to the prompt produce other results, such as backing up a page or searching for a particular pattern.

The **pg** command can be used with the standard input, such as the output of a pipe, if no filenames are provided or if **-** is used as a filename.

If the standard output is not the terminal, **pg** acts like **cat**, except that if there is more than one file, **pg** prints a header for each file to identify it.

To work successfully, **pg** needs to know specific terminal attributes. If the **TERM** environmental variable specifies a terminal type, **pg** scans the **terminfo** database file for the relevant information. Otherwise, it assumes the terminal is the **dumb** type. (UNIX System V usually maintains information about terminals in the **/usr/lib/terminfo** directory.)

COMMON USES You can use **pg** to scan files that are too long to fit a single screen.

OPTIONS The first five options can be strung on the same hyphen.

OPTION	ACTION
-c	Homes the cursor and clears the screen before displaying each page. This option is ignored for terminals not having a clear-screen function defined in the system database that describes terminals.
-e	Doesn't pause at the end of each file.
-f	Doesn't split lines. Normally **pg** splits lines longer than the screen width. This may produce unwanted results when lines contain certain character sequences, such as formatting escape codes.
-n	Doesn't require the <enter> key to be struck for single-letter commands. In this mode, the command is executed as soon as the command key is struck.
-s	Displays messages and prompts in the "standout" mode, which usually is inverse video.
-*n*	Sets the window size (number of lines used) to the integer *n*. For terminals with the usual 24-line display, the default value is 23.

OPTION	ACTION
-p *str*	Normally, **pg** places a : prompt at the bottom of the screen. This option causes the string *str* to be used instead. The character sequence **%d** can be used in the string to stand for the current screen number.
+*ln*	Starts viewing with line number *ln*.
+*/pattern/*	Starts viewing at the first occurrence of *pattern*, which can be a string or a regular expression of the kind discussed under **ed**.

COMMANDS When **pg** pauses at the end of each screenful and displays a prompt at the bottom of the display, you can respond with any of the commands discussed below.

Specifying a Page or Line

All but the last two commands can take an address as a prefix. The address is given in pages or lines, depending on the command. To give an absolute address measured from the beginning of the file, use an unsigned integer, such as **3** to go to page 3, or **50l** (that's **50-el**) to go to line 50. To give a relative address measured from the current page or line, use a signed integer, such as **+3** to move forward or **-2** to move backward. If no address is given, **+1** is assumed. The addresses **+** and **-** are interpreted as **+1** and **-1**, respectively.

COMMAND	ACTION
[*address*]**<return>**	Displays the addressed page. The default address of **+1** causes the next page to be displayed.
[*address*]**l**	Scrolls the screen the number of lines indicated. The default address of **+1** causes the screen to scroll one line forward. When an absolute address is used, the display begins at that line.
[*address*]**d** [*address*]**^D**	Scrolls a half screen. Any non-negative address, including the assumed default of **+1**, means "scroll a half screen forward," while any negative address means "scroll a half screen backward." Only the sign of the address, not the magnitude, matters.
. or **^L**	Redisplays the current screen. This is useful, for instance, after an **h** command. This command does not take an address.
$	Displays the final windowful of the file; this may not work with piped input. This command does not take an address.

Specifying a Pattern

The following commands search for the specified pattern, which can be a simple string or a regular expression (a generalized pattern) as defined under the **ed** entry.

COMMAND	ACTION
n/pattern/	Searches forward for the *n*th occurrence of *pattern*. The default value for *n* is 1. The search begins with the next screenful and continues to the end of the file.
n?pattern?	
*n^pattern^*	Searches backward for the *n*th occurrence of *pattern*. The default value for *n* is 1. The search begins just before the current screen and continues to the beginning of the file. Two notations are provided because some terminals do not handle the ? notation properly.

Normally, the line containing the matching pattern is placed at the top of the screen. Appending an **m** to the command places the line in the middle, and appending a **b** places it at the bottom. These suffixes, once given, continue to be in effect until overriden by another suffix. The **t** suffix restores the top-of-the-screen mode.

Altering the Viewing Environment

The following commands consist of an optional integer followed by a command letter.

COMMAND	ACTION
*i*n	Goes to the *i*th next file. The integer *i*, if present, must be positive. The default value for *i* is 1.
*i*p	Goes to the *i*th previous file. The integer *i*, if present, must be positive. The default value for *i* is 1.
*i*w	Displays the next window of text. If *i* is present, sets the window size to *i* lines.

Miscellaneous Commands

In addition to the three categories of commands already discussed, a few other commands are also available.

COMMAND	ACTION
s *filename*	Saves the input (which could be from a pipe) in the *filename* file. Only the current file is saved. The space between **s** and *filename* is optional.
h	Displays a summary of available commands.
q or **Q**	Quits the **pg** command.
! *command*	Has the command interpreter execute the given *command*. The command interpreter is the one named by the **SHELL** environmental variable. If this variable is not defined, the default command interpreter is used. Typically, this is the shell program you normally use.
^** **<del>	If a quit signal (typically generated by <control-\\>) or interrupt (typically generated by the <del> key or by <control-c>) is generated while **pg** is sending output, **pg** stops sending output and then displays a prompt so that one of the instructions listed above can be given. If one of these signals is sent while **pg** is waiting for terminal input (that is, while the prompt is displayed), it causes **pg** to terminate.

COMMENTS The **pg** command, new with Release 2 of System V, fills a long-standing need for a utility that displays a file a screen at a time. Previously, users had to use an editor to view long files or rely on using <control-s> (stop screen output) and <control-q> (resume screen output). The latter technique became more difficult as terminal communication rates increased. Users of BSD UNIX could use its **more** command, but the old **more** lacked **pg**'s ability to move backward through a file. (Version 4.3 BSD's **more** command, however, can page backward.)

SEE ALSO UNIX Commands: **cat; ed**
UNIX Features: Standard I/O, Redirection, and Pipes; Regular Expressions; Filters

EXAMPLES

1. Peruse some files.

   ```
   pg squid mollusks
   ```

   The **pg** command places an **EOF** message after the prompt when the first file is finished. Hitting <enter> moves **pg** to the next file.

2. Concatentate files along with filenames into a single file.

   ```
   pg in.c out.c mix.c > listing
   ```

   Since the standard output is a file (**listing**) rather than a terminal, the contents of the three files, each preceded by a header giving its name, are sent to **listing**.

3. Create a different prompt.

   ```
   pg -p "%d > " grabbers
   ```

   The **%d** is replaced by the current page number in the prompt. Thus the prompt at the end of the third screen is

   ```
   3 >
   ```

   The double quotes enable the prompt string to include spaces.

4. Move about within a file.

`<enter>`	*Move forward one screen*
`12`	*Move forward to screen 12*
`+12`	*Move forward by 12 screens*
`-`	*Move backward one screen*
`-5l`	*Move backward 5 lines*
`/Ursa/`	*Move to the next line containing* **Ursa**
`5/UNIX/`	*Move forward to the 5th occurrence of* **UNIX**
`5?VAX?`	*Move to the 5th preceding occurrence of* **VAX**

5. Move from one file to another.

`n`	*Move to the next file*
`3p`	*Move backward 3 files*

PURPOSE   Use the **pr** command to format files for printing.

FORMAT   **pr** [*option(s)*] [*file(s)*]

DESCRIPTION   The **pr** command sends the contents of the named files to the standard output (by default, the screen). In the absence of options, the text is organized into pages of 66 lines. Each page begins with a five-line header and ends with a five-line trailer, or footer. The trailer consists of blank lines. The header consists of two blank lines, a line specifying the page number, the date and time, and the filename, and then two more blank lines. Lines that are too wide are truncated. The standard input is used if no files are specified or if - is used as a filename.

     Some options produce separate columns. By default, these columns are of equal width and are separated by at least one space.

COMMON USES   You can use **pr** to format text before sending it to the line printer. Options allow you to merge files and modify file formats.

OPTIONS   The **pr** command has fourteen options:

OPTION	ACTION
+*k*	Begins displaying with page *k*. Here *k* is an integer; its default value is 1.
–k	Uses *k* columns in the output. Again, *k* is an integer, and its default value is 1. This option assumes that options **-e** and **-i** are also used, and is incompatible with option **-m**. The input lines are displayed down the first column and then down the next, and so on, until a page of output is filled. Then the process is repeated for the next page. The width of the columns is determined by the number of columns and the page width.
-a	Arranges multi-column output across the page; that is, the first input line goes to the first column, the second input line to the second column, and so on. Use this option only with the *–k* option.
-m	Merges and displays all input files simultaneously, with one column per input file. This overrides the *–k* option.
-d	Double-spaces the output.

(continued)

OPTION	ACTION	*(continued)*
-eck	Controls the handling of tab characters in the input. Here c is a character and k is an integer; either or both may be omitted. A tab character in the input is replaced by a sufficient number of spaces to move the cursor to the next tab position. If k is 0 or is omitted, tab positions are set at columns 1, 9, 17, and so on; otherwise, the tab positions are set to $k+1$, $2*k+1$, $3*k+1$, and so on. If c is a non-digit character, then that character is treated as a tab character when found in input.	
-ick	Causes tabs to replace spaces in the output, when feasible. Here c is a character and k is an integer. If k is 0 or is omitted, the output tab positions are set at columns 1, 9, 17, and so on; otherwise, they are set to $k+1$, $2*k+1$, $3*k+1$, and so on. If c is a non-digit character, it is interpreted as a tab character on output when present in the input text.	
-nck	Causes the output to be numbered. If the integer k is present, then k digits are used for each number. The default value is 5. If the non-digit character c is present, it is used to separate the number from the following text. The default value is the tab character. The first $k+1$ character positions of each output column are used for the number, except that for **-m** output, the line as a whole is numbered.	
-wk	Sets the line width to k character positions for multi-column output. The default value is 72.	
-ok	Offsets (indents) each line by k character positions. The default value is 0.	
-lk	Sets the page length to k lines. The default value is 66. If not enough lines are allotted to include the header and trailer, they are suppressed.	
-h *header*	Replaces the filename in the header with the string *header*.	
-p	When the output is directed to a terminal, pauses before beginning each page. The **pr** command sounds the terminal's bell and waits for you to hit \<enter\> before continuing.	
-f	Uses a form-feed character to create a new page. Ordinarily, **pr** uses as many line-feed characters as necessary. If the output is to a terminal, pauses before the first page; this is often useful for sending output to a printer.	

OPTION	ACTION
-r	Doesn't report failures to open files.
-t	Suppresses the five-line header and five-line trailer normally supplied with each page. Halts the display after the last line of a file instead of padding with blank lines to the end of the page.
-s*c*	Separates columns with the single character *c* instead of with the appropriate number of spaces. If *c* is omitted, a tab is used.

COMMENTS The **join** and **paste** commands provide alternative approaches to the **-a** option (merging files). The **join** command allows particular fields to be selected from each file, and **paste** allows you to join lines with a tab or other separator instead of producing equal-width columns as with **ps**.

SEE ALSO UNIX Commands: **join; paste**
UNIX Features: Standard I/O, Redirection, and Pipes; Filters

EXAMPLES

The **pr** command normally pads output to full 66-line pages. In the following examples, we've suppressed the blank lines at the end of each page. The examples assume you have the following filenames and files:

```
$ cat names
Dorrie Smeekle
Kirstin Flottle
Doug Deekdup
Tranie Vishicup
$ cat may
106
234
 90
157
$ cat july
116
 87
143
103
```

(continued)

1. Format and display a file.

```
$ pr names

Oct  3 13:07 1986  names Page 1

Dorrie Smeekle
Kirstin Flottle
Doug Deekdup
Tranie Vishicup
```

Note the header.

2. Display a file in columns.

```
$ pr -3 names

Oct  3 13:07 1986  names Page 1

Dorrie Smeekle        Doug Deekdup        Tranie Vishicup
Kirstin Flottle
```

The **pr** command divides the page into three columns of equal width. It divides the number of input lines by three to see how many lines go into each column, and it goes down the first column first.

3. Fill the columns left to right instead of vertically.

```
$ pr -3 -a names

Oct  3 13:07 1986  names Page 1

Dorrie Smeekle        Kirstin Flottle        Doug Deekdup
Tranie Vishicup
```

This is like Example 2 except for the order in which the columns are filled.

4. Merge files side by side.

```
$ pr -m names may july

Oct  3 14:12 1986    Page 1

Dorrie Smeekle          106                116
Kirstin Flottle         234                 87
Doug Deekdup             90                143
Tranie Vishicup         157                103
```

The **pr** command makes three columns of equal width. The **paste** command, which also merges files, simply puts a tab character between columns.

5. Send a file to be printed.

```
pr lunchroom ¦ lp
```

The default header and trailer provide a margin at the top and bottom of each page.

6. Replace tabs in a file with the appropriate number of spaces.

```
$pr -e -t newsletter > newslt
```

The **-t** option means that no headers, trailers, or blank-line padding are added to the text of **newsletter**. The **-e** option means that tabs in **newsletter** are replaced with the correct number of spaces to reproduce the standard tab positions. Using tabs simplifies aligning text, but can complicate editing.

ps

PURPOSE Use the **ps** command to obtain status reports on processes.

FORMAT **ps** [*option(s)*]

DESCRIPTION Since UNIX is a multi-user, multi-tasking operating system, it normally attends to several tasks concurrently. Each such task is termed an "active process." To help keep track of what is going on, the system assigns a process identification number (PID) to each process. The **ps** command reports about such processes. When used without options, **ps** reports on those processes associated with the current terminal. Specifically, it lists the PID, the terminal identifier, the cumulative execution time, and the command name. Options expand the information supplied for each process and alter the number of processes reported.

COMMON USES You can use **ps** to see what jobs you have in the background, and to see what else is happening on the system.

OPTIONS See the Processes section that follows for more on the processes and process group leaders discussed in the list below.

OPTION	ACTION
–e	Displays information about all processes, not just those associated with your terminal.
–d	Displays information about all processes except process group leaders.
–a	Displays information about all processes except process group leaders and processes not associated with terminals.
–f	Generates a "full" listing (see the Listings section below for more details).
–l	Generates a "long" listing (see the Listings section below for more details).
–n *namefile*	Uses a file called *namefile* as the system name file. (Each executable program in UNIX has a "name file" at the beginning that tells where to locate the various variables used in the code. The UNIX system program itself is no exception. The **ps** command uses the "system name file" to find some of the information it supplies. Using a different name file lets you, for example, use **ps** to obtain information about a previous version of the system that has been preserved in a system crash.)

OPTION	ACTION
-t *termlist*	Restricts the listing to processes associated with the terminals named in the string *termlist*. This string consists of device file-names; for example, **tty23** or **co**. If the name starts with **tty**, you can use just the digits; that is, **23** is interpreted as **tty23**.
-p *proclist*	Restricts the listing to processes whose PIDs are given in the string *proclist*.
-u *uidlist*	Restricts the listing to processes whose user ID numbers or login names are given in the *uidlist* list. The UID number is displayed in the listing unless the **-f** option is in effect, in which case the login name is displayed.
-g *grplist*	Restricts the listing to processes whose process group leaders are given (as PIDs) in the string *grplist*.

PROCESSES When UNIX runs a program, it loads the code for the program into memory, and it may allot additional memory for the program to use for data. In addition, it may open various files and connect them to the program. All this, and other related information, comprises a process. Since UNIX is a time-sharing system, it switches back and forth between tasks, which entails keeping track of this information for each process. Currently, UNIX is not a multi-processor operating system, so only one process actually uses the CPU at any one time. Other processes "sleep" while they await their turn, or while they wait for a particular event, such as keyboard input.

Each process is assigned a process identification number (PID) to label it. Some processes start up other processes; for example, the **init** system program starts up a shell program (**sh**) for you when you log in. In such cases, the initiating process is called a "parent process," while the other process is termed a "child." Thus most keyboard commands produce child processes to your shell, making the shell a parent.

The system lumps some processes into a group; for example, your login shell and all the processes it engenders are a group. The parent to the group (here the shell) is termed the "process group leader."

LISTINGS The default use of **ps** produces the following heading:

```
PID TTY TIME COMMAND
```

PID is the process identification number, **TTY** is the terminal from which the process originated, **TIME** is the cumulative execution time, in minutes and seconds, for the process, and **COMMAND** is the name of the command.

The full listing (produced with the **-f** option) has the following heading:

```
UID   PID  PPID  C   STIME TTY  TIME COMMAND
```

Here **UID** is the login name of the process owner, **PPID** is the PID of the parent process, **C** is the processor utilization for scheduling, and **STIME** is the starting time for the command. The remaining headings are as before.

The long listing (produced with the **-l** listing) has the following heading:

```
F S UID PID PPID C PRI NI ADDR SZ WCHAN TTY TIME CMD
```

Here **F** represents flags associated with the process. It is the sum, in octal, of those of the following flags that apply:

FLAG	MEANING
01	In core memory.
02	System process.
04	Locked in core.
10	Being swapped.
20	Being traced by another process.

(In the UNIX environment, not all concurrent tasks can be held in core memory simultaneously. When the system scheduler shifts attention from one process to another, it may have to temporarily "swap" out a process to disk memory to make room for another process, which may be swapped in from disk to memory.)

The next item, **S**, represents the status. Possible values are **R** (for running), **S** (for sleeping), **W** (for waiting), **T** (for terminated), **Z** (for stopped), **I** (for intermediate), and **0** (for nonexistent). **UID** is the process owner's user identification number. **PRI** is a priority value (the lower the number, the higher the priority), and **NI** is the "nice" value, which is used in calculating the priority. **ADDR** is the memory address of the process, and **SZ** is the amount of memory, in blocks, used by the process. **WCHAN** is the event for which the process is waiting, or sleeping; it is given as the address in memory at which the waited-for event will take place.

COMMENTS The **ps** command gives an approximate picture, since things can change while it is running.

SEE ALSO UNIX Commands: **sh**
UNIX Features: Processes

EXAMPLES

---

1. See what processes you have going.

```
$ ps
   PID TTY TIME COMMAND
    34 02  0:06 sh
   281 02  0:04 ps
```

Here the only two processes are the user's login shell (which has a PID of **34**) and the **ps** command itself.

2. Get a full listing.

```
$ ps -f
     UID    PID  PPID  C    STIME TTY  TIME COMMAND
  carolyn    34     1  0 12:50:11 02  0:06 -sh
  carolyn   282    34 80 14:36:06 02  0:05 ps -f
```

Here the user is specified by login name. Note that the parent process (given by PPID) for **ps** is the shell.

3. Get a long listing.

```
$ ps -l
  F S   UID   PID  PPID  C PRI  NI   ADDR SZ  WCHAN TTY TIME CMD
  1 S   202    34     1  0  30  20   319 25   567a 02 0:06 sh
  1 R   202   283    34 61  80  20   382 24        02 0:05 ps
```

This time the user is identified by her user ID number. Note that the **ps** command is running while the **sh** command sleeps.

4. List processes for two terminals.

```
$ ps -t "02 03"
   PID TTY TIME COMMAND
    34 02  0:06 sh
    35 03  0:03 sh
   273 03  0:45 vi
   285 02  0:05 ps
```

Note the use of quotes to make the list of terminals a single argument, and that the **tty** part of the terminal name is not needed. Note, too, how each user has his or her own shell.

(continued)

---

5. List all processes.

```
$ ps -e
  PID TTY TIME  COMMAND
    0   ? 104:21 swapper
    1   ?  0:01  init
   33  co  0:03  sh
   34  02  0:06  sh
   20   ?  0:03  update
   25   ?  0:00  lpsched
   29   ?  0:01  cron
   35  03  0:03  sh
   36  04  0:01  getty
   37  05  0:01  getty
  273  03  0:45  vi
  289  02  0:05  ps
```

Here **co** identifies the console. The **?** refers to system processes not associated with any terminal.

PURPOSE Use the **pwd** command to display the name of your current working directory.

FORMAT pwd

DESCRIPTION The **pwd** command prints the name of the current working directory.

COMMON USES You can use **pwd** to see which directory you are in and to generate the directory name in a shell script.

COMMENTS The **pwd** command may not work if you are in a directory for which you don't have read permission.

SEE ALSO UNIX Commands: **cd**
UNIX Features: Files and Directories; Pathnames and the Directory Tree

EXAMPLES

1. Check your working directory.

```
$ pwd
/usr/tuffy/Forest/Records
```

This can be useful when you have been switching around among directories.

2. Assign the name of the current working directory to a shell variable.

```
CWD=`pwd`
```

This could be part of a shell script. It uses the command substitution (or backquote) mechanism to assign the output of **pwd** to the **CWD** shell variable.

red

PURPOSE Use the **red** command to edit files.

FORMAT red [-] [-p *string*] [*file*]

DESCRIPTION The **red** command is a restricted version of the **ed** editor. It has two limitations. First, it can edit only files in the current working directory. Second, it doesn't allow the !*command* mechanism for running shell commands. Otherwise, the command works like **ed**.

COMMENTS The system administrator may choose to set up a restricted environment for certain users. The **red** editor and the **rsh** (restricted shell) are designed for that purpose.

SEE ALSO UNIX Commands: **ed**; **rsh**

PURPOSE   Use the **rm** command to remove files or directories.

FORMAT   **rm** [**-fri**] *file(s)*

DESCRIPTION   The **rm** command, without options, removes the given file or files from the directory containing them. More precisely, it removes a specified filename from the directory listing. A file can have several names, or "links," and **rm** removes only the specified links. When the final link to a file is removed, the file itself is eliminated.

You must have write permission for a directory before you can remove a file from it; you need not have read or write permission for the file itself. However, if you lack write permission and you give the **rm** command from the keyboard, **rm** prompts you by displaying your permissions (in the octal code described under **chmod**). Type a **y** if you wish to proceed with removal.

The **rm** command does not accept directories as arguments unless you use the **-r** option.

COMMON USES   You can use **rm** to get rid of files you no longer need.

OPTIONS   The **rm** command has three options that can be strung together on a single hyphen:

OPTION	ACTION
-f	Removes files without asking questions, even if write permission is lacking.
-r	Accepts a directory name as an argument. The entire contents of the directory are removed, and then the directory itself is removed. This option works recursively, meaning that all sub-directories, sub-subdirectories, and so on, are emptied and removed.
-i	Removes files (or directories, if **-r** is in effect) interactively, requesting confirmation for each listed file or directory before removing it.

COMMENTS The command **rm –r ..** is invalid. Here **..** is the UNIX shorthand for the parent directory to the current directory.

The consequences of recursively removing the wrong directory can be horrendous. A safer approach is to use **rm** to remove the files in a directory and then to use **rmdir** to remove the directory itself.

To change the mode of the file (to write-protect it, for instance), you must be the file's owner. To remove a file, you must have write permission for the parent directory. Normally, both conditions hold for files you have created. However, if you have used the **chown** command to make another user the owner of a file in your directory, the other user will be able to change the file permissions but not remove the file; on the other hand, you will be able to remove the file but not change the permissions.

SEE ALSO UNIX Commands: **ln**; **rmdir**; **chmod**
UNIX Features: Files and Directories; Shell Scripts

EXAMPLES

1. Remove a file.

```
rm slacks
```

This removes the name **slacks** from the current directory. If **slacks** is the sole name (link) for the file, the file itself is deleted from the system.

2. Remove files interactively.

```
$ rm -i fl*
flak: ? y
flask: ? n
flume: ? y
$
```

Here three files match the **fl*** pattern. The **rm** command prompts for all three, and we agree to the removal of two. Any non-**y** response is equivalent to saying no, so we could have simply hit <enter> to signify that **flask** should be retained.

3. Override write protection.

```
$ rm toys
toys: 444 mode ? n
```

Upon being reminded that **toys** is write-protected, we choose to save it. The **444** mode (see **chmod**) means read-only permission for the owner, group members, and others.

4. Have a shell script use the **-i** option.

```
$ cat ri
rm -i $@
$ ri garbage jewels
garbage: ?y
jewels: ?n
$
```

Here **$@** represents all arguments to the **ri** script. If the **ri** file is made executable and its directory is added to **PATH**, then you can use the **ri** command as shown.

rmail

PURPOSE Use **rmail** to send mail to other users.

FORMAT rmail [-t] *name(s)*
rmail [-oswt] *name(s)*

The first form is for use with Release 2 and the second with Release 3.

DESCRIPTION The **rmail** command is a restricted version of **mail**. It cannot be used to read mail, but it sends mail exactly as **mail** does.

COMMENTS The system maintains a list of commands that can be run on the local system when so directed by a remote system using the **uux** and **uucp** commands. Allowing remote systems to run commands poses security problems to the local system, so many installations restrict the list of commands to just **rmail**. This at least allows the system to participate in remote mail.

SEE ALSO UNIX Commands: **mail**; **uux**; **uucp**

PURPOSE Use the **rmdir** command to remove directories.

FORMAT **rmdir** [**-ps**] *directory-name(s)*

DESCRIPTION The **rmdir** command removes the specified directories. The directories must be empty.

COMMON USES You can use **rmdir** to remove directories you no longer need.

OPTIONS The **rmdir** command has two options:

OPTION	ACTION
-p	Removes the specified directories along with any parent directories that become empty. A message is displayed (sent to the standard output) indicating which directories have been removed. New with Release 3.
-s	Suppresses the message produced by the **-p** option. New with Release 3.

COMMENTS The **rm -r** command removes a directory *and* its files. The **rmdir** command is safer, because it lets you know if you accidentally try to remove a directory that is not empty.

SEE ALSO UNIX Commands: **rm**
UNIX Features: Files and Directories

EXAMPLES

---

1. Remove an empty directory.

   ```
   rmdir Crayfish
   ```

   This works if **Crayfish** is an empty directory.

2. Remove a non-empty directory.

   ```
   $ rm Records/*
   $ rmdir Records
   ```

   These commands first empty the **Records** directory, then remove it. Note that the * notation does not match filenames beginning with a period; any such files in **Records** can be matched by showing the period explicitly, as in .*.

---

rsh

PURPOSE Use **rsh** to create a restricted shell.

FORMAT rsh [*flag(s)*] [*argument(s)*]

DESCRIPTION The **rsh** command is a restricted version of the **sh** command. It works like **sh** with the following differences:

- ☐ Directory changes (**cd**) are not allowed.
- ☐ The shell variable **PATH** cannot be reset.
- ☐ Pathnames and command names containing / cannot be used.
- ☐ Output redirection (**>** and **>>**) cannot be used.

COMMENTS The **rsh** shell is used in setting up accounts with capabilities more limited than those that use the standard shell. The restrictions on pathnames, directory changes, and **PATH** allow the system administrator to create a work environment in which the user has access to a limited menu of commands. For example, the administrator can create a directory containing links to selected commands (such as the **red** restricted editor) and can limit **PATH** to that directory, thus limiting the restricted user to just those commands.

SEE ALSO UNIX Commands: **sh**; **red**

PURPOSE   Use the **sed** command to apply a script of editing commands to the contents of a file.

FORMAT   **sed** [-n] [-e *script*] [-f *scriptfile*] [*file(s)*]

DESCRIPTION   The **sed** command is a stream editor. This means it takes input from a list of files or from standard input, applies editing instructions to each line, and sends the results on to the standard output, which is, by default, the screen. Thus **sed** leaves the original files unaltered. The output, of course, can be redirected to another file or piped to another command.

The editing commands, which are derived from **ed**, can be given as part of the command line, can be taken from specified files, or both. Typically, a command includes an address or address range identified by a line number or pattern and an instruction to be performed on matching lines.

COMMON USES   You can use **sed** to apply a packaged set of editing instructions to a raw file. The versatility of this command makes it a common shell-script tool.

OPTIONS   The **sed** command has three options:

OPTION	ACTION
-n	Suppresses the default output, which is to pass every line, after possible editing, to the output. The **p** command still can be used to print selected lines.
-e *script*	Uses the command-line *script* for editing. If there is only one command-line script and if the -f option is not in effect, the **-e** can be omitted. The *script* consists of one or more editing instructions. Often it is necessary to enclose the script in quotes to avoid confusing the shell. This option can be used successively with several scripts. In this case, each line is acted upon by the first script, each edited line is then acted upon by the next script, and so on.
-f *scriptfile*	Uses the editing instructions found in *scriptfile*. This option can be used successively with several script files. The editing instructions are then applied in the order in which the files containing them are listed.

THE EDITING SEQUENCE AND SPECIAL TERMS   Normally, each line of input is copied into a temporary work area called a "pattern space." Each editing instruction is checked in turn to see if it applies to the copied line. If it does, the editing command is applied before the next instruction is checked. Thus an instruction that would apply to the original

281

line might not apply to the altered line in the pattern space. Note that it is the pattern space, not the original input line, that is edited. Thus we talk about matching and editing pattern spaces rather than lines.

Normally, after the complete list of instructions has been applied, the contents of the pattern space are sent to the standard output, and the pattern space is emptied. Then the next input line is read into the pattern space, and the process repeats. This process of reading an input line into the pattern space, editing it with a succession of commands, outputting the result, and clearing the pattern space is called a "cycle." In the case of multiple scripts, all the commands from all the scripts are included in a single cycle. So **sed** processes the input one line at a time.

Some instructions (**h**, **H**, and **x**) copy text from the pattern space to a temporary storage area called the "hold space." Text stored there later can be placed, in whole or in part, back in the pattern space.

EDITING INSTRUCTIONS Each **sed** instruction has, in general, an address segment and a command. The address segment identifies which text lines are affected, and the editing command specifies what is done. As mentioned earlier, each address and (if applicable) editing command is applied to the pattern space as modified by preceding instructions in the same cycle.

Addresses

There are four forms of address: no address, a numeric address, the special address ($), and a "context" address.

When there is no address, the editing command in the instruction is applied to every pattern space.

A numeric address is interpreted as a decimal line number. When more than one input file is given, the line numbering is consecutive across files. Editing changes to a pattern space may delete lines from or add lines to the output, but they don't alter the line-numbering scheme, which is based on the original input.

The special address $ signifies the last line of input. If there is more than one file of input, $ means the last line of the last file.

A context address consists of a "regular expression," as discussed under **ed**, contained between two slashes. For example, the address /**chocolate**/ selects pattern spaces containing the string **chocolate**, and the address /^[Tt]h/ selects pattern spaces beginning with **Th** or **th**.

The **ed** style for regular expressions is modified somewhat for **sed**. First, a character other than a slash can be used to delimit the regular expression. Starting the address with the combination \c makes c the delimiting character, where c is a character of your choice. For instance, \#**hello**# matches the string **hello**, with # serving as the delimiter. This feature is useful if the pattern itself involves slashes. For instance, **\#/usr/beast/rose#** matches the pathname **/usr/beast/rose**. Of course, the backslash character can be used to "escape" a delimiter (temporarily turn off its meaning), but this is less convenient. Thus we could match the pathname using **/\/usr\/beast\/rose/**.

Second, the "escape sequence" **\n** can be used to match a newline embedded in a pattern space. The pattern space starts as one input line, with one newline character at the end. This terminating newline is not matched by **\n**. But the editing commands can add lines to the pattern space, thereby inserting additional newline characters; these are embedded newlines that are matched by **\n**.

Third, a period matches any character in the pattern space except a terminating newline. (The **ed** command's definition of period behavior also prevents a period from matching embedded newlines.)

When an address specifies a particular pattern space, that pattern space is said to be "selected."

Some editing commands take no addresses, some take one, and some take one or two. When two addresses are used, they are separated by a comma and represent a range that extends from the first pattern space matching the first address through the first subsequent pattern space matching the second address. Thus an address range normally selects at least two consecutive pattern spaces. However, if the first address is a regular expression and the second address is a line number that comes before the line matching the first address, just one line matching the regular expression is selected.

The next selection for a pattern range begins after the last line of the previous range; that is, if the range is **/pat/, /mike/**, the first range runs from the first example of **pat** to the first subsequent pattern space containing **mike**. The lines in this range are edited as directed, then **sed** looks at the lines following the first range for another example of **pat** and **mike**. There is no overlap; the **pat** marking the beginning of the second range must come after the line containing the **mike** that ends the first range.

To apply commands to pattern spaces that were not selected, use the **!** command described later.

Editing Commands

The **sed** command offers several editing commands. Some are borrowed from **ed**, and some are unique to **sed**. Before looking at the commands in detail, let's consider some general matters of syntax.

Multiple commands (an "editing script") must be typed one per line (see Examples 2 and 3). However, if the editing commands are being given on the **sed** command line, you also can use the **–e** option repeatedly (see Example 2).

Three of the **sed** commands (**a**, **c**, and **i**) add text to the output. This text, represented as *text* in the command summaries, consists of one or more lines following the command. All but the final line must end with a backslash (\\), as in this example, which appends two lines of text:

```
a\
Tra la la la\
and goodbye.
```

The backslashes "escape" the newline character generated by the <enter> key; otherwise, the newline character would mark the end of the command. Also use the backslash to protect initial spaces and tabs from being stripped from the text:

```
a\
\ \ \ \ \ Once upon\
a time.
```

Some of the **sed** commands, such as **s** and **G**, alter the pattern space and hence the output. Other commands, such as **a** and **c**, send new text to the standard output while leaving the pattern space unchanged. This difference can be important when you have a series of editing instructions. In particular, text added by a command such as **s** can be altered by a subsequent editing instruction, since the new material is in the pattern space, whereas material added by a command such as **a** is immune to further editing changes because it goes directly to the output and not into the pattern space.

Two commands (**b** and **t**) involve skipping over intervening commands to a label created with the : command. This allows **sed** command sequences to incorporate a degree of flow control.

The various commands differ in the number of addresses they can use. We'll use the following code to indicate the maximum number of addresses they accept:

CODE	ADDRESSES
[*0 adr*]	Takes no address.
[*1 adr*]	Takes no address or one address.
[*2 adr*]	Takes no address, one address, or an address range.

Command Summaries

Here's a list of **sed** commands, each with one of the above address codes.

COMMAND	ACTION
[*1 adr*] a\ *text*	Appends *text* to the output before reading the next input line. Subsequent editing commands don't affect *text*, but they can alter the pattern space.
[*2 adr*] b *label*	Jumps to the : command followed by the string *label*, which can be any sequence of eight or fewer characters.
[*2 adr*] c\ *text*	Deletes the pattern space, sends *text* to the output, and starts a new cycle. Since the pattern space is now empty, there would be no point to trying to match subsequent editing instructions to the pattern space anyway.
[*2 adr*] d	Deletes the pattern space and starts the next cycle.
[*2 adr*] D	Deletes the initial segment of the pattern space through the first newline, and starts the next cycle. This command differs from **d** only when another command, such as **N**, has placed one or more embedded newlines in the pattern space.
[*2 adr*] g	Replaces the contents of the pattern space with the contents of the hold space (see **h** and **H**).
[*2 adr*] G	Appends the contents of the hold space to the pattern space (see **h** and **H**).
[*2 adr*] h	Replaces the contents, if any, of the hold space with the current contents of the pattern space.
[*2 adr*] H	Appends the current contents of the pattern space to the contents of the hold space.
[*1 adr*] i\ *text*	Inserts *text* into the standard output. The text is inserted before the contents of the pattern space if the latter is printed.
[*2 adr*] l	Displays the pattern space on the standard output, representing nonprinting characters with a two-digit ASCII code and "folding" long lines. (Folding means spreading a long line over two or more display lines, if necessary, rather than truncating the line.)
[*2 adr*] n	Sends the contents of the pattern space to the standard output, and replaces the pattern space with the next line of input.

(continued)

COMMAND	ACTION	(continued)

COMMAND	ACTION
[2 adr] N	Appends the next line of input to the pattern space. An embedded newline character separates the appended material from the original. The current line number is increased by one. By placing two input lines in the same pattern space, **sed** can look for a pattern that is spread over two lines.
[2 adr] p	Sends the contents of the pattern space to the output.
[2 adr] P	Sends the contents of the pattern space, up to the first newline, to the output. This command differs from **p** only when another command, such as **N**, has added embedded newlines.
[1 adr] q	Quits. Skips over any remaining editing instructions and doesn't read any more input.
[2 adr] r *rfile*	Reads the *rfile* file and sends its contents to the standard output before reading the next input line. There must be exactly one blank (a space or a tab) between the **r** and the filename, and *rfile* must end the line.
[2 adr] s/*rexpr*/*rstring*/*flags*	Substitutes the replacement string *rstring* for the regular expression *rexpr* (see **ed** for complete discussions of regular expressions and the substitution command). If the **g** flag (described below) is not used, just the first occurrence of *rexpr* in the pattern space is replaced. The optional *flags* argument can be any of the following:

FLAG	MEANING
n	Substitute for just the *n*th occurrence of *rexpr*. Here *n* is an integer in the range 1–512.
g	Substitute for all non-overlapping instances of *rexpr* instead of just for the first. Note that the **g** flag is unrelated to the **g** command. An example of overlapping is the instruction s/s.e/**TUT**/g and the string **ssee**. The overlapping patterns **sse** and **see** both match **s.e**. But **sed** matches the first, then substitutes, so the result is **TUTe**.
p	Print the pattern space if a replacement was made.
w *wfile*	Append the pattern space to the *wfile* file if a substitution was made.

COMMAND	ACTION
	For example, the instruction **s/Fiat/Ford/gp** replaces all occurrences of **Fiat** with **Ford** and prints out each pattern space in which the substitution takes place. Because no address is used, the instruction applies to all pattern spaces. By default, every pattern space is printed anyway, so the **p** causes affected lines to be printed twice. However, if the **-n** option is invoked, the default printing is suppressed; the unaffected lines are not printed at all, and the affected lines are printed once.
[*2 adr*] **t** *label*	Jumps to the **:** command bearing the *label* label if any subsitutions have been made since the most recent reading of an input line or since the most recent execution of a **t** command. Here *label* is a string of up to eight characters. If no label is given, goes to the end of the editing script. This command allows you to write a script whose actions depend on the exact text encountered.
[*2 adr*] **w** *wfile*	Appends the contents of the pattern space to the *wfile* file. There must be exactly one blank (a space or a tab) between the **w** and the filename, and *wfile* must end the line. You can use up to ten distinct write files in a **sed** command script.
[*2 adr*] **x**	Exchanges the contents of the pattern space and the hold space (the **h** and **H** commands are used to place material in the hold space).
[*2 adr*] **y**/*string1*/*string2*/	
	This is a transliteration command. Each character in *string1* is replaced by the corresponding character in *string2*. For example, the instruction **y/cat/dog/** causes every **c** to be replaced by a **d**, every **a** by an **o**, and every **t** by a **g**.
[*2 adr*] **!** *command*	This command is applied only to those pattern spaces that do *not* match the address specification. For example, **/profit/!d** deletes all pattern spaces that do not contain the string **profit**. Note that the **!** command comes between the address and *command*.
[*0 adr*] **:** *label*	Provides a location that a **b** or **t** command can jump to. Here *label* is a string of up to eight characters.

(continued)

COMMAND	ACTION	*(continued)*
[1 adr] **=**	Puts the current line number on the standard output; the number is given its own line.	
[2 adr] **{***commands***}**	When a pattern space is specified by an address, executes all the commands in the *commands* list. Each command must be on its own line, and the closing **}** must be on its own line. Here is an example:	

```
/Idoho/{p
s/Idoho/Idaho/gp
}
```

Each line containing **Idoho** is printed before and after the substitution is made. (This assumes the **-n** option is in effect so that printing occurs only when explicitly requested.)

[0 adr] **#**	If this the first character of the first line of a script file, then the line is treated as a comment. If, in addition, the second character is an **n**, the default output is suppressed. This provides the same effect as using the **-n** option, but limits it to a particular editing script.

When typing editing instructions as part of the command line, it may be necessary to put them in quotes. This is true when special characters, such as **[** or *****, are used, or when more than one line is needed. (See the examples.)

COMMENTS The **sed** command is a useful tool in shell scripts since it is designed as a "filter"; that is, it is designed so that it can take input from the standard input and send it to the standard output.

SEE ALSO UNIX Commands: **ed**
UNIX Features: Command Lines; Regular Expressions; Standard I/O, Redirection, and Pipes; Extending Commands over More than One Line; Filters

EXAMPLES

1. Replace all the occurrences of **Dick** with **Jimmie**.

   ```
   sed s/Dick/Jimmie/g welcome
   ```

   The original **welcome** file is unchanged, and the modified text is sent to the screen. The output could be redirected to another file or piped to another command, as in the following:

   ```
   sed s/Dick/Jimmie/g welcome > newwelcome
   ```

   ```
   sed s/Dick/Jimmie/g welcome ! lp
   ```

2. Use multiple commands while in the command-line mode.

   ```
   $ sed 's/coffee/cocoa/g
   >    s/pancakes/waffles/g' breakfast4
   ```

   Note the use of quoting to allow the command line to extend over more than one line. The **sh** shell displays the **>** prompt (by default) to indicate extended command lines. Since the newline character at the end of the first line is inside the quotes, it does not have its usual special meaning of marking the end of a command line.

   A second approach is to use the **–e** option more than once, as in:

   ```
   $ sed -e s/coffee/cocoa/g -e s/pancakes/waffles/g breakfast4
   ```

   The **–e** explicitly identifies a command-line editing command.

3. Use a script file.

   ```
   $ cat edstuff
   s/Nationel/National/g
   /1981/d
   100q
   $ sed -f edstuff oldstock > oldstock.rev
   ```

   The editing instructions from the **edstuff** file are applied to the first 100 lines of the **oldstock** file.

   (continued)

4. Mix command-line scripts with file scripts.

```
sed -f standard -e 's/Tybold, Inc\./Iago Co./g' bid
```

First the editing commands from the **standard** file are applied to a pattern space, then the command-line substitution command is applied to the pattern space. Switching the order of the **-f** and **-e** options switches the order in which the commands are applied. Note that the period after **Inc** is escaped (**\.**) to distinguish it from the pattern-matching period of regular expressions. The period after **Co**, however, need not be escaped, since it is in the replacement string; the period is special only in the search string.

5. Obtain a list of terminals currently active.

```
who ! sed   's/^[^ ]* *\([^ ]*\).*/\1/'
```

The terminal name is the second item in a **who** listing. The pattern **^[^]*** identifies zero or more non-space characters at the beginning of the line. For **who** output, this is the name of a user. This string ends when the first space is encountered. Then the space followed by * skips over spaces to the next string of non-space characters. This one, the second field in the **who** output, is tagged **\(\)**, so the **\1** in the replacement string refers to it. In the past, **sed** has been used extensively in shell scripts to "parse" lines and select fields in this fashion. The addition of a field-oriented command like **cut** makes these kinds of tasks easier to do.

PURPOSE Use the **sh** command as an interface between you and the operating system.

DESCRIPTION The **sh** command interprets and executes commands typed from the keyboard or read from a file. It is called a "shell," and it acts as an interface between you and the operating system. When you log in, a shell is started up for you. It then interprets the command lines you type and carries out the appropriate actions. Also, you can have **sh** execute a sequence of commands stored in a text file called a "shell procedure," or "shell script." The **sh** program's many features make it a powerful, programmable tool.

The **sh** command itself is not part of the UNIX operating system. It is just one more UNIX command. As mentioned, a shell is started when you log in, but you also can start a new shell after logging in by giving the **sh** command. For example, you might want to start a new shell to run a shell script.

OVERVIEW The basic function of the shell is to run commands. It recognizes simple commands, of course, but it also allows commands to be grouped together and (using the operating system) to be linked together. Furthermore, the shell has programming-language capabilities for setting up loop structures and branching structures involving other UNIX commands.

Here are some other major features of the shell:

☐ It can maintain a list of "shell variables," or "parameters," that can be created by the user.

☐ The shell also uses several standard parameters that take their values from a standard "environment," which is passed to the shell when it is started up. Such variables are called "environmental variables."

☐ In addition to the shell variables and environmental variables, the shell sets and maintains a set of parameters of its own.

☐ The shell has a set of special characters that can be used to create patterns to match filenames. This feature is called "filename generation."

☐ The shell offers several forms of redirection; that is, ways of modifying the routing of input and output of UNIX commands.

☐ The shell has many built-in commands, most of which are designed to assist shell programming.

These and other features are discussed below.

COMMANDS The shell uses a systematic approach for interpreting its input. Describing this approach involves using a specific terminology, so we'll first look at some of those terms:

☐ A "command line" is a line of input that the shell seeks to interpret.

☐ A "blank" means either a tab or a space. The shell uses blanks to divide a command line into separate words.

☐ A "word" is a string of characters with no blanks.

☐ A "name" is a string of characters formed from letters, digits, and underscore characters. A valid name does not begin with a digit. Names generally refer to files, including files containing commands and directory files, or to shell variables.

☐ A "parameter" is a name, a digit, or any of the special characters *, @, #, ?, -, !, and $. A parameter that is a name is a shell variable. A parameter that is a single digit is a "positional" parameter used to represent parts of a command line. The special-character parameters represent information tracked by the shell, such as the shell's process ID number. All these uses will be described later.

SIMPLE COMMANDS AND EXIT VALUES A "simple command" is constructed from words separated by blanks. The first word is the name of the command to be executed. (The shell uses the **PATH** environmental variable, discussed later, to determine which directories to search for the command file.) The remaining words (with some exceptions to be discussed later) are called "arguments" and are passed to the command for it to use. The command name itself is passed as argument number 0.

UNIX commands have an exit status, which is a value returned by the command to the shell to describe how the command functioned. Generally, an exit status of zero indicates all went well, while non-zero values indicate some sort of problem, such as an unopenable file. Each simple command has a "value" that normally represents the exit status. However, if the command terminates abnormally (for example, due to an interrupt signal or a hardware problem), the command value is (in octal) 0200 plus the regular exit value. This feature, which lets a shell script detect system problems even when a command works properly, was new to **sh** with Release 2.

PIPELINES Two or more commands can be linked by a "pipe," represented by the │ character (the ^ character is an alternative, anachronistic choice). A pipe connects the standard output of one command to the standard input of the next. For example ls │ wc routes the output of ls to wc; the number of lines reported by **wc** will be the number of files in the directory, because **ls** prints one file per line. The commands so joined are called a "pipeline." A single command is considered to be a special case of a pipeline, so the term pipeline can be used to encompass both simple and compound commands.

The exit status of a pipeline is the exit status of the final command in the sequence. More generally, the exit status of a compound command is the exit status of the last simple command executed, unless otherwise stated.

COMMAND LISTS: ;, &, &&, AND ¦¦ The next step in complexity in command construction is the "list." A list is a pipeline or sequence of pipelines separated by the character ; or & or the character pair && or ¦¦. (Remember that a pipeline can be a single command.) The & and ; characters also can terminate a list. Thus the following are examples of lists:

```
sleep 30; echo done
awk -f bawk books > report &
grep mars data3 > /dev/null ¦¦ mail tycho > data2
grep plaut nl > /dev/null && sort nl > pl &
```

That's what lists look like, but what do they do?

The ; character causes the commands in the list to be executed synchronously; that is, each command in the list begins after the preceding command finishes. You can use a newline character instead of a ; character to run commands consecutively. In fact, that is the usual approach: you type a command and hit <enter> to generate a newline. The chief difference is that when you use the semicolon, you can type all the commands before execution of any of them begins.

The & causes commands and pipelines to be executed "asynchronously," meaning that the shell does not wait, as it normally does, for the command to finish before prompting you for the next command. Instead, the process is run "in the background," meaning it is placed in the time-sharing queue to await timely processing instead of forcing the shell to wait for it. The usual mode, in which the shell waits for a process to finish, is called running a process "in the foreground." Background processes that normally send output to the screen still do so unless you redirect the output to a file or pipe it to another command, as in this example:

```
awk -f bawk books > report &
```

Here the output of the **awk** program is routed to the **report** file using redirection (another to-be-described-later feature). Meanwhile, as **awk** plugs away, you can perform other UNIX tasks.

The && causes the list following it to be executed only if the preceding pipeline returned a zero (successful) exit status, while the ¦¦ causes the list following it to be executed only if the preceding pipeline returned a non-zero (unsuccessful) exit status. (Recall that each UNIX command returns an exit value for use by the shell.) For instance, consider this example:

```
grep mars data3 > /dev/null && mail tycho < data3
```

The first part of the list has **grep** search the **data3** file for the string **mars**. The output of **grep** (lines containing **mars**) is then redirected to the special file **/dev/null**, which is the UNIX method of discarding the output. The concern of this command is not the actual lines, but whether or not any were found, as indicated by **grep**'s exit status. If the exit value is zero (that is, **mars** was found), then the list following **&&** is executed. In this case, the contents of the **data3** file are mailed to **tycho**.

The **&&** and ¦¦ have the same precedence, which is higher than the precedence of ; and **&**. The latter two have the same precedence as each other. Their precedence determines how commands in a list are grouped. Here's an example:

```
grep plaut nl > /dev/null && sort nl > pl &
```

Because **&&** has higher precedence than **&**, first the **grep** and the **sort** commands are linked with **&&** to form a list, then that list is run in the background. Thus the entire command line is run in the background. To run the **grep** portion in the foreground and the **sort** portion in the background requires the use of one of the grouping notations to override the natural precedence.

COMMAND GROUPING: ( ) AND {} Parentheses and braces both can be used to group commands, but not quite in the same manner.

The format for using parentheses is to include a *list* (as defined above) between them:

(*list*)

For example, we can modify the preceding example to look like this:

```
grep plaut nl > /dev/null && ( sort nl > pl & )
```

This causes the **&** to be associated with just the **sort** portion instead of the entire command line. So the **grep** command runs in the foreground, and when it finishes, the **sort** command runs in the background.

When commands in a list are grouped together, their output is combined. For example, consider this command:

```
( echo Sorted Scores; sort scores ) > scores.sort
```

Without the parentheses, the output of the **echo** command would go to the screen, while the sorted output would go to the **scores.sort** file. With the parentheses, both go to **scores.sort**.

The parentheses mechanism causes *list* to be executed by a subshell; that is, the current shell starts a new shell, which then runs the commands in the list. When the list finishes, the subshell expires, and the original shell takes control again.

The braces mechanism differs in two respects. First, the format is slightly different:

{ *list*; }

The list should be terminated with a semicolon or with a newline. At least one blank is required after the opening brace. Thus

```
$ { date; ls; } > listing
```

is the same as

```
$ { date ; ls
> } > listing
```

Here the first **>** on the second line is the default secondary prompt displayed by the shell to indicate that it expects more input. A newline also could have been used instead of the first semicolon. Anyway, both versions place the current date and current directory listing in the **listing** file.

The opening brace should be the first character, other than initial blanks, at the beginning of a line or after a semicolon.

The second difference between braces and parentheses is that with braces, the commands in the list are executed by the current shell rather than by a subshell. In many cases, this does not affect the eventual outcome of a command, but in some cases it does. The **cd** (change directory) command, for example, is built into **sh**. One implication of this is that each shell keeps track of its own directory changes; that is, if you invoke a subshell, change directories, then return to the parent shell, you'll still be in the original directory. Here is an illustration:

```
$ pwd
/usr/beard
$ ( cd Pantry; pwd ); pwd
/usr/beard/Pantry
/usr/beard
$ { cd Pantry; pwd; }; pwd
/usr/beard/Pantry
/usr/beard/Pantry
```

We begin in the **/usr/beard** directory. In the first case, grouping with parentheses creates a subshell. The subshell makes a directory change, as shown by the output of the **pwd** in the list. But when the subshell finishes, we are back in the original directory. With the braces, however, the current shell makes the directory change, and thus, after the list is completed, we still are in the new directory.

STRUCTURED COMMANDS The shell has several forms of structured commands modeled on those used in traditional programming languages. Each of these structures is considered a single command and can be an element of a pipeline or list. Three of the structures (**for**, **while**, and **until**) create loops, and two (**case** and **if**) offer branching.

The **while** loop has this form:

while *list1*
do
     list2
done

First the commands in *list1* are executed. If the exit status of the last command in the list is zero (the command ran successfully), the commands in *list2* are executed. Then the process is repeated until *list1* produces a non-zero exit status. For example, the command

```
while who ¦ grep godzilla > /dev/null
do
    echo Godzilla is still logged in
    sleep 60
done &
```

keeps you informed every 60 seconds until **godzilla** logs out. The **grep** command searches the output of **who** for **godzilla**. If it finds it, the exit status is zero, and the loop is executed. The **sleep** command causes the loop to wait the specified number of seconds before resuming. Since the entire loop is a single command, we can use an **&** after the **done** to run it in the background.

The keywords **while**, **do**, and **done** must come at the beginning of a line (ignoring any initial blanks) or just after a semicolon (again ignoring initial blanks).

A **while** loop also can be controlled by the value of a shell variable by using the **test** command. This command converts various comparisons of values to a zero exit value if the comparison is true. The **test** command is one of the built-in shell commands and is discussed later. It also is discussed under its own heading in the "UNIX Commands" section. The **until** loop and **if** structure also can use **test**.

The **until** command is just like **while** except that the loop continues as long as the exit status is non–zero. For example, the command

```
until who ! grep godzilla > /dev/null
do
    echo Godzilla is not on the system
    sleep 60
done &
```

reassures you every **60** seconds until the login name **godzilla** shows up in the **who** output.

The exit value of a **while** or **until** loop depends on whether or not the body of the loop is executed. If the body is executed, the exit value of the whole loop is the exit value of the last command executed in the body (*list2*) of the loop. If the body of the loop is not executed, the exit value is zero. This occurs if the test command (*list1*) fails the first time it is attempted. Note that the exit value of *list1* is not used as an exit value for the whole loop command.

The **while** and **until** loops are conditional loops, dependent upon the outcome of a test command. The **for** loop, on the other hand, processes a list of items. Its general form is

> **for** *variable* **in** *values-list*
> **do**
>> *command-list*
> **done**

Here *variable* is a *name*, as described earlier at the beginning of the Commands discussion. Next, *values-list* is a list of words. The first time through the loop, *variable* is set to the first word in *values-list*, and the *command-list*, which may make use of *variable*, is executed. For the next cycle, *variable* is set to the next word in the list, and the process continues until the list of words is exhausted. Here is a simple example:

```
$ for thing in rag mop puppy
> do
>     echo What a GOOD $thing!
> done
What a GOOD rag!
What a GOOD mop!
What a GOOD puppy!
```

As we'll discuss later, if **thing** is the name of a variable, then **$thing** represents its value. The first time through the loop, the **thing** variable is assigned the value **rag**, so in the **echo** command, $thing is interpreted as **rag**. The **>** is the secondary prompt provided by the shell, which knows that a **for** command doesn't end until **done** shows up.

The keywords **for**, **do**, and **done** must be the first words, other than initial blanks, on their lines, or they must appear just after a semicolon; as with **while** loops, initial blanks are allowed.

The *values-list* can be produced several ways. In the above example, we listed the values explicitly, but anything that produces a list of words will do. For example, you can use a shell variable that has been set previously to a list of words. Or you can use command substitution (discussed later) to produce a list. Another possibility is to use filename expansion (also discussed later). For instance,

```
for file in ??
```

sets **file** in succession to all the two-character filenames (represented by **??**) in the current directory.

Another possibility is to use positional parameters (also discussed later). If the **for** command is within a shell script, then the positional parameters represent arguments to the script. Positional parameters can be used explicitly, as in:

```
for file in $*
```

or

```
for file in $@
```

The notations **$*** and **$@**, discussed later, represent different methods of assigning positional parameters. They also can be used implicitly:

```
for file
```

When the **in** *values-list* portion is omitted, **in $@** is assumed.

The **if** statement offers a conditional choice. The simplest form of **if** looks like this:

> **if** *list1*
> **then**
> > *list2*
> **fi**

Here *list1* and *list2* are command lists. First, the commands in *list1* are executed. If the exit status of the final command is zero (it worked fine), then the commands in *list2* are executed; otherwise, they are not. The structure is quite similar to the **while** loop except that it is traversed just once instead of repeatedly.

You can add an **else** segment to an **if** statement to provide a list of commands to be carried out if *list1* yields a non-zero value. The form of an **if else** statement is

> **if** *list1*
> **then**
> > *list2*
>
> **else**
> > *list3*
>
> **fi**

Here is a simple example:

```
if who ! grep godzilla > /dev/null
then
      echo Your friend godzilla is logged on
else
      echo We are godzilla-free
fi
```

An **elif** (short for "else if") segment can be added to provide a series of tests. The form of an **elif** statement is

> **if** *list1*
> **then**
> > *list2*
>
> **elif** *list3*
> **then**
> > *list4*
>
> **else**
> > *list5*
>
> **fi**

First the commands in *list1* are run. If the final command in the list has an exit value of zero, the commands in *list2* are executed. If it doesn't, then the commands in *list3* are executed. If the last command in that list is successful, the commands in *list4* are run; otherwise, the commands in *list5* are run. So for *list5* to run, both the **if** list and the **elif** commands must fail.

You can have multiple **elif** segments, and the **else** need not be present. The keywords **if, then, elif, else,** and **fi** all must come at the beginning of a line or after a semicolon; initial blanks are okay.

The exit value of an **if** command is set to the exit value of the last command executed in a **then** or an **else** segment. If none of these commands is executed, the exit status is zero.

The **if** structure sets up selection on the basis of the outcome of one or more commands. The **case** structure sets up selection on the basis of the value of a string. The general form looks like this:

> **case** *word* **in**
>   *pattern1*) *list1* ;;
>   *pattern2*) *list2* ;;
>   ...
> **esac**

You can have as many patterns as you need. The *word* is checked to see if it matches *pattern1*. If it does, the commands in *list1* are executed, and the **case** statement ends. If it doesn't, *word* is checked to see if it matches the next pattern, and so on. The) separates the pattern from the list of commands, and the ;; marks the end of a command list.

The *word* is a string of one or more characters. Most typically, it is the value of a shell variable. The patterns also are strings; they can make use of the filename-generation mechanisms described shortly. These mechanisms have some limitations: a slash, a leading dot, or a dot immediately after a slash need not be matched explicitly. (In standard filename generation, these characters must be matched explicitly; "wildcard" characters won't do.) Here is a short example:

```
case $SHELL in
        /bin/sh ) echo Your habitual shell is sh ;;
        /bin/rsh ) echo Your habitual shell is rsh ;;
        * ) echo You are a $SHELL user ;;
esac
```

Here **SHELL** is an environmental variable set to the filename of the shell you habitually use. $SHELL represents the actual string. If the string is the same as **/bin/sh**, the command following that pattern is executed. If not, the next pattern is changed. The final pattern is *, which matches all strings, so it acts as a default choice if none of the previous patterns produces a match.

The ¦ character can be used to make two patterns apply to the same choice:

```
case $NAME in
        jake ¦ jillian ) echo administrators ;;
        bob ¦ bernd ¦ don ¦ vic ) echo brains ;;
esac
```

Here if the variable **NAME** is **jake** or **jillian**, the first message is echoed. If it is any of the next four names, the second message is echoed; otherwise, nothing is done. Note that ¦ in this context does not represent a pipe.

The keywords **case** and **esac** must come at the beginning of a line or just after a semicolon, ignoring initial blanks. The exit value of a **case** statement is the exit value of the last statement executed or zero if no choice is selected.

Function Definitions

With Release 2, UNIX System V introduced a function-defining facility. In essence, it allows a single name to represent a list of commands. Here is the format:

name () { *list*; }

This makes *name* a synonym for *list*. The chosen *name* must conform to the same naming conventions that hold for filenames and variable names (see *name* at the beginning of the earlier Commands discussion). You are not allowed to have a function and shell variable with the same name. The parentheses serve to indicate that *name* is the name of a function. There must be a blank after the opening brace.

Here is an example of a function:

```
L () { ls -l | pg; }
```

Once this definition is typed, typing **L** causes a long listing for the current directory to be piped to **pg**. To make the definition more general, you can use positional parameter notation, as in

```
L () { ls -l $* | pg; }
```

Here $* represents the list of arguments given to **L**; that is, the command

```
L /dev /etc
```

is expanded to the following:

```
ls -l /dev /etc | pg
```

Definitions expire when the shell expires, but you can place definitions in your **.profile** file so that they are defined each time you log in. One limitation of functions is that, unlike shell variables, they cannot be exported (exporting a variable causes a child shell to get a copy of it). Thus when you start a subshell, it is ignorant of functions defined in the parent shell.

SHELL SCRIPTS (PROCEDURES) A shell script, or procedure, is a sequence of commands stored in a file. One way to execute a shell script is to invoke **sh** with the filename as its first argument. Here is a sample showing the contents of a shell script file and the mechanism for running it:

```
$ cat hello
echo Hello, my friend.
$ sh hello
Hello, my friend.
```

Note that a subshell, not the current shell, runs the script. Thus the script may run in a different environment (see the Environment discussion later in this section) than that of the current shell.

A second method for running a shell script is to use **chmod** to make it an executable file. Then you merely need to type the filename to run the script:

```
$ chmod u+x hello
$ hello
Hello, my friend.
```

The internal mechanics are the same; however, a subshell is evoked to execute the commands.

Once a script has been made executable, it remains so unless you use **chmod** to remove execute permission.

Commenting Scripts

Often it is useful to insert comments in a shell script. If you begin a word with a **#**, the word and all characters up to the end of the line are ignored by the shell. For example,

```
$ cat howdy
#This program says howdy
echo HOWDY! HOWDY! #this line does the work
$ sh howdy
HOWDY! HOWDY!
```

You also can insert comments in keyboard input, though there is not much point to this.

You may use a system that offers you the option of using Berkeley's **csh** shell. If the first line of a script begins with **#**, **csh** assumes the script is written in the **csh** shell language rather than in the **sh** language. So, since **#** on the first line means "comment" to **sh** and "csh script" to **csh**, you can use the null command (:) instead of **#** to preface a comment that's on the first line of a shell script.

COMMAND SUBSTITUTION Sometimes it is desirable to replace a command with its output. This is done by enclosing the command in a pair of backquotes ('), also called "accents graves." For example, this mechanism can be used to set a shell variable equal to the output of a command:

```
$ DIR=`pwd`
$ echo $DIR
/usr/asimov/Robots
```

Or suppose you wish to run a **for** loop for every word in a particular file. You can do something like this:

```
for word in `cat flowers`
do
    echo A $word is a $word is a $word
done
```

Here **`cat flowers`** is replaced by its output (the contents of the **flowers** file), and **word** is set to each word in **flowers** in turn.

PARAMETERS Parameters are symbolic names that can be assigned values. The shell maintains three kinds of parameters: positional parameters, keyword parameters (also called shell variables), and automatic parameters. All use a $ prefix to indicate the value of the parameter. All values are stored as strings; that is, as a sequence of characters. For instance, the number 24 is stored as the digit character 2 followed by the digit character 4.

Positional Parameters

Positional parameters represent arguments to a command. The first argument is called 1, the second 2, and so on up through 9. The 0 positional parameter refers to the name of the command itself. Positional parameters most frequently are used in shell scripts. The following example illustrates the mechanism (**hi** is an executable shell script):

```
$ cat hi
echo Hi, $1 and $2, from the $0 command
$ hi catherine anne jane
Hi, catherine and anne, from the hi command
```

The first positional parameter is **1** and its value (the first argument, here **catherine**) is represented by $1. Similarly, $3 is **jane**, but the script makes no use of it. Note that $0 represents the command name.

Positional parameters also can be set by the **set** command, which is built into **sh**. The following example shows how this works:

```
$ set paul ringo george john
$ echo $4 $1
john paul
```

303

The positional parameters are set to **set**'s arguments. Incidentally, **$0** is set to **sh**, not **set**, since **set** is just part of **sh**.

More typically, **set** is used in conjunction with command substitution:

```
$ set `date`
$ echo Today is $1
Today is Tue
```

The backquoted **date** is replaced with its output (the date), and the positional parameters are assigned to the consecutive words in the date. The first word is an abbreviation for the day of the week. Since this is Tuesday, **$1** is assigned the value **Tue**.

Keyword Parameters (Shell Variables)

A keyword parameter is identified by its name, which must meet the usual shell standards for a name; that is, it can use letters, digits, and the underscore character, and the first character cannot be a digit. As we mentioned earlier, you can't use the same name for a variable and for a shell function.

To assign a value to a keyword parameter, use the following form:

name=value

There should be no blanks between the elements. To use the value of the parameter, use the $ prefix. The following example illustrates assigning a value to a variable and using it:

```
$ hero=popeye
$ echo Some say $hero is a hero
Some say popeye is a hero
```

Note that in the **echo** command, **hero** is printed literally, but **$hero** is replaced by its value, **popeye**. This is an example of "parameter substitution."

The quoting mechanisms discussed below can be used to assign more than one word to a variable. Filename pattern-matching is not used; that is, a command like

```
files=??
```

does not assign a list of all two-character filenames to **files**; it just assigns the two question-mark characters.

You can use command substitution to assign values:

```
files="`ls ??`"
```

Here `ls ??` is replaced with its output, and the double quotes make the list into a single value so that it can be assigned to **files**.

The shell uses several standard keyword parameters, or shell variables, that normally are assigned values during the login processes. In particular, **PATH**, **PS1**, **PS2**, **IFS**, and **MAILCHECK** are assigned default values. Other parameters may not be defined unless you or the system administrator place a definition in your **.profile** file. Here is a list of these standard parameters and their purpose:

PARAMETER	DESCRIPTION
HOME	The **cd** command, when used without an argument, changes directories to whatever directory **HOME** is set to. **HOME** generally is set to the user's home directory in the default **.profile** file assigned to new users.
PATH	When a shell executes a command, it uses **PATH** to decide which directories to search. Thus **PATH** is called the "search path" for execution. The Command Execution section later in the **sh** entry discusses the format.
CDPATH	Provides the search path used by the **cd** command. If you supply a relative pathname for a directory, the directories in this list are searched in turn for the directory. The format is the same as for **PATH** (see the Command Execution section).
MAIL	If this variable is set to the name of a mail file, the shell informs the user when new mail arrives in that file. With Release 2, this occurs only if **MAIL** is set and **MAILPATH** is not. (See the **mail** and **mailx** commands.)
MAILCHECK	Specifies the interval, in seconds, at which the shell checks for arrival of mail in the files specified by **MAILPATH** or **MAIL**. If it is set to 0, the shell checks before each primary prompt. The default value is 600 seconds. (See the **mail** and **mailx** commands.) New with Release 2.
MAILPATH	Similar to **MAIL**, except you can specify a list of files to be checked for new mail. Use a colon (:) to separate the filenames. In addition, you can follow each filename with a % sign and a message to be printed when new mail is reported. The default message is **you have mail**. New with Release 2.
PS1	The primary prompt string, printed when the shell awaits a command. The default is $.
PS2	The secondary prompt string, printed when the shell expects you to complete a command started on the previous line. The default is **>**.

(continued)

PARAMETER	DESCRIPTION	(continued)
IFS	Internal field separators, used by the shell to identify where words begin and end. The default separators are the space, tab, and newline characters.	
SHACCT	Set this parameter to the name of a file for which you have write permission, and the shell will keep an accounting record in the file of each shell procedure executed. New with Release 2.	
SHELL	When a shell is invoked, it checks its environment (see the Environment section below) for the value of **SHELL**. If the name exists and has an **r** in its basename, the shell is invoked as **rsh** (the restricted shell). New with Release 2.	

Automatic Parameters

The shell automatically sets the values for five parameters, which we have termed "automatic parameters." Most often, this type of parameter is used in shell procedures. Here they are:

PARAMETER	DESCRIPTION
#	The number of positional parameters (in decimal).
−	Flags supplied to the shell on invocation or by the **set** command (see the Built-In Commands and Invoking the Shell later in this entry).
?	The (decimal) command value returned by the last synchronously executed (foreground) command. This value is the exit value of the command if the command terminates normally. If the command terminates abnormally, octal 0200 (decimal 128) is added to the exit value to give the command value.
$	The process identification number (PID) of the current shell.
!	The PID of the last background command invoked.

The automatic parameters can be accessed by using the $ prefix:

```
$ pwd
/usr/games
$ echo The last command had an exit value of $?
The last command had an exit value of 0
```

Parameter Expressions

There are several special notations for using the values of parameters.

NOTATION	MEANING
$parameter	Represents the value of the parameter. As we have seen, it can be used with all three types of parameters. Two special usages are **$*** and **$@**, both of which represent a list of all the positional parameters, starting with **$1** and separated by spaces. They differ in how they behave when quoted (see the Quoting section later in this entry).

${parameter}	Also represents the value of the parameter. The difference between this and the preceding expression is that this form can be embedded in a string without confusion. Here is an example:
	
	```beast=tiger```
	```$ echo See the $beasts```
	```See the```
	```$ echo See the ${beast}s```
	```See the tigers```
	
	In the first case, the shell sought a shell variable named **beasts** and didn't find it. In the second case, **beast** was used.

The behavior of the remaining expressions depends on whether or not a parameter has been set to a non-null value. (Any of the following commands sets a parameter called **name** to a null value:

```
name=

name=''

name=""
```

There are no blanks between the quotes.)

NOTATION	MEANING

${parameter-:word}	The value of this expression is $parameter if parameter is set and non-null; otherwise, it is word. For example,
	
	```$ drink=water```
	```$ food=```
	```$ echo ${food:-cabbage} and ${drink:tea}```
	```cabbage and water```
	
	Here **drink** is set to **water**, so **water** is printed. But **food** is set to nothing, so the alternative (**cabbage**) is printed.

(continued)

NOTATION	MEANING	*(continued)*

Here is a more workaday example:
```
dir=${1:-.}
find $dir -name "*.c" -print
```
This might be used in a shell script to provide a default directory if none is given. If the script is used with an argument, then the first argument is assigned to the **dir** shell variable. If there are no arguments, **$1** is undefined and **dir** is set to ., the current directory. Then the **find** command uses $dir to determine which directory to search.

${*parameter*:=*word*}
Similar to the preceding construction, but has the added feature of assigning *word* to *parameter* if it is not set or if it is set to null. This construction cannot be used to assign values to positional parameters. Here is an example that provides a default value for a shell variable:
```
case $# in
        0) break;;
        *) dir=$1 ;;
esac
echo Directory is ${dir:=`pwd`}
find $dir -name "*.c" -print
```
If the script has no arguments (**$#** is 0), the case statement leaves **dir** undefined; otherwise, it is assigned the first argument. The **echo** statement then assigns the name of the current working directory to **dir** if **dir** is undefined. (Command substitution causes `pwd` to be replaced by its output.)

${*parameter*?*word*}** This has the same value as *$parameter* if *parameter* is set and is non-null; otherwise, *parameter* and *word* are printed and the shell is exited. If *word* is omitted, the default message **parameter null or not set is used. Here is an example:
```
: ${EMERGENCY?'This is no emergency--bye'}
echo stop now
```
If we put these lines in the **pm1.sh** script file and run them, we get this output:
```
pm1.sh: EMERGENCY: This is no emergency--bye
```
Here we use a common construction: the **${?}** form is used as an argument of the null command (:). The null command does nothing except evaluate its arguments. If the variable **EMERGENCY** is undefined, then evaluating the argument causes the message after the ? to be printed and the script to be exited. If **EMERGENCY** is defined, the null command does

NOTATION	MEANING

nothing and the script moves to the next line. If **EMERGENCY** is set outside this script, it must be exported (via the **export** command) so that its value will be known to the script.

${*parameter***:+***word***}**

If *parameter* is set and non-null, the value of this expression is *word*; otherwise, it has a null value. The following example uses the value of the **VERBOSE** parameter to determine whether or not to print a message:

```
echo ${VERBOSE:+'That was a bad choice'\\n}\\c
```

If **VERBOSE** is not set, the script is quiet. If it is set, the message is printed. This avoids having to use an **if** statement. Similar lines could be spread throughout the script, all controlled by the value of **VERBOSE**. The **\\c** construction causes **echo** not to print a blank line when **VERBOSE** is undefined. The **\\n** causes **echo** to print a newline when **VERBOSE** is defined. If **VERBOSE** is set outside the script, it must be exported if it is to be usable to the script.

In all these notations, *word* can be a string or an expression that reduces to a string. For instance, it can be the value of another shell variable or it can be the result of command substitution, as in **${food:=${drink}}** or **${name:='logname'}**. The first case assigns the value of **drink**, which was **water** in our earlier example, to **food** if **food** is undefined. The second assigns the output of the **logname** command to **name** if **name** is undefined. In these cases, the *word* expression is not evaluated unless it is needed; that is, if **food** is defined, the shell does not bother to determine the value of **drink**.

INTERPRETING COMMAND LINES When a command is typed, expressions using parameters are evaluated, command substitutions are made, and a corresponding command line is generated. For example, a command like

```
echo $SHELL `pwd`
```

becomes

```
echo /bin/sh /usr/columbo
```

Word Formation

Having generated the command line, the shell then breaks up this line into separate words using the internal field separators defined by the shell variable **IFS**. Explicit null arguments ("" and ' ') are preserved, but implicit null arguments, such as **$foom**, where **foom** is undefined or null, are dropped.

Several characters besides the **IFS** separators cause the termination of a word unless they are quoted (quoting will be discussed soon). These characters, which have special meaning to the shell, are ;, &, (,), ¦, ^, <, and >. The first five were discussed earlier in the Commands section. The ^ is an alternate symbol for ¦. The < and > are used in redirection (to be discussed later). Because these symbols can terminate words, constructions like

```
who¦wc>namelist
```

work the same as

```
who ¦ wc > namelist
```

Filename Generation

Once parameter and command substitution have taken place and the command line has been separated into words, each word is scanned for the special pattern-matching characters used by the shell: *, ?, and [. (The [is used in conjunction with], but the latter is special only when paired with the former.) A word containing these characters is considered to be a *pattern* that is replaced with those filenames that match it. The filenames are provided in alphabetic order. Certain characters must be matched explicitly: any slash (/), any initial period (.), or any period immediately after a slash. Aside from these restrictions, here is what the pattern-matching characters match:

PATTERN	MATCHES
*	Matches any string, including the null string. For example, the command **ls p*g** lists all files beginning with **p** and ending with **g**, including **pg** (no characters matched by *), **pig** (one character matched by *), and **ping** (two characters matched by *). The initial-period restriction means that ***p*** does not match **.profile**, but **.p*** does.
?	Matches any single character. For example, **h?** matches **ho** and **ha** but not **hat**, and **t??** matches **toy** and **tam** but not **to**.
[*list*]	Matches any single character from the enclosed list. For example, **m[oa]t** matches **mat** and **mot**, but not **moat**, which has two characters between the **m** and the **t** rather than one. A hyphen can be used to indicate a range. Thus **[A-Z]** matches any capital letter (assuming that the system uses ASCII, which encodes the capital letters consecutively.)
[!*list*]	Matches any single character not in *list*. For instance, **h[!k-z]g** matches **hag** but not **hog**.

Quoting

Many characters, such as * and &, have special meaning to the shell. To "quote" a character means to make it simply represent itself, rather than having a special meaning. (Sometimes quoting a character is called "escaping" a character.)

There are three ways to quote characters. The first is to precede the character with a backslash (\). Thus **ls** * lists all files, but **ls *** lists a file with the (poorly chosen) name *.

Normally, the newline character generated by striking the <enter> key marks the end of a command line. Striking \ just before <enter> causes the shell to ignore this special meaning of the newline character. Thus striking the backslash key before hitting <enter> provides one way of extending a command over more than one line.

All characters between two single quotes (except another single quote) are quoted. Thus '(acct$?)' is the same as \\(acct\\$\\?\\). You may find the first form easier to read and type.

Double quotes quote all included characters except \, ", ', and $. This allows parameter substitution, which uses $, and command substitution, which uses ', to take place. The backslash \ can be used to quote \, ", ', and $ within double quotes.

Here are illustrations of some of these properties:

```
$ deity=mars
$ echo '$deity' "$deity" "\$deity"
$deity mars $deity
$ dogs='tana talley'
$ echo $dogs
tana talley
```

Note that quoting allows the inclusion of spaces in words. Also note that the initial $ in the third line comes from the quoted $ in '$deity', and is not the system prompt.

Earlier we saw that $* and $@ both represent the entire list of positional parameters, beginning with $1. The difference between the two notations is in how they are interpreted when enclosed in double quotes:

- ☐ "$*" is the same as "$1 $2 ..."; that is, it puts the whole parameter list into a single word containing embedded spaces.
- ☐ "$@" is the same as "$1" "$2" ...; that is, it is as many words as there are positional parameters.

This distinction often is important in passing arguments in shell scripts.

ARGUMENTS When the shell runs a program, it passes the list of arguments from the command line to a command. For example, suppose you type

```
cat act1 act2
```

The words **act1** and **act2** are passed to **cat** as its first two arguments. As we saw earlier, when the shell passes arguments to a shell script, they are available as $1, $2, and so on.

Quoting can be used to affect how words are arranged into arguments. With the **grep** command, for example, the first argument is a search word and the remaining arguments are filenames. A command like

```
grep ice cream treats
```

causes **grep** to look for the string **ice** in the **cream** and **treats** files. But the command

```
grep 'ice cream' treats
```

causes **grep** to look for the string **ice cream** in the **treats** file. This is because including the space in quotes turns off its usual function as a word separator, making **ice cream** a single word.

The Environment

In addition to passing arguments to a program to be run, the shell passes something called the "environment." This is a list of parameter names and values that can be used by the executing program. When the login shell is invoked, it scans a standard environment provided by the system. For each variable-value pair it finds, it creates a shell variable with the specified name and assigns it the specified value. The environment can be augmented by definitions placed in your **.profile** file. If no changes are made, the standard environment is passed to each command executed by the shell or by any subshells.

An example of such an environmental variable is **PATH**. During the login process, **PATH** is initialized to your home directory, and that information is passed along to any subshells.

You can create new shell variables and modify the values of ones taken from the environment, usually without affecting the environment itself. For example, if you redefine **PATH** and then start a new shell, the original value of **PATH** is given to the new shell (assuming that **PATH** has not been exported, as described next). Then, when you return to the original shell, your redefined value becomes effective again.

However, you also have the option of modifying and adding to the environment. One way is to use the built-in **export** command to identify variables or changes to be placed in the environment. This example shows how **export** works:

```
$ echo $HOME                    Show value of HOME
/usr/granny
$ HOME=/usr/granny/Chips        Redefine HOME
$ DOG=talley                    Define DOG
$ sh                            Start new shell
$ echo $HOME
/usr/granny                     Original value of HOME
$ echo $DOG

                                Ignored; DOG not defined
$ <control-d> $ <enter>         Return to parent shell
$ export DOG HOME               Include in environment
$ sh                            Start a new shell
$ echo $HOME/$DOG
/usr/granny/Chips/talley        New shell knows them
```

Note that **export** accomplished two tasks. First, it added the **DOG** variable to the environment; now subshells of a subshell also will have a **DOG** in their environment. Second, it changed the value of **HOME**, an existing environment member.

The built-in **unset** command (see the discussion of **sh**'s built-in commands) removes a variable-value pair from the environment.

In summary, the environment passed to a command consists of the original environment inherited by the shell plus any changes and additions effected by **export** and minus members removed by **unset**.

Values can be exported down to subshells but not up to parent shells, because each child shell makes a copy of its parent's environment. Any changes made (including unsetting a variable) affect only the copy, not the original. Thus a shell script cannot be used to create or modify shell variables in the parent shell. (See the discussion of the built-in . command later in this section for a method of using a command file to alter the variables in the current shell.)

If you wish to pass an additional environmental variable to a simple command without adding the variable to the current environment, you can prefix the command with the variable's definition. Thus the command line

```
COUNT=25 repro
```

passes the variable **COUNT** and its value of **25** to the **repro** program's environment without affecting the shell's environment. (The **repro** program might be a shell script or C program that makes use of an environmental variable called **COUNT**.)

The built-in **set** command (to be discussed later) has two options that relate specifically to the environment. The **-k** option causes all shell variable definitions to be passed on to a command's environment, even if they follow the command line. Thus, when this option is in effect, the previous command can be written this way:

```
repro COUNT=25
```

Even if **repro** normally takes arguments, **COUNT = 25** is skipped as an argument and is placed in the environment.

The **-a** option for **set** causes all shell variable definitions and changes to act as if they were accompanied by an **export** command.

INPUT AND OUTPUT: REDIRECTION Many UNIX commands take input from the standard input, send output to the standard output, and send error messages to the standard error. The standard input, output, and error are three files that are connected automatically to these commands when they are executed. UNIX treats devices as files, and the standard input file is, by default, the keyboard, while the standard output and standard error are both, by default, the terminal screen (or printer in the case of a teletype-like terminal).

The three standard I/O files are assigned "file descriptor" values of 0, 1, and 2 respectively. (Other files opened by a command are assigned file descriptor numbers, too, with the first additional file being given file descriptor 3.)

The **sh** shell is able to alter the default assignments by using several forms of "redirection." Each of the forms of redirection listed below can appear anywhere in a command, including before or after it. Since they are instructions to the shell rather than to the command, they are not passed to the command; that is, they are not command arguments. Redirection is temporary, confined to the command using it. In the following list, *word* is a filename or something that produces a filename after substitution of values for parameters or of output for a command.

FORM	DESCRIPTION
<*word*	Uses the *word* file as standard input. For example,

<*word*
Uses the *word* file as standard input. For example,
```
tr "[A-Z] [a-z]" < stuff
```
causes the **tr** command to take input from the **stuff** file instead of from the keyboard. The same command could be typed
```
<stuff tr "[A-Z] [a-z]"
```
or even
```
tr <stuff "[A-Z][a-z]"
```
The first form is the usual one. Note that spaces around **<** are optional.

>*word*
Uses the *word* file as standard output. If the file exists already, it is truncated to zero length (wiped out) before the new input is copied in. If it doesn't exist, a new file is created. For example,
```
echo Save this, please. > save
```
redirects the output of **echo** to a file called **save**.

>>*word*
Similar to **>**, except that the output is appended to the *word* file if it already exists.

<<[-]*word*
Reads shell input (that is, input in response to the primary and secondary shell prompts) up to the first line that is the same as *word* or up to an end-of-file. The resulting input, called a "here document," becomes the standard input. Here is an example:
```
$ sort << stop
> boxes
> anterior
> owls
> stop
anterior
boxes
owls
```
As the secondary prompt (the **>**) indicated, the shell continued reading material until **stop** appeared. Then the material, not including **stop**, was sent to **sort** and sorted.

The **-** option causes initial tabs to be stripped from *word* and the document. This is useful in shell scripts, in which tabs may be used to indent the document for aesthetics and readability. Shell scripts sometimes contain "here documents" to provide standard input for commands in the script.

If any character in *word* is quoted, then all characters of the document are treated literally. Something like **$eyes** is treated as a five-character word and not as a shell variable, for instance. Otherwise, parameter substitution and command substitution (the backquote mechanism) are performed when indicated. If no character in *word* is quoted but you want to use a **$**, **'**, or **** literally, quote (escape) the character with a ****.

(continued)

315

FORM	DESCRIPTION	*(continued)*
<&*digit*	Uses the file associated with file descriptor *digit* as standard input.	
>&*digit*	Uses the file associated with file descriptor *digit* as standard output. For example, in shell scripts, the standard output often is routed to the standard error, so that error messages aren't lost if the script output is redirected. This is done using **>&2**, as in	

```
echo That\'s no way to type >&2
```

which sends the message to the terminal (the default file for the standard error) even if regular output is redirected or piped elsewhere.

<&-	Closes the standard input (useful in debugging shell scripts).	
>&-	Closes the standard output (also useful in debugging shell scripts).	

These redirection notations can be preceded with a digit to indicate which file descriptor is being affected. The default values are 0 for input redirection and 1 for output redirection. For example, **< phoo** is a shorter form of 0**< phoo**, and it means to associate the **phoo** file with 0, the standard input. The most common use is to provide redirection for the standard error (file descriptor 2), rather than the standard output. For example, you could use one file to collect regular output and a second file to collect error messages for a background job:

```
bigjob < bigdata > bigout 2> bigerr &
```

Here the **bigjob** program, which runs in the background, collects input from **bigdata**, and sends output to **bigout** and error messages to **bigerr**.

When more than one redirection command is used, they are performed left to right. Suppose, for example, you wish to collect error messages and standard output in the same file. Then you can do this:

```
bigjob < bigdata > bigout 2>&1 &
```

Again, **> bigout** makes **bigout** the standard output (file descriptor 1), but this time **2>&1** sends the standard error to the standard output; thus it also goes to **bigout**.

The commands you run in the background, unless redirected, send output and error messages to their default assignments, the terminal. But background jobs can't take input from the terminal, since terminal input is reserved for foreground jobs. Hence, for background jobs, the default standard input is **/dev/null**. This is an empty file.

THE INTERRUPT AND QUIT SIGNALS Normally, you can send INTERRUPT and QUIT signals to a command invoked from the shell. The INTERRUPT signal is generated by hitting the interrupt key, typically <del>. Usually, the <break> key, or <control-c>, has the same effect (see the **stty** entry and the "UNIX Features" entry about Special UNIX Characters). The INTERRUPT signal causes the program to abort unless the program has been instructed to act otherwise. The QUIT signal (typically generated by typing <control-\>) also aborts a program, but in addition it produces a "core dump." A core dump is a file containing the image (memory contents) of program code and data space at abort time. The built-in **trap** command (discussed later) allows shell scripts to react differently to these signals.

Programs running in the background ignore QUIT and INTERRUPT signals from the keyboard, so the **kill** command is needed to deal with them.

The shell itself ignores the QUIT signal. If run interactively, it also ignores the INTERRUPT signal.

COMMAND EXECUTION What happens when you type a command? First, parameter substitution, command substitution, and filename generation take place. Next, the **sh** shell checks to see if the command is one of the commands built into its program. If it is, **sh** jumps to that part of the program and performs as instructed; no new process is started. If the command is not a built-in one, the shell checks the list of defined shell functions. If it finds the command name there, the shell directly executes the corresponding list of instructions. The arguments to the function are made available to it as positional parameters (**$1**, **$2**, and so on).

If the command is neither a built-in command nor a function, then the shell starts a new process, which attempts to use the **exec( )** system call to run the command. The first task is to locate the file that contains the command. If the command name includes a /, then the file is sought in the indicated directory. For example, the command **/bin/date** causes **exec( )** to use the program found in the **/bin/date** file, and the command **Clab/sumup** causes **exec( )** to look for a file called **sumup** in the **Clab** subdirectory of the current directory.

If, however, you use just a simple filename, the system looks through a series of directories specified by the **PATH** environmental variable for the file. This variable is set equal to a list of directories. The colon (:) is used to separate directories, and a null entry means the current directory. For example, the assignment

```
PATH=:/bin:/usr/bin:$HOME/bin
```

means "first search the current directory (the null entry separated from **/bin** by the first colon) for the command file, then search **/bin**, then **/usr/bin**, then **$HOME/bin**." The last-named directory would be a subdirectory of the user's home directory. As soon as a matching name is found, the search is halted. Thus, if your current directory contains a command called **cat**, when you give the **cat** command, the version in your home directory is run instead of the system version.

If the file found in this manner has execute permission but doesn't conform to the usual executable machine code format, the file is assumed to be a shell script. In that case, a subshell is created to read and execute the commands in the script.

Release 2 added a "hashing" feature. The shell maintains a table of the locations of the commands it has executed so that it won't have to search all the **PATH** directories the next time the command is used. (The term "hash" comes from the name of the algorithm used to construct and search the table.) For example, if you use the **cat** command, **cat** is placed in the table along with the name of the directory in which it was found. The next time you use **cat**, the shell finds it in the table and uses the directory listed there. The built-in **hash** command allows you to view, add to, and delete from the current table. Redefining **PATH** clears the table.

The hash feature causes the shell to ignore **PATH** if the command you type is in the hash table. If the shell "remembers" with the help of the hash table that a command is in a particular directory and you install a new version in a different directory from the old version, the shell won't find the new version. In that case, use the built-in **hash** command to revise the hash table.

BUILT-IN COMMANDS The programming for the shell's built-in commands is part of the **sh** program. Thus the shell doesn't have to start a new process to run them and they therefore are faster to start than regular system commands. As of Release 2, these commands can use I/O redirection.

Most of the built-in commands are intended to provide tools for shell scripts. Some, like **cd**, are built in because it is important that the current shell rather than a new process execute them. Here is the list of built-in commands and what they do:

COMMAND	ACTION
:	The null command. Does nothing and has an exit value of zero. Can be used as a placeholder in program development, and offers an alternate way for making comments, since any words following it are considered arguments with which nothing is done. Another use is as a test command for a **while** loop. Since the null command has an exit value of zero, it always is considered successful, and hence creates an infinite loop. The loop can be broken from within with a **break** command (see below). Also see the example using **{?}** in the earlier Parameter Substitution section.
. *file*	The dot command. Causes the shell to read and execute the commands in *file*. Since the commands are run by the current shell, this mechanism can be used to create or modify shell variables in the current shell. A common use is to execute the commands in the **.profile** file after modifying it. The dot mechanism does not have the full power of standard shell scripts; for example, arguments are not passed to the commands in the file.
break [*n*]	Exits from the enclosing **for** or **while** loop (these loops were described earlier). If the loop is nested within other loops, you can use the optional *n* to indicate how many levels of looping to break through. Thus, if one loop is nested within one other loop, **break 2** breaks through them both. Normally, **break** is selected by a **case** or **if** statement in a loop if a certain condition occurs.
continue [*n*]	Resumes the next iteration of the enclosing **for** or **while** loop. This can be used to skip over part of a loop. The optional *n* can be used for nested loops. For example, **continue 2** means "resume at the next iteration of the loop enclosing the current loop." Normally, **continue** is selected by a **case** or **if** statement in a loop if a certain condition occurs.

(continued)

COMMAND	ACTION	*(continued)*
cd [*directory*]	Makes *directory* the current directory. If no argument is provided, uses the directory specified by the **HOME** environmental variable. If *directory* begins with a /, the indicated absolute pathname is used. If it contains a / but doesn't begin with one, the indicated relative pathname is used. If there is no / in *directory*, **cd** scans the list of directories given by the **CDPATH** parameter for the directory. This list uses a colon to separate directory names, and a null name is interpreted to be the current directory. For example, either of the following instructs **cd** to look first in the current directory, then in the home directory, for a subdirectory:	

```
CDPATH=.:$HOME
CDPATH=:$HOME
```

Each shell has its own concept of the current directory, so changing a directory in a subshell, then returning to the original shell, places you in the last directory remembered by the original shell.

echo	Echoes arguments. (See the **echo** command entry for details. Before Release 2, **echo** was a regular command rather than a built-in shell command.)	
eval [*arg(s)*]	The shell reads **eval**'s arguments and executes them as commands. The **eval** command, like the **{}** mechanism and the **.** command, causes the current shell, and not a subshell, to execute the commands. It differs from **{}** in that **eval** causes the shell to rescan the command line after substitutions have been made. This allows a script to construct a command line using, say, shell variables. For example, consider the following:	

```
cmd=ls
next='¦ wc'
eval $cmd $next
```

The two shell variables are evaluated, and the current shell then executes the resulting command of **ls ¦ wc**.

exec [*arg(s)*]	Here the arguments specify a command and its arguments. The command is executed. No new process is used; the command replaces the current shell process. Thus, when that command exits, control reverts to the parent of the original shell.	
exit [*n*]	Causes the shell to exit with an exit value of *n*. A shell script might use this command to terminate execution under certain circumstances. If no exit value is provided, the exit value of the last command executed by the shell is used. An end-of-file also causes a shell to exit. The end-of-file could be the literal end of a shell script file or the EOF signal generated by striking (typically) <control-d> at the beginning of a line.	

COMMAND	ACTION
export [*name(s)*]	Marks the indicated parameter names for export to the environment of any commands subsequently executed (see the earlier Environment discussion). The parameter itself can be defined before or after the name is marked for export. Function names cannot be exported. If **export** is invoked without arguments, it lists those names currently marked for export.
hash [**-r**] [*name(s)*]	Since Release 2, UNIX System V maintains a table identifying which **PATH** directory contains commands, and commands are added to the table as they are used. Using **hash** with no arguments displays information about the "remembered" commands. If command names are provided as arguments, they are added to the table. If the **-r** option is specified, the table is cleared.
pwd	Displays the name of the current working directory. (This command also is described in its own entry; prior to Release 2, it was a regular command, not a built-in command.)
read [*name(s)*]	Reads one line from the standard input. The first word of input is assigned to a parameter bearing the first name in the list of names. The second word goes to the second name, and so on. Any leftover words go to the last name in the list. Only the characters from the **IFS** shell parameter list are recognized as word delimiters. The command has an exit value of zero unless EOF is encountered.

The **read** command commonly is used for interactive input in a shell script, as in:

```
echo What is your name\?
read NAME
echo Say hey, $NAME
```

Here the entire line entered in response to the question **What is your name?** is assigned to **NAME**, since it is the only argument.

If no argument is given, **read** reads and then discards a line of input.

readonly [*name(s)*]	
	Marks the indicated variable names as read-only, meaning that their values cannot be reassigned later. Thus this command creates named constants. Without arguments, **readonly** causes a list of the existing read-only variables to be displayed.
return [*n*]	When used within a function definition, causes the function to exit with an exit status of *n*. If *n* is omitted, the exit status is that of the last command executed within the function. New with Release 2.

(continued)

COMMAND	ACTION	*(continued)*

set [*flag(s)* [*arg(s)*]]

Performs a variety of functions. First, when invoked with no arguments or flags, it displays the names and values of all currently defined shell variables and the names and definitions of all currently defined functions. Second, when invoked with arguments, **set** assigns the values of the successive arguments to the positional parameters $1, $2, and so on. Third, **set** can be used to set and unset flags that modify the behavior of the current shell. Here's a list of the flags, several of which can be used as debugging tools for shell scripts.

FLAG	ACTION
–a	Marks for export those variables that are modified or created (see the earlier Environment discussion). New with Release 2.
–e	Exits immediately if a command exits with a non-zero exit status.
–f	Disables filename generation, treating *, ?, and [as ordinary characters. New with Release 2.
–h	Locates and remembers commands used in a function when the function is defined. Normally, the commands aren't located by the hashing feature until the function is run. New with Release 2.
–k	Places all keyword arguments (parameter definitions of the form *name=value*), not just those preceding the command name, in the environment of a command (see The Environment discussion above).

The following five flags are useful for debugging.

FLAG	ACTION
–n	Reads commands but does not execute them.
–t	Reads and executes one command, then exits.
–u	Treats unset variables as an error when substituting.
–v	Displays shell input lines as they are read.

COMMAND	ACTION	
	FLAG	ACTION
	-x	Displays commands and their arguments as they are executed, showing them as they look after parameter substitution, command substitution, and filename generation have taken place.
	--	Does not change any of the flags. This option is used when you wish to set $1 to -, as in set -- - Just typing **set -** would make **set** think an erroneous flag had been given.

To unset (turn off) any of the flags, precede them with a **+** instead of -.

The automatic parameter value $- provides the current flag settings. Use **echo $-** to display them.

shift [*n*]	Shifts the positional parameters over *n* places. If *n* is omitted, it is assumed to be 1. Thus **shift** without arguments causes $2 to become $1, $3 to become $2, and so on. And **shift 3** causes $4 to become $1, and so forth. $0 (the command name) is unaffected. Note, however, that the old value of $1 is lost with each **shift**. This command is useful in **while** loops for processing a sequence of arguments.
test	Evaluates conditional expressions so that the exit status of **test** can be used to control **while** loops, **until** loops, and **for** statements. For instance, a comparison that is "true" is converted to an exit value of zero (see the separate **test** entry in "UNIX Commands" for details). This is the opposite of many languages, such as C, which use zero to mean "false."
times	Displays the accumulated user time and system time for processes run from the shell. The cumulative total, not the totals for individual processes, is shown.

(continued)

COMMAND	ACTION	(continued)

trap [*arg*] [*n*] ...   Controls the shell's response to various signals. When signal number *n* is received, the shell reads and executes the commands given by *arg*. More than one signal number can be given. The signal list is system-dependent and typically can be found in the **/usr/include/signal.h** file. Common values are 1 for the signal generated by hanging up a phone line, 2 for the signal generated with the INTERRUPT key (typically <del>, with <break> usually working, too), and 3 for the signal generated by the QUIT key (typically <control-\>).

The **trap** command often is used in shell scripts to modify the default response to signals. For example, if you want the script to remove a temporary file when the script is interrupted, you can place the following command in the script:

```
trap 'rm tempfile; exit 1' 1 2 3
```

If any of signals 1, 2, or 3 is received, the shell running the script carries out the commands in quotes; that is, it removes a file and exits. The quotes serve to make the command sequence a single argument for **trap**.

If *arg* is omitted, the responses to the named signals are reset to the system default values. If *arg* is a null string (''), the shell ignores the indicated signals. If *n* is 0, then the command in *arg* is executed when the shell exits. If no arguments and no signal numbers are given, **trap** displays the signal numbers currently being trapped and the commands associated with them. This is useful for debugging.

type [*name(s)*]   Indicates how *name(s)* would be interpreted if typed as a command; that is, displays the absolute pathname used. This is useful if you have the same command name in more than one directory. New with Release 2.

ulimit [-f *n*]   If the **-f** *n* option is used, sets a size limit of *n* blocks for files written by the shell and its child processes. If no option is used (or if *n* is omitted), displays the current size limit. If *n* is given and **-f** is omitted, it is nonetheless assumed to be present. Most users can use **ulimit** only to decrease the limit; the superuser can also use it to increase the limit.

umask [*nnn*]   Sets the user creation mask to *nnn*. If *nnn* is omitted, displays the current value. (The creation mask is used when permissions are set for a new file. It is a three-digit octal number in the format described in the **chmod** entry. The mask indicates permissions to be denied. The usual default is 022, meaning that write permission for group members and for others is not allowed.)

COMMAND	ACTION
unset [*name(s)*]	Removes the variables and functions listed in *name(s)*. The variables **PATH**, **PS1**, **PS2**, **MAILCHECK**, and **IFS** cannot be unset. New with Release 2.
wait [*n*]	Calls the shell to wait for the process whose process identification number (PID) is *n*, then reports the exit status of the process when it finishes. If *n* is omitted, all child processes that are active are waited for, and an exit status of zero is reported. Since the shell waits for foreground processes anyway, this command is used with jobs that are run in the background.

SPECIAL COMMANDS Two special commands have been added with Release 3.

COMMAND	ACTION
getopts	Used in shell scripts to parse positional parameters and to check for legal options. This command is described under its own entry. New with Release 3.
newgrp	Equivalent to **exec newgrp**. Also described under its own entry. New with Release 3.

INVOKING THE SHELL The login procedure invokes the shell as **-sh**. This causes the shell to first read commands from the **/etc/profile** file and then from the **$HOME/.profile** file, if they exist. Thereafter, you can invoke a subshell by giving the **sh** command. When **sh** is invoked with arguments (and without the **-c** or **-s** flag set), the first argument is assumed to be a file of commands, and the remaining arguments are assumed to be arguments to be used by the command file. For example, a command like

```
sh flipflop can bottle
```

causes the shell to execute the commands in the **flipflop** file and to pass to the commands **can** and **bottle** as positional parameters **$1** and **$2**.

If **sh** is invoked without arguments (other than flags), the subshell takes commands from the standard output. Use **exit** or end-of-file (typically <control-d>) to terminate the child shell and return to the parent.

All the flags discussed under **set** can be used when invoking **sh**. In addition, the following flags are available:

FLAG	ACTION
−c *string*	Reads commands from *string* instead of from a file or from the standard input. For example, the command `sh -c 'date; ls'` runs the **date** command, followed by an **ls** command.
−s	Reads commands from the standard input. Arguments, if present, are assigned to positional parameters. The shell output (other than that from built-in commands) is sent to the standard error.
−i	Makes the shell interactive. This causes a TERMINATE signal (such as that generated by **kill** 0) to be ignored. When this flag is set, **kill** 0 terminates all child processes but not the shell itself. The INTERRUPT signal is ignored by the shell. The QUIT signal is ignored by the shell whether or not **−i** is set.
−r	Invokes the restricted shell (see **rsh**).

EXIT STATUS The shell returns a non-zero status when it detects errors, such as syntax errors. If the error occurs in a shell procedure that is being executed non-interactively, the shell file is abandoned. A shell that terminates normally returns the exit status of the last command executed.

SEE ALSO UNIX Commands: **chmod; ps; test; echo**
UNIX Features: Standard I/O, Redirection, and Pipes; Exit Values; Processes; Command Lines; Command Substitution; Special UNIX Characters; Filename Generation; Shell Variables; Shell Scripts; The Shell and the Kernel; Quoting; Extending Commands over More than One Line; Parameter Substitution

PURPOSE   Use the **shl** command to run more than one interactive shell from a terminal. **shl** allows you to switch back and forth between tasks.

FORMAT   shl

DESCRIPTION   UNIX System V lets you run many tasks in the background. However, normally you can run only one interactive shell in the foreground. (An interactive shell is one that processes your keyboard commands and sends you the shell "ready" prompt.) The **shl** command allows you to set up several interactive shells, known as "layers," to run concurrently. Only one layer can be interactive, or current, at a time, but you can switch back and forth between layers.

COMMON USES   You can use **shl** when you need to work on several tasks concurrently.

OVERVIEW   Invoking **shl** places you in the **shl** command mode. A distinctive prompt (**>>>**) indicates that you are in this mode. Several built-in commands allow you to create, delete, resume, and otherwise manage layers. Once in a layer, which works like a standard shell, you can return to the command level by typing the **swtch** character. This usually is set to <control-z>, but can be set to another character with the **stty** command.

LAYERS AND VIRTUAL TERMINALS   A normal interactive shell is bound to a particular physical terminal; that is, its standard input, standard output, and standard error files are identified with the terminal. But a normal background shell, such as one running a shell script in the background, is not bound to a terminal. A layer is a shell that is bound to a "virtual" terminal; that is, to a "ghost" terminal existing in the imagination of the software but having no physical existence. It can, however, be manipulated like a real terminal, using commands such as **stty**.

Each layer is associated with its own virtual terminal, and there can be up to seven of these pairings. The **shl** commands let you specify one layer to be the "current layer." This makes your actual terminal correspond to the particular virtual terminal associated with the current layer. In essence, the **shl** command and the virtual-terminal system allow your physical terminal to become any one of up to seven terminals, each running its own set of jobs. You then can switch around among the terminals (see Figure 4).

The current layer is the one that receives any keyboard input. Another layer attempting to read from the keyboard is blocked until you switch to that layer. Output from all layers normally is sent to the screen, so that if one layer produces output while you are, say, editing a file in a second layer, the output appears in the middle of your work. Such output does not affect the work you

327

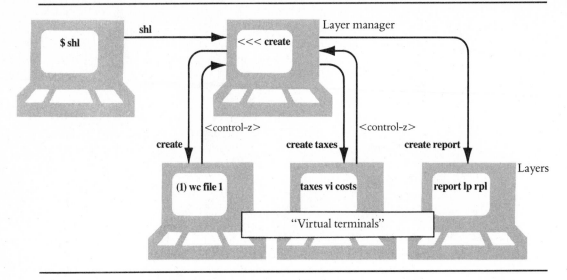

FIGURE 4. *Layers*

are engaged in, but it can muddle the appearance of the screen. To prevent a particular layer from sending output to the screen when not current, switch to that layer (as described later), and use the **stty** flag **loblk** (layer-output block) to block further output. Or you can use the **block** command from the **shl** command mode (see below).

THE shl COMMANDS Most of the following commands make use of a layer "name." A name is a sequence of characters delimited by a space, tab, or newline. Only the first eight characters are significant, so **checkmate** and **checkmatch** would be considered the same name. The names (1), (2), through (7) are reserved for the use of **shl**; they are default names used when no name is provided. The names include the parentheses, but they can be abbreviated to 1, 2, and so on.

The following commands can be issued from the **shl** command mode, which is identified by the **>>>** prompt:

COMMAND	ACTION
create [*name*]	Creates a layer called *name* and makes it the current layer. If *name* is not given, **shl** assigns a name of the form (1), (2), and so forth. The actual digit used is the last digit of the name of the associated virtual terminal. The default prompt provided for the layer consists of the layer name followed by a space.

COMMAND	ACTION
block *name* *[name(s)]*	Prevents each named layer from sending output to the terminal when it is not the current layer. Output is held until you return to the blocked layer.
delete *name* *[name(s)]*	Deletes each named layer. This sends the **SIGHUP** (hang–up) signal to each process originated by the layer. This signal normally causes processes to terminate unless they have been programmed to treat the signal otherwise (see **trap** under **sh**).
help, or ?	Displays a summary of how the **shl** commands are used.
layers [-l] *[name(s)]*	Lists the layer name and its process group for each *name*. This is like doing a **ps** on the specified layers. The –l option specifies a long listing. If no names are given, all existing layers are listed. (See **ps**.)
resume *[name]*	Makes the layer called *name* the current layer. If *name* is omitted, makes the most recently current layer current again.
toggle	Resumes the layer that was current before the last current layer; that is, if you just returned from layer (**3**) and previously had been using layer (**5**), **toggle** returns you to layer (**5**).
unblock *name* *[name(s)]*	Reverses the effects of **block**. Processes running in the specified layers now send output to the terminal.
quit	Exits **shl**, sending all layers the **SIGHUP** signal (see **delete** above).
name	Makes the layer called *name* the current layer.

To go from a layer to the command level, type the **swtch** character, typically a <control-z>.

COMMENTS The **shl** command offers "job control," giving you, in effect, the ability to shift different tasks from foreground to background and back.

SEE ALSO UNIX Commands: **sh; ps; stty**
UNIX Features: Processes; Special UNIX Characters

EXAMPLES

1. Start up the **shl** program.

   ```
   $ shl
   >>>
   ```

   Note the special **shl** prompt.

2. Create a layer from within **shl**.

   ```
   >>> create
   (1)
   ```

   No name is given, so the default name (1) is selected.

3. Run a command in a layer and return to the **shl** command level.

   ```
   (1) ex props
   :a
   We developed four proposals for the Cheddar Chow account, and,
   after careful review, decided to go with one developed by Doris
   Daze's group.
   .
   :<control-z>
   >>> create cheese
   cheese mail doris
   Doris, get your group going with that Cheddar Chow idea.
   .
   (EOT)
   cheese <control-z>
   >>>
   ```

   Now the user can switch to the (1) layer and resume editing the **props** document.

PURPOSE Use the **sleep** command to suspend execution for a while.

FORMAT **sleep** *time*

Here *time* is the time in seconds.

DESCRIPTION The **sleep** command causes a task to wait for the indicated number of seconds before resuming.

COMMON USES You can use **sleep** to delay execution of a command or in a loop to provide a time delay in the performance of a periodic task.

SEE ALSO UNIX Commands: **sh**; **true**; **false**
UNIX Features: Shell Scripts

EXAMPLES

---

1. Delay the execution of a command.

```
(sleep 600; echo TIME TO QUIT) &
```

The parentheses (see **sh**) cause the two commands to be grouped together, and the **&** (again, see **sh**) causes them to run in the background, freeing the terminal for other work. The **sleep** portion causes the system to wait **600** seconds, or 10 minutes, before the **echo** command sends you the specified message.

2. Repeat a command every so often.

```
while true
do
      date
      echo Time is passing, so work harder.
      sleep 300
done &
```

This **while** loop repeats its obnoxious message every 5 minutes. Because it is run in the background (the **&**), you can use the terminal for other business. (The **while** loop is discussed under **sh**, and **true** is a standard UNIX command.)

---

sort

PURPOSE Use the **sort** command for sorting and merging text files.

FORMAT sort [*option(s)*] [*file(s)*]

DESCRIPTION The **sort** command takes input from a list of text files, sorts it by line, and sends the sorted output, by default, to the screen. If more than one input file is supplied, the files are merged during sorting.

Various options determine the sorting order. By default, **sort** uses the "machine collating sequence." This places characters in the order of the numeric codes used in the machine to represent the characters. Most UNIX systems use the ASCII code, in which alphabetic characters have their usual alphabetic sequence, and the uppercase characters, as a group, precede all the lowercase characters. The collating sequence also includes other characters, such as digits, punctuation, the space character, and nonprinting characters, such as the tab character.

Other options determine which portions of a line are used to determine the sorting order. Each portion used is called a "sort key." By default, there is just one sort key: the entire line.

COMMON USES You can use **sort** to sort files alphabetically or numerically, in forward or reverse order, by whole lines or by particular fields in a line. Also, you can use it to merge files and to remove duplicate lines.

INPUT AND OUTPUT Unless the **-o** option is invoked, **sort** sends its output to the standard output, which is, by default, the terminal screen. Redirection can be used to reroute the output to a file, and a pipe can be used to send the output to another command, as in:

```
sort guests1 guests2 > guests
sort maillist ! lp
```

In the first command, the contents of **guests1** and **guests2** are merged, sorted, and redirected to the **guests** file. In the second command, the sorted output is piped to the **lp** command for printing.

Normally, **sort** takes input from the list of files. If no files are listed, **sort** reads the standard input, which is, by default, the keyboard but which can be a redirected file or output piped from another command:

```
who ! sort
```

The hyphen, when used in place of a filename, stands for the standard input. This allows the output from a pipe to be merged with a file:

```
who ! sort oldwho - > newwho
```

The **who** command generates a list of who currently is logged in. The **oldwho** command presumably contains material of the same type saved from a previous **who** command. The **sort** command combines the old material (**oldwho**) and the new (represented by -), and sorts the combined input. The results are placed in the **newwho** file.

OPTIONS The **sort** options fall into three groups: those that alter the general behavior of **sort**, those that describe the ordering to be used, and those that define the sort keys to be used.

Altering the Behavior of sort

OPTION	ACTION
-c	Checks to see if the input file is in sorted order. The exact order expected depends on what other options, if any, are given. There is no output unless the file is not in the order tested for, in which case **sort** informs you that the file is not sorted.
-m	Merges the files in sorted order, assuming the input files already are sorted. (The **sort** command merges multiple files into sorted order by default, but it can do so much faster if it knows the input files already are sorted.)
-u	Suppresses all but one of any lines with the same sort key. Since the sort key is, by default, the whole line, this option suppresses multiple lines unless another key is specified.
-o *output*	Sends the output to the *output* file; this name can be that of one of the input files. Space between the **-o** and the filename is optional.
-y*kmem*	Sets to *kmem* kilobytes the initial amount of main memory set aside for sorting; otherwise, **sort** starts out using a system default memory size. In either case, more memory is used as needed until the administrative maximum is reached. If *kmem* is larger than that maximum or if **-y** with no argument is used, the maximum amount of memory is used. If *kmem* is smaller than the administrative minimum, the minimum amount is used; thus **-y** 0 guarantees that **sort** will start with the minimum amount. The purpose of this option is to maximize performance, because it is wasteful to use a large amount of memory for a small file or to start with a small amount for an extensive file.

Specifying the Ordering

OPTION	ACTION
-d	Uses "dictionary" order. Only letters, digits, and blanks (spaces and tabs) are significant in comparisons; punctuation, for example, is ignored.
-f	"Folds" lowercase letters into uppercase; this causes **uncle**, **Uncle**, and **UNCLE** all to be sorted in the same fashion.
-i	Ignores characters outside the ASCII range 040 (octal) through 0176 (octal) in non-numeric comparisons. The range 040 through 0176 includes letters, digits, punctuation, and other printing characters, such as ¦. It excludes the various control characters.
-M	Compares as months. The first three non-blank characters of each field are treated as uppercase and compared. Thus **January** is compared as if it were **JAN**. **JAN** precedes **FEB**, and so on. Fields that are not months are treated as preceding **JAN**. The -b option automatically is placed in effect. New with Release 3.
-n	Orders numerically; that is, by numeric value rather than by character value. The default order, for example, places 1342 before 3 because the first character of 1342–1–comes before the character 3 in the collating sequence. For numeric sorting to work, the numeric string must come first in the line or, more generally, in the sort field. A numeric string consists of optional initial blanks, which are ignored, an optional minus sign, and zero or more digits, which may include a decimal point. The -n option does not correctly sort exponential numbers, such as 2.314E10.
-r	Reverses the order.

If these options precede sort-key specifications (described next), they apply globally to all sort keys. When they are attached to a particular sort key, they apply to that key only and override any global settings.

Specifying Restricted Sort Keys

By default **sort** works with whole lines. It sorts by the first character in a line. If two lines have the same first character, then the second characters are compared, and so on, until the correct order is found or until it is determined that the lines are identical. Ordinarily, leading blanks (spaces or tabs) count as characters. Since a space character comes before the letters in the ASCII code, a line with an initial blank precedes a line beginning with, say, an A.

You can use a "restricted sort key," which means using just part of the line for sorting. To do that, **sort** divides each line into "fields." By default, the blank (a space or a tab) acts as a field separator, so the line

```
Have a nice pay.
```

consists of four fields. Any blanks preceding the first word are part of the first field, and if subsequently there are two or more sequential blanks, the first blank is a separator and the remaining blanks are part of the next field. Thus the line

```
Have a   nice pay.
```

has " **Have**" for the first field and " **nice**" for the third field.

The following notations are used to indicate which fields to use:

NOTATION	MEANING
+*pos1* [*-pos2*]	Means start the comparison at position *pos1* and end it at position *pos2*. If *pos2* is missing, means go to the end of the line. Here *pos1* and *pos2* are numbers in the form *m.n*, optionally followed by flags that are discussed later. The notation **+***m.n* means start at character *n***+**1 in field *m***+**1. Thus **+**2.3 means start at the fourth character of the third field. Another way of expressing this is to say **+**2.3 means skip two fields and three characters. (See Figure 5.) To start at the beginning of a field, you can omit the *.n* portion. Similarly, the notation *-m.n* means to continue *through* the *n*th character following the *m*th field. The field separator is included in the character count. Omitting the *.n* portion is the same as using *-m.*0, meaning end at the last character of field *m* (the 0th character after field *m*).

FIGURE 5. *Sort-key notation*

You can use multiple sort keys. Lines are sorted first using the first key, then ties are resolved using the second key, and so on. For example, the **sort** command

```
sort +1 -3 +4 -5 suppliers
```

means to begin by sorting the lines on the basis of fields 2 through 3 (skip field 1 and go to the end of field 3). Then sort those lines that have the same first sort key on the basis of the second sort key, field 5 (skip 4 and go to the end of 5).

Any lines that are still considered equal after going through all the sort keys finally are sorted on the basis of the entire line, with all characters considered significant.

Two more options pertain to restricted sort keys:

OPTION	ACTION
-t*c*	Uses the character *c* as the field separator. Each occurrence counts; that is, *cc* is an empty field with a separator on each side. (This is unlike the case for the default blank, where the second blank is considered part of the field.)
-b	Ignores leading blanks when determining the starting and ending positions for a restricted sort key. Placing the -b option before the first +*pos1* argument causes all +*pos1* arguments to be affected. Or it can be attached independently to individual +*pos1* and -*pos2* arguments.

In general, any of the **b, d, f, i, n,** and **r** options can be included in the position arguments. For example,

```
sort +2nr -3 +5fd -8
```

means sort on field 2 in reverse numeric order, then on fields 6 through 8 in dictionary order, folding lowercase into uppercase.

COMMENTS Certain conditions, such as input lines of excessive length or the -c option detecting disorder, cause **sort** to make a comment and terminate with a non-zero exit status.

The **sort** command expects all lines, including the last line, to be terminated with a newline character. Files created by the UNIX text editor automatically terminate this way. If the final newline character is missing, **sort** appends one to the output, issues a message, and continues.

Some commands, such as **comm** and **join**, require sorted input.

The **uniq** command provides a duplicate line service somewhat different from **sort**'s.

SEE ALSO   UNIX Commands: **uniq**; **join**; **comm**
UNIX Features: Standard I/O, Redirection, and Pipes; Filters; The Machine Collating Sequence

EXAMPLES

---

1. Sort a file of names and collect the output in the same file.

```
sort -o porkers porkers
```

Note that while redirection can be used to collect output in a file, it cannot be used to collect output in the original file; that is, a command like

```
sort -o porkers > porkers       Bad command
```

results in redirection clearing the **porkers** file before it gets sorted.

2. Sort a file numerically on the basis of the second field.

```
sort +1n -2 lotto
```

This does not necessarily produce the same order as the following version:

```
sort -n +1 -2 lotto
```

Both versions look at field 2 (skip 1 and go to end of 2) and sort it numerically. The potential difference comes in how ties are resolved. In both cases, lines with the same field 2 are sorted on the basis of the whole line. In the first case, however, the **-n** option applies just to the field, while the second case uses a global **-n** option, so it applies to the whole line. Thus if the first field also is numeric, the second version resolves ties by sorting the lines numerically. But the first version resolves ties by sorting the lines by characters; for example, 245 would come before 31, since 2 comes before 3.

3. Sort a file using another field separator.

```
sort -t: +3n -4 +2n -3 /etc/passwd
```

The **/etc/passwd** file contains information about system users, and it uses a colon as a field separator. The fourth field (delimited by **+3 -4**) is the group ID of a user, and the third field (delimited by **+2 -3**) is the user ID. Thus this command sorts the **/etc/passwd** file by group number. Entries with the same group number then are sorted in order of user ID.

(continued)

---

4. Combine two files, sort them, and eliminate duplicate lines.

```
sort -u team85 team86 > team
```

By default, **sort** merges the sorted output of two input files. The **-u** option eliminates duplicate lines. If we knew that **team85** and **team86** were already sorted, we could use the **-m** option to save time.

5. See if a file is sorted.

```
$ sort -c invites
sort: disorder: Trinkle, Rene
$
```

The line **Trinkle, Rene** is the first line found out of order. If no lines are out of order, **sort** exits without a message.

6. Use **sort** to sort information in a command line.

```
find . -name "*.c" -print ¦ sort ¦ pg ¦ lp
```

This **find** command finds all files in the current directory and its subdirectory tree whose names end in .c. It outputs this list of filenames to **sort**, which places them in alphabetic order. The **pg** command passes on the contents of each file in the list to the **lp** command to be printed, adding the name of each file before its contents. This example illustrates that many UNIX commands are designed to be "filters" and that **sort** is not restricted to working on the contents of regular files.

PURPOSE   Use the **spell** command to check the spelling of words.

FORMAT   spell [*option(s)*] [*file(s)*]

DESCRIPTION   The **spell** command compares words from the indicated files to words in its spelling list. If it cannot find the word in the list or derive it from the list by adding suitable prefixes, inflections, and suffixes, it prints the offending word on the standard output, which is, by default, the screen. This command collects words from the standard input if no files are listed.

COMMON USES   You can use **spell** to check the spelling of a document by obtaining a list of suspect words.

OPTIONS   The **spell** command has five options:

OPTION	ACTION
-v	Prints all words not literally on the list, showing plausible derivations, if any, from words on the list; that is, shows the word along with any plausible prefixes and suffixes that would reproduce it from a root word.
-b	Uses British spelling, such as *behaviour*, *centre*, and *standardise*.
-x	Prints plausible stems (prefixed with **=**) for each word being checked until a matching stem is found or until no candidates remain.
+*sp_file*	Removes any words found in *sp_file* from **spell**'s output. This allows you to supplement **spell**'s list with a personal list of acceptable spellings. The file must contain one word per line in sorted order. Possible derivations are not explored, so placing **Waite** in the list does not catch **Waites**. In the future, this option will be changed to -f*sp_file* to conform with general UNIX practice.
-l	By default, **spell** follows chains of included files requested in **troff** documents, except for those files whose pathnames begin with **/usr/lib**. The **-l** option causes even these files to be included in the spelling check. New with Release 3.

COMMENTS   The **spell** command does not, of course, recognize misspelled words that are correctly spelled for a different context; that is, "Ireland, the Emerald Aisle" passes muster. Nor does the **spell** command suggest correct spellings.

EXAMPLES

1. Obtain a list of potentially misspelled words.

```
$ spell momletter
Crockmorton
thier
```

The output consists of one word per line. Words in the list are not necessarily mis-spelled; they merely may be unknown to **spell**.

2. See what assumptions **spell** is making to match your words.

```
$ spell -v momletter
Crockmorton
thier
+ing        thinking
```

The last line means **thinking** is not in the list, but it can be matched by adding **ing** to **think,** which is in the list.

3. See what assumptions **spell** is making in general.

```
$ cat text
desperately seeking the unknown thenger
$ spell text
=desperately
=desperate
=seeking
=seeke
=seek
=the
=thenger
=thenge
=theng
=unknown
=known
thenger
```

This means, for example, that **spell** sought **seeking** and didn't find it, so it then looked for **seeke.** Not finding that, it looked for **seek.** The word **thenger** is printed at the end because none of the proposed stems was found in **spell**'s dictionary.

PURPOSE Use the **split** command to split a file into smaller pieces.

FORMAT **split** [-*n*] [*file* [*oname*]]

DESCRIPTION The **split** command reads the *file* file (or the standard input if *file* is omitted or is -) and copies it in chunks of *n* lines each into a set of output files. If *n* is omitted, pieces of 1000 lines each are used. If *oname* is provided, the destination file for the first chunk is called *oname***aa**, the file for the second chunk is *oname***ab**, and so on up to *oname***zz**. This provides for up to 26 times 26, or 676, files. If *oname* is omitted, **x** is used instead. If *oname* is used, the name must have at most two fewer characters than the maximum filename length, so that the two extra characters can be tacked on.

COMMON USES You can use **split** to reduce a huge file to more manageable chunks.

OPTIONS The **split** command has only one option:

OPTION	ACTION
-*n*	Splits the output into chunks of *n* lines each. The default value is 1000.

COMMENTS The **csplit** command provides for splitting a file into unequal parts. The line numbers of the break points can be given explicitly, or the break points can be specified by context.

SEE ALSO UNIX Commands: **csplit**

EXAMPLES

1. Split a large file into smaller pieces.

```
split -100 bigrelative br
```

The first **100** lines of **bigrelative** are copied into **braa**, the second **100** are copied into **brab**, and so on.

stty

PURPOSE Use the **stty** command to set and display terminal options.

FORMAT stty [-a] [-g] [*term-flags*]

Here *term-flags* is a list of terminal option settings.

DESCRIPTION Terminals come with a wide variety of capabilities and default behavior. The **stty** command enables you to control various terminal properties, such as the baud rate (rate at which bytes are sent) and the functions of certain keys. When **stty** is typed with no arguments, it displays a selected group of settings. Otherwise, you can include a list of terminal options, or "flags," for it to implement. Some combinations of flags are senseless, but **stty** leaves it to you to avoid such combinations.

COMMON USES You can use **stty** to match the behavior of a particular terminal to your needs.

OPTIONS The **stty** command has two options:

OPTION	ACTION
-a	Lists all flag settings.
-g	Generates a list of current flag settings in a form that can be used as an argument to another **stty** command.

TERMINAL FLAGS The list of settings can be divided into six groups. The majority of the flags, as indicated, are enabled by typing the flag name and disabled by preceding the flag name with a hyphen. In the following descriptions, the actions in parentheses refer to the hyphen form of the flag.

Control Modes

FLAG	MEANING
parenb (-parenb)	Enables (disables) parity generation and detection. The parity of a byte is even if the byte has an even number of 1 bits and odd otherwise. With parity generation, an extra bit is added to each byte when it is transmitted. The extra bit records the parity. When the terminal (or computer) receives a byte, it then can check to see if the parity bit is the same. If it isn't, then there was a transmission error. If the parity is the same, either there was no error or there were two canceling errors, which is much less likely than a single error.

FLAG	MEANING
parodd (-parodd)	Selects odd (even) parity for the parity bit.
cs5 cs6 cs7 cs8	Selects the number of bits used per character ("character size") for transmission and reception. The size does not include parity bits, if any. The 5, 6, and so on indicate the number of bits.
0	Means hang up the phone immediately.
baud	Sets the terminal baud (communication) rate to *baud*, where *baud* is an integer rate supported by the equipment.
hupcl (-hupcl)	Means hang up (don't hang up) the phone when the last process using the line closes the line or terminates.
hup (-hup)	The same as hupcl (-hupcl).
cstopb (-cstopb)	Uses two (one) stop bits per character when sending. Terminals generally communicate one bit at a time; stop bits mark the end of a character byte.
cread (-cread)	Enables (disables) the receiver. No characters can be received unless the receiver is enabled.
clocal (-clocal)	Assumes a line without (with) modem control. A local, direct connection is an example of when clocal should be set.
loblk (-loblk)	Blocks (doesn't block) output from a non-current layer (see shl).

Input Modes

Input here is input from the keyboard. Many of the following flags need to be coordinated with one another. The **icanon** flag, discussed later, "packages" several of the more basic flags together in a rational manner.

FLAG	MEANING
ignbrk (-ignbrk)	Ignores (doesn't ignore) break on input. A break is produced by the <break> key. If ignored, it is not sent on.
brkint (-brkint)	Sends (doesn't send) an INTERRUPT signal upon a break. This assumes that breaks are not ignored.
ignpar (-ignpar)	Ignores (doesn't ignore) characters having parity errors (see the earlier **parenb** discussion).
parmrk (-parmrk)	Marks (doesn't mark) parity errors by prefixing the suspect character with a two-character code.
inpck (-inpck)	Enables (disables) input parity checking.

(continued)

FLAG	MEANING	*(continued)*
istrip (-istrip)	Strips (doesn't strip) valid input characters to seven bits. (The ASCII code only uses the final seven bits of a byte; the eighth bit is needed if the system makes use of non-ASCII characters.)	
inlcr (-inlcr)	Replaces (doesn't replace) **NL** (the newline character) with ASCII **CR** (the carriage-return character) on input.	
igncr (-igncr)	Ignores (doesn't ignore) the ASCII **CR** (the carriage-return character) on input.	
icrnl (-icrnl)	Replaces (doesn't replace) the ASCII **CR** (the carriage-return character) with **NL** (the newline character) on input. This is the opposite of **inlcr**.	
iuclc (-iuclc)	Replaces (doesn't replace) uppercase characters with lowercase characters upon input.	
ixon (-ixon)	Enables (disables) keyboard stop/start control over screen output. A **STOP** character suspends output, and a **START** character causes output to resume. The **STOP** character is <control-s>, and the **START** character is <control-q>.	
ixany (-ixany)	Enables (disables) any input character (not just **START**) to cause suspended output to resume.	
ixoff (-ixoff)	Enables (disables) input stop/start control. When set, the system generates a **START** character when the input queue is nearly empty and generates a **STOP** character when the input queue is nearly full.	

Output Modes

The following flags govern the sending of data to the computer:

FLAG	MEANING
opost (-opost)	Postprocesses (doesn't postprocess) output. If not set, characters are transmitted unchanged; otherwise, they are processed as governed by the following output mode settings.
olcuc (-olcuc)	Maps (doesn't map) lowercase to uppercase on output.
onlcr (-onlcr)	Maps (doesn't map) **NL** (the newline character) to **CR-NL** on output. (**CR** is the ASCII carriage-return character.)
ocrnl (-ocrnl)	Maps (doesn't map) ASCII **CR** (the carriage-return character) to **NL** (the newline character) on output.

FLAG	MEANING
onocr (**-onocr**)	Doesn't (does) transmit ASCII **CR** (the carriage-return character) when it is the first character on a line.
onlret (**-onlret**)	Makes (doesn't make) **NL** (the newline character) appear on the terminal screen as **CR-NL**; that is, outputs a carriage return before outputting a newline. This positions the cursor at column 1 of the next line. If **-onlret** is used, **nl** positions the cursor in the next line but doesn't change the column.

The next few flags relate to "delays." In particular, transmission is delayed to allow for mechanical movement of printer heads or for other factors when certain characters are sent.

FLAG	MEANING
ofill (**-ofill**)	Uses (doesn't use) "fill characters," as defined by **ofdel** below, instead of a timed delay to delay transmission.
ofdel (**-ofdel**)	Uses ASCII **DEL** (**NULL**) as the fill character.
cr0 cr1 cr2 cr3	Selects the style of delay for carriage returns; **cr0** is no delay between the output of a **CR** and the next character, and the others are successively longer delays. This is useful for slow terminals that need time to move the cursor to column 1.
nl0 nl	Selects the style of delay for newline characters; **nl0** is no delay (see the description above), and **nl1** is longer.
tab0 tab1 tab2 tab3	Selects the style of delay for horizontal tabs; **tab0** is no delay, **tab1** and **tab2** are progressively longer delays, and **tab3** causes tabs to be expanded into spaces.
bs0 bs1	Selects the style of backspace delays; **bs0** is no delay.
vt0 vt1	Selects the style of vertical tab delays; **vt0** is no delay.
ff0 ff1	Selects the style of form-feed delays; **ff0** is no delay.

Local Modes

FLAG	MEANING
isig (-isig)	Enables (disables) signals. If **isig** is set, each input character is checked to see if it is a "special control character" (see the Special Control Characters section that follows). If it is, the function associated with that character is performed. When **isig** is not set, characters are transmitted without checking. To disable individual special characters, set them to unlikely or impossible values, such as octal code 0377.
icanon (-icanon)	Enables (disables) canonical input. Canonical input is a standard method of processing input that enables the **erase** and **kill** line editing functions (see the Special Control Characters section below). It controls what happens when a program expects to read input from the terminal. It causes input to be separated into lines by the **EOF**, **eol**, or **NL** character. With **icanon** in effect, input is collected in an input queue that is transmitted when a complete line is detected. Thus a line can be edited before transmitting it.

       If **icanon** is not set, a read request (from a program, for example) does not wait for an end-of-line indication. Instead, the behavior of a read request is controlled by the values of the **min** and **time** variables, as described below. When **icanon** is not set, **min** and **time** values can be set in the fashion of special characters (see the Special Control Characters section below).

       The **min** and **time** quantities can be set up in four styles:

STYLE	ACTION

min > 0 and **time** > 0

        Here **time** serves as a between-character timer that is activated *after* the first character is received and is reset after each subsequent character. If **min** characters are received before the timer expires, the read is satisfied (the characters are transmitted to the requesting program). If the time expires before **min** characters are entered, the characters received up to that time are transmitted to the requesting program.

FLAG	MEANING	
	STYLE	ACTION
	min > 0 and **time** = 0	
		A read is satisfied as soon as **min** characters are received. Then they are given to the requesting program.
	min = 0 and **time** > 0	
		The read operation is satisfied as soon as a single character is received or when the timer expires, in which case no characters are provided.
	min = 0 and **time** = 0	
		Characters are read and made available to a program as they are generated.
xcase (–xcase)	Handles (doesn't handle) upper- and lowercase by the canonical, or standard, method. This is for keyboards with only one case. Lowercase characters are entered by typing the letter, and upper-case characters are entered by preceding the letter with a \. The **icanon** flag must be set, too.	
echo (–echo)	Enables (disables) echoing. Keyboard input is sent to the computer; with echoing, the characters received there are sent back to the terminal so that what you type also appears on the screen. Some terminals handle echoing themselves and shouldn't have this set.	
echoe (–echoe)	Echoes (doesn't echo) the **erase** character as backspace-space-backspace. This causes the character backspaced over to be cleared on the screen, since it is typed over with a space character. If **echo** (see above) is not set, **erase** is echoed as space-backspace. The **icanon** flag must be set for this flag to be used.	
echok (–echok)	Echoes (doesn't echo) **NL** (the newline character) after each **kill** character. The **kill** character negates a line of input, and starting a new line emphasizes that fact. The **icanon** flag must be set for this flag to be used.	
echonl (–echonl)	Echoes (doesn't echo) **NL** (the newline character), even if **echo** is not set. The **icanon** flag must be set for this flag to be used.	
noflsh (–noflsh)	Disables (enables) the "flushing" of input after an INTERRUPT, QUIT, or SWITCH signal. When flushing is enabled, any text typed at the terminal but not read into a running program (because, say, a QUIT signal was generated) is discarded.	

347

Special Control Characters

UNIX has several functions that are effected by striking certain keys. The **stty** command lets you assign particular keys to these built-in functions. The assignments have this form:

name character

Here *name* is one of the terms listed below, and *character* is a character. You can type a control character directly (it may need to be quoted), or you can use an escaped caret to indicate a control character; for example, \^c can be used to represent <control-c>. ^? represents <del>, and ^- means "undefined."

NAME	FUNCTION
intr	Generates an INTERRUPT signal to be sent to all processes under the control of the terminal. Unless trapped (see **sh**), this signal forces the processes to terminate. Typically, the <del> key is used. Note that the **brkint** flag also causes the <break> key to generate an interrupt.
quit	Generates a QUIT signal. This is similar to an INTERRUPT signal, except that a set of abnormal termination routines are started up. Typically, <control-\> is used.
erase	Erases the preceding character. It does not erase back past the beginning of a line. Typically **#** or <backspace> is used.
kill	Deletes the entire line. Typically, **@** or <control-u> is used.
eof	Generates an EOF (end-of-file) signal from the terminal. It flushes (sends to the waiting program) all characters in the input queue without waiting for a newline. If typed as the first character of a line, it produces the end-of-file indication. Typically, <control-d> is used.
eol	The **NL** (ASCII **LF** or the newline character) is the normal line delimiter; **eol** is an additional one. Normally, it is not used.
swtch	The character used by **shl** (see **shl**) to suspend a layer and return to **shl**. Typically, it is <control-z>.
min	The minimum number of characters needed to satisfy a read when the **–icanon** flag is in effect (see the earlier discussion of **icanon**). Although **min** is a number, not a character, the format for setting it is the same as for the special characters.
time	A timing value, in units of 0.10 second, used in the **–icanon** mode (see the earlier discussion of **icanon**). Although **time** is a number, not a character, the format for setting it is the same as for the special characters.

Combination Modes

The following flags represent common combinations of settings.

FLAG	MEANING
evenp or **parity**	Enables **parenb** and **cs7**.
oddp	Enables **parenb**, **parodd**, and **cs7**.
-parity, -evenp, or **-oddp**	Disables **parenb** and sets **cs8**.
raw (**-raw** or **cooked**)	Enables (disables) raw input and output. "Raw output" means that special characters, line editing, and postprocessing of output are disabled.
nl	Unsets **incrnl** and **onlcr**.
-nl	Sets **incrnl** and **onlcr** and unsets **inlcr**, **igncr**, **ocrnl**, and **onlret**.
lcase (**-lcase**)	Sets (unsets) **xcase**, **iuclc**, and **olcuc**.
LCASE (**-LCASE**)	Same as **lcase** (**-lcase**).
tabs (**-tabs** or **tab8**)	Preserves tabs (expands tabs to the equivalent number of spaces) when printing.
ek	Resets **erase** and **kill** to **#** and **@**.
sane	Resets all modes to reasonable values. (Note that there is no **-sane**.)

COMMENTS The **stty** command provides a large number of flags for controlling the terminal interface, but the default settings are the best for most purposes. In any event, you will almost never need to use more than a handful of the options described here. **stty** is usually used to modify the default settings for a special terminal (for example, where parity or lowercase handling is different from the default) or to suit your own tastes (for example, to change the kill character).

SEE ALSO UNIX Features: Special UNIX Characters

EXAMPLES

1. See values for some of your terminal settings.

   ```
   $ stty
   speed 9600 baud; evenp hupcl
   brkint -inpck icrnl onlcr
   echo echoe echok
   ```

   This shows the terminal speed and nine flag settings.

2. See all terminal settings.

   ```
   $ stty -a
   speed 9600 baud; line = 0; intr = DEL; quit = ^\; erase = ^h;
   kill = ^u; eof = ^d; eol = ^` swtch = ^z
   parenb -parodd cs7 -cstopb hupcl cread -clocal
   -ignbrk brkint ignpar -parmrk -inpck istrip -inlcr -igncr icrnl -iuclc
   ixon ixany -ixoff
   isig icanon -xcase echo echoe echok -echonl -noflsh
   opost -olcuc onlcr -ocrnl -onocr -onlret -ofill -ofdel
   ```

   Since **icanon**, rather than **-icanon**, is set, **time** and **min** are not used.

3. Turn off echoing and set **kill** to **<control-u>**.

   ```
   $ stty -echo kill   \^u
   ```

   To set the **kill** character, we type three characters: ****, **^**, and **u**. Or we could have typed the **<control-u>** combination directly; we may need to quote it if **<control-u>** already is a special character.

4. Restore a workable setup after somehow scrambling the settings.

   ```
   stty sane
   ```

   This resets flags to reasonable values.

5. Change the baud rate.

```
stty 2400
```

This causes the computer to transmit information to the terminal at **2400** baud and to expect information to come from the terminal at that speed. Your screen most likely will show gibberish until you also reset the terminal to that speed. This may involve setting DIP switches or using a configuration program built into the terminal.

6. Save the current **stty** settings and restore them later.

```
$ stty -g > stty.save
  ...
$ stty   `cat stty.save`
```

The **-g** option produces output in a form that can be used as an argument to **stty**. Redirection saves this output in the **stty.save** file. The backquote command–substitution mechanism causes the enclosed **cat** command to be replaced by its output, the contents of the **stty.save** file. This ploy makes the contents into command–line arguments for **stty**, which then sets its flags to the values previously saved.

PURPOSE Use the **su** command to become another user.

FORMAT su [-] [*username*] [*arg(s)*]

Here *username* is the name of the user you wish to be (at least as far as the system is concerned). The *arg(s)* are arguments passed on to the new shell.

DESCRIPTION The **su** (switch user) command allows you to become another user (change your UID) without logging out. If you don't supply a *username* argument, **root** is assumed. Unless you are the superuser (for example, you are logged in as **root**), you are asked to provide the password for whichever user you wish to become.

The **su** command changes your real and effective user ID (as reported by the **id** command) to that of the indicated user, and a new shell is started. The shell used is that specified in the indicated user's **/etc/passwd** file; if none is listed, the system default is used.

Your original environment, with the possible exception of **PATH**, is passed to the new shell, so you will have your exported shell variables set (this can be changed by using the - flag described below).

Use <control-d> to reassume your previous identity.

COMMON USES You can use **su** to switch between accounts if you have multiple accounts or need to use someone else's account (presumably with permission). This command frequently is used by system administrators.

OPTIONS The **su** command has only one option:

OPTION	ACTION
-	This option is operational only if the **/etc/passwd** file indicates **sh** is the indicated user's shell. It gives you the environment that it would give the specified user when he or she logs in. For example, you would wind up (most likely) in his or her home directory and with his or her shell variable definitions. When you terminate the change of UID, you return to your shell as you left it.

COMMENTS The system remembers who you logged in as. For example, the **logname** command displays the name you logged in under even when the **id** command identifies you as a different user.

For more about environments, see the **sh** command.

SEE ALSO UNIX Commands: **sh**; **id**

EXAMPLES

---

1. Change your user ID.

```
$ su petunia
Passwd:
$
```

You have to type the password for **petunia**'s account just as if you were logging in directly. Type <control-d> to return to your own account.

---

sum

PURPOSE Use the **sum** command to display a checksum and a block count for a file.

FORMAT sum [-r] *file*

DESCRIPTION One method of checking to see if a file has been (inadvertently) altered is to sum all the byte values and see if the figure has changed from a previously recorded sum. Such a sum, or generalization thereof, is called a "checksum." The **sum** command calculates a checksum for the specified file and displays it, along with the number of 512-byte blocks used by the file.

All UNIX V systems use uniform algorithms so that the value of the checksum depends only on the file and not on the hardware and implementation.

COMMON USES You can use **sum** first on a source file on one UNIX V system and then on a version transmitted to another UNIX V system to check for consistency. If you are a system administrator, you can use it to check for tampering with system files.

OPTIONS The **sum** command has only one option:

OPTION	ACTION
-r	Uses an alternative algorithm.

EXAMPLES

1. Run a checksum.

```
$ sum borrowed
12334 1
$
```

Here the checksum is **12334**, and the file used one 512-byte block.

PURPOSE Use the **tabs** command to set the tab stops on a terminal.

FORMAT tabs [*tabspec*] [**+m***n*] [**-T***type*]

The *tabspec* option specifies the tab settings.

DESCRIPTION Hitting the tab key generates a tab character, which causes the cursor to move to the next "tab stop." Normally, these stops are located every eighth column; that is, at columns 9, 17, 25, and so on. The **tabs** command allows you to select other values.

Tab settings can be specified in three ways. First, you can set tabs arbitrarily for up to 40 positions. Second, you can set up equally spaced tabs with the spacing of your choice. And finally, you can select from "canned" formats corresponding to the standard formats for several programming languages. If no setting is specified, the standard setting of columns 9, 17, and so on is used.

COMMON USES You can use **tabs** to customize the tab settings of your terminal to meet a specific need, providing the terminal has settable tabs.

OPTIONS One set of options, generically termed *tabspec* in the format, specifies the tab settings. These options fall into three groups.

Arbitrary Settings

OPTION	ACTION

n1,n2,...	Here *n1*, *n2*, and so on represent the columns to which successive tab stops are to be set. The first column is always column 1, even on terminals that label the first column with a 0. Up to 40 stops can be set. Note that each number is separated from the next by a comma. Any number, except the first, can have a **+** prefix, in which case it represents an increment over the preceding stop. Thus these two commands
	    `tab 6,16,20,28`
	    `tab 6,+10,+4,+8`
	both set tab stops at columns 6, 16, 20, and 28.

Repetitive Settings

OPTION	ACTION
–*n*	Sets tab stops every *n* columns, beginning with column 1+*n*. The general formula for the columns is 1+2∗*n*. For example, –5 sets the tabs at columns 1, 6, 11, 16, and so on. The default setting for tabs corresponds to the –8 option, and a –0 option clears all tab settings.

Canned Settings

Here we list the settings designed for particular applications:

OPTION	ACTION
–a	Sets tab stops at columns 1, 10, 16, 36, and 72. Used for Assembler, IBM System/370, first format.
–a2	Sets tab stops at columns 1, 10, 16, 40, and 72. Used for Assembler, IBM System/370, second format.
–c	Sets tab stops at columns 1, 8, 12, 16, 20, and 55. Used for COBOL, normal format.
–c2	Sets tab stops at columns 1, 6, 10, 14, and 49. Used for COBOL, compact format (omit columns 1 through 6).
–c3	Sets tab stops at columns 1, 6, 10, 14, 18, 22, 26, 30, 34, 38, 42, 46, 50, 54, 58, 62, and 67. Used for COBOL, compact format with added stops.
–f	Sets tab stops at columns 1, 7, 11, 15, 19, and 23. Used for FORTRAN.
–p	Sets tab stops at columns 1, 5, 9, 13, 17, 21, 25, 29, 33, 37, 41, 45, 49, 53, 57, and 61. Used for PL/I.
–s	Sets tab stops at columns 1, 10, and 55. Used for SNOBOL.
–u	Sets tab stops at columns 1, 12, 20, and 44. Used for UNIVAC 1100 Assembler.

Margin Settings

Some terminals permit the following option:

OPTION	ACTION
+mn	Moves all tabs over n columns and makes column $n+1$ the left margin. If n is omitted, a value of 10 is assumed. Using **+m0** sets the margin to the leftmost setting. For a GE TermiNet terminal, the first value in the tab list must be 1 when this option is used.

Terminal Type

OPTION	ACTION
-T$type$	Here $type$ is the system name for the terminal type. If this option is not given, **tabs** checks the value of the **TERM** environmental variable. If **TERM** is undefined, **tabs** tries a sequence of setting instructions that works with many terminals.

COMMENTS Some terminals behave differently from others. For example, the first tab setting sometimes is interpreted as a left margin setting.

The **tabs** command adjusts tab settings on the terminal; the **pr** command provides for processing tab characters in input and output before printing or piping to other programs.

SEE ALSO UNIX Commands: **pr**

EXAMPLES

1. Set tab stops with a spacing of 5 instead of the standard 8.

   ```
   tabs -5
   ```

   The starting tab position is not changed.

2. Set tab stops to columns 5, 8, 11, 14, 17, and 25.

   ```
   tabs 5,8,11,14,17,25
   ```

3. Set tab stops for FORTRAN.

   ```
   tabs -f
   ```

   This sets the tab stops to values suitable for FORTRAN.

tail

PURPOSE Use the **tail** command to see the end of a file.

FORMAT tail [**+**/-[*number*[**lbc**][**f**]]] [*file*]

DESCRIPTION By default, the **tail** command displays the last 10 lines of a file. Because the standard output is used, **tail**'s output can be redirected or piped to other files and commands. If no filename is given, **tail** reads the standard input. This is, by default, the keyboard, but more typically is the output of a pipe.

You can choose to have **tail** start the display at other points in a file by using the location specifier described below.

COMMON USES You can use **tail** to look at the end of a long file without having to look through all the preceding material. This can be handy for seeing whether or not a file that was transferred over a phone line ends cleanly.

OPTIONS The **tail** options don't fit the usual UNIX mode. There is only one option string with several sections, many of which may be omitted. You also can omit the option string altogether, in which case **tail** begins printing 10 lines from the end of the file.

OPTION	ACTION
-number	Starts the display *number* lines from the end.
+number	Starts the display *number* lines from the beginning.
	For both of the options above, if *number* is omitted, it is assumed to be 10.
l	Counts in units of lines.
b	Counts in units of blocks (512-byte units).
c	Counts in units of characters.
	The unit of counting is, by default, the line (l). Only one of the above three options should be used at a time. As an example, -200c means "start displaying the file 200 characters from the end."
f	When appended to the end of the option string, causes **tail** to enter an endless loop. After printing the requested lines, **tail** waits a second and checks to see if any more lines have been added to the file. If they have, it prints the additional lines. This continues until you terminate **tail** with an INTERRUPT signal or, if **tail** is running in the background, with **kill**. Called the "follow" option, f can be used only when the input file is a regular file and not a pipe. The intent of this feature is to let you monitor the progress of a file that is being written to by another process.

COMMENTS When the starting location is specified relative to the end of the file, the relevant text is saved in a buffer. This limits the maximum length for that form of **tail**.

SEE ALSO UNIX Features: Standard I/O, Redirection, and Pipes

EXAMPLES

---

1. See the last 10 lines of a file.

   ```
   tail spin
   ```

   The last 10 lines of the **spin** file are displayed.

2. Look at the last 20 lines of the sorted output of a file.

   ```
   sort scores | tail -20
   ```

3. Look at a file beginning 50 lines into it.

   ```
   tail +50 treacle
   ```

   To start the display 50 characters instead of 50 lines into a file, use this command:

   ```
   tail +50c treacle
   ```

4. Observe a file as it grows.

   ```
   tail -f logins
   ```

   This shows the last 10 lines of the **logins** file, then shows, at one-second intervals, new lines added to the file. The **f** option can be used with other combinations, such as in **+200cf**, which changes the starting point of the display.

PURPOSE Use the **tar** command to save files in archival form, typically on magnetic tape or floppy disk.

FORMAT **tar** [*function-option*[*modifier*]] [*file(s)*]

DESCRIPTION The **tar** command saves files to an archive and restores files from an archive. An archive combines several files into a single file and maintains a record of where each file is. Files can be added to and deleted from an archive. Also, files can be "extracted," which means a file can be copied from the archive to a directory. The **tar** command creates and manages archive files. If no archive name is provided (via the **–f** option), a system default file is used; normally, the default is a tape or floppy disk drive. (Recall that UNIX treats devices as files.)

A series of options allow you to specify which archival actions you desire. The files to be acted upon are given as arguments to **tar**. When a directory name is used, it refers recursively to the directory's files, its subdirectories and their files, and so on.

COMMON USES You can use **tar** to save copies of your files on tape and to restore saved files to your directories. It also can be used to copy a directory tree (a directory and its recursive subdirectories and files) from one directory to another.

OPTIONS A **tar** option has two parts: a function portion to select the desired action, and an optional modifier.

Function Selection

FUNCTION	ACTION
r	Adds the named *file(s)* to the end of the archive.
x	Extracts (copies) the named *file(s)* from the archive. If a particular filename corresponds to a directory whose contents are in the archive, the entire directory (all subdirectories, and so on) is extracted recursively. If a filename exists in the archive but not in the system, the file is created with the same file mode as the archived file, except that the set-user-ID and set-group-ID modes are not set unless the user is the superuser. If a file exists both in the archive and on the system, the archive version is copied to the system, and the file mode of the system version is retained. If possible, the owner, group, and modification time are restored. If no *file(s)* are listed, the entire contents of the archive are extracted. If the archive contains more than one version of a file, the versions are extracted in turn, with the last file overwriting all others.

FUNCTION	ACTION
t	Lists the names of all the files in the archive.
u	Adds the named *file(s)* to the archive if they are not already there or if they have been modified since last copied to the archive. Any older version is removed. This option implies the **r** option.
c	Creates a new archive, starting the writing at the beginning of the archive instead of after the last file. This option implies the **r** option.

Modifiers

MODIFIER	ACTION
v	Activates the verbose mode, in which **tar** displays the name of each file it processes, preceding it with the function letter. When used with the **t** function, it augments the information supplied.
w	Activates the confirmation mode, in which **tar** displays each action it is about to undertake and then waits for confirmation. Any word beginning with **y** is interpreted as "yes," and the action is performed. All other responses count as "no." This option is not used with the **t** option.
f *file*	Uses *file* as the archive. When this option is omitted, a default file, usually a tape drive or floppy drive, is used. If *file* is **-**, the standard input or standard output is used, depending on whether **tar** is writing or extracting. This feature enables **tar** to be used as part of a pipe. (See the examples.)
f#*s*	Specifies the drive on which a tape is mounted and the tape speed. Replace **#** with the drive number, and *s* with the drive speed (the choices are **l**, **m**, and **h** for low, medium, and high, respectively). For example, if the default drive is **/dev/mt/0m**, then **f31** means "use **/dev/mt/31**." New with Release 3.
b *n*	Uses *n* as the blocking factor for tape records. The default value is 1, and the maximum value is 20. This option should be used only when writing to (raw) magnetic tape archives. When tapes are read (the **x** and **t** options), the block size is determined automatically.
l	Reports when **tar** cannot resolve all links to the files being archived. This option makes sense only with options **c**, **r**, and **u**.

(continued)

MODIFIER	ACTION	(continued)
m	Does not restore the modification time; the new modification time is set to the time of extraction. This option is not valid in conjunction with the **t** option.	
o	Causes the extracted files to have the user and group IDs of the person using **tar** rather than the values stored in the archive. This option is valid only with the **x** option.	

COMMENTS For saving files on tape, many users prefer **tar** to **cpio**. The **tar** command does not use the same archive format as **ar** or **cpio**.

SEE ALSO UNIX Commands: **ar**; **cpio**
UNIX Features: Standard I/O, Redirection, and Pipes; Files and Directories

EXAMPLES

1. Archive a set of files.

```
tar c felt wax Intros
```

Here **Intros** is a directory. The **felt** and **wax** files are copied to the archive along with the **Intros** directory and all its contents. Before giving this command, we should have arranged to have a tape or floppy disk placed on the default drive used with **tar**.

2. Add files to an archive.

```
tar r Silk
```

This appends the **Silk** directory and its contents to the archive.

3. Update an archive.

```
tar u Silk
```

This updates those files in the **Silk** directory that have been modified since the last archiving.

4. Restore a set of files.

```
tar x Silk
```

This copies into the **Silk** directory those files in the archive that belonged to the **Silk** directory when they were archived.

5. Archive a set of files whose names are stored in a file.

```
cat fileset | tar r -
```

This shows how **tar** can be used with a pipe. The output of **cat**, assumed to be a list of files, becomes the input to **tar**.

6. Copy a directory tree.

```
$ cd Dir1
$ tar cf $HOME/temp .
$ cd ../Dir2
$ tar xf $HOME/temp
$ rm $HOME/temp
```

This is the long way. It copies the contents of **Dir1**, including subdirectories, into a temporary archive file, then extracts the contents while in a different directory. The result is that the contents of **Dir1**, including subdirectories, are copied to **Dir2**. The **cd** sequence reflects that **Dir1** and **Dir2** are both subdirectories of the original working directory.

The short way is this:

```
(cd Dir1; tar cf - .) | (cd Dir2; tar xf - )
```

The parentheses group together the commands that are to be run by a subshell. The result is that the **cd** in the first group is confined to the parentheses, so after that group of commands is executed, the current directory is once again the parent directory to **Dir1**. Thus in the second group we can use **cd Dir2** instead of **cd ../Dir2**. The **f** option used with – causes the output (the archived files) of the first **tar** command to be sent to the standard output; the period causes the current directory to be archived. The pipe and the second **f** option cause the output to become input to the second **tar** command, which then restores the archived files in the new current directory.

PURPOSE Use the **tee** command to transmit input to the standard output while diverting a copy of the input to a file.

FORMAT tee [–i] [–a] [*file(s)*]

DESCRIPTION The **tee** command transmits the standard input to the standard output while also placing a copy of the input into a file; that is, a command like

```
sort figures : lp
```

pipes the output of the **sort** command to the **lp** command, while

```
sort figures : tee sortfigs : lp
```

does the same thing and also places a copy of the sorted output in the **sortfigs** file. By default, existing files are overwritten.

More than one destination file can be listed if you want to make more than one copy.

COMMON USES You can use **tee** to save steps when you want to save output and also send it on to another program.

OPTIONS The **tee** command has two options:

OPTION	ACTION
–i	Ignores interrupts. For example, when this option is in effect, the INTERRUPT signal typically generated by the <del> kev is ignored by **tee**.
–a	Appends the output to a file instead of overwriting the file.

SEE ALSO UNIX Features: Standard I/O, Redirection, and Pipes; Filters

EXAMPLES

1. Collect output in addition to sending it on to another program.

   ```
   pr roster ¦ tee roster.pr ¦ lp
   ```

   This collects the output of **pr roster** in the **roster.pr** file and also sends the output on to the **lp** command. If the final pipe (¦ **lp**) is omitted, the output appears on the screen, since the screen is the default standard output.

2. Create three copies of a file and print a copy.

   ```
   cat model ¦ tee muffy didi jocko ¦ lp
   ```

   When more than one file is listed, a copy of the input to **tee** is placed in each.

3. Make a copy of a remote login session.

   ```
   cu 5551000 ¦ tee copycall
   ```

   Since the standard output of **tee** is not redirected, it goes to the default standard output, the screen. Thus to you, the **cu** command seems to work normally, whereas in fact a copy of the output has been placed in the **copycall** file.

test

PURPOSE   Use the **test** command to test conditions in a manner suitable for use in shell scripts.

FORMAT   **test** *expression*

[*expression*]

The bracket form is an alternative, shorter way of expressing the **test** command. Note the use of blanks to delimit the brackets.

DESCRIPTION   Shell script command structures, such as the **while** loop and the **if** control structure, use the exit status of a **test** command to decide what to do next. (See **sh** for a description of these structures.) A zero exit status plays the role of "true," while a non-zero exit status plays the role of "false." Many situations, however, involve conditions that are not ordinarily related to the exit status of a command. For instance, a script may wish to know if two strings are the same or if a file is readable. The **test** command evaluates true-false statements of this sort and returns an appropriate exit value; that is, if **test** is given a true expression, it returns a zero exit status.

In short, **test** converts a true or false expression to a corresponding true or false exit status that is usable by **while**, **until**, and **if**.

COMMON USES   You can use **test** in shell scripts to test for various file permissions and to examine the values of shell variables. The exit status of a **test** command can be used to control **while** loops, **until** loops, and **if** statements.

EXPRESSIONS   The basic expressions used by **test** fall into three categories: file tests, string tests, and numeric tests. Simple expressions of each of these types are called "primaries." Primaries can be combined into larger expressions by using the operators described later. For example, to indicate a read and write test, you must use **-r** *file* and **-w** *file* separately, along with the **-a** operator; you cannot simply use **-rw** *file*.

File Tests

In each of the following, *file* is a filename.

TEST	VALUE
-k *file*	True if *file* exists and has its sticky bit set. (The sticky bit, which can be set only by the superuser, causes the program text of an executable program to be retained in "swap space," so that it is readily available. New with Release 3.
-r *file*	True if *file* exists and is readable.
-w *file*	True if *file* exists and is writable.

TEST	VALUE
-x *file*	True if *file* exists and is executable.
-f *file*	True if *file* exists and is a regular file.
-d *file*	True if *file* exists and is a directory.
-c *file*	True if *file* exists and is a character special file. (A character special file represents a device, such as a terminal, that handles I/O a character at a time.)
-b *file*	True if *file* exists and is a block special file. (A block special file represents a device, such as a tape drive, that handles I/O in blocks.)
-p *file*	True if *file* exists and is a named pipe (FIFO).
-u *file*	True if *file* exists and has its set-user-ID bit set (see **chmod**).
-g *file*	True if *file* exists and has its set-group-ID bit set (see **chmod**).
-t[*fildes*]	True if the open file with the *fildes* file descriptor is associated with a terminal. The default value for *fildes* is 1, which normally is associated with the standard output.

String Expressions

TEST	VALUE
-z *str*	True if the length of the string *str* is zero.
-n *str*	True if the length of the string *str* is non-zero.
str1 **=** *str2*	True if strings *str1* and *str2* are identical. The blanks surrounding **=** are required.
str1 **!=** *str2*	True if strings *str1* and *str2* are *not* identical. The blanks surrounding **!=** are required.
str	True if *str* is not the null string.

Numeric Expressions

Several comparisons can be made on the basis of numeric value:

TEST	VALUE
n1 **-eq** *-n2*	True if the integers *n1* and *n2* are algebraically equal. For example, **22** and **022** are algebraically equal but not equal as strings, since the second has a character that the first lacks.
n1 **-ne** *-n2*	True if the integers *n1* and *n2* are algebraically not equal.
n1 **-lt** *-n2*	True if the integer *n1* is algebraically less than *n2*.
n1 **-le** *-n2*	True if the integer *n1* is algebraically less than or equal to *n2*.
n1 **-ge** *-n2*	True if the integer *n1* is algebraically greater than or equal to *n2*.
n1 **-gt** *-n2*	True if the integer *n1* is algebraically greater than *n2*.

Operators

OPERATOR	DESCRIPTION
!	Unary negation operator ("unary" means it operates on one expression). This operator negates an expression. For example, `! -r notes` is false if **notes** exists and is readable.
-a	Binary AND operator ("binary" means it operates on two expressions). The resulting expression is true only if both contributing expressions are true. For instance, `-r bears -a -w bears` is true only if the file **bears** exists, is readable, and is writable.
-o	Binary OR operator. The expression formed by joining two expressions with **-o** is true if either or both contributing expressions are true. For instance, `-f torts -o -d torts` is true if **torts** exists and is either a regular file or a directory.
(*expression*)	Parentheses are used to group expressions. This may be useful when using more than one of the preceding operators. The order of precedence, from high to low, is ( ) ! **-a -o**. This means the expression `test ! -r bears -a -w bears` is the same as `test ( ! -r bears ) -a -w bears`

OPERATOR	DESCRIPTION

To negate the whole expression, use

```
test ! ( -r bears -a -w bears )
```

Because the **sh** shell has its own interpretation of parentheses, when they are used within **test** they should be quoted; that is, the preceding example could be typed like this:

```
test ! \( -r bears -a -w bears \)
```

Or the whole expression could be enclosed in single or double quotes.

Each operator and expression is a separate argument, so they should be separated from one another by blanks.

COMMENTS The **test** command actually is a built-in shell command. This means that its program code is included in the **sh** program rather than being kept in a file of its own.

The convention that a true statement corresponds to a 0 exit value is opposite to the conventions of many programming languages, such as C, in which 1 is true and 0 is false.

SEE ALSO UNIX Commands: **sh**

UNIX Features: Exit Values; Shell Scripts

EXAMPLES

1. Execute a command if a certain file is readable.

```
if test -r info
then
    cat info
else
    echo You can't read that file
fi
```

The **if** command, discussed under **sh**, will display the **info** file if it is readable; otherwise, it will print a message.

(continued)

2. Execute a command if a certain terminal is used.

```
if test "$TERM" = adm5
then
    echo My, what a naive terminal!
done
```

The **$TERM** environmental variable is used to hold the name of the terminal being used. The double quotes are there to allow for the possibility that **$TERM** is not defined. In that case, the test portion becomes **test "" = adm5**, which compares **adm5** with the null string. Without the quotes, the test becomes **test = adm5**, which is a syntax error.

3. Compare numeric values in a counting loop.

```
LIMIT=200
while test $LIMIT -gt 0
do
    echo I will clean up my directory system
    LIMIT=`expr $LIMIT - 1`
done
$
```

The LIMIT shell variable is set to 1. The **while** loop uses **test** to see if the value of LIMIT is greater than 0. If it is, a message is displayed, and LIMIT is reduced by 1. (The **while** loop is discussed under **sh**.) The **expr** command evaluates numeric expressions, and the back-quote mechanism (discussed under **sh**) replaces the enclosed command with its value. In this case, the value of LIMIT is reduced by 1 each time through the loop.

Note that we could have written the test lines in each example as follows:

```
if [ -r info ]
if [ "$TERM" = adm5 ]
while [ $LIMIT -gt 0 ]
```

The closing] is mandatory.

PURPOSE   Use the **touch** command to update access and modification times of a file.

FORMAT   touch [-amc] [*mmddhhmm*[*yy*]] *file(s)*

Here *mmddhhmm* is the date in month-day-hour-minute format (two digits each). The optional *yy* is the two-digit year.

DESCRIPTION   UNIX maintains information in an i-node, or information node, for each file. The i-node includes the time of creation, time of last access, and time of last modification. The **touch** command allows you to update access and modification times. By default, the **touch** command updates them both, using the specified time, if provided, or the current time otherwise. Also by default, if a named file does not exist, it is created.

COMMON USES   You can use **touch** to update files so that they will not be removed by cleanup programs that delete all files last accessed or modified before a certain time. (The **find** command can be used to construct cleanup programs.)

OPTIONS   The **touch** command's three options can be strung together on one hyphen.

OPTION	ACTION
-a	Updates only the access time.
-m	Updates only the modification time.
-c	Doesn't create a file if the named file doesn't exist.

SEE ALSO   UNIX Commands: **ls**
UNIX Features: Files and Directories

EXAMPLES

1. Update the access time of a file to the present.

   ```
   touch -a phonelist
   ```

   The date of last modification is left unchanged.

2. Set the access and modification times of a file to a particular time.

   ```
   touch 0704202082 twinwit
   ```

   This sets the last access and modification times to July 4, 20:20, 1982.

tr

PURPOSE Use the **tr** command to translate, or substitute for, characters.

FORMAT **tr** [–cds] [*string1* [*string2*]]

Here *string1* consists of characters to be replaced, and *string2* consists of the replacement characters.

DESCRIPTION The **tr** command copies characters from the standard input to the standard output, substituting for or deleting certain characters as directed. It has no provision for reading or writing to files, so normally redirection or pipes are used to connect the standard input and output to other files or programs. Thus a typical **tr** command might look like this:

```
tr "[a-z]" "[A-Z]" < source > result
```

As described below, this replaces lowercase letters with uppercase. Redirection causes input to be taken from the **source** file and output to be placed in the **result** file.

COMMON USES You can use **tr** to convert text to all uppercase or lowercase letters and to perform other acts of text manipulation. For example, sequences of blanks can be replaced by newline characters to produce lists with one word per line.

SPECIFYING
SUBSTITUTIONS The *string1* argument provides a list of characters to be replaced, and the *string2* argument provides the replacement characters. The first character in *string1* is replaced by the first character in *string2*, and so on. Thus

```
tr work play
```

replaces each **w** in the input with a **p**, each **o** with an **l**, and so on.

If the second string contains fewer characters than the first, only the corresponding characters are replaced. Thus

```
tr abcde 1234
```

replaces **a** through **d** with 1 through 4, but **e** is passed through unaltered. (This differs from the behavior of older versions of **tr**, for which any surplus characters in the first string were replaced by the final character of the second string.)

If a character appears more than once in the first string, the last substitution holds. Thus

```
tr hah bit
```

causes each **h** in the input to be replaced by a **t**, not a **b**.

Brackets can be used to indicate a range of characters. For example, **[a-m]** is the range **a** through **m**. Since the shell filename-generation mechanism also uses brackets, you should quote the expressions used by **tr**. For instance, to replace all lowercase letters with uppercase, you can do this:

```
tr "[a-z]" "[A-Z]"
```

Note that the strings are quoted separately so that they will be recognized as two separate arguments for **tr**. The expression

```
"[a-z] [A-Z]"
```

counts as a single string consisting of the characters **a** through **z**, a space character, and the characters **A** through **Z**.

Older versions of **tr** accepted the notation **a-z** (without brackets) to indicate a range.

Brackets can be used with an asterisk and an integer ([$c*n$]) to indicate repetitions of a character. For instance, **[T*5]** stands for five **T**'s. This notation normally is used in *string2* when you wish to replace several characters with the same character. For instance,

```
tr aeiou "[#*5]"
```

is equivalent to

```
tr aeiou #####
```

Either replaces each of the vowels with a **#**.

If the first digit of *n* is 0, then *n* is considered to be an octal number. If *n* is just 0 or if it is omitted, it is taken to be "huge," meaning that the preceding *c* character is to be repeated often enough to take care of any remaining characters in *string1*.

Special characters in a string can be quoted (escaped) with an initial \ to negate special meanings. Also, octal ASCII character codes can be used by preceding them with a \; one, two, or three digits can be used. For example,

```
tr " \11" "[\012*]"
```

replaces each space and each tab character (ASCII code 011 in octal) with a newline character (ASCII 012 in octal).

OPTIONS The **tr** command has three options:

OPTION	ACTION
–c	Uses all characters *not in* *string1*; that is, takes the characters whose codes are 001 through 377 (octal) and forms the list of replacements from those not explicitly given in *string1*. For example, `tr -c "[a-z][A-Z]" "[:*]"` replaces all characters other than lower- and uppercase letters with a colon.
–d	Deletes the characters of *string1* from the input text before sending it to the output.
–s	When a character from *string2* appears two or more consecutive times in the output, "squeezes" the sequence down to a single character.

COMMENTS Any null characters (ASCII code 0) present in the input are not passed on to the output.

SEE ALSO UNIX Features: Standard I/O, Redirection, and Pipes; Filters

EXAMPLES

1. Replace all uppercase characters in a file with lowercase characters.

   `tr "[A-Z]" "[a-z]" < heat0.f > heat1.f`

   Note that the file used to collect the output is different from the input file. Attempting to use the same file for both causes the input file to be erased before it is processed.

2. Convert text to a list of words, with one word per line.

   `tr -cs "[A-Z][a-z]" "[\012*]" < text > list`

   The **–c** option causes all characters other than letters to be replaced. The replacement list consists of ASCII code 012, which is the newline character. So all non–letters are replaced with newlines. The **–s** option causes multiple newlines to be reduced to a single newline.

3. Delete characters.

   `tr -d \$\* < dirty > clean`

   This reads input from the **dirty** file, removes all $ and * characters, and sends the output to the **clean** file. The backslash is used here to turn off the special meanings that $ and * have to the shell.

PURPOSE Use the **true** command to return an exit status of zero.

FORMAT **true**

DESCRIPTION The **true** command returns an exit status of zero.

COMMON USES You can use **true** to construct infinite loops and to test the logic of shell procedures.

COMMENTS In testing shell scripts, you can replace test conditions for **while** loops and **if** statements with **true** and **false** to see how the program behaves with known conditions.

    The convention that a true statement corresponds to a zero exit value is opposite to the conventions of many programming languages, such as C, in which 1 is true and 0 is false.

SEE ALSO UNIX Commands: **false; sh**
UNIX Features: Exit Values; Shell Scripts

EXAMPLES

1. Construct an infinite loop.

```
while true
do
    echo KEEP ALERT
    sleep 600
done &
```

This command displays **KEEP ALERT** every 600 seconds. The **&** causes the command to be run in the background. The **while** loop continues as long as its test command (here **true**) has an exit status of 0, which is for as long as the system functions properly.

tty

PURPOSE Use the **tty** command to obtain the pathname of the current terminal.

FORMAT tty [-ls]

DESCRIPTION In UNIX, devices are treated as files. In particular, each terminal is associated with a file in the **/dev** directory. The **tty** command displays the pathname of the user's terminal.

COMMON USES You can use **tty** to obtain the pathname for your terminal and to determine if the standard input currently is a terminal.

OPTIONS The **tty** command has two options:

OPTION	ACTION
-l	Displays the synchronous line number if the user's terminal is connected to one. New with Release 3.
-s	Inhibits the display of the terminal pathname. Used when you just want the exit value.

EXIT VALUES The **tty** command returns one of the following exit values:

VALUE	MEANING
0	The standard input is a terminal.
2	Invalid options were specified.
1	Neither of the above.

SEE ALSO UNIX Commands: **sh**
UNIX Features: Files and Devices; Exit Values; Pathnames and the Directory Tree

1. Check the pathname for your terminal.

```
$ tty
/dev/tty32
```

   Your terminal is **/dev/tty32**.

2. Check whether the standard input is a terminal.

```
$ tty -s
$ echo $?
0
```

   The **$?** (see **sh**) stands for the exit status of the last command run, here **tty -s**. Of course, since no redirection or pipes are used, the standard input is the terminal. More typically, this command is used in a shell script to tell the script whether or not it is taking input from the terminal.

umask

PURPOSE Use the **umask** command to alter the file-creation mask.

FORMAT umask [*ooo*]

Here *ooo* is a three-digit octal number.

DESCRIPTION When a file is created, it has its file permission mode set (see **chmod**). This mode indicates the read, write, and execute permissions possessed by the file owner, by members of the owner's group, and by others. The actual mode set is the one that is provided by the file-creation process and modified by the "file-creation mask." Different creation processes can provide different base modes; most start with a mode of 0666, which gives everyone read and write permission. The mask indicates permissions that are *not* to be allowed. By default, the mask usually is 0022. As described in **chmod** and below, this octal number stands for write permissions for group members and for others, which are the permissions *denied* by the mask. This mask, combined with a 0666 creation mode, results in a final mode of 0644, which grants read and write permissions for the owner and read-only permission for everyone else. The **umask** command lets you set the creation mask to the value of your choice. When given with no argument, **umask** displays the current setting of the mask.

COMMON USES You can use **umask** to alter the default file permissions. For example, you can use it so that all the files you create are not readable by others.

SPECIFYING THE MASK In the *ooo* three-digit octal number, the first digit represents owner permissions, the second group permissions, and the third permissions for others. (The number optionally can be preceded by a zero.) The codes for the digits are as described in detail under **chmod**, but briefly they are:

CODE	MEANING
1	Execute permission.
2	Write permission.
4	Read permission.

Multiple permissions are formed by combining these basic permissions. For example, 6 is read and write permission (4 and 2).

Permissions described by the mask are withheld from files being created. Superficially, it appears that the final mode is the creation mode minus the mask; for example, a creation mode of 0777 and a mask of 0022 results in a mode of 0755. However, the actual masking only removes modes that are present; that is, a mode of 0644 and a mask of 0022 result in a final mode of 0644, not 0622. This is because 6 is two permissions, a 4 and a 2, so a 2 can be removed. But a 4 is just one permission, read; there is no 2 to be removed.

COMMENTS The creation mask only applies to files being created. Files already in existence do not have their permissions changed when the creation mask is altered.

The **cp** command is not affected by **umask**.

The **umask** command is part of the **sh** command and is discussed briefly in the **sh** entry.

SEE ALSO UNIX Commands: **sh**; **chmod**
UNIX Features: Permissions

EXAMPLES

---

1. Check the current value of the creation mask.

```
$ umask
0022
```

The octal digits 022 mean that user permissions are unaffected, but that write permission (**2**) is withheld for group members and others. Thus if a file is created with mode 666 specified (read and write permissions for everyone), the resulting mode is 644 (read permission for everyone, but write permission only for the user).

2. Modify the creation mask.

```
$ ls -l dink
-rw-r--r--   1 stilton   good           80 Jan 19 10:35 dink
$ umask 066
$ cat dink > newdink
$ ls -l newdink
-rw-------   1 stilton   good           80 Jan 19 10:47 newdink
```

The **umask** command withholds read and write permissions (**6**) from group members and others. Files created subsequent to this command use this mask. Thus a file created using redirection has a permission mode of 0600 instead of the usual 0644. The **ls** command displays permissions using **r**, **w**, and **x** to indicate read, write, and execute permissions for the owner, group, and others.

---

uname

PURPOSE Use the **uname** command to display the name of the current system.

FORMAT uname [*option(s)*]

DESCRIPTION The **uname** command displays the name of the current system. Various options specify the exact information provided.

COMMON USES You can use **uname** to obtain information on the system you are using. This is particularly useful if you are working on a multi-system network.

OPTIONS The **uname** command has six options:

OPTION	ACTION
–s	Displays the system name known to the local installation (the default action if no option is given). Use **–s** along with other options when you don't want the default action overridden.
–n	Displays the node name. This normally is the name by which a system is known to a communications network.
–r	Displays the operating system release number.
–v	Displays the operating system version.
–m	Displays the name of the machine hardware.
–a	Displays all of the above.

EXAMPLES

1. Find the name of your system.

```
$ uname
XENIX
```

This command was run on a XENIX system compatible with System V.

2. Find out information about your system.

```
$ uname -a
sysname=XENIX
nodename=(empty)
release=2.1.3
version=SysV
machine=i80286
```

Here XENIX is being run on an 80286-processor machine. Release 2.1.3 of System V is being used. The system does not belong to a communications network.

PURPOSE Use the **uniq** command to remove duplicate adjacent lines from a file.

FORMAT uniq [-udc] [+*n*] [-*n*] [*input* [*output*]]

DESCRIPTION The **uniq** command reads the input and compares adjacent lines. If two or more adjacent lines are identical, all but one is removed. The resulting text is placed in the output. If two filenames are given on the command line, the first-named file is used for input and the second for output. The same name should not be used for *input* and *output*. If just one name is given, that file is used for input, and the result is sent to the standard output (by default, the screen). If no filenames are given, the standard input and output are used. These can both be connected to other files and programs by using redirection and pipes.

    The default behavior can be modified by the options described below.

COMMON USES You can use **uniq** to clean up files by eliminating redundancies.

OPTIONS The **uniq** command has five options:

OPTION	ACTION
-u	Outputs only those lines that are not repeated.
-d	Outputs only one copy of each repeated line. (Note: This option by itself does not output unrepeated lines. The default behavior of **uniq** is equivalent to the combination -ud.)
-c	Produces output in the default style, but precedes each line with a count of how many times it occurred in the input.
-*n*	Ignores the first *n* fields in a line, as well as initial blanks, when comparing for duplicates. (A blank is a space or a tab. A field is a string of non-blank characters separated from its neighbors by blanks.)
+*n*	Ignores the first *n* characters in a line when comparing for duplicates.

COMMENTS Note that only adjacent duplicate lines are eliminated.

    The **sort** command also has an option for eliminating duplicate lines. However, it also sorts the material (which may or may not be desirable), and **sort** doesn't have the flexibility of **uniq** in specifying the treatment of duplicate lines.

SEE ALSO UNIX Commands: **sort**
UNIX Features: Standard I/O, Redirection, and Pipes; Filters

EXAMPLES

1. Remove redundant lines from a file.

```
$ cat maillist0
Sandor, Filmore:1213 Fortebella St:Pinole, CA 94702
Boeffus, Dilly:343 E. Canfield Ave:Kentfield, CA 94104
Dansen, Shelly:3222 Boston Rd:Fairfax, CA 94122
Dansen, Shelly:3222 Boston Rd:Fairfax, CA 94122
Dansen, Shelly:3222 Boston Rd:Fairfax, CA 94122
Kernef, Gregor:2233 Tsonk Blvd:Sacramento, CA 95833
Bingle, Portentia:987 Clift Dr:Berkeley, CA 94904
Boeffus, Dilly:343 E. Canfield Ave:Kentfield, CA 94104
$ uniq maillist0 maillist1
$ cat maillist1
Sandor, Filmore:1213 Fortebella St:Pinole, CA 94702
Boeffus, Dilly:343 E. Canfield Ave:Kentfield, CA 94104
Dansen, Shelly:3222 Boston Rd:Fairfax, CA 94122
Kernef, Gregor:2233 Tsonk Blvd:Sacramento, CA 95833
Bingle, Portentia:987 Clift Dr:Berkeley, CA 94904
Boeffus, Dilly:343 E. Canfield Ave:Kentfield, CA 94104
```

First we see the contents of the original **maillist0** file. Then **uniq** processes input from that file and places the output in **maillist1**. Finally, we display the contents of the file. Note that only adjacent duplicate lines are removed; the **Boeffus** entry still occurs twice. Sorting the file first would cause all duplicates to be removed.

2. Count the duplicate lines in a file.

```
$ sort maillist0 ! uniq -c
   1 Bingle, Portentia:987 Clift Dr:Berkeley, CA 94904
   2 Boeffus, Dilly:343 E. Canfield Ave:Kentfield, CA 94104
   3 Dansen, Shelly:3222 Boston Rd:Fairfax, CA 94122
   1 Kernef, Gregor:2233 Tsonk Blvd:Sacramento, CA 95833
   1 Sandor, Filmore:1213 Fortebella St:Pinole, CA 94702
```

Using **uniq** without **sort** counts only duplicate lines that happen to be adjacent. By using **sort**, we make all duplicate lines adjacent.

3. Ignore the first field in comparisons.

```
$ cat names
James Kirk
Jim Kirk
James Dirk
Jimmie Dirk
$ uniq -1 names
James Kirk
James Dirk
```

James Kirk and **Jim Kirk** have the same second field, so the second line is deleted from the output.

unpack

PURPOSE Use the **unpack** command to reconstruct files compacted by the **pack** command.

FORMAT **unpack** *name(s)*

DESCRIPTION The **pack** command stores files in a compressed form. The original file is replaced by the compressed version, and **.z** is added to the end of the original name. The **unpack** command reverses the process, replacing the compressed version with the expanded file and removing the **.z** suffix from the name. The unpacked file has the same file permissions, access and modification times, and owner as the packed file.

If the packed file is called *name*.**z**, its name can be provided to **unpack** as *name* or as *name*.**z**.

The **unpack** command may fail if any of the following conditions is true:

☐ The filename (not counting the **.z**) is longer than two characters less than the maximum filename length.

☐ The file cannot be opened.

☐ The file does not appear to have been produced by **pack**.

☐ There already is a file bearing the "unpacked" name.

☐ The unpacked file cannot be created (for example, you could be in the wrong directory).

COMMON USES You can use **unpack** to unpack files compressed by **pack**.

COMMENTS The **pcat** command lets you view a packed file without reconstructing the unpacked version.

SEE ALSO UNIX Commands: **pack; pcat**

EXAMPLES

---

1. Unpack some files.

   ```
   unpack torque.z force
   ```

   Note that the command interprets **force** to be **force.z**.

PURPOSE Use the **uucp** command to transfer files between UNIX systems connected with a direct line or phone line.

FORMAT **uucp** [*option(s)*] *source-file(s) target-file*

DESCRIPTION The **uucp** command transfers files between UNIX systems. You provide the names of the files to be transferred and the name of the destination file or directory; either or both names can contain a system-name prefix to identify the system for the file. **uucp** then takes care of connecting the systems and transferring the files. (Actually, **uucp** acts as a "front end" for a package of programs.)

COMMON USES You can use **uucp** to transfer files to or from other connected UNIX systems, including UNIX bulletin-board services.

OVERVIEW Actual file transfers are handled by a program called **uucico**. The **uucp** program sets up job requests for **uucico** to execute. Once a connection is established between UNIX systems, a **uucico** process from the calling machine establishes a dialogue with a **uucico** process in the called machine. The two processes exchange information and files, and then break off once both have accomplished their assigned tasks. This approach helps make it possible to monitor for transmission errors. Also, the dialogue can be scheduled for times when phone rates and the system load are low. Typically, the system administrator uses **cron** to periodically run **uucico**.

Usually, **uucp** is restricted in the files it can access. This is to protect against unauthorized copying of files. In many installations, files must be copied into a special public directory before **uucp** can access them for sending. Similarly, the destination directory may have to be the public directory on the receiving system. The usual name for the public directory is **/usr/spool/uucppublic**.

SPECIFYING FILES AND SYSTEMS To specify a file on a particular system, use the *system-name!path-name* notation (you can use the **uuname** command to list known system names). If the system portion is omitted, the current system is assumed. For instance,

```
uucp unifoo!/usr/spool/uucppublic/torts   \
/usr/spool/uucppublic
```

copies a file from the **unifoo** system to the current system. (We've used a backslash to extend the command line over more than one line.) The **~uucp** notation, discussed later, can be substituted for **/usr/spool/uucppublic**, so we could also give the command like this:

```
uucp unifoo!~uucp/torts ~uucp
```

385

The destination name can use a series of system names. This is useful when your system "knows" another system, which knows a third system not directly known to yours. For instance,

```
uucp ~uucp/doog unifoo!ugcorp!~uucp
```

forwards the **doog** file from your system to the **unifoo** system, which then sends it to the **ugcorp** system.

The pathname can have any of several forms:

☐ It can be a full pathname, as in **/usr/spool/uucppublic/stanley/baths**.

☐ It can use a ~ notation to indicate login directories. For instance, **~jennie** stands for Jennie's login directory, typically **/usr/jennie**. A special case of importance is **~uucp**. The **uucp** program normally is set up as a system user with the login name **uucp** and with the **uucp** public directory as its login directory. Thus **~uucp** is short for **/usr/spool/uucppublic**, or for whatever other name that directory has. If an invalid login name is used, the system defaults to **~uucp**.

☐ Extending the last method, ~/*name* is interpreted to represent a file or directory called *name* in the public directory. As with **cp**, *name* is interpreted as a destination filename if it is not already a directory name and if just one file is being copied; otherwise, it is interpreted as a directory name. Unlike **cp**, the **uucp** command can create directories. To force *name* to be interpreted as a directory name instead of a filename, use ~/*name*/. Then, under the default **-d** option, a directory called *name* is created if it does not already exist.

☐ Names not beginning with / or ~ are assumed to branch from the current directory.

Keep in mind that while all these forms are acceptable ways of typing a pathname, some may not be acceptable because of system restrictions. For example, you can type **unifoo!~larry/tweet**, but **uucp** may not have permission to read and write files in that directory.

When wildcard characters such as * are used, they are interpreted on the appropriate system. For example, consider this command:

```
uucp *.c  unifoo!~/Trent/Cl*/source
```

The *.c is interpreted on the your system to mean all files ending in .c and in the current directory. The **Cl*** might, for example, be interpreted by the remote system as the **Clanguage** subdirectory of the **Trent** subdirectory of its public directory.

As with **cp**, when the destination is a directory name rather than a filename, the original filename (the basename, not the whole pathname) is used for the copy.

FILE PERMISSIONS The file copies receive universal read and write permissions. The execute permissions for a copy are the same as for the original.

OPTIONS The **uucp** command has eleven options:

OPTION	ACTION
–c	Transfers a local file without first copying it to the **uucp** spool directory (this is the default). The spool directory is used to store temporarily the files that are scheduled for transmission.
–C	Copies each local file to the spool directory and uses those copies for transmission. (You then could remove or modify the original without affecting what eventually is sent.)
–d	Creates directories as needed for the copy; that is, if the destination is ~/**Hilo/rainfall** and if there is no **Hilo** subdirectory, this option creates it. This is the default behavior.
–f	Does not create directories if needed; that is, if the indicated directories do not already exist, this option doesn't copy the file.
–j	Displays the job identification string on the standard output (by default, the terminal). You can use the identification when using **uustat** to determine the job status or to terminate a job. New with Release 2.
–m	Notifies the user by mail when the requested copy has been completed.
–n*logname*	Notifies the user called *logname* on the remote system that a file has been sent.
–r	Just queues the job without actually starting the file transfer. New with Release 2. The transfer will take place next time **uucico** runs.
–g*grade*	Establishes the priority of the job. Here *grade* is a single letter or number. The lower its ASCII value, the earlier the job is transmitted during a "conversation." New with Release 3.
–s*file*	Reports the status of a transfer to *file*, where *file* is a full pathname. New with Release 3.
–x*debug-level*	Produces debugging on the standard output. The *debug-level* parameter is an integer in the range 0–9. The higher the number, the more detailed is the information. New with Release 3.

COMMENTS The **uucp** command differs in strategy from the **cu** command. The latter allows you to log in at a remote site and transfer files. Two drawbacks are that you need an account on the remote system and that the transmission process is not monitored for errors. With **uucp**, you do get transmission monitoring. Also, you don't need an account on the remote system since you never log in there. However, your system needs an account, since it does log in to do the transfers.

SEE ALSO UNIX Commands: **uuname**; **uulog**; **uustat**; **uuto**; **uux**
UNIX Features: Pathnames and the Directory Tree

EXAMPLES

1. Send a file to a remote site.

```
$ cp greatstuff /usr/spool/uucppublic
$ uucp ~uucp/greatstuff unifoo!~/Betty/
```

This assumes that **uucp** on our system is restricted to the public directory, requiring that we place a copy of the material to be sent there first. We place the copy in the **Betty** subdirectory of the **unifoo** public directory, making it easier for user **betty** to find it. The directory is created if it does not yet exist. The slash after **Betty** ensures that the name is interpreted as a directory name.

2. Retrieve a file from a remote site.

```
uucp unifoo!~/Betty/ohyeah ~uucp/Tiger
```

Of course, to give this command, we need to know the pathname for the remote file. Betty could have sent that information earlier by remote mail. This command assumes that **uucp** has restricted access so that it cannot place the copy directly in our home directory.

3. Inform both sender and reciever of a successful copy.

```
uucp -m -nbetty yeah unifoo!~/Betty/
```

The **-m** option informs the sender, and the **-n** option informs the recipient. The **yeah** file is in the current directory. In a restricted **uucp** environment, the current directory should be the public directory or subdirectory.

PURPOSE   Use the **uulog** command to check the log file for **uucp** or **uux** transactions.

FORMAT   **uulog** [–s*system-name*]

              uulog [*option(s)*] **–s***system-name*   *(new with Release 3)*

              uulog [*option(s)*] *system-name*   *(new with Release 3)*

              uulog [*option(s)*] **–f***system-name*   *(new with Release 3)*

              Here *system-name* is the name of a system as listed by **uuname**. Note: With Release 3, the *system-name* must be provided; with Release 2, it is optional.

DESCRIPTION   When the **uucp** command exchanges files between UNIX systems, it maintains a log of its actions. The **uux** command (for remote commands) also maintains a log. The **uulog** command reports on these log files.

COMMON USES   You can use **uulog** to see what action has taken place with your **uucp** and **uux** commands.

OPTIONS   The **uulog** command has four options:

OPTION	ACTION
–s*system-name*	Reports only on transactions involving the system having the name *system-name*.
–f*system-name*	Does a **tail –f** of the file transfer log for *system-name*. The **–f** option of **tail** causes the command to display new material in the file as it is added. Use BREAK to terminate. New with Release 3.
–x	Looks at the **uuxqt** file instead of the default **uucico** file. New with Release 3.
–*n*	Executes a **tail** command to look at the last *n* lines of the file. New with Release 3.

COMMENTS   UNIX Release 2 maintains a single log file, while Release 3 maintains separate log files for each system. As a result, providing a system in the command line is optional in Release 2, but required in Release 3.

SEE ALSO   UNIX Commands: **uucp**; **uux**

EXAMPLES

1. See what's happened with transmissions to and from another system.

```
$ uulog unifoo
liz unifoo (11/8-9:52) OK (startup)
liz unifoo (11/8-9:52) REQUEST (S /usr/liz/C/show.c ~uucp/ liz)
liz unifoo (11/8-9:52) REQUEST (SUCCEEDED)
liz unifoo (11/8-9:52) REQUEST (S D.spatsX0026 X.spatsX0026 liz)
liz unifoo (11/8-9:52) REQUEST (SUCCEEDED)
liz unifoo (11/8-9:52) OK (conversation complete)
```

This is an extract from a system log file (**liz** is a login name for a user). The output indicates the **spats** system reached the **unifoo** system, performed some transactions, and quit. The first request is from **uucp** to transfer a file. The second request is from a **uux** command; the **X** file contains commands to be executed, and the **D** file contains data.

PURPOSE Use the **uuname** command to find the system names usable with the **uucp** package.

FORMAT uuname [–c] [–l]

DESCRIPTION The **uuname** command, by default, prints the names of other UNIX systems connected to yours via the **uucp** package. (This includes **uux** and the remote mail feature for **mail** and **mailx**.) Connections are set up by the system administrators at the two sites.

COMMON USES You can use **uuname** to refresh your memory about system names before using **uucp**.

OPTIONS The **uuname** command has two options:

OPTION	ACTION
–c	Returns the names of systems known to **cu**. By default, the systems known to **uucp** are displayed. New with Release 3.
–l	Displays the local system name.

COMMENTS The sites listed by the **uuname** command are those to which you have direct access. Chaining these names gives you access to sites known by other sites; that is, **unifoo!ugcorp!** takes you to the **ugcorp** site if it is known to **unifoo**.

SEE ALSO UNIX Commands: **uucp**; **uux**; **mail**; **mailx**

EXAMPLES

1. Find your system name.

   ```
   $ uuname -l
   maxivax
   ```

   Other sites should use the **maxivax!** prefix to identify this site.

2. Find out systems known to your system.

   ```
   $ uuname
   berkrep
   well
   hp70
   unifoo
   ```

   You would use the **well!** prefix to identify files or users on the **well** system.

uupick

PURPOSE Use the **uupick** command to process files sent to you by the **uuto** program.

FORMAT uupick [-s *system*]

DESCRIPTION The **uuto** command places any files sent to you into subdirectories marked with your name in the public directory. The **uupick** command scans for such files and reports their names. It displays the name of each file and awaits your response as to what to do with the file. **uupick** gives you a prompt in this form:

> **from system** *sysname*: **file** *filename*
> ?

Here *sysname* identifies the originating system, and *filename* is the name of a particular file that has been sent. Your response, which should be one of the commands listed below, must be typed after the ? prompt.

The sender may package the files he or she is sending you into a subdirectory. In this case, the message has this form:

> **from system** *sysname*: **directory** *filename*
> ?

In this case, the commands you type in response to the prompt apply to the entire directory; that is, the **d** (delete) command described below removes the directory and its contents, and the **c** (copy) command, also described below, copies the directory and its contents. The files within the directory are not handled individually.

COMMON USES You can use **uupick** to process files sent by **uuto**, which sends mail to inform you if files have been sent to you.

OPTIONS The **uupick** command has only one option:

OPTION	ACTION
-s *system*	Looks only at files sent from the system named *system*.

COMMANDS The following are the valid responses to the **?** prompt provided by **uupick**. Here "entry" means the file or directory named in the **uupick** prompt.

COMMAND	ACTION
<enter>	**Goes to the next entry.**
d	Deletes the entry.
m [*directory*]	Moves the entry to the named directory. The current directory is the default if none is given.
a [*directory*]	Moves all files from that particular sending system to the indicated directory. The current directory is the default.
p	Displays the file contents on the standard output (by default, the terminal). If a directory is named, lists its contents.
q	Quits.
EOF	(Stands for "end-of-file"; typically, this signal is generated with a <control-d>.) Quits.
!*cmd*	Causes the shell to execute the *cmd* command.
*	Displays a usage summary for **uupick**.

SEE ALSO UNIX Commands: **uuto**

EXAMPLES

1. Accept and reject files sent to you.

```
$ uupick
from system unifoo: file forks
? m
from system unifoo: file youowe
? d
$
```

Here we move the **forks** file to our current directory and delete the **youowe** file.

PURPOSE Use the **uustat** command to report on or cancel previous **uucp** commands.

FORMAT uustat [*option(s)*]

DESCRIPTION The **uustat** command can display the status of previously given **uucp** commands, and it can cancel them. Also, it can provide a general status report on connections to other systems. Without options, it displays the status of all of your current **uucp** requests.

COMMON USES You can use **uustat** to see if a file has been sent yet, and you can choose to cancel the job if it hasn't yet been processed.

OPTIONS Many of the **uustat** options are mutually exclusive. In particular, the **-q**, **-k**, and **-r** options must be sole options. The **-s** and **-u** options can be used individually or together.

OPTION	ACTION
-q	Lists the jobs queued up for each system. If a status file exists for a machine, displays its date, time, and status information.
-k *jobid*	Kills the **uucp** request having the *jobid* job identification. (This ID can come from the **-j** option of **uucp** or from the **-q**, **-s**, or **-u** option of **uustat**.) Unless you are the superuser, you must have originated the job in order to kill it.
-r *jobid*	Rejuvenates the *jobid* job. Typically, a cleanup program periodically removes old requests. This option resets the time of last modification to the current time, making the request appear new.
-s *system*	Reports the status of **uucp** requests for the *system* remote system.
-u *user*	Reports the status of **uucp** requests made by *user*. The **-u** option is not supported by Release 3.
-a	Outputs all the jobs in the queue. New with Release 3.
-m	Reports the accessibility statuses of all machines. New with Release 3.

SEE ALSO UNIX Commands: **uucp**

EXAMPLES

1. Check the status of your requests.

```
$ uustat
0422 stentor    unifoo      11/07-08:17     11/07-08:17     4000
0420 stentor    unifoo      11/06-08:16     11/06-08:16     4000
0402 stentor    well        11/04-11:52     11/04-11:52     4000
0401 stentor    berkrep     11/04-11:40     11/04-11:40     4000
```

Here the first column provides the job identification number, and the last column provides a status value. On this particular system, **4000** means queued for sending.

2. Kill a request.

```
uustat -k 0401
```

This kills request **0401**, as identified in Example 1.

PURPOSE   Use the **uuto** command to send files to a user on a remote system.

FORMAT   uuto [-mp] *sourcefile(s) system!user*

Here *source-file(s)* represents one or more files on the user's system, *system* is the name of the destination system, and *user* is the login name of the person on that system to whom the files are being sent.

DESCRIPTION   The **uuto** command is similar to **uucp**, except the destination is identified by the recipient's name rather than by a file pathname. To avoid access problems, files are sent to the system's public directory rather than to the recipient's home directory, and the recipient is informed by mail of their arrival.

This command builds up a subdirectory tree in the public directory so as to associate the sent files with a particular recipient and a particular sending system. Specifically, the destination directory is this:

PUBDIR/**receive**/*user*/*system*

Here **PUBDIR** represents the **uucp** public directory (which is typically /usr/spool/uucppublic), *user* is the recipient, and *system* is the name of the sending system.

COMMON USES   You can use **uuto** to send a group of files to someone on another system.

OPTIONS   The **uuto** command has two options:

OPTION	ACTION
-m	Sends mail to the sender when the copying process is completed.
-p	Copies the source file into the spool directory before transmission.

COMMENTS   The **uuto** command is a shell script that is based on **uucp** but is more convenient for sending files to a particular remote user. Note that this command sends files from your system to a remote system but does not allow you to fetch files from a remote system to your system. The **uuto** command is intended to work hand in hand with the **uupick** command, which can be used by the recipient to process files sent by **uuto**.

SEE ALSO   UNIX Commands: **uucp**; **uupick**

EXAMPLES

1. Send a file to someone on another system.

   ```
   uuto crackers unixinu!groucho
   ```

   This sends the **crackers** file to the **unixinu** system. If the sending system is **unifoo**, the file is placed in the **receive/groucho/unifoo** sequence of subdirectories to the **unixinu** public directory. Mail is sent to **groucho**, telling him of the event. He can copy the file directly to his own directory or use **uupick** to obtain the file.

PURPOSE   Use the **uux** command to execute commands on remote systems.

FORMAT   uux [*option(s)*] *command-string*

Here *command-string*, as described below, specifies the commands, files, and systems to be used.

DESCRIPTION   The **uux** command allows you to run commands on a specified system while using files from that or other systems. As with **uucp**, you do not log in on the other systems. Instead, the **uux** command arranges to transmit the required commands and information to the concerned systems.

COMMON USES   You can use **uux** to work with data scattered over several systems.

USING uux   The *command-string* used in **uux** is like an ordinary command, except that each command and each filename may be prefixed with a *system*! notation to identify on which system the command is to be run and in which system the file can be found. If *system* is omitted, the bare ! is interpreted to be the local system. The system names must be taken from the list of names known to the system (see **uuname**). The ~ notation described under **uucp** can be used; that is, ~*user* is the login directory of the person with the login name *user*, and ~/ or ~**uucp** represents the public directory used by **uucp** and **uux**.

For example, here is a command that uses **sort** on the **unifoo** system to sort and merge files from that system and from the local system (we've used a backslash to extend the command line over more than one line):

```
uux "unifoo!sort unifoo!~/jlist !~/klist >  \
unifoo!~/list"
```

The **jlist** file in the **unifoo** public directory and the **klist** file in the local public directory are sorted and merged, using the **sort** command from the **unifoo** system. The output is redirected to the **list** file in the **unifoo** public directory.

Characters with special meaning to the shell, such as **>**, must be quoted. You can quote them individually, as in **\>** or **">"**, or simply quote the whole command string, as above.

The **uux** command has limitations. First, each site can select which commands are usable by **uux**. If a command is not allowed by the remote site, it informs you by remote mail. Second, each site can select which of its directories can be accessed by **uux**. Third, the wildcard metacharacter * and the redirection operations **>>** and **<<** cannot be used. Fourth, a pipe can't be used to connect commands on different systems; that is, a construction like

```
uux "lux!pr lux!~/foo | pop!lp"
```

is not allowed. All subsequent commands must be executed on the same system as the first command.

When a command is run on a particular system, all needed files not already present in that system are copied into a work directory there. Thus, in the example above, the **klist** file has to be copied from the local system to the **unifoo** system. Because of this, you should avoid importing two files with the same name, since one will overwrite the other. For example, the following command is not a good one:

```
uux "!sort mom!~/list pop!~/list > !both"
```

However, it is okay to have an imported file with the same name as a file in the execution system, since the imported file is placed in a different directory.

Some commands can name an output file; in this case, the name of the output file should be enclosed in escaped parentheses. For example, this command

```
uux "pop!sort -o \(!~/stuff\) mom!~/list"
```

uses **pop sort** to sort the **list** file from the **mom** system and places the output in the **stuff** file in the local system. The parentheses let **uux** know that it does not have to fetch the **stuff** file to the **pop** system.

OPTIONS The **uux** command has thirteen options:

OPTION	ACTION
-	Makes the standard input to **uux** the standard input to the *command-string* argument.
-j	Displays on the standard output (by default, the terminal) the job identification string. This string can then be used with the **uustat** command. New with Release 2.
-n	Doesn't notify the user of failed commands.
-a *name*	Identifies the user as *name* instead of by the initiator's user ID (the user is notified). New with Release 3.
-b	If the exit status of a **uux** command is not zero, returns the original standard input to the command. New with Release 3.
-c	Does not copy local files to the spool directory for transfer to a remote machine; this is the default. New with Release 3.

(continued)

399

OPTION	ACTION
-C	Forces local files to be copied to the spool directory for transfer. New with Release 3.
-g*grade*	Here *grade* is a single letter or number that establishes the priority of the job; the lower the ASCII value, the earlier the job is transmitted during a conversation. New with Release 3.
-p	Same as -. Added to conform to the standard UNIX option format. New with Release 3.
-r	Queues the job, but doesn't start the file transfer. New with Release 3.
-s*file*	Reports the status of transfer for *file*. New with Release 3.
-x*debug level*	Produces debugging on the standard output. The *debug level* parameter is an integer in the range 0 through 9. The higher the number, the more detailed the information. New with Release 3.
-z	Notifies the user of success. New with Release 3.

COMMENTS For security reasons, many sites heavily restrict the commands that can be used on them; often **rmail** is the only command allowed. (The remote mail system uses the **uux** command.)

SEE ALSO UNIX Commands: **sh; uucp; uustat; uuname**

EXAMPLES

---

1. Run a command on a remote system.

   ```
   uux "lux!sort nix!~joyce/jlist !~kathy/klist > bigx!~final/list"
   ```

   This command copies the **jlist** file from the **nix** system to the **lux** system, copies the **klist** file from the local system to the **lux** system, has the **lux** system sort and merge the files, and routes the output to the **list** file on the **bigx** system.

2. Pipe information to a **uux** command.

   ```
   pr notes ! uux - unifoo!rmail torpo
   ```

   The - option causes the standard input to **uux**, here the **pr** output, to become the standard input to the *command-string*, here **unifoo!rmail torpo**. Thus the **pr**'ed contents of **notes** are mailed to **torpo** on the **unifoo** system.

PURPOSE   Use the **vi** program when you want to make changes in files that are displayed on your screen.

FORMAT   **vi** [*option(s)*] [*file(s)*]

DESCRIPTION   The **vi** (pronounced "vee-eye") program is a "screen editor." This means it displays a file on the screen and allows you to move freely through it, inserting text and making other changes. Your editing is shown on-screen. In this respect, **vi** is different from the **ed** and **ex** editors, which deal with text on a line-by-line basis.

Like the other UNIX editors, **vi** does its work using a temporary work area called a "buffer." When you decide to save your work, you have the editor copy the buffer contents to a permanent file. (This is called "writing" to a file.)

When you edit an existing file, it first is copied, or "read," into the buffer. The **vi** editor makes the terminal screen a "window" showing part, or all, of the buffer as its contents are being edited. The position of the cursor on the screen indicates the current location within the file. (The cursor is the rectangle of light on the screen that shows where the next character you type will be placed.)

Because the editor must control the screen display to reflect changes in the buffer, the **vi** program needs to know the properties of your terminal. This information is provided by the **TERM** environmental variable, which identifies your terminal using a name stored in a database of terminal information, called **terminfo**, maintained by your system.

The **vi** editor is based on the **ex** line editor, and it is possible to switch between the two while editing. The **vi** editor excels at such tasks as inserting text into a line, changing words, and selectively deleting words, while **ex** is superior for many global editing tasks, such as replacing all occurrences of one word with another.

To invoke **vi**, type **vi**, followed by the options you need, if any, and the name of the file you want to edit. If the file already exists, **vi** provides a copy of it for you to edit. If the file does not exist, it will be created the first time you save the text you type after invoking the editor. If you omit a filename when invoking **vi**, you can use the editor's **:w** command to select a new name for the file, or you can use the **:e** command to select an existing file.

COMMON USES   You can use **vi** to create and edit text files of any kind. It is particularly useful for writing and editing programs, since it makes it easy to correct errors such as omitted parentheses.

OPTIONS Five options can be used with **vi**:

OPTION	ACTION
-r *file*	Recovers *file* after an editor or system crash. (The buffer in which editing work is done is erased when **vi** terminates normally, but not when it terminates because of a crash. The **-r** option uses the preserved buffer to restore your work.) If *file* is omitted, **vi** prints a list of saved files.
-l	Sets the LISP mode, which is used when programming in the LISP language. (This option turns on the **lisp** variable, described under **ex**.)
-w*n*	Sets the window size to *n* lines.
-R	Sets the read-only mode. This allows you to scan through a valuable file, perhaps copying parts to other files, without risking accidental changes to the file.
+*command*	Here *command* is an **ex** editor command; it is executed before regular editing begins.

OVERVIEW The **vi** editor has two modes: the command mode and the text, or input, mode. In the text mode, keystrokes are interpreted as text to be placed in the file, and each keystroke is echoed on the screen, so that you see what you type. In the command mode, keystrokes are interpreted as commands and do such things as delete letters, words, and lines. Most command-mode keystrokes are not echoed (the :, !, /, and ? commands are exceptions).

When invoked, the editor comes up in the command mode. Several commands (including **a**, **i**, and **o**) place the editor in the text mode. The <esc> key takes the editor from the text mode back to the command mode. However, this key is not a toggle; hitting it when you are in the command mode does not put you in the text mode. Instead, it either cancels a partial command or else rings a bell, reassuring you that you are in the command mode. There is no on-screen indication of which mode you are in, so that reassurance is sometimes handy.

Other special keys are those that send an INTERRUPT signal. Typically, these are the <del> and <break> keys. If you are in the text mode, sending an interrupt terminates that mode and places you in the command mode. If you are in the command mode, an INTERRUPT signal cancels incomplete commands and rings the bell if no commands are present. An interrupt, for example, can be used to halt excessive screen scrolling caused by injudiciously holding down a cursor-moving key too long. An interrupt does not terminate the **vi** editor itself, however.

Some lines may be specially marked. When **vi** is invoked with an empty buffer, the screen is nearly filled with lines beginning with a ~. These indicate lines past the end of the file. Some terminals, when a line is deleted, replace the on-screen line with an **@**. This marker indicates space on the screen that does not correspond to lines in the buffer. The **<control-r>** command redraws the screen, eliminating **@** markers.

To learn **vi**, you need to learn how to invoke it, how to change from one mode to another, and how to use at least some of its commands. We've already covered the first two topics; next we'll take a look at its commands.

COMMANDS We'll discuss the commands in (extended) alphabetic order, but first, here's an overview. Aside from the :, /, and ? commands, **vi** commands do not require that you hit the <enter> key to activate them; they take effect as soon as you strike the appropriate key or keys. The commands can be grouped in terms of what they do and how they are used. The following sections are one possible grouping; they illustrate the general range of commands and provide a short summary of each one. For a more complete description, read the Command Summaries section.

Group I Commands

The following commands leave **vi** in the text mode. The characters you type after issuing one of these commands appear within the text. Some of these commands add text, and others replace it.

COMMAND	ACTION
a	Appends text after the cursor.
A	Appends text at the end of the line.
i	Inserts text before the cursor.
I	Inserts text at the beginning of the line.
o	Opens a new line below the cursor.
O	Opens a new line above the cursor.
R	Replaces text ("typeover").
s	Substitutes for the character under the cursor.
S	Substitutes for the whole line.
c	Changes the indicated text.
C	Replaces to the end of the line.

Group II Commands

The following commands alter the text (delete, replace, and move material) but leave **vi** in the command mode. (Groups III through VI also leave **vi** in the command mode.)

COMMAND	ACTION
d	Deletes the indicated text.
D	Deletes to the end of the line.
x	Deletes the character under the cursor.
X	Deletes the character in front of the cursor.
y	Makes a copy of ("yanks") the indicated text.
Y	Yanks the current line.
p	Puts text after (or below) the cursor.
P	Puts text before (or above) the cursor.
"	Used with y, **Y**, **d**, **D**, **p**, and **P** to indicate a buffer.
J	Joins lines.
>	Shifts text to the right.
<	Shifts text to the left.
!	Processes text with a UNIX command, replacing the text with the output of the command.
=	Reindents for LISP.
r	Replaces the character under the cursor.
u	Undoes the last change.
U	Undoes all recent changes on a line.
.	Repeats the last change-producing command.

Group III Commands

The following commands, termed "movement" commands, control the position of the cursor on the screen. Note that they move the cursor, not text (see Figure 6 on page 406).

COMMAND	ACTION
0	Moves the cursor to the beginning of the line.
$	Moves the cursor to the end of the line.

COMMAND	ACTION
h	Moves the cursor to the left.
j	Moves the cursor down.
k	Moves the cursor down.
l	Moves the cursor to the right.
^H	Moves the cursor to the left (backspace).
[space]	Moves the cursor to the right.
f	Moves the cursor forward to the indicated character.
F	Moves the cursor backward to the indicated character.
t	Moves the cursor forward to just in front of the indicated character.
T	Moves the cursor backward to just after the indicated character.
;	Repeats the last f, F, t, or T command.
,	Reverses the last f, F, t, or T command.
¦	Places the cursor in the indicated column.
%	Finds the matching parenthesis or brace.

Note: In the commands that follow, **W**, **B**, and **E** use a more general definition of "word" than do **w**, **b**, and **e** (see the Command Summaries for **b** and **B**).

w	Moves forward to the beginning of a word.
W	Moves forward to the beginning of a word.
b	Moves backward to the beginning of a word.
B	Moves backward to the beginning of a word.
e	Moves forward to the end of a word.
E	Moves forward to the end of a word.
)	Moves forward to the beginning of a sentence.
}	Moves forward to the beginning of a paragraph.
)	Moves backward to the beginning of a sentence.
}	Moves backward to the beginning of the preceding paragraph.
<enter>	Moves down.
-	Moves to the first non-white-space character in the previous line.
+	Moves to the first non-white-space character in the following line.

(continued)

COMMAND	ACTION	(continued)
'	Moves to the marked line.	
`	Moves to a marked character.	
H	Moves to the top of the screen.	
L	Moves to the bottom of the screen.	
M	Moves to the middle of the screen.	

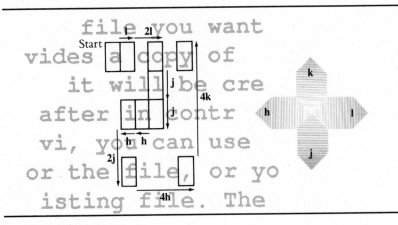

FIGURE 13. *Simple cursor movement*

Group IV Commands
The following commands position the window in the file.

COMMAND	ACTION
^F	Scrolls the window forward one screen.
^B	Scrolls the window backward one screen.
^U	Scrolls the window backward one half-screen.
^D	Scrolls the window forward one half-screen.
^E	Scrolls forward one line.
^Y	Scrolls backward one line.
G	Moves to the indicated line.
n	Moves to the next instance of the search pattern.

COMMAND	ACTION
N	Reverse of **n**.
?	Scans backward for the search pattern.
/	Scans forward for the search pattern.
]]	Moves forward to the next section.
[[	Moves backward to the previous section.

Group V Commands

The following commands adjust the screen.

COMMAND	ACTION
^L	Clears and redraws the screen.
^R	Redraws the current screen.
z	Redraws and repositions the screen.

Group VI Commands

Group VI has only one command, which is used to mark lines in the text.

COMMAND	ACTION
m	Marks lines in the text.

Group VII Commands

The following commands can be given from the text mode.

COMMAND	ACTION
^H	Moves backward one space.
^W	Moves backward one word.
\<esc\>	Returns to the command mode.
\<del\>	Returns to the command mode.
^D	Backs up over indentation.
^V	Escapes, or "quotes," the next character; that is, takes the next character literally, rather than treating it as a command.

Group VIII Commands

The following commands exit the editor and save your work.

COMMAND	ACTION
:wq	Saves your work and exits.
:x	Saves your work and exits.
ZZ	Saves your work and exits.

The : command is of special note, because it allows you to execute most **ex** commands (see the short discussion of this command in the Command Summaries). The **:w** and the **:q** commands may be used separately, too.

Many **vi** commands optionally can be prefixed by a number to indicate how many times the command is to be repeated. For instance, **x** deletes one character and **10x** deletes ten characters. Such a prefix is termed a "count."

Several **vi** commands (**c**, **d**, **y**, **<**, **>**, and **!**) involve giving a command letter followed by a "movement command" (Group III above) indicating the extent of the text to be affected. For example, **dl** means "delete a letter," **dw** means "delete a word," and **d$** means "delete to the end of the line." Other boundaries (sentence, paragraph, and section) are described later.

Command Summaries

In the following summaries, commands that accept an optional numeric prefix are identified as "taking a count."

Several commands refer to variables and options used by the editor. These variables and options are described under the **ex** command. You can use the **:set all** command to display the current values of all such parameters.

Depending on the value of the **redraw** variable, insertions and appends may appear on the screen as typeovers until you strike <esc>.

The term "white space," when used in the following discussion, refers to spaces, tabs, and newlines.

The entries for **b** and **B** explain the two definitions of "word" used by **vi**.

Control characters are indicated with a caret (**^**); that is, <control-d> is represented as **^D**.

The following commands are given in the command mode unless otherwise indicated. Note that a few commands can be given in either the text or command mode, with the effect depending on the mode.

COMMAND	ACTION
^B	Scrolls backward to display the window before the current one. If possible, a two-line overlap is kept. You can use a count to indicate how many windows the editor should go back.
^D	In the command mode, causes the screen to scroll forward one half-screen. To scroll just *n* lines, use *n*^D. The value of *n* is remembered by future ^D and ^U commands during the current editing session. In the text mode, this command causes the cursor to back up over indentation. The indentation can come from the ^T command or the **autoindent** feature. The cursor is backed **shiftwidth** spaces over the indentation (see the discussion of **ex** for an explanation of **autoindent** and **shiftwidth**).
^E	Scrolls forward one line. If possible, the cursor is left in the same position relative to the text.
^F	Scrolls forward one window. If possible, there is a two-line overlap. A count, if used, indicates how many windows to scroll forward.
^G	Displays the current filename and line number, and the total number of lines.
^J	Moves the cursor down one line in the same column. Use a count to move more than one line. Same as ^N and **j**.
^L	Clears and redraws the screen.
^M	Moves forward to the first non-white-space character on the following line. A count can be used to move further than the following line.
^N	Same as ^J and **j**.
^R	Redraws the current screen, eliminating screen lines that are not in the file. The editor temporarily marks these lines with an **@**.
^T	A text-mode command. If the cursor is at the beginning of a line or preceded only by white space, inserts **shiftwidth** white spaces. In general, the most efficient combination of tabs and spaces is used. (The **shiftwidth** parameter, discussed under **ex**, is set to the number of columns to be shifted.)
^U	Scrolls up through the text one half-window. To scroll a certain number of lines instead of a half-window, use a count to give the number of lines. The count is remembered for subsequent uses of ^U and ^D.

(continued)

COMMAND	ACTION	*(continued)*

COMMAND	ACTION
^V	A text-mode command. Used to "quote" (or "escape") special characters so that they can be placed in the text. For instance, the sequence **^V\<esc\>** (where \<esc\> is the escape key) places the \<esc\> character in the text; otherwise, \<esc\> terminates the text mode.
^W	A text-mode command. Backs up one word. The characters backed over are deleted from the buffer but remain displayed.
\<esc\>	(Also generated by **^[**.) When given in the command mode, cancels an incomplete command, or sounds the bell (or beeper) if there is no command in progress. With the :, /, and ? commands, terminates input and executes the command.
\<esc\>	When given in the text mode, returns the editor to command mode.
[space]	Moves one space to the right, but not past the end of the line. A count can be used when you want to move more than one space. Same as the l command.
!*movement cmd*	Processes text lines with a UNIX command or other program. The ! is followed by a movement command to indicate the scope; for example, !j means "process text up to the end of the next line." (The scope must go beyond the current line; !$ is not valid.) Next comes the command to be executed, then the \<enter\> key. The affected text becomes input to the command and is replaced by the output of the command. For example, the sequence **!}sort\<enter\>** causes lines from the current line to the end of the paragraph, indicated by the **}**, to be replaced by the same lines in sorted order.
	When a !*movement cmd* command is given, the editor displays a ! on the bottom line *after* the scope is given. The rest of the command (but not the scope) appears on the bottom line as typed.
	A count typed before the ! is passed on to the movement command. Thus **3!)sort** is the same as **!3)sort**; both sort the next three sentences, indicated by the), line by line.
	To process a given number of lines, start with a count and use two ! marks. For instance, **10!!sort** sorts 10 lines, beginning with the current line.
"	Indicates that a named buffer will be used (see Named and Unnamed Buffers later in this entry).
$	Moves to the end of the current line. Use a count to move to the end of a later line. For instance, 2$ moves to the end of the next line.

COMMAND	ACTION
%	Moves forward or backward to the parenthesis or curly brace that matches the parenthesis or curly brace at the current position of the cursor; that is, it finds the next) for a (and the preceding (for a). This is particularly valuable for programming in C, which uses nested parentheses and braces.
&	Repeats the previous **ex** substitute command; that is, repeats a substitution initiated with a **:s** command. It does not repeat substitutions made using, for example, **vi**'s **s**, **r**, and **c** commands.
'*c*	Here *c* is a lowercase letter. Moves forward to the line marked by *c* using the **m** command, and places the cursor at the first non-white-space character in the line. When used as a **move** command for an operator such as **d**, the scope includes the whole line; that is, **d'g** deletes through the whole line marked with a **g**.
' '	Returns to the line of the previous context and places the cursor at the first non-white-space character there. For instance, '**x** takes the cursor to the line previously marked with an **x** (using the **m** command), and ' ' takes the cursor back to its location just before the '**x** command was given. Note that this command consists of two single quotes (' ') and not of a double quote (").
'*c*	Like '*c*, except the cursor is placed at the exact character position marked by the *c*.
` `	(Two backquotes.) Like ' ', except the cursor is placed at the exact character position marked by the *c*.
[[	Backs up to the previous section boundary. Section boundaries are defined by the **sections** variable, as discussed under **ex**. Lines starting with a form-feed character (**^L**) or a left brace ({) mark section beginnings in any case. When the lisp option (**-l**) is set in the command line or when the **lisp** variable described in the **ex** entry is set, each (at the beginning of a line is a section boundary.
]]	Moves forward to the next section boundary (see]] above).
^	Moves forward to the first non-white-space character that is on the current line.

(continued)

COMMAND	ACTION	(continued)

(Moves backward to the beginning of a sentence. A sentence end is defined by a period, exclamation mark, or question mark followed by the end of the line or by at least two spaces. To allow for quotations, single and double quotes between the punctuation and the end of the line or the spaces are ignored. Paragraph and section boundaries also count as sentence beginnings.

      If you provide a count, the command moves the cursor backward that number of sentences.

      When **lisp** is set (see **ex**), moves to the beginning of a LISP "s-expression."

)   Moves to the beginning of the next sentence. If a count is used, moves forward that number of sentences. (See (above for the definition of a sentence.)

{   Moves backward to the beginning of the preceding paragraph. Paragraph boundaries are defined by the **paragraphs** variable, as discussed under **ex**. Additionally, a completely empty line and a section boundary (see [[above) always count as paragraph boundaries. You can use a count to indicate how many paragraphs to move.

}   Moves forward to the beginning of the next paragraph. You can use a count to indicate how many paragraphs to move. (See { above for the definition of a paragraph.)

n| Moves the cursor to column *n* if possible. The | command requires a count *n*.

+   Moves the cursor to the first non–white-space character in the next line. Use a count to move more than a line. Same a ^M or a <return>.

,   (Comma.) Reverses the last **F**, **f**, **T**, or **t** search command, moving the opposite direction in the current line. Use a count to repeat the action several times.

–   (Hyphen.) Moves backward to the first non–white-space character in the preceding line. Use a count to specify how many lines to move back.

.   (Period.) Repeats the last command that produced an editing change (cursor- and screen-movement commands are ignored). If a count is given, it is passed to the repeated command.

COMMAND	ACTION
/str	Searches for the next occurrence of the string *str*. The search starts with the line after the current line and wraps around to the beginning of the file if necessary. In general, the string *str* can be a regular expression (as defined under **ex**). Thus **/the** finds the next occurrence of **the**, and **/[Tt]he** finds the next occurrence of **the** or **The**. The / and the string appear on the bottom line of the screen. The \<enter\> key or \<esc\> key must be used to terminate the string entry and start the search. The search continues until the string is found, until it is determined that the string is not present, or until an interrupt signal (typically \<break\> or \<del\>) is given. To move the cursor to a certain number of lines before or after the pattern, use a suffix of the form */-n* or */+n*, where *n* is the number of lines. For example, **/Sincerely/+2** places the cursor on the second line following the next line containing **Sincerely**. The / can be used with operators such as **d** to define the range to be affected. The defined region is from the current cursor position to just before the matched string. If one of the two numeric suffixes mentioned above is used, whole lines are affected.
0	Moves to the first character on the current line.
:	Used to initiate an **ex** command. The : and the command are displayed on the bottom line of the screen. To terminate the command-line input and initiate the command, hit \<enter\> or \<esc\>. (See the short discussion of the : command following this section.)
;	Repeats the last **f**, **F**, **t**, or **T** search command. A count can be used to request a number of repetitions.
<	Shifts a line **shiftwidth** columns to the left (**shiftwidth** is a variable discussed under **ex**). Follow this command with a second **<** or an \<enter\> to shift the current line to the left; otherwise, follow it with a movement command that specifies additional lines to be affected. For example, **<j** shifts the current line and the following line to the left. A count is passed through to the movement command, so **2<j** shifts the current line and the next two.
>	Shifts a line **shiftwidth** columns to the right; otherwise, similar to **<**.

(continued)

413

COMMAND	ACTION	*(continued)*
=	Used with the **lisp** option. Reindents the specified lines as if they had been typed with **lisp** and **autoindent** set (these variables are discussed under **ex**). To specify how many lines, precede the command with a count or follow it with a movement command.	
?str	Scans backward for the pattern *str*. The reverse of / (see /**str** above for more details).	
A	Appends at the end of the line, leaving the editor in the text mode.	
B	Backs up one word and places the cursor at the beginning of the word. A "word" is any sequence of characters without white space (the similar **b** command uses a different definition of a word). For example, **hot.429** is a word. Use a count to specify how many words to move.	
C	Changes the rest of the current line. A $ appears, indicating the end of the affected text. Type the new text, hit <esc>, and the old text is replaced by the new.	
D	Deletes from the cursor to the end of the current line.	
E	Moves forward to the end of the current word. Here a word is any sequence of characters without white space (See **B**; the otherwise similar **e** command uses a different definition of a word). Use a count to indicate the number of words to move.	
F*c*	Here *c* represents a character. Scans backward in the current line to the character *c* and, if *c* is found, places the cursor there. Use a count to indicate how many characters to move backward.	
*n*G	Here *n* is a line number. Moves to line *n*. If *n* is omitted, moves to line 1.	
H	Moves the cursor to the top of the screen and places the cursor at the first non-white-space character on the line. If a count is given, goes to that number of lines from the top. When used to specify the scope of a command, whole lines are affected, as in **dH**, where even initial white spaces are deleted.	
I	Inserts at the beginning of the line, leaving the editor in the text mode.	
J	Appends the next line to the current one, supplying spaces as needed so that words and sentences are not run together. Use a count to specify how many lines should be joined.	

COMMAND	ACTION
L	Moves the cursor to the first non–white-space character of the last line on the screen. If a count is given, moves the cursor to that many lines from the bottom. When **L** is used to specify the scope of a command, whole lines are affected, as in **dL**, where text from the current cursor position to the end of the last screen line is deleted.
M	Moves the cursor to the first non–white-space character on the middle line of the screen.
O	Opens a new line above the current cursor position, places the cursor there, and enters the text mode.
P	Places the last deleted text back on the screen. If whole lines were deleted, the replaced text is placed above the current cursor position; otherwise, it is placed just before the cursor. This command can be used with ” to fetch the contents of named buffers (see the discussion of named buffers below).
Q	Quits the **vi** mode and enters the **ex** mode. (The : command lets you give one **ex** command, but **Q** leaves you in the **ex** editor.)
R	Replaces on-screen characters with typed characters until <esc> is struck. This is a type-over mode.
S	Replaces the entire current line with the text typed subsequent to this command. Type <esc> to end the substitution.
T*c*	Here *c* is a character. Scans backward in the current line for the character *c* and places the cursor just after the character. Use a count to indicate how many times the search should be repeated.
U	Undoes all changes made to the current line since the cursor was last moved to it.
W	Moves forward to the beginning of a word. If a count is used, moves the indicated number of words. A word is a sequence of characters without any white spaces (see **B**; the otherwise similar **w** command uses a different definition of a word).
X	Deletes the character before the cursor. To delete more than one character on the current line, use a count to indicate the number of characters.
Y	Copies, or “yanks,” the current line and places the copy in an unnamed buffer. You can use ” to specify a named buffer (see the discussion of named buffers below).

(continued)

COMMAND	ACTION	*(continued)*
ZZ	Exits the editor. If the buffer has been edited since the last write, saves the edited contents.	
a	Switches to text mode. Text is placed after the current cursor position. If the new text is limited to one line, a count can be used to enter several instances of it.	
b	Backs up to the beginning of a word. A count can be used to specify how many words to back up. A word, in this case, is a string of letters and digits or else a string of non-letters and non-digits containing no white spaces (the similar **B** command uses a different definition of a word). Thus **dormouse** and **#$%^*** are words, and **hot.429** is three words: **hot**, **.**, and **429**.	
c	Changes text. This command is followed by a movement command to indicate the range to be affected. For example, **c$** means "change text up to the end of the line," and **cw** means "change text up to the end of a word." A $ appears on the screen to mark the scope of the change, and the editor enters the text mode. After you have finished typing the replacement text, hit <esc> to replace the old text with the new and to return to the command mode. The replacement text can be any length. A count can be passed through to the movement command. Thus **3cw** means "change three words."	
d	Deletes text. This command is followed by a movement command to indicate the range affected. For example, **d0** means "delete from the current cursor position to the beginning of the line." A count can be passed through to the movement command. Thus **5dw** means "delete five words." If more than part of a line is deleted, the deleted text is saved in a numbered buffer (see the discussion of buffers below).	
dd	Deletes the current line. Use a count to delete more than one line. (A special case of the **d** command.)	
e	Moves forward to the end of a word (as defined under **b**). A count can be used to tell how many words to move.	
f*c*	Here *c* is a character. Moves the cursor forward to that character, if it is found after the cursor and on the same line. Use a count to repeat the search.	
h	Moves the cursor to the left. Use a count to tell how many characters to move.	
i	Switches to text mode. This command is like **a** except that the text is placed to the left of the cursor.	

COMMAND	ACTION
j	Moves the cursor down one line in the same column. (If the next line has fewer characters than the current column, the cursor won't be able to go all the way to the column position.) Same as **^J** and **^N**.
k	Moves the cursor one line up in the same column. Same as **^P**.
l	Moves the cursor one character to the right. Same as **[space]**.
m*c*	Here *c* is a lowercase character. Marks the current cursor position with a *c*. This enables you to refer to the line as '*c* and to the exact cursor position as `*c*. Typing either of these combinations in the command mode takes you to the indicated line or cursor position.
n	Repeats the last **/** or **?** search command.
o	Opens a line below the current cursor position, moves the cursor to the beginning of the new line, and enters the text mode.
p	Like **P**, except that this command puts text after or below the current cursor position.
r*c*	Here *c* is a character. Replaces the character currently under the cursor with the character *c*, which may be a newline (this is one way to break one line into two). If an *n* count is given, then *n* characters are replaced with *c*, beginning with the one under the cursor and counting to the right.
s	Deletes the single character under the cursor and enters the text mode. Text entered up to <esc> then replaces the deleted letter. To replace a longer block of characters, use a count to indicate how many characters to delete.
t*c*	Here *c* is a character. Searches forward in the line for *c* and places the cursor just before it. A count repeats the search the indicated number of times.
u	Undoes the last editing change to the current file. If repeated, it restores the buffer and screen to the preceding state. If text from more than one line is deleted, it is saved in a numbered buffer (see the discussion of buffers below). If you strike **u** again before making other changes, it toggles you back to the state of affairs before the first **u**.
w	Moves to the beginning of the next word (a word is defined as for the **b** command). Use a count to move forward more than one word.

(continued)

COMMAND	ACTION	*(continued)*
x	Deletes the character under the cursor. If an *n* count is given, deletes *n* characters from the cursor forward, but does not continue to the next line.	
y	Copies, or "yanks," the specified text into a buffer. This command should be followed by a movement command to indicate the range to be yanked. For instance, **ye** yanks from the cursor to the end of the current word. The unnamed buffer is used. If the command is preceded with "*c*, the text also is placed in the buffer called *c* (see the discussion of buffers below).	
yy	Yanks the current line. (A special case of the **y** command.)	
z	Redraws the screen. If **z** is followed by an <enter>, places the current line at the top of the screen. The combination **z.** places the current line in the center of the screen, and **z-** places the current line at the bottom of the screen. An *n* count immediately after the **z** means "use a window *n* lines long." An *m* count before the **z** means "place line *m* at the top, bottom, or center of the screen, depending on the suffix."	

ex Commands

You can access the **ex** commands in two ways. You can use the **Q** command to switch the editor to the **ex** mode, or you can use the **:** command to give one **ex** command and still stay in the **vi** mode. The **ex** commands are discussed in detail under **ex**, but you should be aware of the commands listed below. We present them here as they would be typed in the **vi** command mode, with a prefatory **:**.

COMMAND	ACTION
:w[*name*]	Writes the current contents of the editing buffer to the *name* file. If *name* is omitted, uses the current remembered filename (if you invoked **vi** with a filename and haven't changed files, that is the file used). The **:w** command can be given during an editing session to update the original file or at the end, in the form **:wq** as a save and quit command. It also can be used to transfer text to another file by providing the file's name. When used with an address or address range, it copies just the indicated lines to the named file. Note: The **w** command overwrites the previous contents of the *name* file.
:w >> *name*	Appends text to the *name* file.

COMMAND	ACTION
:q	Quits the editor. The editor protests if changes have been made since the last write. If you really want to quit anyway, use :q!.
:q!	Abandons the editing session, ignoring all changes made since the last write.
:e *name*	Edits the file called *name*, replacing the current edit buffer contents with material from the *name* file. Normally, you would precede this command with a :w command to save the current contents of the editing buffer. Using :e allows you to change files without reinvoking the editor. The contents of the named buffers (see below) are saved, so they can be used for transferring blocks from one file to another.

Other useful **ex** commands worth looking into are :**r** for reading in contents of other files or the output of commands, :**s** for global substitutions, and :**map** for mapping a key to represent several keystrokes.

UNNAMED AND NAMED BUFFERS The **vi** editor maintains several buffers. The editing buffer contains the text currently being edited, the "unnamed buffer" is a default temporary storage location, and the "named buffers" are two types of temporary storage locations (numbered buffers and alphabetic buffers) that you can use with certain **vi** commands.

Specifically, the unnamed and named buffers are used by the yank (**y** and **Y**) and put (**p** and **P**) commands, and by commands that delete text (**d**, **x**, **c**, and so on). In particular, yank and delete commands place material in the buffers, and put commands copy material from the buffers to the editing buffer. The contents of these storage buffers are not changed by put commands, so the same buffer can be copied into text repeatedly.

The Unnamed Buffer
By default, text that is deleted or yanked is placed in the unnamed buffer and, also by default, the put commands place the contents of the unnamed buffer back in the text buffer near the current cursor location. Thus the combination **dw** followed by a movement command followed by **p** deletes a word from one location and appends it in another. Similarly, the combination **yw** followed by a movement command followed by **p** copies a word from one location to another.

The Numbered Buffers

When a **d** command deletes more than a part of a line, a copy is placed in a numbered buffer, which is one type of named buffer. The numbered buffers are numbered 1 through **9**, and buffer 1 contains the most recently deleted material. When new material is placed in the numbered buffers, the old contents are bumped up one buffer, with the old contents of buffer **9** being discarded. For instance, giving the **dd** command four times in succession fills buffers 1 through 4. But a command like **4dd** counts as a single command, and all four deleted lines are stored in a single buffer.

The contents of a numbered buffer can be recovered by using the sequence "*n*p or "*n*P, where *n* is the number of the buffer. This enables you to recover deleted material that is beyond the scope of the **u** (undo) command. The sequence "*n*p **u** can be used to view the contents of a buffer and then take it back off the screen.

Alphabetic Buffers

The second class of named buffers is designated by the names **a** through **z**. By using a "*c* (where *c* is a lowercase letter) prefix to a **d** or **y** command, you can place the deleted or copied material in the buffer named *c*. Material can then be copied from the named buffer to the editing buffer using a **p** or **P** command with the same prefix. For example "**a10dd** deletes 10 lines, copying them into buffer **a**. The cursor then can be moved to another location, and the "**ap** command can be used to copy the deleted material to the new location.

THE ex/vi ENVIRONMENT The **ex** editor has a working environment with many adjustable parameters, as does **vi**. In particular, it has over two dozen option variables that control its behavior, covering such matters as the window size, tab settings, autoindentation, screen redrawing, automatic right margin, and so on. The **vi** command **:set all** shows the names and setting of these parameters, and **:set** can be used to change the settings (see **ex** for more details).

You can customize **vi** by establishing your own default settings for these option parameters. When **vi** is invoked, it checks to see if an **EXINIT** shell parameter has been defined. If so, it executes the initialization commands found there. Then the editor checks to see if there is a file named **.exrc** in the current directory. If so, it executes the initialization commands found there. If it doesn't find a **.exrc** file there, it checks your home directory for a **.exrc** file and uses it, if present. Because the **.exrc** file is read after **EXINIT**, settings in **.exrc** override **EXINIT** settings.

COMMENTS Cursor movement is limited to locations already occupied by text (spaces count as text).

The **vi** editor has an imposing number of commands. In the command mode, practically every keystroke does something, and learning all of these commands is a daunting undertaking. In fact, very few users do learn them all. A sensible approach is to begin by learning the most essential commands: **a**, **i**, and **o** for adding text; **x**, **r**, and **d** for editing text; **h**, **i**, **j**, and **k** for cursor movement; **ZZ** for quitting and saving; **q**! for abandoning a file; and, very importantly, **u** for undoing a command. Then, as you have time, sample the other commands. You will use the ones you find most useful the most often, and thus will learn them without undue effort.

Although the **vi** editor shows you on-screen the editing changes you make, it is not a word processor. For one thing, it does not reformat text when you make insertions or deletions. The standard UNIX method for document processing is to use an editor, such as **vi** or **ex**, to create a file containing text embedded with the formatting commands for UNIX's **nroff** or **troff** text processor.

SEE ALSO   UNIX Commands: **ex**

EXAMPLES

Note: It is difficult to show screen-oriented examples without showing large numbers of drawn screens. Here we make no attempt to simulate **vi**'s sequences of responses, only to show some of the characters you can expect to see on the screen when you give certain commands.

1. Start up a file.

```
$ vi stuff
"stuff" [New file]
~
~
~
~
~

...
"stuff" [New file]
```

The first **"stuff"** line is displayed while **vi** is taking care of such things as preparing the buffer. Then **vi** clears the screen, prints tildes (many more than shown here), places the second **"stuff"** line at the bottom of the screen, and places the cursor at the beginning of the first line. The editor is in the command mode.

(continued)

2. Enter some text and quit.

```
<a>
You should bring the following stuff along:
a softball mitt, a bat, insect repellent,
a cushion, some Ace bandages, a canteen, a
portable radio.<esc>
~
~
~
:wq
```

The **a** command does not actually show on the screen, but the next letter typed (here a **Y**) does appear, because the editor now is in the text mode. Similarly, the <esc> key does not show on the screen, but it does put you in command mode. The :**wq** (write and quit) command does show on the screen.

3. Give some sample commands in the command mode.

`10dd`	*Delete 10 lines, starting with current line*
`20G`	*Go to line 20*
`p`	*Place contents of unnamed buffer into text*
`/potato`	*Go to next line containing **potato***
`5e`	*Advance to end of 5th word*
`D`	*Delete from cursor to end of line*
`j`	*Go down one line*
`fk`	*Move cursor to next letter **k***
`rc`	*Replace letter under cursor with a **c***
`?leek`	*Seek backward for line containing **leek***
`de`	*Delete to end of word under cursor*
`u`	*Undo last change*

All these commands leave you in the command mode. If given in the order shown, the **p** command inserts the text deleted by the **10dd** command. Also, the **u** command restores the word deleted by the **de** command.

4. Use the **c** command.

c w	*Replace the word under the cursor with new text*
c $	*Replace text to the end of the line with new text*
3 c w	*Replace three words with new text*

In each case, whatever text is typed after the command is given is the replacement text. Type <esc> to terminate the replacement text and to return to the command mode. The replacement text need not match the deleted material in length. Five words can replace two, and vice versa.

For more examples, see those given for the **ex** editor. **ex** commands can be given from **vi** by prefixing them with a colon (:) while in the **vi** command mode.

PURPOSE Use the **wait** command to cause the shell to wait for processes to complete.

FORMAT wait [*pid*]

DESCRIPTION The shell program (see **sh**) handles the interface between you and the system. Normally, when you use **&** to run a task in the background, the shell resumes processing subsequent commands. The **wait** command, when given with no arguments, causes the shell to resume only after all background processes are complete. If a PID (the process identification number reported when a background job is started and by **ps**) is given with the **wait** command, and if that PID identifies a background job, then the shell waits for just that particular process to be completed. If the PID does not identify a background process, then the shell waits for all processes to be completed.

COMMON USES You can use **wait** in a shell script to ensure that certain commands are not given until a particular process is finished.

COMMENTS The **wait** command is a built-in **sh** command, which means its coding is included in the **sh** program and is not kept in a separate file.

SEE ALSO UNIX Commands: **sh**
UNIX Features: Shell Scripts; Processes

EXAMPLES

---

1. Have a shell script wait for an action to be complete.

```
spell $1 > stmp &
echo Here is the $1 file
cat $1
wait
echo Here are the misspelled words
cat stmp
```

These commands would be placed in a file, and **$1** would be the first argument when the file was executed as a shell script (see **sh**). The script starts the **spell** program in the background and displays a message and the contents of the file specified by **$1**. Then the script waits until the spelling check is complete before displaying the results. (This is a simplistic example, but it does show one technique for using **wait**.)

PURPOSE Use the **wall** command to write to all users.

FORMAT /etc/**wall**

DESCRIPTION The **wall** command reads the standard input (by default, the keyboard) until an end-of-file signal (usually <control-d> at the beginning of a line for keyboard input) is detected. The text then is sent to all currently logged-in users, except those who have denied you access through **mesg** or **chmod**. (When run by the superuser, this command overrides all such denials.)

The message is preceded by a heading of this form:

Broadcast Message from *login-name*

Thus messages are not anonymous.

The system administrator may (and often does) limit other users' access to this command.

COMMON USES The **wall** command usually is used by the system administrator to warn all users of some imminent action, such as shutting down the system.

COMMENTS The **wall** command is not found in the usual command directories provided by the **PATH** shell variable (see **sh**), so the full pathname is used.

EXAMPLES

1. Send a message to everyone who is open to receive it.

```
$ /etc/wall
A flying saucer has just landed out front.
<control-d>
$
    Broadcast Message from welles
A flying saucer has just landed out front.
```

Note that the message is sent to its sender, too.

PURPOSE Use the **wc** command to count characters, words, and lines in a file.

FORMAT wc [-lwc] [*filename(s)*]

DESCRIPTION The **wc** command counts the number of characters, words, and lines in the named files. If more than one file is named, **wc** provides the individual counts and a grand total; the counts for each file are labeled by filename. If no file is specified, **wc** uses the standard input, in which case a pipe typically is used to connect the standard output of another command to **wc**.

Here words are defined in terms of "white space" (white space is a space, tab, or newline). A word is a string of characters containing no white space and bounded by white space. Thus **WOW!** counts as one word, but **WOW !** counts as two.

COMMON USES You can use **wc** to count words in a text document.

OPTIONS Three counting options are available with **wc**:

OPTION	ACTION
-l	Counts lines.
-w	Counts words.
-c	Counts characters.

The default is equivalent to **-lwc**.

When more than one option is given, the counts are listed in order of the options. Thus **-lw** displays the line count, then the word count, while **-wl** displays the word count, then the line count.

SEE ALSO UNIX Features: Standard I/O, Redirection, and Pipes; Filters

EXAMPLES

1. Count the words in a file.

   ```
   $ wc beans
   ```

2. Count the number of files in a directory.

   ```
   $ ls ! wc -l
   32
   ```

   With no filename given, **wc** reads the standard input, which here is the output of the **ls** command. Since **ls** lists one file per line, counting the lines gives the number of files. Normally, counting the number of words also would give the number of files. However, it is possible to create a name containing a space, which would count as one line but two words. (You can use quotation marks to create a filename with a space, as in **cp a "a b"**, but this is not recommended.)

who

PURPOSE   Use the **who** command to find out who is logged in on the system.

FORMAT   **who** [*option(s)*] [*filename*]
who am i
who am I

DESCRIPTION   The **who** command, by default, lists the login names, terminal lines, and login times of users who currently are logged in to the system. Various options cause other information to be displayed, too. Normally, the **who** command obtains information from the **/etc/utmp** file, but it takes it from the *filename* file if the name is provided as an argument.

If you type **who am i** or **who am I**, the command identifies who the system thinks you are.

COMMON USES   You can use **who** to see if a particular person is on the system, and to check the general level of activity.

OUTPUT FORMAT   The output format depends on the option you use. The format can have up to eight fields:

FIELD	CONTENTS
name	Gives the user's login name.
state	Indicates whether others can write to the terminal (using **write**, for example). A **+** means the terminal is writable, a **-** means it is not writable, and a **?** indicates a bad line.
line	Gives the line or terminal being used, as identified in the **/dev** directory.
time	Indicates the time when the user logged in.
activity	Gives the number of hours and minutes since the last activity on that line. If the terminal has seen activity within the last minute, a dot (.) is displayed. If more than 24 hours have elapsed since the line was used or if it has not been used since the last system boot, the word **old** is displayed.
pid	Indicates the process identification number (the same as provided by **ps**, for example) of the user's login shell.
comment	Displays the contents of the comment field, if there is any, from the **/etc/inittab** file. The field might, for example, say where a terminal is located, the type of terminal it is, and so on.
exit	If present, contains the termination and exit values of dead processes (see option **-d**).

OPTIONS Unless otherwise stated, the following options display the **name**, **line**, **time**, **activity**, and **pid** fields, and, if defined, the **comment** field. Several options are of more interest to the system administrator than to the general user. The default behavior is the same as the –s option.

OPTION	ACTION
–u	Lists only those users currently logged in.
–T	Adds the **state** field to the fields listed. If this is the only option, the rest of the fields are as in the –s option.
–l	Lists only those lines for which the system is waiting for someone to log in. **LOGIN** is displayed in the **name** field, and the **state** field is not displayed.
–H	Displays headings above each column. New with Release 2.
–q	The quick **who**; just displays the names and the number of users, ignoring all other options. New with Release 2.
–p	Lists other currently active processes started by the system **init** program.
–d	Lists processes that have died and have not yet been respawned by **init**. The **exit** field is displayed; this may help to determine why a process terminated.
–b	Gives the time and date of the last reboot.
–r	Displays the current run level of the **init** process.
–t	Indicates the last change to the system clock.
–a	Turns on all options except **–q** and **–s**.
–s	Lists just the **name**, **line**, and **time** fields.

SEE ALSO UNIX Commands: **ps**; **write**

EXAMPLES

1. See who is on the system.

```
$ who
root          console      Oct 28 06:48
pickles       tty03        Oct 28 15:15
citizen       tty02        Oct 28 09:24
slow          tty04        Oct 28 13:45
```

2. Get more extensive information.

```
$ who -HuT
NAME        LINE         TIME              IDLE    PID  COMMENTS
root      - console      Oct 28 06:48      .       10
pickles   + tty03        Oct 28 15:15      0:20    37   Tonga Room
citizen   + tty02        Oct 28 13:44      .       36
```

Here **pickles** and **citizen** can be written to.

3. Get a quick list.

```
$ who -q
citizen pickles root
# users=3
```

The user count is more useful for systems with many users.

PURPOSE   Use the **write** command to communicate with another logged-in user.

FORMAT   write *user* [*terminal*]

DESCRIPTION   The **write** command causes lines you type on your terminal to be echoed on the recipient's terminal. The recipient can use the **write** command to communicate back to you. To terminate your end of the "conversation," use an INTERRUPT signal (typically generated by <break> or <del>) or the EOF signal (typically a <control-d> at the beginning of a line.)

COMMON USES   You can use **write** to communicate interactively with someone else currently on the system.

USING write   To initiate the **write** command, type **write** followed by the login name of the person you want to communicate with. This causes a message with this form to be displayed on the recipient's terminal:

> **Message from** *sender* (*ttynn*)

Here *sender* is your login name and *ttynn* is your terminal. (Some systems may display more information, such as the date and the system name.) When the connection is completed, two bell signals are sent to your terminal. After that, each line you type is sent to the other terminal when you hit the <enter> key.

To terminate **write**, send an EOF signal (usually a <control-d> at the beginning of a line) or an INTERRUPT signal (typically <break> or <del>). The **write** command then displays **EOT** on the other terminal.

To deny others the right to write to you, use the **mesg n** command, which also terminates any writing to your terminal that is currently taking place. The **mesg y** command reestablishes your accessibility to others. (The superuser can write to a terminal regardless of its write permission settings.)

If a user is logged in on more than one terminal, a terminal argument can be used to indicate which terminal to use. For example,

```
write rona tty12
```

writes to **rona** on terminal **tty12**.

You can temporarily suspend the **write** process and run a command by typing a ! character at the beginning of a line. The writing mode resumes when the command completes.

COMMENTS The **write** command provides a simple, interactive, and immediate means of corresponding with someone else on the system. The **mail** command, on the other hand, works whether or not the recipient is currently logged in and provides messages that the recipient can save.

You can use the **who** command to see if the person you wish to talk to is logged in.

SEE ALSO UNIX Commands: **mesg**; **mail**; **who**
UNIX Features: Files and Devices; Special UNIX Characters

EXAMPLES

1. Write to another user.

```
$ write zeke
What was the name of that book that helped you? -o-
    Message from zeke (tty11)
It's Advanced UNIX -- A Programmer's Guide;
I'll bring a copy by later. -o-
Thanks, I'll be in my office until 4. -oo-
<control-d>
Okay, see you at 3:30. -oo-
EOT
```

Note that this is a two-way conversation. A common convention is to type **-o-** ("over") to indicate when you have finished one part of the conversation and to type **-oo-** ("over and out") when you intend to quit.

UNIX Features

Introduction

When we discuss the UNIX commands, we find that many UNIX features come up repeatedly. For example, a large number of commands use the "standard input" and the "standard output," and many commands make use of "regular expressions." In this section of the book, we will look at these recurring topics.

Many of the "UNIX Features" topics refer to other topics and to relevant commands. Because the topics tend to be interdependent, some material is discussed in more than one place. Also, in the "UNIX Commands" section, we refer to topics in "UNIX Features" whenever they relate to a particular command.

Because of all these interrelationships, we decided to put the "UNIX Features" topics in alphabetic order so that when you encounter a reference to a particular feature, you can quickly find its discussion. Most likely, you will turn to this section only when you need more information about a particular topic, but if you do sit down to read it from start to finish, be warned: we designed *UNIX System V Bible* as a reference book and have made no attempt in this section to maintain a narrative flow from one topic to the next. Each is intended to be a stand-alone discussion—concise, but as complete as possible.

Command Lines

To give a UNIX command from the keyboard, you type the name of the command along with any information, such as a filename, that the command requires, and hit the <enter> key. The typed line is called a "command line." To interpret what you mean when you type a command line, UNIX uses a program called a "command-line interpreter," or "shell." When you log in, UNIX starts up a shell program just for you. It is this program that displays your prompt and that interprets the command lines you type. Several shells have been developed for UNIX. The most common, and the one used by default in System V, is the Bourne shell, which has the command name **sh**. In this book, we assume that **sh** is the command-line interpreter you are using.

Now let's look at the more important characteristics of command lines and at how **sh** interprets them.

COMMAND-LINE ELEMENTS The usual components of a command line are the command name and the "arguments" (see Figure 7). Arguments provide additional information for use by the command. Common forms of arguments are filenames, directory names, and options. Options, in UNIX, usually are indicated by a hyphen prefix; they usually modify the behavior of the command. For example, consider this command:

```
sort -r titles
```

Here **sort** is the command, **-r** is an option indicating that sorting should be done in reverse order, and **titles** is the name of the file to be sorted. Both **titles** and **-r** are arguments, but only **-r** is an option.

The elements of a command line should be separated from one another by blanks; that is, by spaces or tabs. The following examples are not valid command lines:

```
sort-r titles
```
Missing blank before -r
```
ls -s-i
```
Missing blank before -i

FIGURE 7. *A command line*

If you require more than one option, you can type them separately:

```
ls -a -s -i
```

Note that each option is separated by a space from its neighbors. In many cases, multiple options can be strung together after one hyphen, as in the following command:

```
ls -asi
```

Here there are no spaces between the options. However, it is not always possible to string options together in this fashion; you'll have to read the "UNIX Commands" discussion of a particular command to see whether it is permitted.

OTHER COMMAND-LINE FORMS Command lines can be more complex than the examples we've given so far. They can use "redirection" and "pipes" to reroute the flow of information, as discussed under Standard I/O, Redirection, and Pipes, and under **sh** . They can contain control statements that create shell programs; the control statements recognized by the **sh** shell (**while, for, if, until,** and **case**) are discussed under **sh**. And the command lines can direct the shell to run programs "in the background," as discussed under Processes and under **sh**.

Whether a command line is simple or complex, it is the shell's duty to interpret that command line. Here are further examples of the kinds of things the shell has to deal with.

☐ The Filename Generation entry describes how you can use special "wildcard" characters in a command line; the shell must match them to filenames.

☐ The Shell Variables and Parameter Substitution entries describe how you can use shell variables in a command line; the shell must replace them with their values.

☐ The Command Substitution entry discusses a mechanism by which a command in a command line can be replaced by its output.

☐ The Quoting entry discusses ways to deactivate special characters by quoting them.

There are a variety of other special notations recognized by **sh** and discussed under that command.

Historically, most UNIX commands have been fairly standard in the way that they required their options to be specified, but there have been variations. System V, Release 3 sets forth a uniform command-line syntax that all new commands must obey. Not all old commands conform, but many are being brought into line with new releases.

The new standard has thirteen rules. In general, they assume that the command line has three or four elements:

☐ A command name.

☐ Options consisting of a hyphen and a single character, as in -**p**. The single character is the option's name.

☐ Options consisting of a hyphen and a single character followed by one or more option arguments, as in -**o sfile**. Here the option name is **o**, and the option argument is **sfile**.

☐ Other arguments to the command.

Here are the thirteen rules:

1. Command names must be between two and nine characters long.

2. Command names should consist of only lowercase characters and digits.

3. Option names must be one character long.

4. All options are preceded by a hyphen (-). Thus -**b** and -**f** are examples of options bearing the option names **b** and **f**, respectively.

5. Options with no arguments may be grouped after a single hyphen. Thus -**b** and -**f** can be represented as -**bf**.

6. The first option argument following an option must be preceded by white space. Thus -**o sfile** is valid, but -**osfile** is not.

7. Option arguments cannot be optional. For instance, if the **o** option normally requires a filename argument, the command cannot assume a default argument if none is given. Omitting the argument is a syntax error.

8. If an option takes more than one argument, these arguments may be separated by commas (no spaces) or be separated by white space and be quoted; that is, if a -**f** option is to be used with the arguments **past**, **now**, and **next**, either of the following is valid:

```
-f past,now,next
-f "past now next"
```

9. All options must precede other arguments on the command line.

10. A double hyphen (--) may be used to indicate the end of the list of options.

11. The order of the options relative to one another should not matter.

12. The relative order of the remaining arguments may be significant, depending on the command.

13. A lone hyphen preceded and followed by white space (-) should be used only to mean standard input.

Again, you should bear in mind that many existing UNIX commands do not conform to all these rules.

SEE ALSO UNIX Commands: **sh; getopts**
UNIX Features: Command Substitution; Directory Abbreviations; Extending Commands over More than One Line; Filename Generation; Parameter Substitution; Processes; Quoting; The Shell and the Kernel; Shell Scripts; Shell Variables

Command Substitution

The shell provides a mechanism for replacing a command in a command line with its output. When a command appears within "backquotes" (also known as "accents graves"), it is replaced by its output. For example, consider this command:

```
$ now=`date`
```

Here **now** is a shell variable being assigned a value. Without the backquotes, **now** would be set to the word **date**. But with them, **now** is set to the output of the **date** command:

```
$ echo $now
Tue Dec 29 1986 14:18:21 PST
```

Command substitution often is used in shell scripts. Here is a simple example of a line that could be used within a script:

```
echo $0 program used `date` >> logfile
```

Suppose this line is in a shell script file called **pickup**. The $0 represents the name of the shell script file containing this line, so in this case, $0 is set to **pickup**. The **echo** command puts together a message of the form

```
pickup program used Wed Dec 30 1986 03:22:18 PST
```

and redirects it to a log file.

SEE ALSO   UNIX Commands: **sh**
UNIX Features: Command Lines

Directory Abbreviations

UNIX uses a single period to denote the current directory and two consecutive periods to denote the parent directory of the current directory. For example, to copy a file called **bunbun** from a directory called **/usr/burney** to your current directory, you could type this:

```
cp /usr/burney/bunbun .
```

The next example shows how you can use the .. abbreviation to change to the parent directory:

```
$ pwd
/usr/burney/Bilge
$ cd ..
$ pwd
/usr/burney
```

Note that since **usr/burney/Bilge** is your current directory in this example, the effect of **cd ..** is the same as that of **cd /usr/burney**.

A directory is really a special form of file that lists the filenames and corresponding i-node values for all the files and subdirectories in a directory. The . and .. abbreviations are used in this listing to represent the current and parent directories. For instance, the **Bilge** directory file from the last example would associate . with the i-node number of the **Bilge** directory file and .. with the i-node number of the **burney** directory file. The **burney** directory file, however, would refer to itself as . and to **Bilge** as **Bilge**. Its .. would refer to the i-node of the **usr** directory.

The shell makes use of another directory abbreviation, the environmental variable **HOME**, which normally is set to the user's login directory.

SEE ALSO UNIX Commands: **mkdir; cd; pwd**
UNIX Features: Files and Directories; Pathnames and the Directory Tree; Shell Variables

Exit Values

UNIX commands have exit values (also called "exit status" and "return values"). These are numeric values returned to the system when a command completes. Typically, a command returns an exit value of zero if it proceeded normally, and it returns a non-zero value if something went awry. For example, the **grep** command returns an exit value of 0 if it found a matching line, 1 if it failed to find a matching line, and 2 if there are syntax errors or inaccessible files.

Shell programs can use the exit value of a command to determine what to do next. For instance, the **while** loop of the shell continues to cycle as long as the exit value of a test command is zero. As an example, the program

```
while who ! grep tinka > /dev/null
do
      echo LOG OUT NOW, TINKA > /dev/tty21
      sleep 30
done
```

keeps sending the message *LOG OUT NOW, TINKA* to terminal **tty21** (presumably Tinka's) every 30 seconds until she logs out. As long as she is logged in, **grep** finds **tinka** in **who**'s output and returns a 0 exit value. When she logs out, **grep** no longer finds her name, the exit value becomes 1, and the loop quits. The redirection of **grep**'s regular output (the matching lines) to **/dev/null** discards the output; otherwise, the matching line would be displayed on the screen. (Redirection to **/dev/null** is a common practice when you are interested in the exit value of a command rather than its normal output.)

The **until** and **if** structured commands also utilize the exit values of commands, as do the **sh** notations ¦¦ and **&&** (see **sh**).

The shell keeps track of the exit value of the last command; you can access it with the $? notation. Here is an example:

```
$ grep bagels togo
$ echo $?
1
```

Here **grep** sought for the string **bagels** in the **togo** file and did not find it; echoing $? reveals that the exit value of the **grep** command was 1. Had the **togo** file not existed, then the session would have looked like this:

```
$ grep bagels togo
grep: can't open togo
$ echo $?
2
```

If you write a shell script, you can explicitly specify exit values by using the **exit** command. For example, **$#** represents the number of arguments to a shell script. The following program fragment reports an error and causes the program to quit if there are no arguments:

```
case $# in
     0) echo Usage: $0 files... 1>&2 ; exit 1;;
esac
```

This **case** statement goes to the line whose label has the same value as **$#**. So if that is 0, the line labeled 0) is executed. Here **$0** represents the name of the file containing the script, and **1>&2** makes sure the message is sent to the screen (see Standard I/O and **sh**). The exit value is 1 in this case.

If you don't provide for the exit value of a shell script, it will have the exit value of the last command performed in the script before it quit.

If you are programming in C, you can use C's **exit( )** function to provide an exit value for your C program. By using exit values for C programs and shell scripts, you make it possible for those programs to be used in the loops and **if** statements of other programs. You can have your program generate whichever exit values you choose, but it makes sense to comply with the UNIX practice of using zero to indicate that the program ran successfully; then you can use the program with the shell's structured statements.

SEE ALSO UNIX Commands: **sh**
UNIX Features: Shell Scripts

Extending Commands
over More than One Line

Normally the newline character, which is produced by striking the <enter> key, marks the end of a command line. To extend a command over more than one line, type a backslash before striking <enter>. The **sh** shell then displays its secondary prompt to indicate that it expects more input. By default, the primary prompt is $ and the secondary prompt is **>**, so an extended command might look like this:

```
$ echo She who laughs last \<enter>
> laughs best<enter>
She who laughs last laughs best
```

The backslash causes the command line to extend to the next line, as shown by the secondary prompt **>**. Because the second line ends with a regular <enter>, the command line ends there. The shell gathers up the arguments and delivers them to **echo**; then **echo** echoes them.

Certain shell control commands automatically generate the secondary prompt:

```
$ for file
> do
>     rm $file
> done
$
```

The shell knows the syntax of the **for** command and provides secondary prompts until **done** is reached (see **sh** for more details).

The shell also provides the secondary prompt on the next line if you have an odd number of single quotes or an odd number of double quotes, since it expects quotation marks to appear in pairs. This is useful for commands like **sed**, which accepts one editing command per line:

```
$ sed 's/Ed/Ted/g
>       s/Vi/Sue/g
>       s/Cal/Tex/g' assignments
```

SEE ALSO UNIX Commands: **sh**
UNIX Features: Command Lines; Quoting

File Systems

The Files and Directories entry describes how a directory tree is used to organize files logically and how i-node blocks are used to organize files physically. A "file system" involves both forms of organization. Let's look at the physical aspect first.

Often a system uses more than one hard disk or partitions a disk into more than one part. In these cases, each partition on each hard disk (or other storage device) is allocated its own "i-node block," its own file storage space, and a "superblock." This collection of superblock, i-nodes (information nodes), and files is called a "file system." The superblock contains information about the i-node block (how many i-nodes, where they are), just as the i-nodes in the i-node block contain information about the files. Thus all files in the same file system have to reside on the same physical device.

Files in a file system also share a logical relationship; they all belong to a particular directory and its subdirectories. The root directory and the essential UNIX files and directories usually constitute one file system, which is "mounted" on the root directory, meaning that its directory tree is based on the / directory. Other file systems are added by mounting them on other directories. For example, if all the **usr** files and directories were in a single file system, that system would be mounted on the **/usr** directory; that is, **/usr** would be the "root" of that file system. Mounting the system, then, connects it with the rest of the tree. You can visualize mounting a file system as grafting it to a particular location on the directory tree. Figure 8 on the following page shows an example.

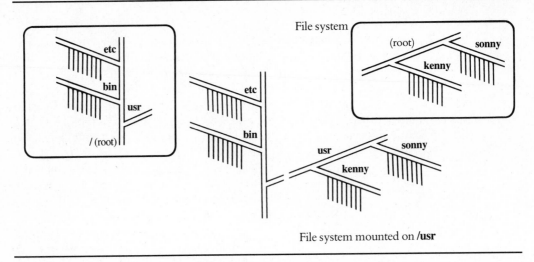

File system

File system mounted on **/usr**

FIGURE 8. *Mounting a file system*

Multiple file systems complicate the operating system's duties in that the same i-node number can be used with different file systems. The user normally is shielded from this problem, but because file aliases (as set up with the **ln** link command) require that all the aliases refer to the same i-node number, you cannot create a link in one file system to a file in a second file system. This is because an i-node block describes just one file system and any i-node entry in a directory file can refer only to the file system to which that directory belongs.

This situation also complicates moving a file from one file system to another. Ordinarily, an **mv** command alters just a directory entry or two. But if the target file is placed in a different file system, the file must be physically transferred from one disk to the other, and the i-node blocks for both file systems must be updated. Fortunately, the **mv** command does all this for us without demanding any attention on our part.

SEE ALSO   UNIX Commands: **ln; mv; df**
UNIX Features: Files and Directories

Filename Generation

You can use certain "wildcard" characters (or "metacharacters") to generate patterns for the shell to use when matching file and directory names. A word containing these characters is replaced with an alphabetic list of all file and directory names matching the pattern. This process is called "filename expansion" or "filename generation." By using this process, you can refer to a set of related files by typing just one pattern. The following are the wildcard metacharacters:

WILDCARD	ACTION
*	Matches any string, including the null string.
?	Matches any one character.
[*list*]	Matches any one character in *list*.
[!*list*]	Matches any one character not in *list*.

A string is any sequence of characters; a null string is a string of no characters. The *list* can be a string of letters, as in **[aeiou]**, or a hyphen can be used to indicate a range, as in the pattern **[a-z]**. You can combine both forms in a list; for example, **[a-zQMT]** denotes the letters **a** through **z** and the letters **Q**, **M**, and **T**. Note that case matters: **A** and **Z**, for example, would not be matched by this pattern.

You can use more than one metacharacter in a command. For example,

```
cat *
```

displays the contents of all files in the current directory, but

```
cat [aeiou]*[z]
```

displays the contents of those files whose names both begin with a vowel and end with **z**.

With these rules come a few exceptions:

☐ A period (.) at the start of a filename must be matched explicitly.

☐ A period immediately following a slash (/.) must be matched explicitly.

☐ The slash character itself (/) must be matched explicitly.

Filenames beginning with . normally aren't included in expansions; you have to include the initial . in the command line, as in these examples:

```
ls .*
ls .[a-z]
```

449

The first command lists the filenames beginning with . and the second lists the filenames consisting of . followed by a lowercase letter.

The initial period in a filename gets special treatment in order to protect important files like **.profile**. Files with initial periods normally aren't shown by the **ls** command when you list files. Thus, you might forget the existence of such a file and give a command like this one:

```
rm *file
```

Without the requirement to match the period explicitly, this command would remove the **.profile** file. Also, . and .. are abbreviations for your current working directory and its parent (see Directory Abbreviations).

Since / is used to separate parts of the pathname (as in **/usr/joy**), and since expansions apply only to individual parts, or "components," of the pathname, expansions don't include the slash. For example, **/usr/jo*** and **/u*/joy** will both expand to include **/usr/joy**, but **/u*y** will not, because the * stops matching at a /.

To see how the filename generation feature works, suppose the **ls -a** command shows the following files (the **-a** option lists all files, even those whose names begin with a period):

```
.profile      bagfile       bgfile        canfile
ashcan        bigfile       boogfile      sleepy
```

Here are some wildcard patterns and the filenames from the list that match them:

PATTERN	MATCHING FILENAMES
*file	bagfile bigfile bgfile boogfile canfile
.*file	.profile
*ashcan	ashcan
b?gfile	bagfile bigfile
b*gfile	bagfile bigfile bgfile boogfile
can	ashcan canfile
b[aou]gfile	bagfile
[ac]*	ashcan canfile
[c-t]*	canfile sleepy
[!ac]*	bagfile bigfile bgfile boogfile sleepy

There are several points to note here. First, ***file** does not match **.profile** because wildcards do not match an initial period. Second, since ***** matches even a null string, ***ashcan** matches **ashcan**. But **?ashcan** would fail to match **ashcan** since it requires exactly one character before the first **a**. Third, the **[]** construction, like **?**, matches exactly one character. Thus **b[aou]gfile** matches **bagfile** but not **boogfile**, since the latter has two characters between the **b** and **g**. For the same reason, it will not match **baogfile**.

SEE ALSO UNIX Commands: **sh**; **ls**

Files and Directories

The documents, programs, and data collections you may create are stored in files. The programs for the various UNIX commands are stored in files. The UNIX operating system itself is stored in files. The sheer number of files contained on a typical UNIX system makes it necessary to have some system for organizing them.

UNIX has two forms of file organization. The first is physical: which file is found where on which hard disk (or other storage device). The second is logical: which file belongs to whom. For physical organization, UNIX uses a set of tables called "i-nodes" (information nodes). For logical organization, it uses a directory-tree system.

As a user, you deal mainly with the logical organization of files, so we will cover that first.

DIRECTORIES In UNIX, a directory is a specialized form of file that contains a list of all the files and directories in that particular directory. However, this information is not stored in text form, so you can't use text commands like **cat** or **vi** to read the list.

For each of its files and directories, the directory also contains an internal file identification number, called the "i-node number," which is used by the computer to identify the file. The list also includes the directory's own i-node number and the i-node number of the directory that contains it. We'll discuss i-nodes further in a moment.

Directories organize files in two ways. First, each file belongs to a particular directory. Thus, you can set up one directory to hold files of correspondence, another directory to hold program files, and so on. Second, the directories themselves are organized into a hierarchical, or tree, structure. A directory contained in another directory is called a subdirectory, and the containing directory is called the parent directory.

UNIX maintains one master directory from which all others branch, either directly or indirectly. This directory is called the "root directory," or "root," but it is typed as /. Several standard subdirectories, including **bin**, **usr**, and **etc**, typically come with UNIX systems. You can visualize them as branching off the / directory (see Figure 9). Each of these directories can contain files and subdirectories. In Figure 9, we represent the directories with heavy lines and the files with thin lines.

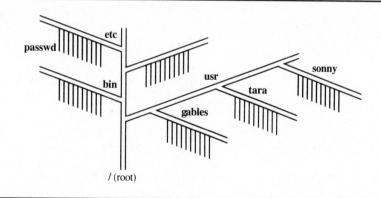

FIGURE 9. *The directory tree*

PATHNAMES AND THE CURRENT WORKING DIRECTORY

To specify a particular file, you can use its "full pathname," which tells UNIX how to find the file by prefixing its filename with the list of directories leading from the root directory to the file. The root directory is represented by a slash, and subsequent directory names and filenames are separated by more slashes. Thus, **/usr/flint/rebop/toot** indicates that the file **toot** is in the **rebop** subdirectory of the **flint** subdirectory of the **usr** subdirectory of the root directory (/). See the Pathnames and the Directory Tree entry for more details.

UNIX keeps track of which directory you are currently working in. You can access a file in your "current working directory" by using just its basename—the part of the full pathname that follows the final slash. For instance, continuing with the previous example, if **/usr/flint/rebop** is your current working directory, then you can access the **toot** file by using just the basename **toot**.

Normally, when you log in, your current working directory is set to your "home directory." This is a directory set up by the system administrator for you, and it usually has the same name as your login name. Typically, it is a subdirectory of **/usr** or, perhaps, **/u**.

FILE AND DIRECTORY OPERATIONS

To make the directory system effective, UNIX allows you to establish your own system of subdirectories in your home directory, and lets you "move" from one directory to another. Moving to a directory means that the directory you've moved to becomes your new current working directory.

UNIX also lets you create files (with **ex** and **vi**, or using redirection, for example), copy files (with **cp**), rename files (with **mv**), move files from one directory to another (also with **mv**), and establish multiple pathnames for the same regular file (with **ln**). You also can control access to particular files (with **chmod**). See the "UNIX Commands" section for details.

FILES AND DEVICES UNIX treats devices such as terminals, printers, and disk drives as files. Each device connected to a UNIX system is represented by a "special file" in the **/dev** directory. When the computer displays something on your screen, it actually is "writing" in the special file that represents your terminal. This "device-as-file" feature is the basis for such UNIX features as redirection and pipes, which let you divert material from the screen to a file or a program. The Special Files entry discusses this topic further.

FILE ORGANIZATION From the user's standpoint, files are organized into directories and subdirectories in a logical structure. From the computer's standpoint, files need to be organized physically on the system storage devices. The physical arrangement of files on, say, a hard disk does not parallel the logical organization into directories. A new file goes to the first available space on the disk and need not be anywhere near existing files in the same directory. (It would be horrendously inefficient to have to rearrange everyone's files on a hard disk each time a new file was placed in an existing directory.)

To make the file system workable, the operating system has to tie together the two methods (logical and physical) of organizing files. UNIX accomplishes this by maintaining tables of file information and by storing relevant information in the directory files. To see how this is done, let's take a look at what happens (in simplified steps) when we create a file and place it in a particular directory.

Suppose, for example, that we are in the **/usr/vulcan** directory and that we have just created a text file called **nifty**. Information about this file is stored in three places. First, the actual file contents are placed on the permanent storage medium, which we will assume is a hard disk. Second, an i-node entry is made in the i-node block—a section of the hard disk reserved for that purpose. Each i-node is assigned an i-node number, and the i-node itself is used to store information about the file. It holds, for example, the location on the hard disk of the file; the size of the file in bytes; the various access permissions for the file; the type of file (regular or directory, for instance); the times of creation, last access, and last modification; and the number of links to the file (more on links soon). The i-node does not contain the filename.

Finally, an entry is made in the **vulcan** directory file, containing two pieces of information: the name of the new file (**nifty**) and the file's i-node number. The i-node number is used internally by UNIX to identify the file, and the directory entry "links" the user's label for the file (**nifty**) to its i-node number. In short, the pathname **/usr/vulcan/nifty** reflects the file's logical location, and the i-node number specifies its physical location.

This brief discussion provides us with some insight into how the **mv**, **cp**, and **ln** commands work. These commands respectively change the name of a file, copy a file, and provide an additional name for a file. The **mv** command changes the link; the file itself stays the same and the i-node number and i-node stay the same, but the original directory entry for the file is removed and a new one is created, possibly in a different directory. The **cp** command creates a new file, a new i-node entry, and a new directory entry. The **ln** command leaves the file and the original directory entry unchanged, but creates a new directory entry using a new filename but the same i-node number. It also changes the i-node entry in the i-node block, showing that the number of links has been increased by one.

Incidentally, the number of files that can be stored on a hard disk is limited not only by the space set aside to store files but by the space set aside to store i-nodes, since one i-node is needed for each file. Thus the **df** command, which reports on available disk space, provides information about both available space and available i-nodes.

SEE ALSO   UNIX Commands: **mkdir**; **cd**; **cp**; **mv**; **ln**; **df**
UNIX Features: Pathnames and the Directory Tree; Special Files; File Systems

Filters

Many UNIX commands are designed to be "filters"; that is, they are designed to read the standard input, process it in some manner, and then write the transformed input to the standard output. You can think of raw information flowing in one end of the command and filtered information flowing out the other end. For example, the **tr** command takes characters from its standard input, transforms them as directed, and sends the results to the standard output.

One important advantage of filters is that they can be used with redirection and with pipes (see Standard I/O, Redirection, and Pipes). Thus filters can be used with keyboard input or file input, or with output from another command. The output can be shown on the screen, saved in a file, or piped to another command. For example, consider this command:

```
grep 'Main Street' Reno | sort | tee mslist | pr | lp
```

First **grep** finds the lines in the **Reno** file that contain the string **Main Street**. These lines are piped to **sort**, which sorts them, piping the results to the **tee** command. This command saves the sorted results in the **mslist** file and also sends them on to **pr**, which formats them and passes the text on to **lp** for printing.

This example illustrates the flexibility that makes possible a "building-block" approach to UNIX, in which simple commands can be linked together to perform complex tasks.

SEE ALSO   UNIX Commands: **tr; sed; cat; grep; awk**
UNIX Features: Standard I/O, Redirection, and Pipes

Groups

Part of the UNIX administrative approach is to divide users into classes called groups. This feature stems from the Bell Labs environment for UNIX, in which UNIX was (and is) used in research and development. People working on the same project would be placed in the same group. Nowadays UNIX exists in a variety of work environments, but the group feature is still useful.

When the system administrator created your system account, he or she assigned you to a group. The **/etc/passwd** file, which contains your login name and encrypted password, also contains your group ID—your group's identification number. The **/etc/group** file contains a list of groups, their corresponding group IDs, and group membership information.

The group scheme is more than an organizational classification, since it is used by UNIX's file-protection scheme. Just as each user is assigned to a group, each file is identified with a group by being assigned a group ID. Access to a file is defined for three separate classes of users: the file's owner, members of the group with which the file is identified, and the remaining users. By using **chmod**, you can set file permissions so that a file can be read or otherwise used by group members while access to it is denied to others.

A file's group ID normally is your group ID at the time you create the file. Your group ID normally is the group that you are associated with in the **/etc/passwd** file; that's the group ID you are assigned when you log in. However, you can use the **newgrp** command to change temporarily to any other group that lists you as a member in the **/etc/group** file. You can also use the **chgrp** command to change the file's group ID without changing your own group ID.

In short, each user has a group ID, each file has a group ID, and UNIX explicitly defines access privileges for group members to files of the same group ID. Your group ID, the group for files you create, and the group access permissions all have default values, but you can alter them using UNIX commands. For example, you can change from one of the groups to which you belong to another using **newgrp**, "give" a file to another group using **chgrp**, and allow or deny access to a file, based on group, using **chmod**.

SEE ALSO UNIX Commands: **chmod**; **chgrp**; **newgrp**
UNIX Features: Permissions

The Machine
Collating Sequence

Computers use a numeric code to represent the various characters they recognize. These characters include uppercase letters, lowercase letters, digits, punctuation, the space character, and various nonprinting characters, such as the tab and form-feed characters. The machine collating sequence is the arrangement of these characters in order of increasing numeric code; it is, essentially, an extended alphabetic order.

The code most commonly used in UNIX systems is ASCII (American Standard Code for Information Interchange), which uses the numeric values 0 through 127 to represent a set of 128 characters. Mainframe IBM computers use a different code called EBCDIC, which allows up to 256 characters to be represented. As a result, programs like **sort**, which use the machine collating sequence, may produce different results on an EBCDIC system than on an ASCII system.

The ASCII system is shown in Figure 10. This table lists the decimal, hexadecimal, and octal values for each character, the ASCII labels assigned to the control characters, and the names used in this book for some keystrokes, such as the backslash.

DECIMAL	HEXADECIMAL	OCTAL	ASCII LABEL	KEY(S)	NAME
0	0	0	NUL	^@	
1	1	1	SOH	^A	
2	2	2	STX	^B	
3	3	3	ETX	^C	
4	4	4	EOF	^D	
5	5	5	ENQ	^E	
6	6	6	ACK	^F	
7	7	7	BEL	^G	
8	8	10	BS	^H	\<backspace\>
9	9	11	HT	^I	\<tab\>
10	A	12	LF	^J	\<line feed\>
11	B	13	VT	^K	
12	C	14	FF	^L	

FIGURE 10. *Table of ASCII values*

DECIMAL	HEXADECIMAL	OCTAL	ASCII LABEL	KEY(S)	NAME
13	D	15	CR	^M	\<enter\>
14	E	16	SO	^N	
15	F	17	SI	^O	
16	10	20	DLE	^P	
17	11	21	DC1	^Q	
18	12	22	DC2	^R	
19	13	23	DC3	^S	
20	14	24	DC4	^T	
21	15	25	NAK	^U	
22	16	26	SYN	^V	
23	17	27	ETB	^W	
24	18	30	CAN	^X	
25	19	31	EM	^Y	
26	1A	32	SUB	^Z	
27	1B	33	ESC	^[	\<esc\>
28	1C	34	FS	^\	
29	1D	35	GS	^]	
30	1E	36	RS	^^	
31	1F	37	US	^_	
32	20	40	SP	Spacebar	
33	21	41		!	
34	22	42		"	
35	23	43		#	
36	24	44		$	
37	25	45		%	
38	26	46		&	
39	27	47		'	
40	28	50		(	
41	29	51		)	
42	2A	52		*	
43	2B	53		+	

(continued)

FIGURE 10. *Table of ASCII values*

DECIMAL	HEXADECIMAL	OCTAL	ASCII LABEL	KEY(S)	NAME (continued)
44	2C	54		,	
45	2D	55		–	
46	2E	56		.	
47	2F	57		/	<slash>
48	30	60		0	
49	31	61		1	
50	32	62		2	
51	33	63		3	
52	34	64		4	
53	35	65		5	
54	36	66		6	
55	37	67		7	
56	38	70		8	
57	39	71		9	
58	3A	72		:	
59	3B	73		;	
60	3C	74		<	
61	3D	75		=	
62	3E	76		>	
63	3F	77		?	
64	40	100		@	
65	41	101		A	
66	42	102		B	
67	43	103		C	
68	44	104		D	
69	45	105		E	
70	46	106		F	
71	47	107		G	
72	48	110		H	
73	49	111		I	
74	4A	112		J	
75	4B	113		K	

FIGURE 10. *Table of ASCII values*

DECIMAL	HEXADECIMAL	OCTAL	ASCII LABEL	KEY(S)	NAME
76	4C	114		L	
77	4D	115		M	
78	4E	116		N	
79	4F	117		O	
80	50	120		P	
81	51	121		Q	
82	52	122		R	
83	53	123		S	
84	54	124		T	
85	55	125		U	
86	56	126		V	
87	57	127		W	
88	58	130		X	
89	59	131		Y	
90	5A	132		Z	
91	5B	133		[	
92	5C	134		\	\<backslash\>
93	5D	135		]	
94	5E	136		^	\<caret\>
95	5F	137		_	\<underscore\>
96	60	140		`	\<backquote\>
97	61	141		a	
98	62	142		b	
99	63	143		c	
100	64	144		d	
101	65	145		e	
102	66	146		f	
103	67	147		g	
104	68	150		h	
105	69	151		i	
106	6A	152		j	
107	6B	153		k	

(continued)

FIGURE 10. *Table of ASCII values*

461

DECIMAL	HEXADECIMAL	OCTAL	ASCII LABEL	KEY(S)	NAME *(continued)*
108	6C	154		l	
109	6D	155		m	
110	6E	156		n	
111	6F	157		o	
112	70	160		p	
113	71	161		q	
114	72	162		r	
115	73	163		s	
116	74	164		t	
117	75	165		u	
118	76	166		v	
119	77	167		w	
120	78	170		x	
121	79	171		y	
122	7A	172		z	
123	7B	173		{	
124	7C	174		¦	<pipe>
125	7D	175		}	
126	7E	176		~	<tilde>
127	7F	177		DEL	<del>, <rub>

FIGURE 10. *Table of ASCII values*

SEE ALSO   UNIX Commands: **sort**

Parameter Substitution

As discussed under the Shell Variables entry, the shell maintains a list of variables, or parameters. Some are set by the system, but they also can be created by the user. For example, the command

```
pal=Horatio
```

creates a parameter called **pal** having the value **Horatio**. When a parameter name is prefaced by a $ and used in a command line, it is replaced by its value; this is called "parameter substitution." If the $ is omitted, the parameter name is used literally. Let's use **echo** to illustrate this mechanism:

```
$ echo The parameter pal is set to $pal
The parameter pal is set to Horatio
```

You can use braces around the parameter name. This is necessary when the parameter is embedded in a longer string, as the following examples show:

```
$ echo $pals

$ echo ${pal}s
Horatios
```

The first **echo** command prints a blank line because the shell looked for, but did not find, a parameter named **pals**.

The shell also provides for more elaborate forms of parameter substitution; see **sh** for details.

SEE ALSO   UNIX Commands: **sh**
UNIX Features: Command Lines; Shell Variables

Pathnames and
the Directory Tree

As you work with UNIX, you tend to generate a large number of files, which produces a need for file organization. The organizational framework UNIX supplies is the directory system. Conceptually, the multitudes of files on the UNIX system are organized into separate directories, which are in turn organized into a tree-like structure. There is one master directory, called the "root directory." Various subdirectories branch off this root, and sub-subdirectories can branch off the directories. Usually each directory also contains files. (The Files and Directories entry provides a deeper look at the directory system.)

Each user is assigned a "home directory." When you log in, your home directory becomes your "current working directory." Files you create are stored in this directory, and commands you give are assumed to apply to files in this directory. Using the **mkdir** command, you can create subdirectories to your home directory, thus extending the tree structure.

UNIX has a file-naming convention that goes along with the directory tree structure. Each UNIX file has a "full pathname" and a "basename." The full pathname locates exactly where the file can be found in the directory tree. It is an "absolute" label, in that it does not depend on your current directory. The basename is used for files in the current working directory. It is a "relative" label. For example, when you run the **ls** command, it lists the basenames of the files in the current directory.

A full pathname prefixes the basename with a list of directories leading from the root directory to the file. For example, home directories typically are subdirectories of the **usr** directory (or of the **u** directory in many systems). The **usr** directory is a subdirectory of the root (/) directory. Suppose, then, that a **bells** file originally is in a home directory called **tara** (your home directory normally has the same name as your login name). The full pathname for this file would be **/usr/tara/bells**. The first / stands for the root directory. The subsequent slashes serve as separators between directory names and filenames (see Figure 11). So this particular pathname says that

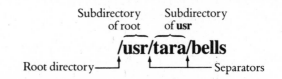

FIGURE 11. *The anatomy of a pathname*

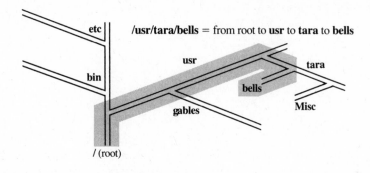

FIGURE 12. *Translating the /usr/tara/bells pathname*

bells is found in the **tara** subdirectory of the **usr** subdirectory of the root directory (see Figure 12).

Suppose we move (using **mv**) the **bells** file to the **Misc** subdirectory of **tara**. The file still has the same basename (**bells**), but now its full pathname becomes **/usr/tara/Misc/bells** (see Figure 13).

Because the full (or "absolute") pathname specifies exactly where a file can be found, it can be used in any working directory. Suppose, for example, we still are in the **tara** directory and want to use **cat** to see the contents of the

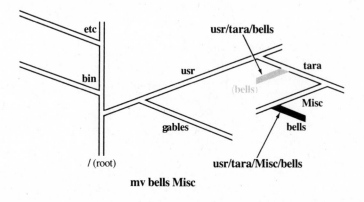

FIGURE 13. *Relocating the bells file*

bells file. The following example shows an invalid and a valid method for looking at it.

```
$ pwd
/usr/tara
$ cat bells                      Use just the basename
$ cat: cannot open bells         Doesn't find it
$ cat /usr/tara/Misc/bells       Use full pathname
Some bells ding, some bells dong.
Put them together, and get a song.
$
```

If the file or directory you wish to investigate is on a continuation of your current directory path, you can use a "relative pathname." A relative pathname provides a path relative to your current directory; tacking it onto the end of the pathname of the current directory gives the full pathname. In our example, we could use the relative pathname **Misc/bells**, as shown here:

```
$ cat Misc/bells
Some bells ding, some bells dong.
Put them together, and get a song.
$
```

Note that there is no initial / for the relative pathname. UNIX would interpret **/Misc/bells** as an absolute pathname, with **Misc** branching off the root directory.

You can use both relative and full pathnames with **mkdir** to divide your subdirectories by creating sub-subdirectories:

```
$ mkdir Correspond/Friends       Create subdirectory
$
```

Here we used a relative pathname to specify that we want to create a **Friends** subdirectory in the **Correspond** directory, which is our current working directory.

In short, you can use the basename if the file is in your current working directory. You can use a relative pathname if the file is in a subdirectory or chain of subdirectories branching off your current directory. And you can always use the full pathname.

SEE ALSO UNIX Commands: **mkdir; mv; basename; dirname**
UNIX Features: Files and Directories

Permissions

The forms of access different users have to a UNIX file are controlled by the file "permissions." Each file is described by a "file mode," a 16-bit number in which individual bits describe different aspects, including individual permissions. This gives rise to terminology like "set the user-execute bit," which means "grant the user permission to execute."

UNIX recognizes three classes of permissions: permission to read a file, permission to write or modify a file, and permission to execute a file. The **ls -l** and **chmod** commands call these permissions **r**, **w**, and **x**, respectively. If the file is a directory, these permissions become permission to list the contents of the directory (**r**), permission to add or remove files from the directory (**w**), and permission to look at files and subdirectories in the directory (**x**).

UNIX also recognizes three classes of potential users, based on the identifications (IDs) associated with the file. A file has a user ID and a group ID (see the Groups entry). By default, the creator of the file is the user (or owner), and the group ID is that of the user's group at the time he or she creates the file. However, the ID values can be changed using the **chown** and the **chgrp** commands.

The first class of potential users recognized by UNIX is the "user," or owner, of the file. The second class is the "group"—those users having the same group ID as the file. The third class is "others"—everyone else.

THE PERMISSION MODE   The three permissions are assigned to each of the three classes separately, producing nine permissions altogether. The **ls -l** command produces a listing that includes a file mode entry detailing the permissions. Here are two sample modes:

```
-rwxr-xr--
drwxr-xr--
```

The first character indicates the type of file; **-** is a regular file and **d** is a directory. Next comes a set of three characters detailing user permissions; **r** is read, **w** is write, and **x** is execute. If permission is not granted, a **-** is shown instead of a letter. The next set of three characters describes permission for group members. In the example, they can read and execute the file, but they cannot write in the file (**r-x**). The last set of three characters applies to other users. In the example, they can read the file or **ls** the directory, but do nothing else (**r--**).

OCTAL REPRESENTATION OF THE MODE The mode often is described by a three-digit octal (base 8) number. The first digit specifies user permissions, the second specifies group permissions, and the third specifies permissions for others. The basic values for a digit are these:

DIGIT	MEANING
04	Read permission.
02	Write permission.
01	Execute permission.

(The initial 0 is the C programming language convention for indicating an octal number.) You indicate combined permissions by adding the corresponding values. Thus read and write permission is 06 (04 + 02). A mode value of 0644, then, means read and write permission for the owner (the 6), and read only permission for the group and for others (the two 4s).

CHANGING THE MODE You can use the **chmod** command to set the permissions to the values you desire. For example, the command

```
chmod 0700 predator
```

gives the owner read, write, and execute permissions for the **predator** file while denying all permissions to the group and to others. You also can use a symbolic method for changing the mode. For instance,

```
chmod go-r memo.213
```

revokes read permission for group members (**g**) and other users (**o**) for the **memo.213** file. Read the entry for the **chmod** command for more details on using this command.

THE CREATION MASK The **chmod** command lets you set permissions *after* a file has been created. The **umask** command regulates permissions when a file is created by providing a "creation mask" that disallows certain permissions. The mask uses the octal code just described to indicate forbidden permissions. For example, a creation mask of 0022 (the default value) means that write permission (02) for the group and for others is disallowed when a file is created. The **umask** command lets you set the creation mask value. For example, the command

```
umask 0000
```

sets the creation mask to 0000, which does not disallow any permissions.

Using the **umask** command when a file is created does not prevent you from using the **chmod** command later to grant the previously forbidden permissions.

SET-USER-ID AND SET-GROUP-ID Sometimes it is useful to allow a user to modify a file that he or she is not ordinarily permitted to alter. For example, when you change your password, you need to update the **/etc/passwd** file, even though, if you are an ordinary user, you don't normally have permission to access this file. UNIX solves this problem by providing the set-user-ID permission bit. If you set this bit for one of your executable files, anyone who uses the program in that file will have *your* file permissions while running the program. This allows you to set things up so that other users can alter another file *only* by using that particular program, and not directly. (This is much better than handing out passwords.)

The octal value for setting this permission is 04000. Here is an example of how it can be used:

```
$ chmod 0600  folio
$ chmod 04755 invest
```

Here **folio** is a data file and **invest** is a program that can read and alter the **folio** file. First we set the **folio** mode to 0600, giving us (the owner) read and write permission for the file, but preventing anyone else from seeing or altering the file contents. Then we set the **invest** mode to **04755**, giving us read, write, and execute permission for **invest**, and allowing everyone else to read and execute it. In addition, because we have set the set-user-ID bit, anyone using **invest** has our permission settings and thus can alter **folio**. Once **invest** terminates, their original permissions apply and they are kept out of **folio**.

The set-group-ID bit works similarly, except that it gives a user the permissions in effect for the group instead of the permissions in effect for the owner. Its octal value is 02000.

Using set-user-ID and set-group-ID can lead to security problems. If, for example, your program allows a user to start up a shell while the set-user-ID bit is set, then that shell will have your access to your files. Since the shell executes commands, people using that shell could run any command they liked, using your files just as if they were their own.

Note that set-user-ID and set-group-ID work for executable programs but not shell scripts. (Some versions of UNIX allow set-user-ID/set-group-ID shell scripts, but because of the problems just described, it's usually not a good idea to use them unless you plan to spend a lot of time making your scripts secure.)

SEE ALSO UNIX Commands: **chgrp**; **chmod**; **chown**; **ls**; **umask**
UNIX Features: Files and Directories; Groups

Processes

A process is a running program. Because UNIX is a multi-user, multi-tasking system, it can run several processes at once. So one important duty for the operating system is to schedule the various processes and keep track of them.

Actually, the UNIX time-sharing system involves switching back and forth among the various tasks, so that the CPU deals with only one process at a time. The system maintains a list, or "queue," of current processes, devotes some time to one process, puts it on hold, works on another, and so on.

FOREGROUND AND BACKGROUND PROCESSES

A foreground process works under the control of the person at the terminal. It may, for example, require interactive input from the keyboard. While a process is in foreground, you cannot use the terminal except as input/output to that process; once a foreground process terminates, you can move to another task.

A background process is one that is placed in the process queue but is removed from terminal control. The computer takes care of scheduling the process for execution; meanwhile, you can use your terminal for other tasks.

Since a background process is disassociated from your terminal, it will have problems if it expects to read keyboard input. You should therefore use redirection or a pipe to provide any input that might be needed.

A process that ordinarily sends its output to the screen will still do so when run in background. You should therefore use redirection or a pipe to send the output elsewhere.

The traditional UNIX way to run a job in the background is to use the **&** symbol:

```
$ sort enormous > enormous.s &
5234
$
```

The system reports back that **5234** is the process identification number (PID), then prints the shell prompt, showing that you can proceed with another command.

The **kill** command can be used to terminate background processes from the keyboard.

Under UNIX System V, logging out normally terminates background jobs. This can be avoided by using the **batch** or **nohup** command.

Release 2.0 of System V added the **shl** (shell layer) command, which allows you to run up to seven shells simultaneously, switching them back and forth between foreground and background modes.

THE SHELL PROCESS One process of particular note is your shell. This is an interactive program that acts as an interface between you and the system. When you log in, a shell process is started up for you. When you run another program, such as **cat** or **vi**, from the shell, it arranges to start up that program as a new process. The shell process waits until the new process finishes, then starts up again.

THE ps COMMAND The **ps** command displays a list of those processes that belong to you. Various options provide more information about these processes and allow you to display other processes, too.

SEE ALSO UNIX Commands: **ps; sh; kill; batch; nohup; at; crontab**
UNIX Features: The Shell and the Kernel

The .profile File

The **.profile** file contains startup instructions for your login shell. When you log in, the shell reads and executes the commands in this file. Normally, the system administrator provides new users with a standard **.profile** file when their accounts are established. To see if you have one, use the **ls -a** command. **ls** (list) ordinarily does not list files whose names begin with a period, but adding the **-a** option instructs it to list all files.

One common use for **.profile** is to set up environmental variables. Suppose, for example, that you want to change the primary and secondary prompts that UNIX displays when it is waiting for a command. These are defined by the **PS1** and **PS2** variables, and their default values are $ and **>**. To change them, you can place these lines in **.profile**:

```
PS1='WHAT NOW? '
PS2='PLEASE COMPLETE COMMAND '
export PS1 PS2
```

The first two lines define the new prompts, and the third line causes the definitions to stay in effect when you create new subshells by running the **sh** command.

Normally, the **.profile** file is only read when you log in, so any changes you make to the file will not go into effect until then. However, you can use sh's **.** (dot) command to read and execute the file immediately:

```
. .profile
```

SEE ALSO   UNIX Commands: **sh**
UNIX Features: Shell Variables

472

Quoting (Escaping)

Many characters have special meanings to the shell. Sometimes you may wish to override those special meanings. The **sh** shell lets you do this by using single quotes, double quotes, or a backslash to "quote," or "escape," the characters that have special meanings. Let's see how this works.

THE BACKSLASH (\)   The backslash is used to make the character that follows it an ordinary character. For instance, the shell normally interprets **?** to be a "wildcard" character (or "metacharacter"), but interprets **\?** to be an ordinary question mark. Let's use the **echo** command to see how the backslash works. The **echo** command prints out, or "echoes," its arguments, as in:

```
$ echo VAX 750 is my name - UNIX is my game.
VAX 750 is my name - UNIX is my game.
$
```

Try using **echo** with a question:

```
$ ls
file1
file2
file3
$ echo Which file?
Which file1 file2 file3
$
```

Here the argument **file?** is replaced by filenames fitting that pattern. Actually, the **sh** version of **echo** is pretty clever: if there are no filenames matching an **echo** argument that includes a **?**, the **?** is printed literally; that is, if our directory did not contain **file1**, **file2**, **file3**, or any other file with a name that matched the pattern, the interaction would have gone like this:

```
$ ls
popcorn
$ echo Which file?
Which file?
```

Obviously, you should not depend on such good fortune in order for your programs to work. The safest course is to use the backslash to turn off the pattern-matching property of the question mark:

```
$ echo Which file\?
Which file?
```

This form of the command works regardless of whether or not we have matching filenames in our directory.

Sometimes it is more convenient to use single quotes for overriding special meanings; everything between the open and close quote is affected. Note that the open and close quote are the same character: the forward quote. Don't use the backquote, which is an accent grave (`); it has another special meaning in UNIX (see Command Substitution).

Besides turning off metacharacters, single quotes also make everything between them a single argument, because the space character no longer has its special meaning as an argument separator. We can use **echo** to see how this aspect works:

```
$ echo a) fresh fish            b) hamburger
a) fresh fish b) hamburger
$
```

The **echo** command prints its arguments with a space between each argument. In our example, there are five arguments: the first is **a)**, the second is **fresh**, and so one to the fifth, **hamburger**. All the spaces between **fish** and **b)** merely serve to separate the two arguments and are not themselves arguments. Thus **echo** puts only one space between the arguments when printing them out.

Now let's place the whole argument in single quotes:

```
$ echo 'a) fresh fish           b) hamburger'
a) fresh fish           b) hamburger
$
```

This time, everything between the two quotes, including all the spaces, counts as a single argument, so it is printed in its entirety.

Single quotes often are required to clarify command lines. For example, the **grep** command searches for patterns in a file. Its first argument normally is the pattern and the remaining arguments are the files to be searched. Consider the following two commands:

```
grep high school ferdy

grep 'high school' ferdy
```

The first searches for the single word **high** in the files **school** and **ferdy**. The second searches for the phrase **high school** in the file **ferdy**. The quotes make **high school** into one argument instead of two.

Another common use for single quotes is with pattern-using commands like **grep**, **sed**, and **awk**. These commands can use pattern-matching wildcard characters in a manner similar, but not identical, to the shell's use. If you want to sneak a pattern past the shell to the command, use single quotes.

For example, suppose you want to search for the words **sunset** and **Sunset** in a particular file. The **grep** command can use a bracket pattern to specify a lower- or uppercase **s**:

```
grep '[Ss]unset' maui
```

This command searches the **maui** file for either form. If the single quotes were omitted, the shell would try to replace **[Ss]unset** with matching filenames.

The shell expects single quotes to come in pairs. If you include just one and then hit the <enter> key, the **sh** shell displays the secondary prompt, which, by default, is the **>** character followed by a space. This prompt tells you that the shell expects you to finish an incomplete command. Suppose, for example, you omitted the close quote; you would see something like this on your screen:

```
$ echo 'The tiger walks alone<enter>
>
```

The shell pauses until you either cancel the command by striking the <del> key or complete the command, as here:

```
$ echo 'The tiger walks alone<enter>
> on cloud-feet'<enter>
The tiger walks alone
on cloud-feet
$
```

DOUBLE QUOTES (" ") Double quotes work much like single quotes except that a few metacharacters are not affected by them. In particular, they do not override the backquote (') used for command substitution or the dollar sign ($) when it is used in parameter substitution (see the Command Substitution and Parameter Substitution entries).

Let's use **echo** to illustrate the difference. First, suppose **TERM** is a variable with the value **ansi**. We use the dollar sign to represent the value:

```
$ echo TERM is $TERM
TERM is ansi
```

Let's further suppose the current directory has a file called **peppy** in it. The next example shows the effect of no quotes, single quotes, and double quotes:

```
$ echo This is a pep* $TERM
This is a peppy ansi
$ echo 'This is a pep* $TERM'
This is a pep* $TERM
$ echo "This is a pep* $TERM"
This is a pep* ansi
```

The single quotes override * and $, but the double quotes override only *.

Double quotes are useful when you need both quoting and parameter substitution. Suppose you have a shell script containing this line:

```
grep $pattern somefile
```

The intent is to have **grep** search the **somefile** file for **pattern**. But suppose **pattern** is set to a string containing spaces; for instance, **Mr. Schmoo**. Then parameter substitution converts this line to the following:

```
grep Mr. Schmoo somefile
```

This causes **grep** to seek **Mr.** in the **Schmoo** and **somefile** files. However, suppose we use double quotes:

```
grep "$pattern" somefile
```

After parameter substitution, the command expands to this:

```
grep "Mr. Schmoo" somefile
```

The double quotes allow the substitution and preserve **Mr. Schmoo** as a single argument.

If you wish to pass quotes as arguments to a command, you need to quote them. For example, the command

```
$ echo '
```

doesn't work because the shell expects quotes to come in pairs. But the next two approaches do work:

```
$ echo \'
'
```

```
$ echo "'"
'
```

Similarly, you can use a \ or single quotes to quote a double quote.

SEE ALSO   UNIX Commands: **sh**
UNIX Features: Command Lines; Command Substitution; Parameter Substitution; Extending Commands over More than One Line

Regular Expressions

Many commands, including **ed**, **ex**, **sed**, **vi**, **awk**, **grep**, **egrep**, **expr**, and **pg**, use character patterns called "regular expressions." Most of these commands search a file for a "string," or sequence of characters, that fits the pattern. If one is found, the regular expression is said to "match" the string. How the regular expression is used depends on the command. For example, **grep** finds lines in a file matching a regular expression, while **ed** can use a regular expression to locate text that is to be replaced with something else.

A regular expression is a series of characters. Most characters, including letters of the alphabet, simply represent themselves. For example, the regular expression **men** matches any string containing these three letters in sequence, so it would match the **men** sequence in the words **men**, **women**, and **demented**.

A few "special characters," however, have more general meanings. A period, for instance, matches any one character, so the regular expression **d.n** matches any string containing a **d** that is followed by any one character followed by an **n** . Thus **d.n** matches the corresponding three–letter sequences in **don**, **good night**, and **done**. Note that the space between **good** and **night** counts as a character.

The commands that use regular expressions don't all recognize the exact same set of special characters. The most basic specification of regular expressions is that of the original **ed** command, which defines "limited regular expressions." **awk** and **egrep** recognize additional special characters, defining "full regular expressions." However, limited regular expressions are not quite a subset of full regular expressions, since they use a couple of patterns not used in full regular expressions.

BASIC REGULAR EXPRESSIONS First, let's look at the common core of limited and full regular expressions. We might consider this core a set of basic building blocks.

SYMBOL(S)	MEANING
c	Any character that isn't a special character matches itself. The special characters are \, [, ., and sometimes *, ^,], and $, as described below.
.	Matches any one character.
\	Overrides the special nature of a special character. Thus, . matches any character, but \. matches just the period character. The \ is said to "quote," or "escape," the following character.

(continued)

SYMBOL(S)	MEANING	_(continued)_
[_list_]	Matches any one character from _list_. Here _list_ can be a series of characters, as in [aeiou], or can use a hyphen to indicate a range, as in [a–z], or can do both, as in [AEIOUa–m]. Note that this construction stands for a single character: m[ea]t matches **met** and **mat**, but not **meat**.	
[^_list_]	Matches any one character not in _list_. For example, m[^ea]t matches **mutt**, **mottled**, and **I'm tired**, but not **met** or **mat**.	
*	Matches zero or more occurrences of the single–character regular expression it follows. Thus go*d matches **gd**, **god**, **good**, and so on. Note that the * applies just to the **o**, not to the **go**; that is, the pattern go*d does not match **gogod**.	
	The single–character regular expression can be one of the other special characters. Thus the pattern g.*d matches **gd**, **gad**, **god**, **gold**, **gould**, and so on. The difference between go*d and g.*d is that, for the first pattern, the only letter that can used between **g** and **d** is **o**, while in the second pattern, any character can be used. In general, the longest possible match is selected; that is, if the expression is g.*d and the line is **gould's gold is bad**, then the whole line is matched, since that is the longest string starting with **g** and ending with **d**.	
^	When this is the first character of a regular expression, the rest of the expression must match the beginning of a line. For example, ^joey matches only lines beginning with **joey**, and ^[a–z] matches only lines beginning with lowercase letters.	
$	When this is the last character of a regular expression, the rest of the expression must match the end of a line. For example, ^abc$ matches only those lines that contain the string **abc** with nothing else on the line.	

You can string together these building blocks to form larger regular expressions; this is called concatenation. Let's look at some more examples:

PATTERN	POSSIBLE MATCHES
[Bb]ird	Matches **Bird** or **bird**, but not **Bbird**. The bracketed list represents just one character from the list.
[Bb][ai]rd	Matches **bird**, **Bird**, **bard**, and **Bard**, but not **Baird**.

PATTERN	POSSIBLE MATCHES
s[aeiou]*t	Matches any string starting with **s**, ending with **t**, and having zero or more vowels and nothing else in between; for example, **st**, **set**, **soot**, and **suit**. Note that having the first vowel be a **u** does not require that the next one be a **u**, too; any vowel from the list can be used.
^\.	Matches any line beginning with a period. Note that the period is "escaped" to preclude its interpretation as a special character.
^$.*\.$	Matches any line beginning with a dollar sign, ending with a period, and having any number of any other characters in between. (Only the final $ in a pattern is a special character, so we don't have to escape the first $ in this pattern.) Thus both **$12.69 for the old vase on the desk.** and **$1000.** would be matched.
^[a–z]* 100	Matches any line beginning with zero or more lowercase letters followed by a space, followed by **100**. Thus **tony 100 jan 18, 1988** would be matched, and so would **100 is enough**, but **Gena 100** would not be matched. This is because regular expressions are case sensitive, and **G** is not lowercase.

LIMITED REGULAR EXPRESSIONS: TAGGED EXPRESSIONS

Limited regular expressions, as used by **ed**, **ex**, **sed**, and **grep**, have a provision for "tagging" expressions. Once an expression has been tagged, it can be referred to by number. To tag an expression, precede it with \(and follow it with \). The first tagged expression, reading from left to right, can be referred to as \1, the second as \2, and so on. Consider, for example, this regular expression:

```
Rin \(Tin\) \1
```

Here **Tin** is tagged, so \1 represents **Tin** and the regular expression matches **Rin Tin Tin**. Similarly, the regular expression

```
\(ding\) \(dong\) \2 \1
```

matches **ding dong dong ding**.

In an editor substitution command, the \n form can also be used in the replacement string. For example,

```
s/\(UNIX System\) III/\1 V/
```

replaces **UNIX System III** with **UNIX System V**.

479

This \n convention looks just like an abbreviation, but it's really more powerful than that. For example,

```
s/\([a-zA-Z]*\)'s/\1 lost a/
```

changes the lines

```
Jacki's coat
John's car
```

to

```
Jacki lost a coat
John lost a car
```

FULL REGULAR EXPRESSIONS Full regular expressions, as used by **egrep** and **awk**, do not recognize tagged expressions. But they do add the following notations to the basic set:

SYMBOL	MEANING
+	Matches one or more occurrences of the preceding regular expression. Thus **go+d** matches **god**, **good**, and **goood**, but not **gd**.
?	Matches zero or one occurrence of the preceding regular expression. Thus **go?d** matches **gd** and **god**, but not **good**.
¦ or newline	Matches either of two regular expressions separated by the ¦ or the newline character. Thus the regular expression **cat ¦ dog** matches either **cat** or **dog**. Or, similarly, if **cat** and **dog** were placed on separate lines, either of them would be matched.
()	Parentheses are used to group a regular expression so that *, +, ?, or ¦ can be applied to the whole expression. Thus **(go)?** matches **go** and **gogo**, while **go?** matches **go** or **goo**.

The () symbols have the highest precedence, followed by the * ? + group, followed by concatenation, followed by ¦ and the newline (see the examples below).

Because parentheses are special characters when they are used with full regular expressions, you must use \(and \) to match literal parentheses in a string. That, in turn, means that \(and \) are not available for tagging expressions; that is, in limited regular expressions, \(and \) are a special notation for tagging and (and) are ordinary parentheses. In full regular expressions, (and) are special, and \(and \) are ordinary parentheses.

Let's look at a few examples of full regular expressions.

PATTERN	POSSIBLE MATCHES
[a–z] +[0-9]	Matches any sequence where a lowercase letter is followed by one or more spaces followed by a digit; for example, c 8 and t 5 are matched, but k9 is not matched, because it lacks a space.
[a–z]+[0-9]?	Matches any series of one or more lowercase letters followed by zero or one digits; for example, be4, you, and f8 are matched, but c 8 is not matched, because it has a space.
Tony ¦ Anthony	Matches Tony or Anthony, as does Tony Anthony
Tony ¦ Anthony Quinn	Matches the string Tony or the string Anthony Quinn. Concatenation (joining the characters from the beginning of Anthony to the end of Quinn) has higher precedence than ¦ , so two names separated by a space are treated as a unit. Note that Tony Quinn is not matched.
(Tony ¦ Anthony) Quinn	Matches Tony Quinn or Anthony Quinn. The parentheses have higher precedence than concatenation, so the expression in parentheses is treated as a unit.
(so?)+	Matches a series of one or more elements, each of which is an s or so; for example, so, sos, sso, soso, and sossssosos all are matched. But soo and soos are not matched, because no combination of s and so produces two consecutive o's.

AN EXTENSION TO LIMITED REGULAR EXPRESSIONS

The System V ed, sed, and grep commands recognize an extension to limited regular expressions. You'll recall that * means zero or more occurrences of the preceding single-character regular expression. The extension allows you to specify the number of occurrences more precisely. It has these three forms (n and m are integers):

NOTATION	MEANING
\{n\}	Matches exactly n occurrences of the preceding single-character regular expression. Thus t\{2\} matches tt.
\{n,\}	Matches at least n occurrences of the preceding single-character regular expression. Thus t\{2,\} matches tt, ttt, tttt, and so on.
\{n,m\}	Matches from n to m occurrences of the preceding single-character regular expression. Thus t\{2,3\} matches tt and ttt.

The longest possible match is selected. Suppose, for example, a line contains the string **seeeed**. Next, suppose we apply this **ed** editing command to it:

```
s/e\{2,\}/x/
```

The first two **e**'s match the pattern, but the longest match is all four **e**'s, so all four are replaced by the single **x**. Thus, **seeeed** becomes **sxd**. Now suppose this editing command is applied to the line with **seeeed**:

```
s/e\{2\}/x/g
```

This time, exactly two **e**'s are matched, so first the initial two **e**'s are replaced, then the next two are replaced. Thus **seeeed** becomes **sxxd**. The **g** (global) suffix causes all pairs of **e**'s on a line to be replaced.

ex EXTENSIONS   The **ex** editor does not recognize the **\{\}** notation, but it has some extensions of its own:

SYMBOL(S)	MEANING
\<	Matches the beginning of a "word."
\>	Matches the end of a "word."
~	Matches the replacement string from the most recent **ex** substitute command.

To be considered a "word," a string can use only letters, digits, and underscore characters. The beginning of a word is one of these characters preceded by a newline character or a character that is not a letter, digit, or underscore. Similarly, the end of a word is marked by a newline character or one of these non-word characters. Consider, for example, the following line:

```
It is a catch22 day, isn't it? 248 12.19
```

The "words" in this line are **It, is, a, catch22, day, isn, t, 248, 12,** and **19.** Spaces, of course, act as word delimiters, but so do punctuation characters such as the comma, apostrophe, question mark, and period.

These extensions are useful for avoiding embedded strings in a search. Thus the pattern **\<men\>** will find the string **men** in **men** or **men?** but not in **women** or in **demented.**

We've seen the main features of regular expressions. Specific commands may modify their use slightly, as discussed in the "UNIX Commands" section.

SEE ALSO   UNIX Commands: **awk; ed; egrep; ex; expr; grep; pg; sed; vi**

The Shell and the Kernel

The shell is a program that acts as an interface between you and the kernel, which is a system of programs that manage a computer's resources. The kernel is the heart of the UNIX operating system, while the shell, like **cat** and other commands, is an extension. Let's look at an example that illustrates the distinction between the shell and the kernel. Suppose you want to copy a file by giving a command like this one:

```
cp /usr/fott/*.c .
```

When you type this command, it's the shell's job to interpret it. It figures out which filenames are matched by the ***.c** combination and which directory the lone period represents. It finds where the **cp** program is kept, and it starts the execution of the program. In short, the shell acts as a "command-line interpreter."

The kernel, on the other hand, takes care of the nitty-gritty work. It puts the command in its process queue and schedules when it will be run. It finds hard-disk space for storing the copies. It creates the proper i-node entries to describe the locations of the files and such properties as time of creation, file sizes, and file permissions. And the **cp** command uses calls to the kernel to copy the bytes from the original files to the copies.

The kernel starts up when the computer is started up, or "booted." One of the kernel's tasks is to start up a shell program for you when you log in. Each user gets his, her, or its (some "users" actually are programs) own shell. Thus, typically one kernel and several shell programs are running at any one time.

Several shells have been developed for UNIX. The standard shell for System V is **sh**, and it is the only one discussed in this book.

In addition to being a command-line interpreter, **sh** is a programming language. It recognizes several programming constructs, including loops and conditional statements. Traditional programming languages are oriented toward manipulating numeric values, but **sh** manipulates UNIX commands.

SEE ALSO UNIX Commands: **sh**
UNIX Features: Shell Scripts; Shell Variables; Command Lines; Processes; Filename Generation; Parameter Substitution; Quoting; Command Substitution

Shell Scripts

A shell script, also called a shell procedure or a shell program, is a sequence of shell and UNIX commands. Typically, a shell script is saved in a file so that it can be used when needed.

Writing shell scripts is a form of programming. The main programming elements are UNIX commands, and the **sh** shell provides constructs such as loops and conditional statements for structuring programs.

Shell scripts have several advantages over programs written in conventional programming languages. They are easy to put together and to modify; you need only a text editor instead of a compiler. Since scripts can make use of any UNIX command, they have very powerful tools at their disposal, but they don't require much room in memory, because they call upon UNIX commands that already are stored in the system. And scripts are easily transferred from one UNIX system to another. Since they are simple text files, they can, for example, be transmitted by electronic mail from one UNIX system to another, even if the other uses different hardware.

The chief disadvantage of shell scripts is that they are slower than compiled programs, but often that is not an important consideration.

Here we will look primarily at how shell scripts are put together and used, rather than at programming details.

RUNNING A SHELL SCRIPT The simplest form of shell script would be one containing straightforward UNIX commands. For example, we can place these commands in a file called **tp** (for "time and place"):

```
date
pwd
```

Then, to have these commands execute, we can do this:

```
$ sh tp
Tue Dec 15 1987 04:21:15 PST
/usr/troll
$
```

This starts up a new shell process; our old shell becomes inactive. When **sh** is invoked with a filename as an argument, it executes the commands in the file. After executing the last command in the file, the new shell expires, returning control to the old shell.

You can use **chmod** to make the shell script file executable:

```
chmod u+x tp
```

Once that is done, you can run the **tp** program just by typing its name:

```
$ tp
Tue Dec 15 1987 04:23:53 PST
/usr/troll
$
```

MAKING A COMMAND DIRECTORY

So far, the **tp** command works just in the directory containing it. If we switch to some other directory, we have to use the full pathname of the command so that the system can find it:

```
$ cd /usr/gnome/rocks
$ /usr/troll/tp
Tue Dec 15 1987 05:51:37 PST
/usr/gnome/rocks
$
```

To make shell scripts (and the other programs you write) easier to use, you can create a command directory and place it in your **PATH**. **PATH** is a shell environmental variable that tells the shell which directories to search for commands. Typically, your **.profile** file contains a line like this:

```
PATH=.:/bin:/usr/bin
```

This instructs the shell to look in the current directory (.) for the command. If the command is not there, the shell searches **/bin**. If it is not there, the shell searches **/usr/bin**. The colons serve to separate the pathnames (see **sh** for more details).

What you can do is create, say, a **bin** subdirectory to your home directory and place your executable programs there. Then you need to modify your **.profile** file to read as follows:

```
PATH=$PATH:$HOME/bin
```

Here, **$PATH** stands for the original search path and **$HOME** stands for your home directory (see Shell Variables). Now, after searching the other directories for a command name, the shell searches your personal command directory for it. Note: The new path value does not become effective until the system rereads the **.profile** file. This will happen the next time you log in. Or, to speed things up, you can use the **sh .** (dot) command:

```
. .profile
```

This causes the current shell to run through the instructions in the **.profile** file, just as if you had logged in.

Incidentally, the following command does not have the desired effect:

```
sh .profile
```

This creates a new shell that executes the commands in the **.profile** file. However, the assignments made to shell variables, such as **PATH**, are effective in that new shell, not in the original one, and the new shell expires as soon as it finishes reading the file. So the original shell is left with the same values it had before.

USING COMMAND-LINE ARGUMENTS

Consider this shell script:

```
ls -l ¦ pg
```

Suppose we place it in a file named **L** in our command directory and that we use **chmod** to make the file executable. Then, if we give the **L** command, we get a long listing piped through the **pg** command. If a directory contains many files, this lets us see just one screenful of listing at a time.

But what if we are in, say, our home directory and give a command like this one?

```
L /
```

The command still lists the files in our home directory, not the files in the / directory. This is because the script itself does not include any filename arguments. Fortunately, UNIX lets us convey command-line arguments to a shell script. The scheme is straightforward. The first argument on a command line is referred to as **$1** in the script, the second argument is **$2**, and so on through **$9**. In addition, **$0** signifies the name of the command itself, and both **$*** and **$@** signify everything in the command line except the command name.

Here is one possible modification of the **L** command:

```
ls -l $1 ¦ pg
```

With this modification, a command like

```
L /
```

is translated to this:

```
ls -l / ¦ pg
```

But the next version is better:

```
ls -l $* ¦ pg
```

This allows us to give commands like this:

```
L -i / /bin
```

The whole command line is transmitted to the script, yielding this final command:

```
ls -l -i / /bin ¦ pg
```

Thus we can apply **L** to several files and bring in additional options.

The difference between **$*** and **$@** lies in how they behave when enclosed in double quotes. The expression "**$***" is expanded to a single argument of many words, while "**$@**" is expanded to the original number of arguments. For example, consider this short script:

```
# seekdata -- searches datafile
grep "$*" datafile
```

The **#** marks a comment line; here we indicate the name and use of the script. Now suppose we give this command:

```
seek July 18, 1976
```

This becomes the following:

```
grep "July 18, 1976" datafile
```

That is, the whole date is treated as a single argument to be sought by **grep**. If we use "**$@**" instead of "**$***", the final command is this:

```
grep "July" "18," "1976" datafile
```

Here the original three arguments are still three arguments, and **18** and **1976** are interpreted by **grep** to be filenames. This is the wrong choice here, but sometimes the **$@** construction is the one that is needed.

OTHER SHELL SCRIPT TOOLS The **sh** shell offers several tools for making shell scripts more powerful and convenient. First, there are a variety of programming structures, including the **while**, **until**, and **for** loops; the **if elif** conditional statement; and the **case** selection statement. In addition, the **echo** and **read** commands, which are built into the **sh** command, allow you to construct interactive scripts. And the **–v** and **–x** options to **sh** facilitate the debugging of shell scripts. Also, the shell allows you to create and use variables. All these tools are detailed in the "UNIX Commands" section under **sh**, and shell variables also are discussed under that "UNIX Features" topic. The **test** command is another useful tool; it tests file types and the values of shell variables in a manner compatible with **sh** structures such as the **while** loop and **if** statement.

SEE ALSO UNIX Commands: **sh**; **test**
UNIX Features: Command Lines; The Shell and the Kernel; Shell Variables

Shell Variables

The shell maintains a table of variables and their values. These variables are called "shell variables," or "shell parameters." Several variables are created for your shell when you log in. They do things like specify your prompt string, specify what kind of terminal you are using, set up search paths for commands, and specify your home directory.

CREATING A SHELL VARIABLE To create a shell variable, you first need to choose a name. You can use upper- and lowercase letters, digits, and the underscore character in a name, but the name must not begin with a digit. Thus **sam**, **PUDGE**, **last_num**, and **G8** are valid names, but **8ball** is not.

Having chosen a name, you assign a value to it:

```
sam=yes
PUDGE='ginnie mae'
last_num=88
G8=rusty!
```

Note that there are no spaces around the **=** sign. The values are strings, or series of characters. Any character in your computer's character set can be used, but characters with special meanings should be quoted. Thus, **ginnie mae** is in quotes in the above example because the space, like the newline character, otherwise serves to mark the end of an assignment. The value of **last_num** is the string **88**; that is, two **8** characters. Note, however, that some shell commands interpret numeric stings arithmetically.

ACCESSING A SHELL VARIABLE Use a $ prefix to indicate the value of a shell variable:

```
$ echo G8 is $G8
G8 is rusty!
```

Here **G8** is printed literally, but **$G8** is replaced by its value, as discussed under Parameter Substitution.

The variable's name can be enclosed in braces to clarify the grouping. Compare these commands:

```
$ echo $sammy

$ echo ${sam}my
yesmy
```

In the first case, the shell looks for and fails to find a variable called **sammy**. There is no error message, but the shell produces a blank line. In the second case, the braces show that the **sam** variable should be used.

EXPORTING VARIABLES When you create a variable like **sam**, it is local to the current shell. If, say, you start up a new shell by giving the **sh** command or by running a shell script, the new shell will not know about **sam** unless you "export" the variable. This is accomplished using the **export** command:

```
$ sh              Start up a new shell
$ echo $sam

                  Doesn't know sam
$ <control-d>     Return to first shell
$ export sam
$ sh
$ echo $sam
yes               Now sam is known
$
```

What happens is that each shell maintains its own set of variables. When you export a variable, any new shell you create in turn creates its own variable of the same name and value. One consequence of this is that if you change the value of an exported variable in a child shell, you only change the value of that copy. When you return to the original shell, the original value still holds:

```
$ sam=maybe       Still in new shell
$ echo $sam
maybe
$ <control-d>     Return to original shell
$ echo $sam
yes               Old value
$
```

ENVIRONMENTAL VARIABLES When the shell is invoked, an "environment" is passed to it. The environment of a program is the set of variables and values passed to it. You can type **set** to see what variables your shell starts up with. Here are some of the common ones:

VARIABLE	DESCRIPTION
HOME	The home directory; used as the default argument for the **cd** command.
PATH	Specifies the directories that the shell will search for command files.
PS1	The primary prompt string; typically set to $.
PS2	The secondary prompt string; typically set to **>**.

489

One reason for calling these "environmental variables" is that they help shape your work environment. The system sets up default values for these variables, but you can redefine them. For instance,

```
PS1='What now? '
```

resets your prompt so that the shell asks **What now?** whenever it is waiting for a command. If you place this line in your **.profile** file, the prompt will be set to this string each time you log in.

You can change the environment by adding new variables to it; just define the variables and export them. If you want to add them permanently, place the definitions and export commands in your **.profile** file.

What if you create a new shell? The new shell is handed the same environment as the original, unless you have changed the environment in the meantime, and even then changes you make in the original environment are not carried forward unless you export them. Thus, in the **PS1** example above, the prompt for a new shell would revert to $ unless you also export **PS1**. Note that **PS1** behaves differently from **sam**. If **sam** is not exported, the new shell will have no **sam** variable; if **PS1** is not exported, the new shell will have only the default **PS1** variable, which doesn't reflect any changes to **PS1** made in the parent shell.

There are several contributors to the environment. Some variables, such as the **PS1** prompt string, are provided to each shell that is started. Other environmental definitions may be contained in the **/etc/profile** system file and your home directory **.profile** file.

Variables Used by UNIX Commands

Several UNIX commands can make use of shell variables. For example, the **lp** command, by default, uses the printer specified by the **LPDEST** environmental variable, if it is defined; otherwise, it uses a system default. Thus this variable allows you to customize your environment. If you wish to have a different default from the system default, define the **LPDEST** variable in your **.profile** file and export it.

The **EXINIT** variable is another example of a way in which you can customize your environment. This variable can be set to a string of initialization instructions used by the **ex** and **vi** editors. This allows you to set up the default behavior you want for the editors; for example,

```
EXINIT="set list"
```

causes the **vi** editor to set the **list** option each time the editor is started up.

SEE ALSO   UNIX Commands: **sh**
UNIX Features: The Shell and the Kernel; Parameter Substitution; Shell Scripts; Quoting

Special Files

In UNIX, devices are treated as files, with a unique file representing each device. These special files normally are found in the **/dev** directory. For example, the file **/dev/tty02** represents a terminal. Elsewhere, we've noted that the default standard input and standard output files are both the terminal; this means that a file like **/dev/tty02** can be opened for reading and writing.

To gain some insight into how devices are treated as files, let's look at some sample listings for files in the **/dev** directory. We'll use the **ls -il** command. The **-i** option lists the i-node number for each file, and the **-l** option produces a long listing with a lot of information. There are many files in **/dev**, but we'll just show a few:

```
140 brw-rw-rw- 3 bin  bin    2, 52 Dec  8 15:00 fd0
 32 brw-rw-rw- 2 bin  bin    2,  4 Aug 12 20:31 fd048
 32 brw-rw-rw- 2 bin  bin    2,  4 Aug 12 20:31 fd048ds9
140 brw-rw-rw- 3 bin  bin    2, 52 Dec  8 15:00 fd096
140 brw-rw-rw- 3 bin  bin    2, 52 Dec  8 15:00 fd096ds15
136 crw-rw-rw- 3 bin  bin    2, 52 Sep  1 14:04 rfd096ds15
103 crw-rw-rw- 1 root root   3,  0 Dec 22 14:54 tty
108 crw--w--w- 1 ragu good   0,  1 Jan  7 09:40 tty02
109 crw--w--w- 1 arly good   0,  2 Jan  7 09:39 tty03
117 crw-rw-rw- 2 uucp bin    5,  0 Jan  3 17:50 tty11
```

Let's look at the entry for **tty02** first; it's the third listing from the bottom. The **108** is the i-node number. The file system maintains an i-node (information node) for each file, and the i-node number identifies which i-node entry corresponds to a particular file. Here i-node **108** describes the file **/dev/tty02** (see the Files and Directories entry for more on i-nodes).

Next comes the file mode: **crw--w--w-**. The first character in the mode indicates the kind of file: **-** indicates a regular file, **d** a directory, **c** a character special file, and **b** a block special file. A "character special file," such as **tty02**, indicates a device that transfers information character by character. A "block special file" indicates a device that transfers data in blocks, typically of 512 or 1024 bytes each.

Strictly speaking, a block special device does read/write requests through a "file system buffer cache" and a character special device does not. One common way to distinguish between them is that all terminal devices and networking devices are character special, transferring one byte at a time, while disks that contain mounted file systems use the buffer cache and are block special. Unless you find yourself creating files in /dev using the **mkmod** command, the distinction won't be important.

The rest of the characters in the mode indicate read, write, and execute permissions, just as for regular files. Note that the default setting allows you to read your terminal and to write to it. It also allows others to write to your terminal, which makes the **write** command possible. (The **mesg n** command turns off the write permissions of others, disabling **write** to your terminal.)

After the file mode comes the number of links to the file, 1 in this case. Then comes the owner of the file; this is the login name of the person who logged in on that terminal (when the terminal is inactive, the owner is **root**). Then comes the user's group name.

Next, where we would have the file size for a regular file, we have the major and minor device numbers, separated by a comma; here they are 0 and 1. (We'll come back to these numbers in a minute.) Then comes the date and time of the most recent access and, finally, the filename.

DEVICE NUMBERS AND DEVICE DRIVERS Somewhere, the computer needs programs to tell it how to communicate with a device. Such programs are called "device drivers." The **tty02** file is not itself a device driver, but the major and minor device numbers listed for the **tty02** file (0 and 1, in this case) indicate where to find the drivers.

The major device number identifies the set of drivers to be used for the device. The kernel contains device tables labeled by major device number. For each device number, the table indicates which driver routines are to be used for the various I/O routines. For example, **tty02** uses the routines labeled 0, whereas **fd0** (a floppy disk drive) uses the routines labeled 2.

The minor device number is used to differentiate among devices that use the same driver. Thus **tty02** has a minor device number of 1, while **tty03**, which has the same major device number (0), has a minor number of 2.

MULTIPLE FILES The same device can be referred to by more than one special file. For instance, in our example **fd0**, **fd096**, and **fd096ds15** all refer to the same device. In fact, they are the same file; they all have the same i-node number, and the listing indicates the file has three links. This is a matter of convenience. The third version (**fd096ds15**) fully specifies the drive: drive 0, 96 tracks, double-sided, and 15 sectors. The other two versions are easier to type in. If a 48-track, double-sided, 9-sector drive had been installed instead, **fd0** would be linked to **fd048ds9**.

492

Looking back at the **ls –il** listing, you'll see that the **rfd096ds15** special file also refers to the disk drive, but this is a different file from the **fd096ds15** file. For one thing, it has a different i-node value; for another, it is a character special file, while **fd096ds15** is a block special file. But the two files have the same major and minor device numbers, so they refer to the same device. The difference is that they provide for different ways of communicating with the device. The kernel has separate device tables for character devices and block devices, so although the same device number (**2**) is used to look up which routines to use, a different table is used. Thus **fd096ds15** is used to access this disk through the buffer cache, while **rfd096ds15** bypasses that cache. File-system utilities, such as **fsck** and **mkfs**, tend to use **rfd096ds15** because it provides "raw" access to the disk.

USING SPECIAL FILES You can use special files just as you use regular files. Suppose **/dev/lp0** is a special file for a printer. If you are writing a C program to use the printer, you can use **open( )** or **fopen( )** to open **/dev/lp0**, and you can use **write( )** or **fprintf( )** to write on the printer (assuming you have the necessary file permissions).

You can use redirection with special files. If you have write permission for the printer, then

```
cat guts > /dev/lp0
```

sends the contents of **guts** to the printer. Or if you have write permission to terminal 3, you can use

```
cat guts > /dev/tty03
```

to display the contents of the **guts** file on that terminal.

/dev/tty AND /dev/null So far, the special files we have discussed refer to specific physical devices. UNIX also has special files that are more conceptual in nature. One such file is **/dev/tty**. You can use it to mean the terminal that you are using. Suppose, for example, you are on terminal **tty02** and Grendel is on **tty04**. Then for you **/dev/tty** means your terminal, while to Grendel **/dev/tty** means her terminal. This notation is handy for shell scripts; when you use **/dev/tty** in a shell script, it will refer to your terminal, no matter which one you happened to log in on.

Another special file is the **/dev/null** file, which refers to a "null" device. This is a handy device, sometimes called a "bit bucket," into which you can dump unwanted output. For example, here is a **while** loop that tests to see if **grep** finds a certain name in the output of **who**:

```
while who ! grep sligo > /dev/null
    do
        . . .
    done
```

The **while** statement uses the exit status of **grep** but is not interested in the regular **grep** output. By redirecting the output to **/dev/null**, we discard the output rather than having it displayed on the screen.

Also, if you want to clear a file, setting it to zero length, you can do this:

```
cat /dev/null > proposal
```

The **/dev/null** file has 0 length, so this command replaces the contents of **proposal** with nothing.

SEE ALSO   UNIX Commands: **ls; mesg**
UNIX Features: Files and Directories; Standard I/O, Redirection, and Pipes

Special UNIX Characters

UNIX recognizes several special characters. The **sh** shell makes use of a host of "metacharacters," including the wildcard characters discussed under File-name Generation and the redirection symbols discussed under Standard I/O, Redirection, and Pipes.

There also are characters recognized by the UNIX kernel, such as the interrupt character and the quit character. These characters normally are caught and processed by the kernel and never reach other programs. They are the topic of this section.

Because these characters are represented by different keys on different terminal keyboards, they have descriptive names. We'll look at these characters now, along with what they do and what their common defaults are.

CHARACTER	DESCRIPTION
Interrupt (Intr)	Sends an INTERRUPT signal to whatever process is currently being run from the keyboard. Normally, this signal causes the process to terminate, although programs can be instructed to ignore it. (Editors and interactive shells, for example, ignore the INTERRUPT signal.) The keys most commonly used for this purpose are <del> and <rub> (but also see the discussion below of the break character).
Quit	Sends the QUIT signal. It is similar to the interrupt character but, in addition to terminating the currently running program, it produces a file, called a core dump, that contains an image of the process at quit time. The core dump shows the program's code and what the values of the various variables were, and can be used for debugging. The usual default for the quit character is <control-\>.
Break	Usually has the same effect as the interrupt character. However, the **stty** command controls the interpretation of the break character in two ways. First, if the **ignbrk** flag is set, the break character is ignored. Second, if the **brkint** flag is set, a break is interpreted as an interrupt. Usually, **ignbrk** is set to off and **brkint** to on. The break character is generated by the <break> key or by <control-c>.

(continued)

CHARACTER	DESCRIPTION	_(continued)_
EOF	Simulates an end-of-file condition. Many UNIX commands process input until they reach the end of the file. If the input is from the keyboard, a way is needed to indicate the end of the input. That way is to type the EOF character, usually <control-d>, at the beginning of a line.	
	Incidentally, when the **sh** shell is used interactively, it treats the keyboard as an input file. Thus, typing the EOF character at the beginning of a line terminates input to the shell, causing it to quit. If the shell is your login shell, this logs you out.	
Erase	Erases the preceding input character. Terminals with screens usually use the <backspace> key or <control-h> for this purpose. Terminals with paper displays usually use the <#> key.	
Kill	Erases input back to the beginning of the line. The usual key for screen terminals is <control-u>, while teletype-like terminals generally use the <@> key.	
Switch	Used to go from a shell layer to the **shl** command level when **shl** is running. The usual value is <control-z>.	
Stop	Temporarily suspends output to the terminal. This character typically is <control-s>. If the **stty** is used to turn off the **ixon** flag, this feature is also turned off.	
Start	Causes output halted by the stop character to resume. This character typically is <control-q>. However, **stty** can be used to set the **ixany** flag, in which case any input character will restart the screen output.	
Newline	Generated when the <enter> or <return> key is struck. Normally, the newline marks the end of a command, and flushes the input line, sending it on to be processed further.	

The interrupt, quit, erase, kill, EOF, and switch characters can be assigned new values by using the **stty** command. For example,

```
stty kill @
```

sets the kill character to the @ character.

SEE ALSO   UNIX Commands: **stty**; **shl**
UNIX Features: Standard I/O, Redirection, and Pipes

Standard I/O,
Redirection, and Pipes

Programs that take input and produce output need to have communication channels to transport that information. Sometimes this is accomplished by having a program explicitly "open" a particular file. For example, suppose you type this command:

```
sort gradelist
```

This causes the **sort** program to open the **gradelist** file so that **sort** can read the file for input.

Many UNIX commands, including **cat**, **grep**, **wc**, and **sort**, automatically open three files, called the "standard input," the "standard output," and the "standard error." As their names imply, these three files are used for providing input, receiving regular output, and receiving error messages, respectively. In UNIX, devices are treated as files, so these three standard files can be devices; indeed, by default, they are devices. The standard input is the keyboard, and the standard output and standard error are the screen of your terminal. However, redirection can change these assignments so that the standard files are ordinary files instead.

WHEN STANDARD FILES ARE USED Commands that use the standard input, standard output, and standard error files typically use them unless explicitly told to do otherwise. For example, the command

```
sort
```

expects input to come from the standard input, which is, in this case, the keyboard. However, the command

```
sort contributors
```

causes the **sort** program to open the **contributors** file and to take input from it instead of from the standard input. The **sort** command, like most UNIX commands that accept standard input, interprets command-line arguments, like **contributors**, to be the names of files to be used instead of the standard input.

Similarly, the command

```
sort contributors
```

normally sends its output to the standard output, which is, in this case, the screen. However, the **-o** option in the command

```
sort -o contrib.sort contributors
```

causes **sort** to open the **contrib.sort** file and to route the sorted output to that file instead of to the screen.

In short, many commands use the standard input and output by default, but some may use other files instead if they are explicitly provided.

TERMINATING KEYBOARD INPUT AS STANDARD INPUT Commands that process files normally read to the end of the file. But if the standard input is the keyboard, there is no obvious end-of-file indication, so a method is needed to signal the end of the file from the keyboard. In UNIX, this is accomplished by typing <control-d> at the beginning of a line, which causes an end-of-file (EOF) signal to be generated. This signal terminates input from the keyboard.

REDIRECTION Although some commands, such as **sort**, have built-in options for specifying output files, and many commands allow you to specify input files on the command line, UNIX offers a more general mechanism that is extremely useful: redirection.

As we mentioned earlier, UNIX redirection allows you to reassign the standard files. A program still is connected to the three standard I/O files, but the identities of the files can be changed. Consider, for example, a command like **cat**, which uses the standard output. We can use the "greater than" symbol (**>**) to make the standard output a regular file. For example, the command

```
cat sam and janet > evening
```

concatenates the three files **sam**, **and**, and **janet** and sends the results to the standard output. The notation **> evening** causes the standard output file to be the **evening** file instead of the screen. This is an example of output redirection.

Standard output redirection creates the output file, providing that there is not already a file by that name. If the specified name is the name of an existing file, the file is erased first before being used, so *be cautious with output redirection to avoid accidentally erasing treasured files.*

The spaces around the redirection operator are optional. All of the following are equivalent:

```
cat toad frog > amphibs
cat toad frog >amphibs
cat toad frog> amphibs
cat toad frog>amphibs
```

Input redirection works much like output redirection, except that the "less than" symbol (**<**) is used to reassign the standard input. For example, the command

```
sort < contributors
```

causes the **contributors** file rather than the keyboard to be the standard input. This reassignment lasts for the duration of the **sort** command. The standard output still will be displayed on the screen, because no other destination has been specified.

How does redirection differ, say, from this command?

```
sort contributors
```

In this example, the presence of a filename tells **sort** to actually open the **contributors** file so it can use **contributors** instead of the standard input. Thus two input files are open: **contributors** and the standard input, though the latter is not used (but it can be, as we will see later).

With redirection, however, the **contributors** file *is* the standard input, and only one input file is open. Also, with redirection, the *operating system* opens the **contributors** file, while with the previous example, the **sort** *command* opens the file; that is, in the latter case, the programming for opening a file is included in **sort**'s code.

Redirecting the standard output does not affect the standard error, and error messages are still sent to the screen. Suppose the **newt** file does not exist but **frog** does, and that we give this command:

```
cat newt frog > amphibs
```

The contents of **frog** are redirected to the **amphibs** file, and a "no **newts**" error message is sent to the screen:

```
newt: No such file or directory
```

Standard error redirection is possible, however, and we'll cover that shortly.

Only one file each can be used for standard input and standard output redirection, because each command is joined to just one standard input and one standard output. We can use redirection to change the connections but not to add additional ones.

MULTIPLE REDIRECTION Input and output redirection can both be used in the same command. For example, the transliteration command

```
tr "[a-z]" "[A-Z]" < act1 > bigact1
```

takes input from the **act1** file, sends it to the **tr** command, and routes the output to the **bigact1** file. This particular **tr** command replaces all lowercase letters in the input with uppercase letters in the output. With the **tr** command, redirection is particularly important, because **tr** uses only the standard I/O files. So if you want to apply **tr** to a file, you have to use redirection (or perhaps a pipe construction; see below).

The order in which redirection instructions are given is immaterial. Both of the following are equivalent to the original command above:

```
tr "[a-z]" "[A-Z]" > bigact1 < act1
< act1 tr "[a-z]" "[A-Z]" > bigact1
```

However, the customary and most readable order is to put the command first, then the arguments, then input redirection, then output redirection.

Here **< act1** means "make **act1** the standard input." Similarly, **> bigact1** means "make **bigact1** the standard output." These actually are commands to the **sh** shell, which has the task of interpreting the command line. So the shell makes these connections before running the rest of the command.

PIPES Redirection links a command to a file. The UNIX pipe facility links one command to another command. More specifically, it makes the standard output of one command the standard input of another. The pipe symbol (¦) is used to establish a pipe. For example, the command

```
wc reports* ¦ sort -n
```

takes the output of the **wc** (word count) command (in this case, the individual and total line, word, and character counts for all files whose names begin with **reports**), and sends it to **sort** to be sorted numerically (the **-n** option). What finally appears on the screen is the count results in ascending order.

Pipes can be combined with redirection. For instance, the command

```
wc reports* ¦ sort -n > rep_counts
```

acts like the preceding example, except that the sorted counts are sent to the **rep_counts** file instead of to the screen. In this example, **sort** is linked to the **wc** *command* by a pipe and to the **rep_counts** *file* by redirection.

COMBINING FILES WITH STANDARD INPUT As we have seen, many UNIX commands can use the standard input as well as accept a list of files for input. Consider the following three commands:

`lp goulash`	*Command opens* **goulash**
`lp < goulash`	*Command uses standard input*
`cat goulash ¦ lp`	*Command uses standard input*

All three print the **goulash** file, but they go about it differently. The first command opens **goulash** and ignores the standard input. The second causes the shell to open **goulash** and call it the standard input. The third makes the standard output of the **cat** command become the standard input for **lp** (see Figure 14).

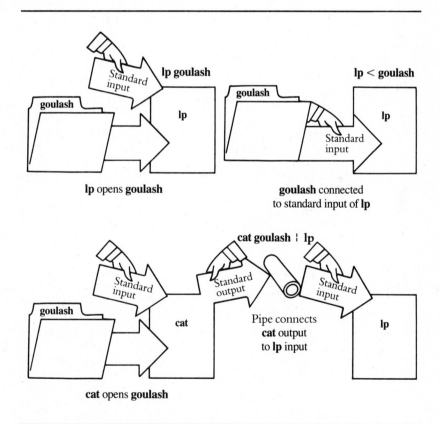

FIGURE 14. *Arranging input for the* **lp** *command*

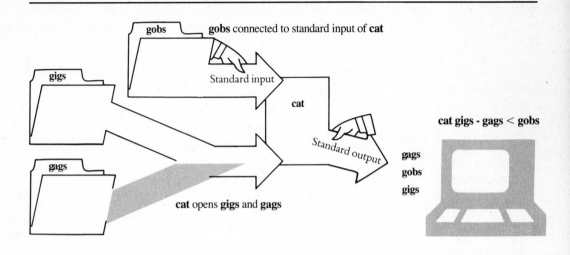

FIGURE 15. *Combining file lists with standard input*

Usually, as in the previous examples, you use either the standard input or a list of files, but several UNIX commands allow you to use both simultaneously. The trick is to use a lone hyphen (-) to represent the standard input in a list of filenames. For example, suppose you give this command:

```
cat gigs - gags < gobs
```

Then the **cat** command opens the **gigs** and **gags** files, but the shell opens the **gobs** file and supplies it as the second of three input files (see Figure 15). This is not a realistic example, since the following command is simpler and produces the same result:

```
cat gigs gobs gags
```

The hyphen notation is useful when you wish to combine a pipe with a file-opening process. Suppose, for example, you want to print the three files **gigs**, **gags**, and **gobs**. Further, suppose you want to print **gags** in sorted order, but you don't want to keep the sorted copy of the **gags** file. You can give this command:

```
sort gags | lp gigs - gobs
```

The output of **sort gags**, which is the file in sorted order, becomes the standard input of **lp**. The hyphen informs **lp** that the second file to be printed is the standard input, so **lp** prints **gigs**, then the sorted version of **gags**, then **gobs**. (If the hyphen were the first argument, then the sorted **gags** would be printed first.)

Not all UNIX commands that use the standard input recognize this hyphen usage; check the command entry in the "UNIX Commands" section if you have any doubts.

OTHER FORMS OF REDIRECTION The **>** and **<** forms of redirection are the most common, but UNIX offers several others.

Append Redirection: >>

The append form of standard output redirection (**>>**) is used when you wish to add to the end of an existing file. For example,

```
cat newclients verynewclients >> clients
```

adds the contents of the **newclients** and **verynewclients** files to the end of the **clients** file. If the destination file does not exist when you give the append instruction, the file is created.

"Here File" Redirection: <<

Suppose you have a standard message you have to mail regularly to other users. You can set up a shell script like this:

```
# mailmesg -- sends standard message to users
mail $* < message
```

The **#** marks a comment and **message** is a file containing the standard message. In this case, $* represents arguments to the shell script. Thus the command

```
mailmesg sam sally sue stu
```

substitutes the list of names following the command for the $*.

A problem with this script is that the commands and the message text are in two separate files. If you were to reorganize your directory system, the files might get separated. However, you can avoid this problem by using **<<** redirection to place the text in the same file as the commands. The text so included is called a "here document" because it's right here. The new script might look like this:

```
# mailmesg -- sends standard message to users
mail $* << stop
Please remember to pay your monthly
file insurance -- Big Jake
.
stop
```

Here's how it works. The word following **<<** acts as a halt signal. Text beginning on the next line and up to (but not including) the first line that consists of the halt signal is used as the standard input. In this case, we used **stop** as the signal, so the two lines of text are mailed and the lone period terminates **mail**.

What happens if the halt word is omitted? Then input continues to the end of the file, which often is fine. But having a marker word like **stop** allows us to use additional commands after the here document, as in

```
# mailmesg -- sends standard message to users
mail $* << stop
Please remember to pay your monthly
file insurance -- Big Jake
.
stop
echo $* reminded on `date` >> $HOME/fi.log
```

Here we redirect information to a log file. The actual date is substituted for `date` (see Command Substitution).

File Descriptors and Standard Error Redirection: 2>

Sometimes it is desirable to redirect error messages. For example, running a task in the background does not alter where the output goes. Suppose you give a command like this:

```
spell odd_tales &
```

The **spell** program works in the background (freeing the terminal for other tasks), but the list of candidates for misspelled words goes to the standard output, which still is your terminal. This could garble the appearance of whatever else you are doing at the time. Suppose you give this command instead:

```
spell odd_tales > odd_sp &
```

Then the normal output is collected in the **odd_sp** file, but error messages are sent to the standard error file, which still is the terminal; confusion still can occur. To collect error messages in a file, we need standard error redirection, and that requires using "file descriptors."

File descriptors are integers used internally to identify files. Each of the three standard files is assigned a file descriptor. Here is the scheme used:

DESCRIPTOR	FILE
0	Standard input
1	Standard ouput
2	Standard error

If you want to redirect error messages, you can combine the file descriptor with the redirection symbol, as in

```
mv datsun nissan 2> cperrs
```

This command says to redirect any error messages to the **cprerrs** file.

Going back to the **spell** example, you can save both regular output and error messages by giving this command:

```
spell odd_tales > odd_sp 2> odd_err &
```

You would be able to examine the **od_sp** and **odd_err** files later to see what happened.

Combining Output: 2>&1

Sometimes you may wish to redirect both the standard output and the standard error to the same file. For instance, in the previous example, the chances are that you will get a list of misspelled words or an error message, but not both. So it would be simpler to use just one file. This can be done with the **2>&1** combination, which merges file descriptor 2 (the standard error) into file descriptor 1 (the standard output). For example, the command

```
spell odd_tales > odd_sp 2>&1 &
```

results in the routing of both regular output and error messages to **odd_sp**.

Note the order of redirection. First, the standard output is redirected to the file **odd_sp**, then the standard error is merged with the standard output. The **2>&1** operator does not itself redirect output to a named file; it simply merges the standard error into the standard output. Regular redirection is used to send the combined flow to a named file.

What if we reverse the order of the redirection instructions?

```
spell odd_tales 2>&1 > odd_sp &
```

Redirection is effected in left-to-right order. Here, the standard error is merged into the standard output, which at this point is still the terminal. Then the standard output is redirected to **odd_sp**. This *does not* reconnect the standard error to **odd_sp**. The **2>&1** operation connects the standard error to the same file the standard output is attached to at the time; it doesn't tie the standard error to the standard output itself. So with this example, the error message goes to the terminal, and the misspelled words go to **odd_sp**.

What the **2>&1** notation actually means is that file descriptor 2 is now a duplicate of file descriptor 1; that is, both are now the standard output. Similarly, **1>&2** makes both into the standard error.

The **sh** entry provides some further details on redirection.

THE tee COMMAND   The redirection and pipe operations we have investigated are properties of the UNIX operating system and of the shell. But there also is a UNIX command specifically designed to work with them. It is the **tee** command, and its purpose is to save the intermediate results of a pipe sequence. Suppose, for example, that we wish to send the output of **sort** to the line printer and that we also wish to save a copy in a file. This can be done in two steps:

```
? sort things > sthings
$ lp sthings
```

The **tee** command lets us do this in one step:

```
sort things ! tee sthings ! lp
```

First, **tee** sends its standard input on to its standard output; in this case, it sends **sort**'s output on to **lp**. Second, **tee** places a copy of its standard input into the named file, here **sthings**. That accomplishes the file-saving part of the task.

SEE ALSO   UNIX Commands: **sh**
UNIX Features: Files and Directories; Processes; Special Files

The Superuser

A superuser is a user who is not restricted by file permissions, and thus can read, write to, and remove any file he or she pleases. The superuser can shut the system down. Typically, the superuser logs in as **root**. Superuser status generally is confined to those responsible for administering the system.

Index